Smoking Typewriters

SMOKING TYPEWRITERS

*The Sixties Underground Press
and the Rise of
Alternative Media in America*

John McMillian

OXFORD
UNIVERSITY PRESS

OXFORD
UNIVERSITY PRESS

Oxford University Press, Inc., publishes works that further
Oxford University's objective of excellence
in research, scholarship, and education.

Oxford   New York
Auckland   Cape Town   Dar es Salaam   Hong Kong   Karachi
Kuala Lumpur   Madrid   Melbourne   Mexico City   Nairobi
New Delhi   Shanghai   Taipei   Toronto

With offices in
Argentina   Austria   Brazil   Chile   Czech Republic   France   Greece
Guatemala   Hungary   Italy   Japan   Poland   Portugal   Singapore
South Korea   Switzerland   Thailand   Turkey   Ukraine   Vietnam

Copyright © 2011 by Oxford University Press, Inc.

Published by Oxford University Press, Inc.
198 Madison Avenue, New York, NY 10016

www.oup.com

Oxford is a registered trademark of Oxford University Press.

Library of Congress Cataloging-in-Publication Data
McMillian, John Campbell.
Smoking typewriters : the Sixties underground press
and the rise of alternative media in America / John McMillian.
    p.   cm.
Includes bibliographical references and index.
ISBN 978-0-19-531992-7
1. Underground press publications—United States—History—20th century.
2. Radicalism—United States—History—20th century.
3. Press and politics—United States—History—20th century. I. Title.
PN4888.U5M35   2011
071'.309046—dc22   2010026243

9 8 7 6 5 4 3 2 1

Printed in the United States of America
on acid-free paper

For Harry Reed

Contents

Acknowledgments   ix
A Note on Sources   xiii

Introduction   1

1   "Our Founder, the Mimeograph Machine":
*Print Culture in Students for a Democratic
Society*   13

2   A Hundred Blooming Papers: *Culture and
Community in the 1960s Underground Press*   31

3   "Electrical Bananas": *The Underground Press
and the Great Banana Hoax of 1967*   66

4   "All the Protest Fit to Print": *The Rise of
Liberation News Service*   82

5   "Either We Have Freedom of the Press . . .
or We Don't Have Freedom of the Press":
*Thomas King Forcade and the War against
Underground Newspapers*   115

6   Questioning Who Decides: *Participatory
Democracy in the Underground Press*   140

7   "From Underground to Everywhere":
Alternative Media Trends since the Sixties   172

Afterword   186

Notes   *191*
Bibliography   *249*
Index   *261*

Acknowledgments

IT'S A THRILL to be able to finally acknowledge the many people who have helped with this book. Let me first thank Alan Brinkley, my graduate advisor at Columbia University, who has done a wonderful job of helping me to shape this project from its beginning. Eric Foner has likewise provided wise and trusted counsel during my graduate career at Columbia and beyond. I am so fortunate to have worked work under the supervision of these two distinguished historians. I would also like to thank Todd Gitlin, Casey Blake, and James Miller for generously serving on my dissertation committee. Manning Marable likewise provided valuable feedback, as well as indispensable financial assistance through Columbia's Institute for Research in African-American Studies.

Going back further, I had some truly outstanding professors at Michigan State University, without whom I would not have acquired the skills or the confidence necessary to pursue a scholarly career. They include James Madison College professors Ken Waltzer, Katherine O'Sullivan See, and history department professors David Bailey, Christine Daniels, and Mark Kornbluh. The same must be said about John VanLooy, my high school English teacher. I was very sad to learn, recently, that Professor Doug Hoekstra, another great influence on me, passed away in 2006. I'm pleased that the James Madison College has established an endowment in his name. More than any of my past teachers, though, Harry Reed has been an inspiration, friend and mentor. Had we not crossed paths during my sophomore year at MSU, my life might have taken a different and far less rewarding path. A long time ago, I declared that I would dedicate my first scholarly monograph to Dr. Reed, and I am happy to at last fulfill that promise.

I would also like to thank my editor, Susan Ferber, who has lived up to her legendary reputation. She read every page of this manuscript with an eagle eye and provided valuable suggestions about how it could be improved. Plus, her patience rivals Job's. I am also grateful for the stellar feedback that was provided by my three peer reviewers, one of whom later identified himself to me as Professor Jeremi Suri. And I was the recipient of some truly top-notch copyediting from Ben Sadock.

Many people helped with the research for this book. I would like to thank Chip Berlet, at the Political Research Association in Somerville, Massachusetts; Ron Grele and Mary Marshall Clark at Columbia's Oral History Research Office; and Brett Eynon, for letting me examine his oral history interviews at the Bentley Historical Library in Ann Arbor, Michigan. I had a great time meeting John Holmstrom in NYC's East Village, where he provided me with a trove of papers that helped me to write Chapter 5. Similarly, Rob Chalfen lent me some material from his private archives that contributed to my analysis in Chapter 7. As this project was nearing completion, Harvard's Division of Continuing Education provided me with a fabulous and energetic research assistant, Arwen Downs. And when the book was in its copyediting phase, Ridhi Kashyap helped me tidy up some stubborn footnotes. Cherie Braden did the outstanding index for this book.

I owe a big thanks to everyone who agreed to be interviewed. But I am especially grateful to Allen Young, Thorne Dreyer, and Clif Garboden, who all took a special interest in this project and helped by answering questions, supplying me with contact information, and occasionally putting in some good words on my behalf. Thorne and Clif also contributed some excellent photos. Photographer David Fenton was exceedingly generous with me, and I likewise appreciate the friendly help I received from his assistant, Lely Constantinople. I also received assistance with photographs from Tom Fels, Chris Green, Leni Sinclair, Mark Goff, Dustin Byerly, David Buehrens, John Wilcock, Andy Marx, Peter Simon, and Robert Altman. Allen Ginsberg (R.I.P.) provided me with this book's title.

This book was written while I was teaching virtually full time at Harvard University, mostly in the Committee on Degrees in History and Literature, where Steve Biel and Jeanne Follansbee Quinn cheerfully extended me every consideration. It was also a pleasure to briefly work with Tom Jehn and Karen Heath in Harvard's Expository Writing Program. Living in Quincy House for seven years was a great blessing of my life, and I am grateful to House masters Lee and Deb Gehrke for their tremendous support. The same goes for residential dean Judith Flynn-Chapman, Sue Watts, Larry Peterson, and Susan Hamel, all good friends. As this book was going into production, I was warmly welcomed into the history department at Georgia State University, and I'm thrilled to be here.

So many others have been supportive, whether by reading parts of this manuscript, helping me out with favors, or otherwise extending their friendship. They include: Zoe Trodd, Stuart Perkins, Richard Griffin, Jesse Lemisch, Richard Karpel, Ben Mathis-Lilley, Chris Parris-Lamb, Marc Favreau, Frank Rich, Lizzie Simon and her wonderful parents, Toby and Peter Simon, Gustavo Turner, David McBride, Brendan O'Malley, Jeremy Galen, Daniel Liss, Mana Kia, Dan Sullivan, Ben and Jane Ebert, Nick Bromell, Paul Barksdale, Alex Burns, Fotini Christia, H. M. Naqvi, Jason Appelman, Eddie Stern, Rich Van Tol, Matt Holcomb and Kari Zimmerman, Caitlin Casey, Bill Higgins, Paul Buhle, Bob Kirschner and Jayne Loader, Andrea Mainguy, Renne Richardson Gosline, Jeff Janowick, Richard and Robin Parker, the Wesche family, the Campbells, Leon Neyfahk, Katy Cox, Heidi Julavits, Ariane Tschumi, Zach Stone (computer genius), Elaine Mar (MS Word expert), and my dear friend Rebecca O'Brien. When this project was in its dissertation phase, Carolyn Rathjen provided crucial support. (Pablo S. Torre, I am pleased to acknowledge you, too.) Extra special thanks go to my buddies Nick Meunier, Aaron Buchner, and Brandon Tilley, all of whom would occasionally pry me from my desk in order to provide such wholesome recreational opportunities.

I have three comrades in this profession, however, who have been helpful above all. In addition to often providing cogent readings of my work, Tim McCarthy, Mike Foley, and Jeremy Varon have greatly enriched my life with their trustworthy support, rich humor, and abiding friendship. Jeremy, especially, labored over almost every page of the manuscript, and has helped me to navigate some intellectual, personal, and professional challenges. Whitney Hoke has likewise been a tremendous source of love and encouragement for which I shall always be very grateful.

Finally, I'm happy to pay special thanks to my wonderful parents, Harlon and Judy McMillian. It is safe to say that neither of them feels very favorably toward radical youth culture or political protest in the 1960s, and yet they have always been wonderfully supportive of my academic endeavors. I am so grateful for all they have done for me.

A Note on Sources

A FEW THINGS TO KEEP IN MIND: Throughout this book, when I write about "the Sixties" (spelled out, capital "S") I'm talking about the Sixties as an era, or historical period, with all of its implied associations. When I refer to the "1960s," I'm referencing the actual decade. Also, when quoting texts from the 1960s and 1970s, I typically render passages that originally were underlined in *italics*. It looks better this way. Careful readers of footnotes should also bear in mind that when it came to putting dates on issues, or numbers on pages, some underground newspaper staffs were very sloppy. And sometimes in archives, I came across undated clippings or documents. If, in a very few instances, I'm missing some information about my sources, it may not be my fault.

This book would not be possible without Bell & Howell's Underground Press Collection on microfilm, and virtually all of the underground newspapers and Liberation News Service (LNS) news packets that I draw from can be found there. Recently, however, some LNS veterans have begun establishing a web archive that promises to digitize every LNS news packet from 1968 through 1981; it can be found at http://www.lns-archive.org. Meanwhile, people associated with some of the underground newspapers that are discussed in this study, including Austin's *Rag*, Boston's *Avatar*, and Atlanta's *Great Speckled Bird*, are likewise beginning to make back issues available on the web.

Hopefully, others will follow their lead. In addition to learning something about the underground press, I hope readers of this book will come to understand that the New Left's tabloids comprise an amazing trove of primary-source material, capable of affording insight into a wide range of issues.

Way back in 1968, Allan Katzman, a cofounder of the *East Village Other* (*EVO*), said as much: "in the future," he remarked, "people will be able to look back and understand this period, get a good feel for what it must have been like, by reading the *EVO*."[1] Later, literary critic Morris Dickstein wrote, "The history of the sixties was written as much in the *Berkeley Barb* as in the *New York Times*."[2]

As Mary Ryan has pointed out in *Civic Wars*, her study of American public culture in the nineteenth century, newspapers can by read as "the printed nexus of an extended, multivoiced conversation," and as a result, they may be "as close as historians can get to the voice of the public."[3] This observation would seem to carry special force vis-à-vis the hundreds of youth-oriented papers of the 1960s, which were so much a product of the grass roots. Again and again, the fullest and most revealing record of the behaviors, manners, and beliefs of New Leftists can be found in the pages of the underground press.

Smoking Typewriters

Introduction

"STONES CONCERT ENDS IT," blared the front-page headline of the underground *Berkeley Tribe*, dated December 12–19, 1969. "America Now Up for Grabs."

The Rolling Stones concert that the *Tribe* described was supposed to have been a triumphant affair. Coming just four months after half a million hippie youths drew international attention by gathering peaceably at Max Yasgur's farm, some had even hyped the free, day-long event—which was held at Altamont Speedway, some sixty miles east of San Francisco, and which also featured Santana, the Jefferson Airplane, and the Flying Burrito Brothers—as "Woodstock West."

But this was no festival of peace and love. As almost everyone knew, the idea for the free show only came about after the Stones were nettled by criticisms that they had alienated fans with exorbitant ticket prices and arrogant behavior on their 1969 American tour. What's more, Altamont proved to be a dirty, bleak space for a rock festival, almost completely lacking in amenities for the 300,000 concertgoers. People practically clambered over each other to get near the hastily built, three-foot-high stage, and by almost every account, "bad vibes" were regnant among the concertgoers. Asked to guard the performers—allegedly in exchange for a truckload of beer[1]—the Hell's Angels motorcycle gang went on a drug-and-booze soaked rampage, assaulting countless hippies with weighted pool cues and kicks to the head.

When the Stones finally started their set after sundown, they found it impossible to gain momentum; they could only play in fits and starts, as the Angels roughed up spectators and commotion swirled around them. Albert and David Maysles' classic concert documentary, *Gimme Shelter*, captured

Mick Jagger nervously trying to soothe the crowd: "Brothers and sisters, come *on* now. That means *everybody*—just *cool out*." "All I can do is ask you—*beg* you—to keep it together. It's within your power." "If we *are* all one, let's fucking well *show* we're all one!"

But Jagger's entreaties were in vain. Just as the Stones were starting "Under My Thumb," the Angels set their sights on an African American teenager in a flashy lime-green suit: Meredith Hunter. By one eyewitness account, the whole thing began when a heavyset Angel was toying with Hunter, laughing as he yanked him by the ear and by the hair. Then, when Hunter pulled himself away, he ran into a pack of perhaps four more Angels, who started punching him. Trying to escape, Hunter whipped out a long-barreled revolver and held it high over his head; in an instant, an Angel plunged a knife between his neck and shoulder. Autopsy reports confirmed that Hunter was tweaking on methamphetamines when he was killed. His last words, supposedly, were: "I wasn't going to shoot you."[2]

Ever since, writers and historians have found it tempting to describe Altamont as a generation-shattering event, the proverbial "end of an era."[3] If the early Sixties was a time of gauzy idealism, characterized by JFK's youthful vigor, righteous lunch-counter sit-ins, and the first flush of Beatlemania, then the Altamont disaster ranks alongside the 1968 Democratic National Convention riots, the Manson Family murders, and the Weather Underground's townhouse explosion as evidence of the era's swift decline.

Less well known, however, is that the trope arose in the underground press.[4] "Altamont . . . exploded the myth of innocence for a section of America," wrote twenty-one-year-old George Paul Csicsery (now a respected filmmaker) in the *Tribe*'s lead article. Just a little while earlier, he said, it had been "cool" for large groups of youths to assemble at parks and rock festivals. "People would play together, performing, participating, sharing and going home with a feeling that somehow the communal idea would replace the grim isolation wrought on us by a jealous competitive mother culture." But on the bleak, dry hills around Altamont, the feeling was entirely different: "Our one-day micro society was bound to the death-throes of capitalist greed." The Angels' violence had "united the crowd in fear" while Jagger strutted on the stage like a "diabolical prince." To Csiscery, the concert was a metaphor for a society on the brink: "Clearly, nobody is in control. Not the Angels, not the people. Not Richard Nixon, or his pigs. Nobody."[5]

Elsewhere in the *Tribe*, readers could find several more pieces on the Altamont debacle, all of them written by participant-observers, all of them done in a familiar, even informal style. Several writers made liberal use of the editorial "we" (as in, "We're turning into a generation whose thing is to be an

Audience, whose life-style is the mass get-together for 'good vibes.'") Others sprinkled their reports with song lyrics, hallucinatory images, or whimsical asides. The *Tribe* also featured an elliptical poem about the Altamont debacle, as well as a comic strip by the artist Greg Irons that skewered a local radio station for irresponsibly hyping the event and then fulminating against it after things went bad. Almost all of this material struck a portentous tone; the *Tribe*'s radical politicos and youth-culture aficionados who caravanned to Altamont came away feeling grubby, mortified, and concerned. "I realize some people just had a good time," said one writer. "Me, I saw a guy get killed."[6]

Altamont received front-page attention in the *San Francisco Examiner*, too, but nothing like the blanket coverage that was found in the *Tribe*, and besides, the Bay Area's leading evening paper completely missed the concert's significance; its reports and analysis could not have been more wrong-headed.[7] On December 6, the *Examiner* stressed that the biggest problem associated with the concert was the traffic headache it caused on Interstate 5/580; it specifically added that police reported "no violence."[8] The next day, the paper mentioned that one person had been killed, but in fact four people died: two were run over by a car while sitting at a campfire, and another drowned in a swift-moving irrigation canal while zonked out on drugs. "But for the stabbing," the *Examiner* reported, "all appeared peaceful at the concert. . . . The record-breaking crowd was for the most part orderly, but enthusiastic. The listeners heeded the advice of the Jefferson Airplane: 'We should be together.'"[9]

Then on December 9, the paper's editorial writers fumbled to explain why 300,000 youths would even want to attend a free rock festival headlined by the Rolling Stones in the first place. They literally could not come up with an explanation that they deemed fully satisfactory.[10] Finally, on December 14, Dick Nolan, an op-ed columnist, stressed that the event had been a disaster for the counterculture, but his tone was so priggish and excoriating that it's hard to imagine very many younger readers taking him seriously. "Maybe it's wishful thinking," he wrote. "But to me that Altamont rock fiasco looked very much like the last gasp of the whole hippie-drug thing." There were the Stones, he said, "peddling their idiot doggerel and primitive beat," before "that most mindless of animals, the human mob." Altamont was just another manifestation "of the rock-drug-slobbery cult," to which Nolan could only say good riddance.

This is not a book about Altamont, of course. But by quickly glancing at how two local newssheets covered the Stones concert, we can begin apprehending the powerful appeal of the underground press in the late 1960s and early 1970s. Amateurishly produced by a collective of unabashed radicals, the *Berkeley Tribe* had a fleet of reporters who actively *participated* in the events they covered. Lacking any pretense of objectivity, they put across forcefully opinionated accounts of events that mattered deeply to them—that grew out of their culture—and they used a language and sensibility of their own fashioning; their hip vernacular was something they shared with most of their readership. By contrast, the professionals who staffed the *Examiner*—the flagship of the Hearst newspaper chain—approached Altamont with a prefabricated template. Their first instinct was to cloak the free concert in gooey, Woodstock-style sentimentalism. Then after that proved untenable, their editorialists proved totally uncomprehending of the rock and youth cultures they sought to explain.

It is little wonder, then, that many New Leftists never bothered to read daily newspapers, at least not when they wanted to know what was going on in their own milieu. Instead, beginning in the mid-1960s, in cities and campuses across the country, they began creating and distributing their own radical community newssheets, with which they aimed to promote avant-garde sensibilities and inspire political tumult. Amplitude and conviction were hallmarks of the underground press: this is where they set forth their guiding principles concerning the unfairness of racism, the moral and political tragedy of the Vietnam War, the need to make leaders and institutions democratically accountable, and the existential rewards of a committed life. And their success was astonishing. According to cultural critic Louis Menand, underground newspapers "were one of the most spontaneous and aggressive growths in publishing history."[11] In 1965, the New Left could claim only five such newspapers, mostly in large cities; within a few years, several hundred papers were in circulation, with a combined readership that stretched into the millions.[12]

In addition to trying to build an intellectual framework for the Movement's expansion, New Leftists imbued their newspapers with an ethos that socialized people into the Movement, fostered a spirit of mutuality among them, and raised their democratic expectations. The community-building work that New Leftists brought about in this way was neither incidental nor marginal. Instead, it played a crucial role in helping youths to break away from the complacency and resignation that prevailed in postwar America, in order to build an indigenous, highly stylized protest culture. Given the obstacles confronting those who have attempted to build mass democratic movements in the United States, this was a considerable achievement.[13] Simply put, much of what we associate with the late 1960s youth rebellion—its size, intensity, and contrapuntal expressions of furious anger and joyful bliss—might not have been possible without the advent of new printing technologies that put the cost of newspaper production within reach of most activists, or without the institutions they built that allowed their press to flourish.

WE HAVE NO SHORTAGE OF BOOKS seeking to explain how so many American youths grew restless and dissatisfied with their country in the early 1960s and why they became so intensely radical in the mid-1960s. Surely, demographics can account for part of the answer. Growing up in a time of unprecedented prosperity, baby boomers developed a keen sense of their own generational potency, a confident "can-do" attitude that inspired them to tackle the problems troubling public life.[14] The civil rights movement was also pivotal. When African Americans bravely stood up against attack dogs, cattle prods, fire hoses, and lynch mobs, they dramatically demonstrated the power of collective action to foster social change. Meanwhile, the sterile culture that the Cold War helped to produce, in which middle-class youths were expected to march lockstep into impersonal bureaucracies and circumscribed gender roles, prompted some to reflect critically upon the supposed promises of the American Dream. The escalation of the Vietnam War, the draft, and the gruesome images that were transmitted from Southeast Asia's jungles into American living rooms led many activists to ramp up their protest activities. So too did the era's frightening urban unrest, which some traced back to the federal government's unwillingness to address the more far-reaching demands of the civil rights movement. The fact that it was liberals, rather than conservatives, who presided over the catastrophic war, and who failed to bring about genuine racial equality, prompted some youths to direct indiscriminate animus against "the Establishment."

The New Left's development, however, can't be accounted for by these factors alone; it has also been necessary for scholars to examine the internal dynamics that propelled the Movement. In the late 1980s, a small corpus of books arrived that greatly shaped thinking on this subject. Foremost among them are James Miller's *Democracy Is in the Streets: From Port Huron to the Siege of Chicago*, and Todd Gitlin's *The Sixties: Years of Hope, Days of Rage*.[15] Both of these penetrating and beautifully written works helped to establish what I have elsewhere called "the New Left consensus"—the reigning narrative explaining the intellectual and sociocultural forces that account for the Movement's rapid rise and precipitous decline.[16] Both studies, however, focus heavily upon the institutional history of SDS—especially in its early years—when in fact much of the decade's political energy arose from the grass roots, and it wasn't until the mid and late 1960s that the New Left became a mass movement.[17] As a result, these books shaped the research designs of an even more recent body of scholarship, which has begun to present a fuller historical accounting of the youth rebellion by de-centering SDS, examining the Movement at the local level, and exploring other groups within the organized Left.[18]

By showing how underground newspapers educated, politicized, and built communities among disaffected youths in every region of the country, this book contributes to a broader revisionist effort. SDS played a major role in the Sixties, but the strategic and intellectual debates that preoccupied its national officers must have seemed removed from the concerns of many grassroots activists. By contrast, radical newspapers engaged local, hot-button issues, and sometimes inspired devoted regional followings. Moreover, since most of these papers were interconnected—whether through a loose confederation called the Underground Press Syndicate (UPS) or a radical news agency called Liberation News Service (LNS)—they also became the Movement's primary means of internal communication. Absent such newspapers and organizations, the New Left could not have circulated its news, ideas, trends, opinions, and strategies without having them "strained through a mainstream filter."[19]

Unlike, say, the covert and highly illegal newspapers attacking the Nazi occupation of France and the Netherlands during World War II, the vast majority of radical papers produced during the Vietnam era circulated openly.[20] The "underground" moniker arose because some of the first of them—including the *Los Angeles Free Press* (established in 1964), the *Berkeley Barb*, and New York City's *East Village Other* (both established in 1965)—appealed to self-styled cultural outlaws: freelance intellectuals, dissenters, artists, and folk and jazz musicians, who clustered in taverns and espresso houses in low-rent neighborhoods. Many of these papers, however, could seem genuinely subversive, openly flouting society's conventions and, by the late 1960s, championing the revolutionary overthrow of the United States government. Also, many of those who produced and sold such newspapers became targets of harassment from federal and local authorities.

A writer for Vancouver's *Georgia Straight* observed in 1968 that although underground papers were highly critical of capitalism, they represented "some of the greatest examples of practical free enterprise."[21] Before the 1960s, newspaper copy had to be set in hot type on a Linotype machine—a procedure that was both costly and difficult. But with the advent of photo-offset printing, newspaper production suddenly became cheap and easy. All one needed was a competent typist, a pair of scissors, and a jar of rubber cement with which to paste copy onto a backing sheet, which was then photographed and reproduced exactly as it was set. For just a couple hundred dollars, one could print several thousand copies of an eight- or sixteen-page tabloid.[22] The Offset Revolution also allowed for creatively designed layouts, whereby prose could be fitted around swirling drawings and photo collages. Some of the more mystically oriented papers, like the San Francisco *Oracle*—which was rumored to receive funding from Owsley Stanley, the famous underground LSD chemist—pioneered split-fountain printing techniques that allowed them to blend colorful inks and create beautiful rainbow effects on their pages, no two of which were ever exactly alike.

As newspaper production suddenly became more accessible, amateurs filled the staffs of most of the papers, learning the mechanics of layout, distribution, sales, and advertising as they went along. Though they worked feverishly, most of them were jaundiced to the very idea of profit making; according to a 1969 survey, 72 percent of underground papers reported they made no profit whatsoever.[23] "Financially, it is nearly impossible to expect a small underground publication to pay for itself," one radical editor observed.[24] By the late 1960s, however, a few well-made tabloids in radical hotbeds like Los Angeles and Northern California did quite well.

Even when they were only barely solvent, the papers were often highly visible in their communities. They lined the shelves of head shops and offbeat bookstores, and street vendors sold them in hip neighborhoods or at public gatherings: "poetry readings, political meetings, art gallery openings, light-shows and other freakouts—anywhere [there was] a captive audience."[25] Most underground papers also had back-page calendars that alerted people to such events. Especially in smaller communities, which lacked the pageantry and intellectual ferment that accompanied the youth revolt in urban areas, underground papers could impart to their readers a sense of connection and belonging to the New Left. Thomas King Forcade, who would become something of a legend in underground publishing, nurtured his early fascination with the Movement through underground newspapers he was able to obtain while living in right-wing Phoenix, Arizona. David Armstrong, who later wrote a book about alternative media, recalled an epiphanic moment when, as an undergraduate at Syracuse University, he picked up "a thin weekly published on the West Coast called the *Berkeley Barb*." It was the first paper he'd ever seen that covered things like the Vietnam War, the draft, and the Black Power Movement "with anything approaching the intensity and urgency" that he and his friends felt.[26]

The failure of the nation's glossy magazines and daily newspapers to cover the youth rebellion adequately also helped to fuel the subterranean press. By the early 1960s, newspaper ownership, once diverse, had become highly concentrated, mainly because newspapers were such valuable properties. Those who could afford to buy them up and consolidate them—the Hearsts, the Annenbergs, the Chandlers—did so. By 1962 twelve managements controlled one-third of the circulation of newspapers in the United States. Large cities that could earlier boast of having multiple newspapers began to have only one or two. Furthermore, the corporate structures that girded these newspapers (and also television news programs, which in 1961 became the main source of news for most Americans) favored employees who were better educated and more "sophisticated" than previous generations of writers and editors.[27] The result, in this new era of consensus and conformity, was a ubiquity of increasingly bland, cautious, and professionally balanced journalism. Angry and iconoclastic opinions, which flourished in a formerly diverse world of newspapers, were largely restricted from the news diets fed to most Americans.

This helps to explain why the underground's media activists were united in their disdain for Establishment journalists—those who resided, as Hunter S. Thompson combatively put it, "way out there on the puzzled, masturbating edge, peering through the keyhole and selling what they see to the big wide world."[28] By contrast, New Leftists claimed for themselves a kind of epistemic privilege, arguing that only those from within the Movement could take its true measure. Typically, underground press writers actively participated in the events they wrote about, sometimes with considerable fervor. By coloring their stories with their subjective responses, they pioneered a literary style closely resembling that of the era's celebrated New Journalists.[29] Commenting on the underground press's widespread appeal in 1968, writers Joan Didion and John Gregory Dunne remarked, "It is the genius of these papers that they talk directly to their readers. They assume that the reader is a friend, that he is disturbed about something, and that he will understand if they talk to him straight; this assumption of a shared language and a common ethic lends their reports a considerable cogency of style."[30]

Numerous successful journalists working today got their start with underground papers. Among them are the celebrated investigative reporters Lowell Bergman (formerly of 60 *Minutes*, currently of PBS's *Frontline*) and Jeff Gerth (formerly of the *New York Times*), and foreign correspondent Mike Shuster (of NPR). Columnist Joe Conason (*New York Observer* and *Salon*) edited a monthly underground-style paper when he was still in high school. The work of Hunter S. Thompson and humorist P. J. O'Rourke appeared in underground newspapers before they became famous, and the same is true for novelists Tom Robbins, Ishmael Reed, Charles Bukowski, rock critic Lester Bangs, and sex educator Susie Bright. Some esteemed poets occasionally contributed to underground papers, including Diane DiPrima, d. a. levy, Gary Snyder, and Allen Ginsberg, and some of today's best-known graphic artists, including Robert Crumb and Art Spiegelman, launched their careers writing underground "comix." The list of notable left-wing scholars who edited or regularly contributed to underground rags includes Maurice Isserman, Todd Gitlin, Paul Buhle, Chip Berlet, Michael Kazin, Jon Wiener, Clayborne Carson, and Ann Gordon. Sometimes unlikely voices appear in the radical newssheets, like Jon Landau (Bruce Springsteen's manager), David Stockman (Ronald Reagan's budget director), and Cameron Crowe (the Hollywood director who referenced the underground press in his loosely autobiographical film *Almost Famous*).

However compelling underground papers could seem, by conventional standards they usually weren't of very high quality. "People involved with movement papers generally see themselves as activists or organizers first, and journalists second," observed Thorne Dreyer and Victoria Smith, both radical journalists themselves.[31] Nor is it surprising that, amid the great rush of events that characterized the 1960s, New Leftists had such little use for belletrists. As Tocqueville remarked, it is a rare thing when the "the literature of democracy" exhibits "the order, regularity, skill and art characteristic of an aristocratic" (or professional) literature. More commonly, writers "will be more anxious to work quickly than to perfect details. . . . Authors will strive more to astonish than to please, to stir passions than to charm taste."[32]

Certainly underground journalists could be fiercely polemical, and some critics easily dismissed the overzealous tones favored by some newspapers. But it bears remembering that young radicals hardly cornered the market on highly ideological agendas. In 1970, Allen Ginsberg stressed this point in a letter to PEN American Center president Thomas Fleming, who had recently released a statement condemning the attempts of authorities to suppress underground newspapers. Fleming hadn't risen to the New Left's defense because he was a fan of the radical tabloids (he was not); he was simply defending their right to free speech. And although Ginsberg was grateful for Fleming's statement, he couldn't help but add,

> I would've taken exception, were it my place, to [the] adjective "inflammatory" applied wholesale to "New Left" literature outside the context of equally inflammatory ideology displayed in, say, *Reader's Digest* with *its* historically inflammatory cold war fury or odd language about "dope fiends"; or *NY Daily News* which in editorials

has proposed atombombing China counting 200 million persons at their own estimate as reasonable; or for that matter the *New York Times* whose business-as-usual reportage in this era of planetary ecological crisis occasionally inflames my own heart to fantasies of arson. Be that as it may it's a minor quibble with your text. Merely to say that I find "aboveground" language as often inflammatory as I find "New Left" underground rhetoric, as [would] W. C. Fields.[33]

Furthermore, most New Leftists understood that even the rude and untutored papers still brought people into the Movement's fold, shored up political communities, and inspired organizing efforts and militant actions.[34] In some instances, newspapers played this role in areas that previously had not seen much radical activity. By welcoming rank-and-file participation in all aspects of newspaper production, and by generally opening their pages to whoever wanted to air their left-wing views, they helped to bring radicals and bohemians into communion with one another. "For writers, editors, photographers, [and] artists," Todd Gitlin recollects, the underground press "was a marvelous adventure, full of infectious enthusiasm."[35]

Oftentimes, street-corner papers drew attention to issues, inflamed opinions, and fomented dissent through heated prose and old-fashioned muckraking. In some instances, they were so provocative, inflammatory, or "obscene" that they became targets of censorship or harassment, thereby becoming local *causes célèbres*. Because these were often the only newspapers that radicals identified with, they were read with unusual intensity.[36] Sometimes the communal homes or offices where the papers were produced doubled as meeting spots for local activists, or stopping-off points for hippie travelers. Barry Miles, who helped launch Europe's first underground paper, *International Times* (abbreviated as either *IT* or *it*), recalled that his most enduring memories of the underground press have to do with the "warmth and camaraderie" of the people who worked within it. "I remember arriving in Los Angeles in January 1969 and walking unannounced into the offices of *Open City*, and saying I was from *it*," Miles recalled. "Immediately I was offered a place to stay and more invitations to events and meals than I could hope to use."[37] In a few robust youth culture enclaves, enterprising hippies could nearly earn a living by hawking underground newspapers.[38]

No doubt because they were so effective, underground newspapers were targeted by the FBI, as well as by local authorities, campus administrators, and even a few vigilante groups, sometimes with devastating effect. As appendages of the New Left, the radical newssheets could not have outlived or surpassed the youth rebellion anyhow; their fate was always intertwined with that of the larger Movement (and when they labored to win the affection of the broader Left, or purged their ranks of amateurs, they ceased being "underground"). But they might have been even more effective, or lasted a bit longer, if they'd constituted themselves a little differently.

Many papers functioned as collectives, in which entire newspaper staffs participated in all levels of decision making. Initially these decentralized working environments must have held a certain appeal, but most people who toiled within them eventually discovered they could also be burdensome, inefficient, and alienating. And when the papers were *exceedingly* coarse, brash, or harshly militant—that is, when they violated even the counterculture's loose standards of civility and propriety—they gave people good cause to turn their noses up at the Movement. Finally, in their organization and content, most underground newspapers mirrored the sexism and homophobia of the dominant culture. As a result, they caused unnecessary divisions and deprived themselves of valuable talent. When the gay and women's liberation movements hit full force in the very late 1960s and early 1970s, no one should have been surprised when some New Leftists lit out for new ideological territory and quickly established their own formidable network of more narrowly focused publications.[39]

WHEN DISCUSSING THE SOCIAL REBELLIONS of the 1960s, it is sometimes necessary to draw distinctions between the strategically oriented New Left, which was made up of "politicos" who wanted to change society, and the counterculture, which consisted of lifestyle radicals, or "hippies," who self-segregated from society. Although the two groups shared certain obvious commonalities, including a basic skepticism toward the dominant culture and a yearning for "authenticity" in personal relations, the underground press sometimes underscored their differences. Papers like San Francisco's *Oracle* and New York's *East Village Other*, which promoted psychedelic drugs with millenarian intensity, were probably not so compelling to activists who were consumed with finding the right formulas for halting the Vietnam War, fighting racism, and restructuring American universities. However, just as most of those who contributed to the 1960s youth rebellion didn't operate exclusively at one or the other end of this spectrum, most of the era's underground newspapers presented an intermingling of aesthetic and tactical radicalism.[40] This became increasingly true in the late 1960s, when it became harder to distinguish precisely between the New Left and the counterculture, and when many formerly hippie-oriented papers began adding more specifically political content to their pages.[41] When the term "New Left" appears in this study, it is used maximally, to describe the whole constellation of predominately white, nonconformist, college-aged youths of the 1960s who rebelled against American racism, imperialism, and bourgeois social relations.[42]

While some might be troubled by the lumping together of hippies and politicos, others may object that this definition of the New Left is too narrow, since it doesn't include many African Americans, multicultural activists, or feminists.[43] The New Left's relationship to these groups demands special comment. Without a doubt, activists of color were potent sources of inspiration for New Leftists, and combating racism was a central component of their politics. The United States in the 1960s, however, was culturally and politically segregated to an enormous degree, and black and white radicals often operated on parallel tracks. Even as white militants labored to win the trust of African Americans, they frequently acknowledged and lamented the exclusivity of their activism. And although second-wave feminism was among the most important protest traditions to emerge from the 1960s, strictly speaking, it was not part of the New Left. Very few male radicals developed progressive gender politics in the 1960s. In fact, much of the energy that fueled the women's liberation movement arose *in response* to the patriarchy and sexism they encountered in the New Left—and, especially, in its underground newspapers.[44] In this book, I've tried to present the New Left accurately, as a largely white, broad-based, and male-dominated movement, while nevertheless recognizing the crucial influence of the civil rights movement and the important contributions of women.[45]

For some scholars, it has also been a matter of concern that the most influential writing on the New Left has been produced by Sixties veterans who have remained basically sympathetic to the lofty idealism that anchored their activism in the Port Huron Era.[46] By lack of birthright, I am not capable of having participated in the New Left, but I will cop to sharing the assumptions of some of its activists—particularly those who believed (as goes the cliché) that a genuine democracy is not possible in the absence of an informed, engaged citizenry. I also won't mind if this book helps to remind people that there was a time in recent American history when the political left soared with confidence. Whatever the New Left's deficiencies, the underground newspapers they left behind breathe of a more hopeful time, when the problems troubling American public life were addressed by a great mass of young citizens who thrust themselves into the public discourse, and who ached with ethical worry about the society in which they lived. Today, it seems necessary to recapture that spirit. Nevertheless, I hope my distance from the material that I analyze will be clear.

1

"Our Founder, the Mimeograph Machine"

Print Culture in Students for a Democratic Society

IT SCARCELY MATTERED whether it was day or night—people just kept coming and going. Amid the frequently ringing phones, the tap-tap-tap of perhaps a dozen typewriters, and the periodic rumble of a nearby elevated train, they worked, ate, and talked in dimly lit rooms, perched on wobbly chairs, surrounded by sheaves of paper and battered desks.[1] Flyers, posters, and newspaper photographs nearly papered over the chipped plaster walls. Some of the wall decorations—a charcoal drawing of Eugene Debs, stickers from the Industrial Workers of the World, and a print by the social-realist artist Ben Shahn—represented the American left of previous years. But other ephemera—a photograph of Bob Dylan, a political cartoon from the *Village Voice* by Jules Feiffer, and the bumper-sticker slogan "Make Love, Not War"— gave the headquarters of Students for a Democratic Society (SDS) a sense of political currency. One journalist who visited its national office, which in the mid-1960s was at the edge of Chicago's West Side ghetto, described it as something between a newsroom and a flophouse, drawing attention to "an unmade cot, several laundry bags, a jar of instant coffee, and a half-eaten chocolate bar." But one artifact, above all, caught his attention. Taped to one of the walls was a picture of a mimeograph machine. Just beneath it someone had written the words "Our Founder."[2]

SDS leaders were nothing if not irreverent, but here we find a metaphor that speaks volumes about how they conceived of themselves, their history, and their mission.[3] Seeing as it was not unusual for SDS organizers to imagine themselves working in the reflected glow of the left-wing luminaries they pasted on their walls, they could scarcely afford to be anything but confident about the agency of the written word and the power and authority of fresh ideas. Various and multihued pamphlets and flyers, densely printed newspapers, crude bulletins, circular letters, and delicate, smudgy carbons—this was the stuff through which SDS aimed to change the world.

On the whole, members of SDS wrote easily. Throughout the organization's various permutations, melodramatic zeal was rarely in short supply; reticence was. Even in SDS's earliest years, when it was a more intellectually minded organization than it became, the group's frustrations with American society sometimes registered awkwardly in print. Increasingly braying tones became more familiar toward the mid-1960s, and by about 1968 its literature frequently displayed such a violence of feeling that writers literally took to calling their pamphlets "shotguns." (As in, "My first project was to write a shotgun on political prisoners.")[4] From this perspective, an analysis of SDS's published writings could easily replicate, and even amplify, the familiar story line about how the New Left betrayed its roots in liberalism and participatory democracy and eventually self-destructed.[5]

Through an examination of SDS's internal printed communications, however, we can tell an altogether different story, one that helps us understand how SDS established itself as a community of participatory democrats and, in the process, fashioned a political style that ended up greatly influencing the underground press of the late 1960s and early 1970s. This point has not quite been made before. Typically, people argue that underground papers owed much of their inspiration to liberal and satirical publications that came before them: the *Village Voice*, Paul Krassner's *Realist*, and even, to some degree, *Mad* magazine.[6] Though there is some truth to this, SDS needs to be brought into the discussion as well. This was the organization that set the template for underground newspapers that functioned as open forums, to which virtually anyone could contribute. Many underground rags likewise functioned as democratic collectives; the people who staffed the papers were also the ones that determined how they should be run. In professional journalism, there was little, if any, precedent for these approaches. It was SDS that helped to make them seem attractive.

Efforts to explain SDS's wide-ranging appeal have sometimes touched upon its highly *verbal* culture—its seemingly endless meetings and debates and late-night bull sessions, inspired by the existential politics of the civil rights movement, as well as C. Wright Mills's famous dictum that "personal troubles . . . must be understood in terms of public issues."[7] SDS's meetings, however, frequently left much to be desired. Some people loved them, but others found them tedious, windy, unfocused, cliquish, sexist, and prone to being commandeered by whoever was most charismatic and articulate. Written conversations could be similarly skewed, but overall, SDS's print culture may have been better suited to its goal of eliciting genuine membership participation and reinforcing its inclusive and deliberative ethos.

To be sure, this spirit was sometimes strained. Resources in SDS were constantly stretched thin, the federal government waged a relentless dirty-tricks campaign against the group, and certain internal debates—concerning SDS's structure, strategy, and programs—were all too predictable.[8] But even amid all of this, SDS never lacked various internal newsletters that helped to raise people's stakes in the organization. Although a few New Leftists tried to reach a wide public audience with their writings, in scrutinizing SDS through the lens of print culture, our attention turns not just to *ideas* set forth in the SDS's published works, but also to the *cultural work* they accomplished through their printed materials. In addition to trying to build an intellectual framework for the Movement's expansion, SDS created an ethos surrounding its printed communications that welcomed people into the movement and encouraged their democratic activity. This was no small thing; before long, underground newspapers in every region of the country began playing a similar role.

STUDENTS FOR A DEMOCRATIC SOCIETY was officially founded in 1960, but for all intents and purposes, the group launched itself in June 1962 at a United Auto Workers camp in Port Huron, Michigan, when fifty-nine of its members gathered there to complete the Port Huron Statement—a twenty-four-thousand-word manifesto that was originally drafted by Tom Hayden.[9] Today a certain mystique surrounds the document, some of which is deserved, some perhaps not.[10] On the one hand, only a cynic would deny the romantic appeal of young intellectuals writing a political *cri de coeur* from the edges of a Michigan forest. But the popular notion that the Port Huron Statement rekindled a moribund left is overblown.[11] It actually appeared during a rising tide of political activism and cultural nonconformity among young people, and while the new student radicalism was a fertile topic for journalists in the early 1960s, few of them regarded SDS's manifesto as especially important.[12] Finally, while more than a few 1960s veterans claim that their readings of the Port Huron Statement provoked a certain frisson, others found it rather dull. Those SDS leaders who have admitted that they found sections of it "tedious" or "boring" are probably more representative of the New Left as a whole.[13]

But if it is true that an essential ingredient of politics is timing, then the Port Huron Statement's authors were maestros. The manifesto's celebrated opening salvo—"We are people of this generation, bred in at least modest comfort, housed now in universities, looking uncomfortably at the world we inherit"—put into prose the smoldering discontent of countless students in the Cold War era.[14] Its dour conclusion—"If we appear to seek the unattainable . . . then let it be known that we do so to avoid the unimaginable"—captured a sense of moral urgency among young leftists.[15] Its impertinence—the notion that it represented an "agenda for a generation"—reflected the outsized ambitions of many baby-boomers idealists.[16] Its strategic call for "realignment" (which meant replacing the Democratic Party's Dixiecrats with left-liberals) struck a familiar chord, but its suggestion that students themselves could be the driving forces for social change was novel.

Finally, the Port Huron Statement popularized participatory democracy, the idea that people should have some say over the decisions that affect their lives.[17] Participatory democracy did not originate in the New Left; many whites gleaned the concept from the civil rights movement, particularly the Student Nonviolent Coordinating Committee's emphasis on consensus building and "group-centered leadership."[18] Others had been educated in the virtues and pleasures of civic engagement through their encounters with theorists like Arnold Kaufman and C. Wright Mills. As SDS biographer James Miller argues, participatory democracy was never adequately defined, and eventually the concept became hopelessly tangled up with the New Left's calls for direct action and personal "authenticity."[19] Nevertheless, it provided a rationale for any number of left-inflected political activities in the 1960s, and it offered a simple way of critiquing all sorts of existing institutions.

Equally important, it promised to frame social relations within the New Left itself.[20] Whatever different shades of meaning participatory democracy may have had in the 1960s, on this point the Port Huron Statement seems reasonably clear. One of the "root principles" of participatory democracy, it said, was the idea that "decision making of basic social consequence [must] be carried on by public groupings." Furthermore, politics should be "seen positively, as the art of collectively creating an acceptable pattern of social relations" and bringing people "out of isolation and into community."[21] If participatory democracy remained rather vague as a macropolitical analysis, as a basic interactional model within SDS it was easily understood and implemented. Of course, people could (and did) quibble about the details: Did participatory democracy mean that decisions should be made by consensus, or simply by consensus-building methods? Should leadership positions be frequently rotated, or abolished altogether? Who knew? But participatory democracy did not need to be crisply formulated to function effectively as a bedrock ideal; certainly very few New Leftists ever called for centralized decision making, entrenched leadership, or rigid hierarchies.[22]

Members of SDS gathered in small groups to refine various sections of the Port Huron Statement that Hayden had already drafted with help from others, and they finished their work in three days. For decades afterward, many of those who collaborated on the project retained glowing memories of the whole experience. Dorothy Burlage recalled, "People kept operating out of idealism and their instincts about what would create a better world. It was a rare moment in history, and we were blessed to be given that opportunity."[23] Barbara Jacobs (later Barbara Haber) remembered feeling "like the luckiest person on earth for having had either the good luck or the good sense" to have made it to Port Huron; the conference, she said, was "dazzlingly exciting."[24] An often-overlooked preface to the Port Huron Statement underscores its democratic spirit. "This document represents the results of several months of writing and discussion among the membership," it begins. The preface goes on to explain that the manifesto should not be regarded as the final word on SDS's ideology, but rather as "a *living document* open to change with our times and experiences. It is a beginning: in our own debate and education, [and] in our dialogue with society."[25] In other words, the Port Huron Statement was itself a product of the collaborative ethos that it championed in its text. It offered a critique of society and specific strategies for change, as well as being a symbol and an embodiment of participatory democracy itself.

Although SDS began establishing a democratic print culture with the Port Huron Statement, the ethos they built around their printed communications did not become a pronounced force in the organization right away. Instead, it evolved gradually, over the course of several years, in an effort to retain the harmonious social relations that characterized SDS when it was founded. To understand how this happened, it is necessary to briefly examine SDS's institutional history in the period following the Port Huron conference, as it began growing into a larger, more heterogeneous organization.

For a time, the same sense of camaraderie that marked the group's retreat to the Michigan woodlands continued to propel SDS. As one former member recalled, Tom Hayden and Al Haber personally drew many people into their fold. "They would go find people they . . . connected with on a gut level. It wasn't 'Do you believe in the principles of unity?' It was, 'You feel good to me. I have the feeling you're very bright and you're spirited and we see things basically the same way.' So this was a hand-recruited bunch of people who really wanted to use their lives to change the world, and who loved finding each other."[26] Frithjof Bergmann, a professor at the University of Michigan in the early 1960s, said much the same thing: "The nucleus attracted good people."[27] Most were high achievers—student government leaders, editors of campus newspapers, and precocious intellects—who were united by friendship and mutual admiration.[28] As a result, dialogue was eased by a "mutual awareness." As Dick Flacks put it, "You could trust each other, even if you disagreed."[29]

SDS meetings were typically thorough and intensive. Jeremy Brecher, who attended his first SDS National Council meeting in New York City in 1963 while he was an undergraduate at Reed College, found himself enthralled by the group's "freewheeling discussions," not least because they seemed scrubbed clean of the Old Left's sectarianism. "They weren't talking about the history of Soviet-American relations and who was right in 1956," he said. Instead, meetings provoked "emotional and political responses that were relevant" to people's lived experience.[30] Alan Haber's influence seemed particularly notable. According to Brecher, Haber "was the one who taught [SDS activists] to be thoughtful and argumentative without being sectarian. . . . He had set the tone of a place that was committed to open discussion and yet also politically committed."[31]

Moreover, so long as SDS remained very small, there was room for deeply felt personal conversations. Ann Arbor peace activist Elise Boulding recalled one memorable evening when "eight or ten" SDSers attended a New Year's party at her home one year. After her husband, the economist Kenneth Boulding, read aloud Alfred Lord Tennyson's "Ring Out Wild Bells" at the stroke of midnight, a group gathered on the living room floor in front of the fireplace:

> They began asking each other how they might have dealt with situations each had faced, like having police dogs unleashed on them. How do you protect yourself from a police dog that is taught to leap at your throat? . . . For middle class students who had come from protected families, this was the first time they had faced raw violence. They were totally unprepared for it. This was a time for them to share with each other what it meant to them, how much it had hurt them inside— much more than the outside hurt—and what it meant to feel afraid. The tone of the dialogue impressed me profoundly, because there wasn't a trace of defensiveness or even hostility. It was beyond all that. . . . Their conversation went on for hours. I just sat, barely breathing. I felt I was tapping another dimension of human experience that was very rare. One just didn't hear people sharing at that level.[32]

This very same group, however, could also appear cliquish and self-absorbed. Looking back, one SDS veteran even characterized himself this way: "I honestly walked around with the feeling, as narrow and group-centered as it was, that if you weren't in SDS your life was empty and you were not perceiving what was really happening," he said.[33] Another former member, Barry Bluestone, said that his first impression of SDS was that it was dominated by "purely political people [who] had no other interests at all." When he attended an SDS retreat in 1962, it only seemed to confirm his negative assessment. "It seemed to me there was more to life than debating . . . infinitely detailed political nuances," he recalled. Only later did he learn that "you could get intensely involved and entwined with political struggle and yet still lead a full and active and enjoyable life."[34]

Another problem arose from the fact that although elitism was officially discouraged in SDS, the group maintained an obvious internal pecking order. According to Brecher, while "there was no intimidation about arguing" with the so-called "heavies" in the organization—people like Tom Hayden, Al Haber, Dick Flacks, Paul Potter, "and to some degree Steve Max"—it was often a foregone conclusion that "obviously their rap was going to take the way [and] your rap wasn't."[35] Moreover, no matter how inclusive SDS aimed to be, some members *were* intimidated, simply because others shined so brightly. Jacobs recalled a summer afternoon when Hayden—in many respects the early New Left's *beau ideal*—cockily announced (with his feet on the desk, while reading the *New York Times*) that the Democratic Party's "realignment" was all but imminent, "and [so] it was time for him and Al [Haber] and Casey [Hayden] to get in the car and drive down to Washington." When Jacobs read the same newspaper article without managing to reach a similar conclusion, she thought to herself, "'Boy, he's a genius and I'm dumb. He knows how to read the *New York Times* and then he has the guts to go down and talk to congressmen,' which I never would have the guts to do."[36] Another SDS veteran, looking back with almost two decades of hindsight, said, "I still consider [SDS's founders] to be some of the most brilliant people of our generation, and I still, in some ways, idolize those folks."[37]

Finally, although the issue of sexism within the New Left had yet to emerge as a topic of conversation, women generally took secondary roles in SDS. Today, SDS veterans sometimes disagree over whether women were muscled aside or simply acquiesced to prevailing gender stereotypes, but almost everyone acknowledges that that they were less vocal than men, and that they handled the great majority of what the New Left called "shit-work" (which could include anything from routine office tasks to cooking and cleaning).[38] Cathy Wilkerson recalled that she "first became conscious of the issues around men and women" at the SDS meetings she attended at Swarthmore College in 1963. "I noticed that no women were in leadership positions. No women were really listened to. . . . I realized that to be accepted, you had to date one of the men."[39] Another woman who says she belonged to "a very typical chapter of SDS," recalled that "men tended to dominate all the discussions and women tended to run the mimeograph machine, and would sort of be expected to screw and make meals."[40]

In December 1962, Al Haber and his fiancée, Barbara Jacobs—who, perhaps not coincidentally, was among the women who felt her talents were not being recognized—expressed some of these concerns in a Cassandra-like letter that they distributed among the SDS inner circle. "We have, each in different ways, felt isolated, missed communication from the national office or from projects, missed a sense of membership activity and élan, and squirmed with a feeling of in-groupishness," they said. SDS was "still an association of friends, and not yet an organization where the individual member has dignity and respect and is the concern of the 'leadership.'"[41] Although a few SDSers resented the letter's tone, its general thrust was hard to refute. SDS may have described itself as a "national" organization in 1962–63, but this was an obvious conceit: It was barely solvent and basically jerry-built, with only four hundred members and nine chapters rigged together through a combination of meetings, conferences, and occasional visits from field secretary Steve Max.[42]

Moreover, the Haber-Jacobs missive arrived at a propitious moment, as the October 1962 Cuban Missile Crisis had had a truly unsettling effect on SDS—most obviously because it raised the horrible specter of nuclear war, but also because it threw into sharp relief the enormous chasm between SDS's outsized ambitions and its organizational capabilities. In New York City, SDS activists could do little more than greet the nuclear standoff with mordant humor.[43] In Ann Arbor, students responded by converging on Tom and Casey Hayden's home, where they ran up a massive phone bill trying to keep tabs on protest activity that unfolded elsewhere; all they accomplished locally was to organize a tiny demonstration at the University of Michigan, where they were pelted with eggs and tomatoes by an opposing group of students.[44]

Much of what SDS required in this period was obvious: "A lot of plain dirty fundraising and a lot of laborious chapter organizing."[45] But SDS leaders also recognized that if their group was to grow stronger and more cohesive, it would need to experiment with new approaches.[46] The democratic idealism that fueled the Port Huron Statement would not be enough. As a result, they began promoting new ways of communicating with the membership through print. In short, they tried to replicate on paper what was attractive about SDS meetings (the warm, honest, probing discussions that helped to build a store of trust and a sense of community), while mitigating those qualities that hampered the organization (its ineffectuality, clannishness, and unequal participation). SDS may have been infused with a collaborative spirit from the beginning, but the values and assumptions that governed many of its communications, and that in turn bonded many people to SDS, evolved out of a painful recognition that participatory democracy—like any form of democracy—did not unfold naturally. It would have to be promoted and protected.

To a considerable degree, SDS expressed its egalitarian social theories through its attitudes toward written correspondence. Although we frequently think of letters as among the most private of communications, in SDS epistolary exchanges were shared liberally. This was true from the beginning, when Tom Hayden sent the very first drafts of the Port Huron Statement to a select group of colleagues, who in turn mailed back their responses, which he retyped, mimeographed, and distributed to the entire group "for the purposes of dialogue and cross fertilization."[47] In subsequent years, however, letters carried on and informed SDS conversations in such unusual ways that Arthur Waskow, a prominent peace activist, asked a friend whether anyone had ever considered the possibility that the New Left was inventing a "new literary form."[48]

Sometimes, SDSers passed letters around by hand (and since they were frequently typed with carbons, multiple copies abounded). National secretary Clark Kissinger once acknowledged that unless his missives from the Chicago national office were marked "personal," he expected them to be circulated in this way.[49] On other occasions, New Leftists orchestrated an exchange of letters on a particular issue, intending their correspondence to be distributed to others, so as to expose the student community to differing points of view. At Swarthmore College, which had a strong SDS chapter, activists launched a small, mimeographed magazine called *Albatross* that was made up entirely of letters that students had also sent to campus and public officials "on such matters as the Cuban situation, the Un-American Activities Committee, the Peace Corps, foreign policy in Africa, and the sit-ins." Recipients of these letters were told that duplicate copies were slated to be reprinted in *Albatross*, a magazine read by "several thousand students and adults." The idea "was not only to make Congressmen attentive to the letters but to inform and consolidate student opinion."[50] Similarly, New Leftists sometimes used the epistolary form when writing for a larger audience, say by publishing dispatches from their travels or open letters to the SDS community.[51] Finally, letters originally intended as private exchanges sometimes appeared in print later on, in one of SDS's various newsletters, or in its official newspaper, *New Left Notes*.[52]

Usually this happened with the author's blessings, but not always. The democratic sensibilities of some New Leftists were such that they could be remarkably casual about copyrights, permissions, and rights of privacy.[53] Occasionally, letter writers even took special care to indicate that they did *not* want to see their correspondence published.[54] Certainly Steve Max was not pleased when, on several occasions, SDS officers published his private letters. The final straw came when someone at *New Left Notes* took the liberty of printing a personal letter sharply critical of a recent essay by someone Max admired—the distinguished author and labor activist Sidney Lens. "Listen you sons of bitches, if I wanted my letter on the Sid Lens piece printed, I would have asked to have it printed," Max exclaimed. "Unlike some people in SDS there is nothing wrong with my toilet training and I don't feel the need to communicate my every thought to the entire world. When I write for publication, I try to write in a bit more reasoned and careful way than when I dash a note to you screwups." (To Sidney Lens, Max added, "I must apologize . . . for my unfortunate use of the word 'didleywack.'")[55]

The question of just how much confidentiality SDS's letter writers could expect provoked a revealing discussion at a 1964 National Council meeting. The issue came up when Vernon Grizzard, head of one of SDS's Economic Research and Action Projects, suggested that certain sensitive correspondence relating to their work should be stored in locked file cabinets.[56] But others strenuously disagreed; Shelly Blum worried that the proposal made SDS look like an "autocracy" and argued that "there should be some leniency in who sees what." Robert Ross was even more adamant: "Any dues paying member should be able to see all [SDS] correspondence," he said. "As soon as confidential files not open to all are established, a new elite is set up. People should feel that they know what is happening in the organization."

When someone else noted that there were important security considerations to take into account, Doug Ireland dismissed the claim as "old left conspiratorialism." "The FBI won't be prevented from getting information from a locked file," he scoffed. Another member suggested the group should simply rely on the good judgment of SDS's elected officers to decide which letters should be kept confidential, but added that, of course, the files should be left "fairly open." Only Todd Gitlin said flatly, "It should be the right of a member to decide who will read what he writes." When Dickie Magidoff argued that the case for confidentiality should not hinge on political considerations, but rather upon "pragmatic and functional" ones (apparently having to do with that fact that a few "nuts" were beginning to hang around the office), Ross amplified his argument that the very idea of holding letters in locked file cabinets was antithetical to SDS values. SDS would not be treating people equally if the National Council allowed one group of people to see its letters, but not others. "We're acting like people who attach more importance to little things without some concern for the way we do business," he added. The discussion finally wound down when the group settled on a compromise: SDS's files would be left open to the membership, except for certain sensitive materials that could be stored elsewhere "at the discretion of the president and national secretary." Although Ross's position didn't fully carry the day, the National Council clearly took special care to protect SDS's reputation as a democratic community.

The National Council also helped to establish SDS's print culture at a meeting in Columbus, Ohio, in 1962, when it voted to launch a newsletter called the *Discussion Bulletin*. Unlike SDS's *Membership Bulletin*, which aimed to keep people up to date on SDS's activities, the *Discussion Bulletin*—often called the "*DB*" for short—was designed to stimulate discussion on the Port Huron Statement, although it soon opened itself up to a much wider range of concerns.[57] The National Council charged the group's indefatigable assistant national secretary, Don McKelvey, with putting the *DB* in motion.[58] Having graduated from Haverford College in 1960, McKelvey was slightly older than most of SDS's members, and as a former National Secretary for the Student Peace Union, he had prior experience working in a highly democratic organization.[59] At the same time, he had an almost sentimental attachment to the *Discussion Bulletin*, and in his frequent correspondence with new and prospective members he promoted it zealously. Later, the *Membership* and *Discussion Bulletins* were streamlined into a single *SDS Bulletin*, and Helen Garvy and then Jeff Shero took turns as editors, until the entire operation was scrapped in 1966 to make room for SDS's tabloid newspaper, *New Left Notes*. Regardless of who was at the helm, these newsletters welcomed input from anyone who wanted to contribute, even if they were not SDS members.[60] This easygoing editorial policy aimed to generate a steady flow of ideas in SDS, but it served another important purpose as well; as McKelvey put it at the time, people's written contributions were thought to facilitate the "creation of community."[61] Garvy agreed, but added that the *Bulletin* likewise functioned as a countervailing force against SDS's testosterone-fueled meetings. "I saw it as an equalizer," she recalled. "Sometimes meetings were dominated by whoever talked the loudest,"[62] and from her perspective, the *Bulletin* represented a way "to bring members into the mainstream of the organization—into its thoughts and discussions."[63]

The *Discussion Bulletin* appeared irregularly, and no one expended much effort on its design. At first McKelvey printed it from SDS's headquarters on East 19th Street in New York City on a hand-cranked mimeograph machine; later, Garvy produced it on colored paper through an offset printer after SDS moved its operations to Chicago. Only when Jeff Shero took over in late 1965 did the *Bulletin* begin featuring a few photographs, illustrations, and sidebars. (Later Schero became heavily involved in the underground press, and from 1968 to 1970 he edited New York City's second major underground paper, the *Rat*.) One gets a sense of the special role it played by how the SDS faithful described it—almost never as a newsletter, but rather as an "organ of intellectual exchange," a "dialogue," a "forum," or a "medium."[64] Just as it was an article of faith in SDS that politics grew out of personal experiences rather than entrenched ideologies, the *Bulletin* was spurred on by the notion that the very process of writing—of sitting down, laboring over one's prose, and putting ink to paper—often helped people to sharpen thinking, crystallize viewpoints, and generate new discoveries.[65] When a student from Georgia State University inquired about how to go about building an SDS chapter there, McKelvey suggested he might begin by asking new members to write critiques of the Port Huron Statement. This was "most important," he said, because "those who write . . . are, hopefully, stimulated to thinking and writing on their own."[66] To a student at Rutgers University, he underscored "the importance to you and others . . . of examining what you're doing in order to articulate your thoughts about it."[67]

The opinions of newcomers were particularly welcomed. As McKelvey told one student, "We especially need the comments of people who were not involved in the writing of the [Port Huron Statement]."[68] Similarly, editors took special care to solicit commentary from grassroots members, reminding them that they, too, had a stake in the SDS's future. When Garvy took over the *Bulletin* in October 1964, one of the first things she did was draft an editorial announcing, "The SDS program and analysis are neither static nor complete. There is a continuing dialogue within SDS and it should not be limited to . . . members who are active at the national level."[69] The *Bulletin* also sometimes published local chapter reports, which gave members an idea of the scope of SDS's activity and a sense of connection to a larger movement.

But the *Bulletin*'s editors especially prized dissenting opinions, iconoclastic proposals, and sharply argued theories—anything at all, in fact, to keep SDS ideas from calcifying into orthodoxy.[70] As McKelvey said at the time, SDS must avoid presenting itself "as a package of set ideas and dictated actions."[71] When a student wrote to ask whether SDS had any connections to the Communist Party, McKelvey answered that it did not, but he added that he worried that "overconcern with communism . . . contributes to an atmosphere in which young people . . . fear to inquire in 'unsafe' ways."[72] By contrast, SDS depended on its vigorous spirit of inquiry. When another student wrote in announcing he would like to join SDS, but that he didn't always see eye-to-eye with everyone in the organization, he might have been surprised at McKelvey's reply: "I am more than glad to hear that you disagree with several of our members' published opinions," he said. The student was encouraged to give full vent to his disagreements in the *Bulletin*.[73]

So accessible were the *Bulletin*'s pages that its editors rarely fulfilled all of the duties their titles implied. "I really ain't no editor," McKelvey once confessed. "In fact, one of the reasons the *SDS Bulletin* has gotten so big . . . has been my general refusal to edit things, to cut things out, my desire to include everything. I have *compiled* an increasingly good—and now excellent—Bulletin; I've edited nothing, really."[74] Shero, a colorful activist (who once campaigned for an end to segregated toilets at the University of Texas at Austin under the slogan "Let My People Go") proved equally reticent to exercise his editorial hand. "I've no fixed policy on editing copy, but tend to want to edit as little as possible," he wrote. "I conceive [of the *Bulletin*] as a democratic publication growing from the membership's concerns rather than a news magazine [coming] from the national office." When on one occasion an especially prolix letter arrived, Shero asked its author for permission to pare it down, adding humorously, "[t]his confronts my budding neo anarchist tendencies with severe and difficult mental problems."[75]

Shero recognized the obvious dilemma that arose from such a laissez-faire editorial approach: "A democratic publication sacrifices professionalism so that all the voices, even the halting and poorly expressed, can be heard, yet at the same time a shoddy production will not serve the needs of the membership."[76] Most of the *Bulletin*'s contributors were college aged, and while some were very talented, it was rare that their work would not have profited from an editor's red pen. With such minimal editorial oversight, the *Bulletin* always had a certain stitched-together quality. One typical issue covered an ongoing New York City newspaper strike, U.S. relations with China and Cuba, the peace movement, and the McCarren Internal Security Act of 1950.[77] Another issue ran an analysis of the 1964 congressional elections, a debate on SDS's Peace and Research Education Project, correspondence between two SDSers about how to organize the unemployed, and a news report about a misadventure that Tom Hayden had with the Newark Police Department.[78]

Another persistent problem that the *Bulletin*'s editors grappled with was that in spite of their eagerness to accommodate SDS writers, they frequently had difficulty getting rank-and-file members to contribute the kinds of material they hoped for. During their tenures, all three of the *Bulletin*'s editors—McKelvey, Garvy, and Shero—made urgent appeals for more writing, and sometimes they seemed convinced that printed discourse was as essential to SDS's survival as food and water are to living creatures. In one unsigned editorial, someone said that writing "substantive pieces" for the *Bulletin* was as important as attending SDS's upcoming national convention, for without such writings "SDS cannot build the politically and socially conscious base on campuses which it must build in order to attain even the most modest success."[79] Around the same time, McKelvey circulated a memo flatly telling SDS organizers that if they didn't participate in conversations through the *Bulletin*, "the organization won't grow and be cohesive."[80] Garvy similarly pleaded with SDS's inner circle to produce copy for the *Bulletin*. "I really feel strongly [that] there should be more discussion—and in a public way, involving as many members as possible. . . . And I'm really at a loss as to how to get this going."[81]

The editors may well have been laboring under unduly high expectations, since during most of the time that the *Bulletin* was in operation SDS remained relatively quiescent. This changed rather quickly after the Berkeley free speech movement got under way in September 1964. Then in March 1965, students and faculty at the University of Michigan organized an all-night teach-in against the Vietnam War that attracted some three thousand students. Similar events were soon replicated on dozens of campuses. The following April, SDS spearheaded the first national rally against the Vietnam War in Washington, DC. Expecting a turnout of about five thousand, organizers were amazed when the gathering, on a balmy spring afternoon, attracted upwards of twenty thousand. Meanwhile, several major magazines and newspapers published long articles describing the new student intelligentsia.[82] As a result, membership in SDS swelled from 29 chapters and just one thousand members in June 1964 to 124 chapters and more than four thousand official members by the end of 1965.[83]

From SDS's perspective, the only problem with this upsurge was that it came on so suddenly that it proved difficult to manage. To cite but one telling anecdote, when former SDS president Todd Gitlin embarked on a speaking tour through several Great Plains states in the fall of 1965, he discovered three functioning SDS chapters that no one in the national office even knew existed.[84] Brecher summed up the exigencies SDS faced in an internal memorandum:

From an organization almost non-existent outside of the East Coast and Middle West, we have become an outfit with a severe case of national sprawl—so spread out we can hardly keep in touch across the continent. We have grown so much in size that whereas less than two years ago almost everybody knew everybody else, now hardly anybody but the "old gang" knows anybody else. Our function has grown from an organization where people got together to talk about the things they were doing in various movements to one [that] has its own extended program on half-a-dozen fronts, involving wildly different kinds of people and approaches.[85]

Implied, but unstated, was the widely shared sense that the influx of these "wildly different kinds of people" had produced a *Kulturkampf* in SDS. Far removed in both temperament and background from the doughty, often well-heeled progressives who helped found SDS, this new generation of radicals—sometimes called the "prairie power" faction of SDS because many of them came from the South and the West—were mainly novices. More likely to be guided by urgent moral considerations than by any ideological traditions, some among them lacked the old guard's sophistication, urbanity, and *savoir faire*.[86] Many years later, former SDS national secretary Greg Calvert, who was closely aligned with the prairie-power faction, still bristled at the memory of being treated by some of SDS's old guard with "upper middle class arrogance," as if he were "some sort of ignorant bum"—a galling experience for anyone, but especially so for Calvert, who grew up in severe rural poverty but held a PhD in history from Cornell University.[87]

In a surprisingly unguarded letter to SDS benefactors, national secretary Paul Booth pointed out the shift in member profile:

From a movement of theorists we have become largely a movement of activists. . . . Where two years ago, the model SDS personality was someone doing a master's thesis on C. Wright Mills, today he is a college dropout. Where we used to spend months prior to an SDS convention debating the preparation of a document of political analysis and strategy, today . . . activists with radical humanist values implement whatever analysis strikes them as appropriate.[88]

Booth's letter injected a dose of hyperbole in the situation, for at no point was SDS ever in jeopardy of being overrun by a scrum of college dropouts.[89] But others echoed his concern that the new members who were surging into SDS might have something of the effect of a downhill stream, loosening its agenda and carrying its nonhierarchical tendencies into uncharted waters. In a

National Guardian article, Steve Max grumbled that SDS's "fantastic growth" and heterogeneity carried a hidden cost: an "anything goes" ethos that threatened to undermine its political coherence. A "high degree of programmatic consensus" in the Port Huron Era had given way, he said, to a "Pandora's Box of theories of social change."[90]

SDS's disastrous national convention at Kewadin, Michigan, in June 1965 stoked Max's fear; by almost all accounts, newcomers felt excluded, old guarders were threatened, and discussions proved tedious. Robert Pardun—a fresh arrival to SDS—recalled the Kewadin meetings "tended to be dominated by a few articulate men who spoke often and seemed to enjoy the political bantering." This might have been tolerable enough, but Pardun also found something discrepant about the fact that these old guarders were so concerned with "winning" their various debates. By this time, Pardun had already reached an understanding—strongly encouraged in SDS writings—that "democracy and winning aren't the same thing. Winning is about overwhelming the opposition while democracy, as we defined it, encouraged everyone to participate in making collective decisions."[91]

The sudden upsurge in SDS also put a new strain on the *Bulletin*. Originally designed to promote membership participation and organizational dialogue, it now tried to keep tabs on the widening range of SDS activities; to function, in short, much more like a traditional news bulletin. Complaints that SDS wasn't keeping its members up to date were particularly pointed when coming from members who lived in regions where SDS had yet to gain a significant toehold. As one letter writer put it, "Being out in the wilderness like this makes one feel lost to the national tone of SDS."[92] Similarly, a regional organizer from San Francisco complained, "The longer I am on the West Coast the more I become concerned over the lack of communication between the [national office] and SDS in general. . . . I am completely in the dark as to what has been happening in the East over the last two or three weeks."[93]

The National Council responded to these concerns by revamping the *Bulletin* so that it would appear weekly rather than monthly. In the summer of 1965, Shero was elected vice president of SDS largely on the basis of his pledges to do just this.[94] Shortly thereafter, he sent out a note promising that the "new" *Bulletin* would give "the widest possible view" of recent SDS activity.[95] Here again we see evidence of SDS's confidence in the power of printed material, but as sociologist Francesca Polletta points out, with hindsight, this may seem a rather small-scale solution to the divisions that were plaguing SDS.[96] Besides, even the "new and improved" *Bulletin* failed to meet everyone's expectations. One supposedly lackluster issue prompted a reader to snap, "People's literature isn't sacred merely because it comes from the people's [*sic*]! . . . If SDS is growing as rapidly as everything we read would have us believe, why the hell isn't there more substantive news about the chapters?"[97] In this same period, the national office received at least two more letters from members who claimed they learned more about what was happening in SDS from major newspapers and magazines than from SDS itself.[98]

After only a few more months, the *Bulletin* folded, this time for good. (Most members learned of its demise in January 1966 when its tabloid replacement, *New Left Notes*, arrived in their mailboxes with a front-page headline reading "SURPRISE!")[99] As the chief means of internal communication among the growing number of chapters that were operating more or less independently, *New Left Notes* marked a turn in the history of SDS's print culture. Whereas SDS had once relied on printed dialogues as a way of shoring up its identity as a democratic organization, by the mid-1960s its character and temperament were no longer in question. The new challenge for the national office was simply to keep tabs on SDS as it outgrew its cosseted childhood to become an established force in the organized Left. Nevertheless, *New Left Notes* still bore more than a passing resemblance to its predecessor. Edited at first by Shero, it featured on its masthead the old Economic Research and Action Project slogan, "Let the People Decide," in its masthead, and, as SDS historian Kirkpatrick Sale quipped, "In terms of how the paper presented itself that is exactly how it was edited. Almost any scrap of news, any letter, any essay or comment that came into the paper found its way into print."[100]

In this way, SDS was living up to its democratic promise. The group never quite had a fixed identity—its own members sometimes described it as amoeba-like, as an *"organism* as well as an *organization"*[101]—but in its early years, the social processes that guided SDS's printed communications contributed to its reputation as an accessible, egalitarian New Left organization. True, this spirit was present at SDS's founding, when fifty-nine of its charter members contributed to the redrafting of Tom Hayden's Port Huron Statement. Not only was the manifesto written collectively; its supple-minded authors also conceived of it as a "living document," subject to future deliberations by SDS's membership. But it was only later, in response to specific exigencies, that SDS fashioned a culture of print that granted liberal access to its records, in which letters were freely circulated, editors deferred to writers, and newsletters were regarded not as official organs but as running dialogues to which everyone was welcome to contribute.

Of course, this ethos carried its own built-in biases; just as not everyone had the force of personality or "mystique" that was required to be an SDS leader, not everyone in the New Left had the wherewithal to capably express themselves in print. Nevertheless, by the mid-1960s, SDS was known on the Left as a group that "passed the charisma around."[102] Its print culture is part of the reason why. Soon, underground newspapers would begin playing a very similar role, affording a basis for community among activists and avant-gardists, and helping to democratize the youth rebellion. With this in mind, the notion that the New Left was founded not by any individual, nor even by any group of persons, but rather by SDS's mimeograph machine, is so rich a metaphor that if it hadn't already been suggested, one would almost feel compelled to invent it.

2

A Hundred Blooming Papers

*Culture and Community in the 1960s
Underground Press*

METAPHORS, OF COURSE, are supposed to be revealing, and when radical
journalist Walt Crowley observed that by the summer of 1966, underground
newssheets were "popping up . . . like mushrooms after a spring rain," he was
no doubt aiming to convey his enthusiasm for the underground press.[1] Similarly, *Time* magazine revealed something about its standpoint when it commented on precisely the same phenomenon in July 1966, only it had the
papers "popping up like weeds."[2] Either way, it's clear that by the mid-1960s,
the climate for youth-oriented, antiestablishment newspapers had quickly
become fertile. Although these papers varied widely in terms of their quality,
size, and style, together they documented the New Left's efflorescence and
subjected defenders of the established culture to unprecedented levels of
scrutiny and ridicule. Along with the new gravitas in rock and roll, the rising
tide of campus-based activism, and the outré countercultural style, underground newspapers began contributing mightily to the New Left's sense that
it stood at the heart of a new society.

An examination of the early histories of three of the New Left's "prototyp-
ical" newspapers—the *Los Angeles Free Press*, East Lansing, Michigan's, *The
Paper*, and the *Rag*, from Austin, Texas (established in 1964, 1965, and 1966,
respectively)—reveals some of the ways that they emboldened activists and
dissenters in their own communities.[3] Each of these tabloids grew out of relatively isolated regional subcultures, and they originally presented themselves

as *community* newspapers, aiming to defend local avant-gardists, provide forums for neighborhood activists, and irritate campus administrators or municipal officials. Ironically, their provincialism was the main source of their influence and prestige. As SDS officer Jeff Shero remarked, the "early underground papers were very powerful because they were generally started locally and dealt a lot with what people knew, that electrified people."[4] But their bloom was brief; after playing a vital role by strengthening the activist movements in their own backyards, many underground newspapers became mouthpieces for militant New Leftists and third-world revolutionaries, and in turn lost much of their distinctive local flavor. Having hitched their fortunes to the national youth rebellion, they could not survive its collapse, and by the early 1970s the nation's underground newspapers melted away with all the sound and fury of a fading flower. The metaphor is deliberate; as goes an ancient Chinese proverb, at the peak of a blossom's beauty comes an intimation of the beginning of its decline.

UNDERGROUND JOURNALISTS of the 1960s sometimes drew self-serving comparisons between themselves and their earliest forebears, the pamphleteers of the American Revolution. Pamphlets had the virtue of flexibility—George Orwell once quipped that they need only be "topical, polemical, and short"[5]—and after the Port Huron Statement, many more New Left pamphlets found their way into print. But they were usually written by individuals rather than groups, and they were not always the preferred literary form among young people aiming to build a movement based on cooperation and democratic participation.

Another comparison can be drawn between the underground press and the very first types of dissident newspapers in American history—the labor-movement weeklies that appeared during the market revolution and the celebrated abolitionist papers of the antebellum period. As media historian Roger Streitmatter suggests, pioneering organs like Philadelphia's *Mechanic's Free Press*, New York's *Working Man's Advocate*, and Boston's *Liberator* all faced obstacles that radical papers of the 1960s grappled with, including severe financial hardship and unvarnished hostility from the mainstream press. The underground newspapers also generally regarded their papers as an open forum, as had their radical ancestors. "Having themselves been denied access to mainstream papers," Streitmatter writes, "the earliest dissident editors were committed to publishing not only their own ideas but also those of their readers—including ideas in direct conflict with their own."[6]

In the early twentieth century, the country's most widely read radical newspaper was *Appeal to Reason*, a Kansas-based socialist organ that at one point boasted a paid circulation of over 750,000, thanks largely to the efforts of its massive "salesman army" of volunteers who doggedly peddled the paper in public meeting places, parks, and on street corners—the same types of places where hippies and activists later hawked their underground newspapers.[7] Meanwhile, out of New York City's Greenwich Village came the *Masses*, a sophisticated monthly journal edited by Max Eastman that advertised the styles and sensibilities of the pre–World War I avant-garde.[8]

The journalistic guerillas of the 1960s, however, had more direct influences than the tradesmen and abolitionists of the nineteenth century, or the lyrical left of the early twentieth century. First, there were those outspoken thinkers and writers who directly challenged American culture and values in the 1950s and early 1960s: beat-generation scribes, trenchant social critics like C. Wright Mills and Paul Goodman, satirical novelists like Joseph Heller and Kurt Vonnegut Jr., dramatists like Lorraine Hansberry and Leroi Jones (later Amiri Baraka), and writer-activists like James Baldwin, each of whom produced work that rested uneasily alongside popular characterizations of the Eisenhower era as one of tranquility, optimism, and innocence.

Existential literature also came into vogue in the late 1950s and early 1960s, as disaffected youths wrestled with shallowness, boredom, competition, the struggle for meaning and purpose, and other conundrums of modern living.[9] In 1953 maverick journalist I. F. Stone launched *I. F. Stone's Weekly*, his own muckraking newsletter. Instead of attending press briefings or cultivating high-powered sources, Stone meticulously scoured public documents in order to uncover official hypocrisy, mendacity, and various abuses of the public trust, all hidden in plain sight. The next year, Irving Howe and Lewis Coser began publishing *Dissent*, a quarterly journal popular with New York intellectuals that aimed to combat what the editors called "the bleak atmosphere of conformism that pervades the political and intellectual life of the United States."[10] Meanwhile, the artists and writers who put together the satirical comic book *Mad* formed a kind of "alternative New York intellectual circle" that presaged the 1960s counterculture.[11]

But more than any other publications, lower Manhattan's *Village Voice* and Paul Krassner's satirical magazine, the *Realist*, helped to pioneer the kind of offbeat and subversive approaches that youthful journalists of the 1960s mimicked and amplified. The *Voice* came first. Founded by Ed Fancher, Dan Wolf, and Norman Mailer in 1955, the liberal weekly sold for five cents and was at first only available downtown. Few would have predicted its success; Fancher was the only one of the three who had ever dabbled in journalism, but he'd never come close to managing or publishing a newspaper. Wolf was an unaccomplished forty-one-year-old, known throughout Greenwich Village as a brilliant conversationalist, but clearly lacking in marketable skills. And though Mailer was famous for writing *The Naked and the Dead* in 1948, his two subsequent novels were poorly reviewed flops, his second marriage was floundering, and his personality was becoming increasingly erratic from his overconsumption of alcohol, marijuana, barbiturates, and amphetamines. According to *Village Voice* historian Kevin McAuliffe, none of the three had a clear idea "of what the hell they were doing or what they were getting themselves into."[12] They all agreed, however, that the *Voice* would be a *writer's paper*. That is, they would simply publish the best material they received, with minimal editorial oversight or interference.[13] Wolf "was a brilliant editor because he didn't edit," a friend recalled. "Every writer was crazy about him."[14] According to Wolf, the paper's amateurish quality reflected its mission. "The *Village Voice* was originally conceived as a living, breathing attempt to demolish the notion that one needs to be a professional to accomplish something in a field as purportedly technical as journalism. It was a philosophical position."[15]

The *Voice*'s news coverage sometimes aped what could be found in the suburban press, but its "back of the book" pages—which featured theater, film, and book reviews—attracted numerous talented writers who turned the paper into an acknowledged force.[16] To some who were sensitive to the cultural narrowness of the Cold War era, it was like manna from heaven. One reader later described it as a "godsend . . . a weekly hint that there existed a real place . . . full of people who wouldn't think I was a Commie weirdo every time I opened my mouth."[17] Also noteworthy was the "letters" section, which drew from the Village's reservoir of well-educated, colorfully opinionated habitués. By the paper's third number, McAuliffe writes, "A whole new tradition had been born—the *Village Voice* letter column as community sounding board, as exchange of dialogue and dialectic with its writers, as a repository for random outrageous opinion."[18] Finally, Mailer's darkly comic weekly columns—full of parenthetical asides, personal digressions, and vituperative attacks on his readers—gave the paper an edgy quality that distinguished it from previous Village weeklies.[19] Mailer stayed only about four months at the *Voice*, however, before storming off, ostensibly because of several spelling and typesetting errors in his columns; in fact, the real cause of his departure was his different vision of what the *Voice* should become.

Although the *Voice* in its early years had many qualities that underground newspapers later replicated—a light editorial hand, an interest in the cultural fringes, and a close rapport with its readers—both temperamentally and politically, it was always a liberal paper rather than a radical one, a home to some eccentric thinkers and top-notch writers, but never an outpost for subversives. Mailer, on the other hand, said he wanted to "reach an audience in which no newspaper had yet been interested."[20] In one of his last *Voice* columns, he professed that "after years of the most intense pessimism," he felt "the hints, the clues, the whispers of a new time coming." Accordingly, he wanted to align himself with "the destructive, the liberating, the creative nihilism of Hip, the frantic search for potent Change [that] may break into the open."[21] In short, Mailer wrote, "They wish this newspaper to be more conservative, more Square—I wish it to be more Hip."[22]

At the other extreme from the *Voice*'s hidebound liberalism was Krassner's *Realist*, an irreverent humor magazine that fashioned itself as a kind of adult alternative to *Mad*.[23] For someone who would later be inducted into the Counterculture Hall of Fame (at the Cannabis Cup festival in Amsterdam in 2001) Krassner's background was unusual. A violin prodigy, he became at the age of six the youngest concert artist ever to play Carnegie Hall. When he first started printing the *Realist* in 1958, he was twenty-six years old, still living with his parents, and still a virgin—although as he points out in his autobiography, by then he'd acquired enough experience with the formularies of "heavy petting" to write a very funny sex manual for teenagers—it was called *Guilt without Sex*.[24] Novelist Ken Kesey once said of Krassner, "[He] doesn't imbibe. Not in alcohol, caffeine, or nicotine anyway. Nor have I even known him to pop an aspirin, drop a downer, or plop-plop an Alka-Seltzer."[25]

But like his friend and fellow comedian Lenny Bruce, Krassner had a penchant for biting political humor.[26] His goal with the *Realist*, he said, was to "combine entertainment with the First Amendment," thereby helping to break the "shackles" that constrained humorists during the Cold War.[27] Madison Avenue pitchmen, religious zealots, white supremacists, and McCarthyites were frequent targets of Krassner's wicked humor, but his taste for the absurd meant that people on *both* sides of an issue were often made to seem ridiculous. Around the time of the Cuban Missile Crisis, Krassner ran a cartoon on the cover of the *Realist* that pictured a gorgeous nude woman lying seductively before two unattractive men; the woman was drawn to represent the globe (with longitudinal and latitudinal lines across her round buttocks) while the men were stand-ins for the United States and the Soviet Union; as the American gestures toward the Russian, he tells her, "It's his turn now and then me again."[28] Another time Krassner simultaneously offended prudish conservatives and doctrinaire leftists by printing a star-spangled poster bearing the unlikely slogan: "Fuck Communism."[29]

The *Realist* featured interviews with people who were popular among disaffected youths, in which Krassner unfailingly broached controversial or taboo topics. It also ran fake interviews and imaginary dialogues between famous people that were sometimes hard to recognize as satire—the idea being to prompt readers into reexamining what passes for "normal" in every-day life.[30] Humorous commentary on a wide range of current events and controversies likewise helped define the magazine. And as the parameters governing what was acceptable humor loosened in the middle and late 1960s, the *Realist* continued to press beyond them, sometimes with flagrantly offensive and crudely sexist material.[31] Although some radicals later complained that Krassner's "satirizing everything" approach "lacked the commitment and advocacy" that the underground press movement required, the magazine grew in popularity through most of the 1960s, and at one point its subscribership reached 100,000.[32] But its influence extended even beyond its own readership, for by then countless underground press writers had already set off on their own adventures, looking to explode pieties, confound expectations, and knock over sacred cows. Many years later, when *People* magazine ran a flattering profile identifying Krassner as the "father of the underground press," he replied, "I demand a blood test."[33]

IT CAN BE TEMPTING to regard all of this social criticism and artistic ferment as a kind of nebulous intellectual phenomenon, as if the sentiments and values that nourished the underground press simply drifted over the landscape in an ethereal mist. In fact, many of the ideas that gave rise to New Left journalism had an important material context—they were generated in urban spaces. Iconoclastic thinkers, subversive humorists, and cultural critics in the back pages of the *Village Voice* lived and found their audience in offbeat neighborhoods where like-minded people clustered together. In New York City, Greenwich Village was the magnet for romantics, politicos, artists, and freelance intellectuals (although low rents in the East Village would soon exert a pull of their own).[34] San Francisco's hip district was in North Beach; in Los Angeles, it was Venice. "Other cities," Russell Jacoby writes, "boasted small, sometimes tiny and ephemeral, bohemian sections that served as way stations for young intellectuals."[35] Often, these settlements—later called "hip zones" (or, in a more extreme formulation, "liberated territories")[36]—sprang up alongside college campuses, which could also be welcoming environments for bright and curious young people who weren't necessarily students. Their infrastructures were nothing more than places where people could hang out and mingle with one another—public areas like parks or quadrangles, or commercial establishments, such as bookstores, taverns, music halls, and coffee shops.[37]

Many of the New Left's leading writers and activists had their first inklings that society was heading toward a period of increased emotional and intellectual vitality through their exposure to these hip zones. Several years before he helped to draft the Port Huron Statement, Dick Flacks recalled that he spent considerable time reading and lingering at an independent bookstore in Ann Arbor, Michigan, which specialized in highbrow paperbacks (a new phenomenon in the 1950s) and seemed far removed from the beer-swilling, sports-loving fraternity culture that prevailed on campus.[38] "People of our cultural type would always be there," Flacks said. "I felt that the amount of talk in the bohemian world about the hypocrisy of American life couldn't just go on without there being some expression of this, besides just talk, or sitting around in coffee houses. I couldn't figure out what it would be, but I began to change my feelings that nothing would change in the United States."[39] Jim O'Brien, an SDS activist at the University of Wisconsin who became involved with several radical publications, noted that before his campus witnessed any activism, there was "a change in lifestyle and mood of a critical mass of students" that banded together in a three- or four-block area along Mifflin Street—a veritable "center of nonconformist youth culture."[40] While visiting New York City from the Midwest in 1965, *Radical America* founder Paul Buhle encountered several small, quirky storefronts on St. Mark's Place that sold political buttons and were "in some vague way forerunners of [the] counterculture . . . just little glimpses of something."[41]

But it wasn't just that these hip zones exposed future underground press writers to new ideas or social styles; as they increased in number and visibility in the 1960s, they also provided the main impetus for the underground press itself. They supplied an audience that allowed the papers to grow and flourish, and to the extent that these communities reflected a new mood and a new tonality among young people—who were unfulfilled by mainstream American life, but energized by their political commitments and the promise of a greater personal freedom—they gave the underground press something to write about. A glance at the early histories of three of the "original" underground newspapers—the *Los Angeles Free Press*, East Lansing's *Paper*, and Austin's *Rag*—illustrates the mutually dependent relationships they had with their local communities. In each instance, a nascent left-wing or avant-garde community provided the rationale for a local radical paper. In turn, the paper accelerated the growth and development of the community that birthed it.

FOUNDED BY ART KUNKIN in 1964, the Los Angeles *Free Press* (often called the *Freep*) is widely considered to be the youth movement's first underground newspaper. Certainly it was among the most successful. Whereas most underground rags were of the "here today and gone tomorrow" variety, the *Freep* ran steadily and remained solvent until August 1969, when Kunkin unwisely published the names, addresses, and home telephone numbers of eighty undercover narcotics agents employed by the state of California as a "public service announcement." The predictable legal wrangling that ensued sent the *Free Press* into a tailspin, but at its peak it was the leading radical paper in the city that some felt had the liveliest underground newspaper trade in the country.[42] In 1967 a *New Yorker* journalist went so far as to call it "*the* newspaper of the New Left."[43] The following year, a West Coast record executive who did business with Kunkin suggested the *Freep* was better characterized as a "barely above-ground" newspaper.[44] By the decade's end it boasted nearly 100,000 paid subscribers and a readership said to be more than double that number.[45] Initially, though, the *Free Press* appealed mostly to L.A.'s hip cognoscenti, and its survival was far from certain.[46] It won its wider readership by simultaneously championing the local movement's artistic productions (mainly rock music), filling gaps in local news coverage, and allying itself with youths who made claims on contested public space. "A great part of [its] success," a local scenester remembered, "came from the presence of long-haired teenagers everywhere on the Sunset Strip."[47]

During the Sixties, Kunkin was a rare type: half-Marxist, half-hippie. A writer for *Esquire* magazine once described him as "stocky, with a workman's thick-fingered hands, and . . . horn-rimmed glasses. The overall impression he makes is that of a dedicated, strong-willed, slightly harried German music professor."[48] Born in New York City in 1928, where he attended the prestigious Bronx High School of Science, he later worked as a machinist and became a devoted Trotskyite, joining the Socialist Workers Party and managing its newspaper, the *Militant*. He was also a member of the Congress of Racial Equality, and he occasionally wrote for two other small labor papers, *News and Letters* and *Correspondence*. But his first experience with a locally oriented newssheet came after he moved to Los Angeles, where he started writing for the Mexican American *East L.A. Almanac* in the early 1960s. "For the first time in my life, I was writing about garbage collection and all kinds of community problems," he recalled.[49] As appealing as this work seemed, Kunkin was also attracted to the street life in Venice, a neighborhood that was said to have anticipated San Francisco's "Summer of Love" by almost a decade, thanks in part to Lawrence Lipton's *The Holy Barbarians*, a popular guide to the local beat scene that was published in 1959.[50]

In addition to his print journalism, Kunkin also regularly delivered radio commentaries for KPFK, a beloved community radio station run by the Pacifica Foundation, which broadcast eclectic programming and left-wing viewpoints throughout the region. Since the station survived on financial support from local listeners, Kunkin was well attuned to the climate of opinion among Southern California's liberal population. (Later on, one of the "major arguments" he used to attract investors to the *Free Press* drew attention to the fact that "KPFK managed to pay its bills while broadcasting programs of little more than 'underground' interest.")[51] Meanwhile, Kunkin became a frustrated reader of the *Village Voice*. Although he admired its investigative journalism and cultural commentary, as a refugee from the Old Left, he loathed its reflexive support of liberal Democrats. To his mind, this made it an "Establishment" paper—but it also convinced him of the need for a radical alternative.[52] Others agreed. Lionel Rolfe, a Los Angeles writer who has documented the area's bohemian scenes, recalls frequently gathering with friends at the Xanadu coffeehouse in the early 1960s "to complain about how badly a new newspaper was needed."[53] "The difference between Kunkin and everyone else at the Xanadu," Rolfe adds, "was that Kunkin actually went out and started the paper the rest of us just talked about."[54]

The *Freep*, then, was simply a stripped-down, radicalized version of the *Village Voice*, geared toward Southern Californians, which Kunkin launched with just a few hundred dollars that he rounded up from friends (in contrast to the $50,000 that Mailer supposedly put up for the *Voice*).[55] "I wanted a paper that would draw together all the diverse elements in the community, that would be not only political, but cultural as well," Kunkin later remarked. "I had been hanging around the coffee houses and the poetry groups, the small theaters and so forth, so I knew there was a whole life there."[56] Others, though, were less optimistic, telling Kunkin that L.A. "was too spread out, and unlike most other large cities, had no closely knit Bohemian neighborhood that would immediately support such a venture."[57] Attempting to prove otherwise, Kunkin distributed the very first issues at a KPFK-sponsored festival known as the Renaissance Pleasure Faire, at which some three thousand revelers converged on a fairground in San Bernardino to take part in historical reenactments celebrating European culture while drinking copious quantities of old English ale. Although the Faire was never billed as a political event, its co-creator, Phyllis Patterson, acknowledged that it attracted a liberal and socially conscious crowd. When Kunkin asked Patterson for permission to hawk the first issues of his paper there, she consented, under the condition that the paper would not be "controversial." "I was not interested in an issue [of the paper] that was making issues," Patterson recalled.[58]

To her annoyance, Kunkin didn't quite keep up his end of the bargain. At first glance, the *Free Press* looked like a simple spoof of a paper from the Middle Ages. Its masthead presented the paper as the *Faire Free Press*, and its humorous front-page articles were all datelined as if they had been written in the sixteenth century. (For instance, one article described an obscenity charge

against a "self-styled poet" named "William Shakspur.")[59] But inside the tabloid, readers found the real *Free Press* masthead and logo, along with a note
announcing that the new paper aimed to help unify Los Angeles's "liberal-
intellectual population," and a subscription blank that basically said, "if you
want a paper like this, send us money."[60] Kunkin's prospectus for the paper
was ambitious: He promised a weekly calendar of events, coverage of left-
wing political movements, muckraking articles on issues of local concern,
and "a full weekly report on the new productions in small theater, poetry,
experimental cinema, painting, music and sculpture." Last, and seemingly
most important, Kunkin pledged that his paper would "provide a place for
free expression and critical comment and for dialogues between creative figures
who have pertinent and humorous things to say about everything and anything . . . but who presently have no local outlet in which to print such provocative writing."[61]

Put another way, Kunkin aimed to attract writers and build a following
from L.A.'s nascent underground scene. The longest article in the first issue,
headlined "Puritanism Scores a Victory," discussed an obscenity conviction
against a twenty-five-year-old theater manager who screened Kenneth
Anger's *Scorpio Rising*, a homoerotic biker film.[62] Kunkin also reprinted a
letter that the folksinger Joan Baez wrote to the Internal Revenue Service
explaining her refusal to pay 60 percent of her 1963 federal income taxes—
the portion, she said, that goes toward military expenditures.[63] ("We sort of
stole [that item] from a small college newspaper," Kunkin later admitted.)[64]
An obituary for a local jazz musician and an anguished article describing an
African American's daily encounters with racism both signaled Kunkin's
determination to cover issues of concern to L.A.'s black population, which
was isolated by the city's tangled freeway system and largely ignored by the
mainstream press.[65]

In the second issue, Kunkin stressed the paper's democratic mission,
pledging "that if anyone has anything to say on an important community
issue and can say it well and with documentation, he or she will have their
day in print. That is why we call ourselves the *Free Press*." And while he promised to promote a climate of journalistic integrity, he understood this as something more than simply hiring honest and fair writers; *Free Press* staffers could
also be expected to oppose racism and support freedom of speech and expression. In language redolent of the Port Huron Statement, Kunkin proclaimed
himself "committed to the principles inherent in the democratic ordering of
society wherein all citizens have the right to meaningfully participate in
community political and social life." In that spirit, he said the paper would
avoid becoming an organ of any particular group. "As a public newspaper free

of organizational commitment, we are going to print the shots as our writers call them . . . and then invite comment and rebuttal"—the appropriate stance for what he said was "fundamentally a community newspaper."[66]

This wasn't just lip service. From the beginning, Kunkin anchored the *Free Press* in L.A.'s underground community, in part by locating the newspaper's offices in the basement of the "notorious" Fifth Estate coffeehouse on Sunset Strip. As historian David McBride explains, the Strip was at the very "heart of the city's coalescing hippie Bohemia," and the Fifth Estate in particular was "a central gathering point for cultural rebels."[67] It opened each evening at 7 PM and closed the following morning at 6 AM; it regularly hosted folk musicians and hootenannies, screened classic films, and displayed arts and crafts. With the purchase of just a single cup of coffee, customers could stay all night. Meanwhile, KPFK and the *Free Press* were closely connected, with broadcasters doubling as columnists and vice versa.[68] Finally, the *Freep* had friendly interactions with the bookstore Papa Bach, which was known as "a meeting place and a cultural institution in its own right."[69] Established in 1964, Papa Bach sold not just books, but also esoteric records, pipes, and imported tobacco. The bookstore regularly advertised in Kunkin's paper; in turn, the *Freep* sometimes reviewed high-quality trade paperbacks of the type that Papa Bach specialized in.

Although many came to regard Southern California as a hippie mecca, in the early 1960s it was still a bastion of what McBride calls "high" bohemianism. "Significantly, the *Free Press* . . . hardly ever discussed youth-oriented popular culture at first." During its first year or so, "cultural critics focused on little-known and 'challenging' works, especially modern jazz and art, European film, and avant-garde composers. Among many articles on these subjects were pieces on John Cage, the west coast jazz 'cool school,' and Italian director [Michelangelo] Antonioni." The paper also sponsored several avant-garde concerts and exhibits, "including one devoted to the archetypical 'difficult' composer, Arnold Schoenberg," aimed at democratizing the avant-garde.[70]

This is not to suggest, however, that L.A.'s esoteric underground scene lacked political direction. Al Mitchell, owner of the Fifth Estate, made at least two agitprop film documentaries, one of which was a polemic against the Los Angeles Police Department called *Blue Fascism*.[71] Meanwhile, Papa Bach's owner, John Harris, cut his political teeth working for a federal job-training program and, like Mitchell, regularly allowed activists to post literature and hold meetings on his property.[72] Kunkin was a devoted Marxist, an ardent civil-rights supporter, and an early critic of the Vietnam War, as anyone who read the *Free Press* would have known.[73] "For all its "countercultural bluster," McBride writes, the *Freep* was "essentially the local New Left paper. As a source of information on racial injustice, SDS, local New Left schools, demonstrations, and antiwar activities, [it] was authoritative."[74] Early issues drew from KPFK radio commentaries and gave special emphasis to the Berkeley free speech rebellion, which ushered in a new era of campus-based activism that, from Kunkin's perspective, was fortuitously timed.[75] Had he launched the *Free Press* six months earlier, he later said, it might not have survived; as it happened, the sensational story coming out of Berkeley gave the *Free Press* a crucial lift.[76]

Its pièce de résistance, though, was its coverage of the Watts riot, which exploded on August 11, 1965, after a police officer clubbed a black bystander during a routine traffic stop; in the resulting mayhem, which lasted for nearly a week, thirty-four people were killed, four thousand more were arrested, and some $200 million worth of property was destroyed. Hardly anyone outside Watts saw the violence coming. According to one historian, one of the reasons that so many Americans regarded L.A. as a paragon of prosperity in the 1950s and 1960s is because its impoverished black and Hispanic residents were left out of its carefully constructed, mass-mediated image (and were in fact literally shielded from the view of motorists by railings along the city's expansive highways).[77] A pair of sociologists who analyzed L.A.'s two daily newspapers, the *Los Angeles Times* and the *Los Angeles Herald-Examiner*, discovered the local press gave scant attention to local blacks, and its coverage of African Americans had actually diminished in the years leading up to the Watts rebellion.[78] By contrast, the *Free Press* covered civil-rights issues from its inception and strongly opposed Proposition 14, a 1964 California ballot initiative that repealed a state law prohibiting housing discrimination.[79]

"I built up personal capital in the black community," Kunkin remembered, "so as soon as Watts happened there were people there writing for the paper."[80] While not quite condoning the rebellion, Kunkin's post-riot analysis stressed its sociopolitical significance. Whereas mainstream media organizations described a week of riotous anarchy in Watts, Kunkin referred to the uprising as "demonstrations in the streets" that "have completely ended the myth that the Negroes of Los Angeles are the happiest in the whole country." He went on:

> It has been an election without ballot boxes and the Negroes have cast their votes. Whether or not the white majority likes this vote, it is time for the analysis [that] follows every election. It is time to listen to the Negro.
>
> Attempts to simply establish "law and order," to simply establish the pre-demonstration status quo, are doomed to failure. Anyone who

thinks in these terms is fundamentally anti-Negro and will be understood as such by the vast majority of Negroes.

The real "tragedy," Kunkin added, was that "government officials and the major news media have not understood what has happened." Rather than addressing the rebellion's underlying causes, he said, the stage was being set "for reprisals against the Negro community."[81] By contrast, a *Los Angeles Times* editorial called the riots "criminal terrorism" and dismissed even the "inference" that it was an "inevitable result of economic and sociological pressures."[82] In addition to taking a charitable stance toward the rioters, the *Freep* presented an urban black perspective that was sorely lacking in other media outlets.[83] To cite but one example, Bob Freeman, a local CORE activist, wrote a first-person account of walking through Watts during the riot, where he talked with residents who described the anger that had been festering in the community as a result of longstanding poverty and police brutality. "Many of the young men to whom I spoke said if they must go to Vietnam to fight for freedom, they might as well fight and die in Watts for freedom," he reported. "In everyone I spoke to I saw an undaunted courage and fearless determination to make their desires known to the officials of this city."[84]

Discussing the *Freep*'s Watts coverage, one writer credited the paper with laying bare "the obtuseness of local officials, the insensitivity of the police and the inability of the major news media to grasp the seriousness of the event."[85] "Watts proved that this was a serious paper, not a sheet about Happenings attended by two hundred people," Kunkin boasted.[86] In subsequent years Kunkin's paper was the place to turn for coverage of ghetto unrest, black nationalism, and the multicultural Left.[87]

In the months after Watts, the *Free Press* was also caught up in the Sunset Strip's transformation from a bland corridor of fast food joints, cheap motels, and tacky billboards into a hub of hip bohemia.[88] Several forward-looking tavern owners set the change in motion by persuading Los Angeles County to let them make rock and dance clubs more accessible to baby-boomer youths. Several such venues opened near the Strip in the early 1960s, beginning with P.J.'s in 1961 ("an event with which any reputable future historian has got to mark the beginning of Renaissance Hip in Los Angeles," a local writer opined.)[89] Before long, youth-oriented clubs like the Hullabaloo, the Action, and the Trip were nurturing a bevy of sophisticated rock acts—including the Byrds, Buffalo Springfield, Love, the Doors, and the Seeds—whose songs were far removed from the bouncy, angst-free hymns to surfing and cruising that the Beach Boys and Jan and Dean popularized just a few years earlier.[90] Meanwhile, motorcycle groups started prowling around the Strip's congested streets, modish teens fraternized with "serious longhairs" along the sidewalks, and late-night crowds lingered in nearby coffeehouses and diners, especially Canter's Restaurant and Ben Franks (sometimes called Ben *Freaks*).[91] Although local writers began describing Sunset Strip as a coalescing bohemia in 1965, by the following year the youthful takeover of this once stodgy territory attracted attention in *Look*, *Life*, *Newsweek*, and *Time*, with the last magazine declaring it "the perfect place for flaunting rebellion, for catching the latest underground movie . . . and trying on the newest fads."[92]

Naturally, the *Free Press* wrote more exuberantly about the so-called "Strippies," particularly around late 1965, as the paper started evincing greater enthusiasm for rock and roll, and its back page calendar was increasingly festooned with notices concerning the neighborhood's art showings, film screenings, rock concerts, and "happenings"—loose and improvisational gatherings that typically involved some combination of experimental music, performance art, and (by the mid 1960s) drugs.[93] Later on, Kunkin opened his own bookstore near the Strip, called Kazoo, which specialized in "obscure works" on politics, drugs, and Eastern religions, and also sold buttons, posters, bumper stickers, and countercultural ephemera.[94] One *Free Press* writer boasted that the Strip belonged to "a throng of Renaissance Rockers . . . who take the street as their open-air hallway."[95] In December 1965, the paper began running a regular column by Jerry Farber, called "Making It," which was devoted to documenting the Strip's efflorescence.[96]

When crime rose in the area and local authorities resurrected an arcane curfew law in order to clear the Strip, the *Free Press* covered the crackdown and editorialized against the police's overzealous tactics. One *Free Press* article claimed that a recent photograph in the *Los Angeles Times*, which purported to show sheriff's deputies questioning curfew violators, was actually staged before the cameras as a publicity stunt designed to counter criticisms that authorities had received in a recent *Life* article.[97]

Away from the camera's gaze, however, police malpractice was said to be commonplace. The *Free Press* frequently railed against police harassment of juveniles and once ran a firsthand account of citizens being "viciously clubbed and beaten" by officers who stormed into a crowd of youths outside the Fifth Estate. "There was no plan or purpose evident in the beatings or subsequent arrests," the reporter claimed. "It seemed the handiest people, with no regard given to age, sex, or social position, were clubbed, kicked, punched, and/or arrested."[98] Tensions mounted as policemen continued arresting scores of teens on weekend evenings, and in November 1966 perhaps a thousand irate youths spilled into streets and waved placards, while a much smaller number of delinquents ("no more than twenty or thirty," the *Free Press* said) scuffled with bystanders, scrawled anti-police graffiti slogans, climbed upon a city bus while it was full of passengers, and unsuccessfully attempted to light an empty bus on fire. Though certainly a major disturbance, most Strippies seemed to regard it as something less than the "scene of anarchy" the *Los Angeles Times* described.[99] Estimated total damages from the "riot" amounted to only $200, and according to eyewitnesses, local TV crews encouraged the attacks on the buses.[100] According to a *Free Press* reporter who watched the scene unfold, "There was not the wholesale rioting that the newspapers and mass media implied. The great majority of the teen-agers . . . were orderly and lawful, with the possible exception of creating a traffic jam by congregating in the streets."[101]

County officials nevertheless revoked the licenses that allowed minors to dance inside clubs that served alcohol, while police intensified their nightly patrols and shut down Pandora's Box, a local coffeehouse popular with nonconformist youths. Meanwhile, an ad hoc protest organization that Mitchell ran out of his Fifth Estate coffeehouse coordinated several large-scale demonstrations at which youths asserted their right to freedom of expression (even if that meant, in this case, "the right of freaks to roam freely").[102] Many of their pugnacious slogans, including "A Better Police Force = A Better Police State," "Peace if Possible," and "The Police are Full of Shit," mimicked complaints and suspicions about lawful authority that first circulated in the *Free Press*.[103] True to its mission, the *Freep* also served as an open forum for community activists, and in the weeks and months after the riot, its letters-to-the-editor page sizzled with angry commentary.[104] (Local rock band Buffalo Springfield also weighed in with their baleful anthem "For What It's Worth," one of the era's iconic songs.)[105]

Eventually, the cops and longhairs on Sunset Strip reached a rapprochement, thanks in part to assistance from a local task force chaired by Jim Dickson, a local rock impresario, and Fred Rosenberg, the leader of a neighborhood association of restaurant owners—both of whom shared an interest in preserving the Strip's commercial vitality. Arrests declined, protests fizzled, merchants prospered, and the Sunset Strip basically returned to its "pre-riot status quo."[106] But one institution changed markedly in the months and years after the Strip protests cooled—Art Kunkin's *Free Press*. As late as October 1966, Kunkin could claim only nine thousand readers, and no one on his staff drew a regular paycheck. In an interview with a local journalist, Kunkin even belabored the fact that his paper was barely solvent.[107] Six months later, its circulation was said to have reached fifty thousand.[108] "The fantastic success story of 1967 has been the growth of the *L.A. Free Press*," said a writer for the *Los Angeles Underground*, one of two additional underground newspapers that appeared in Los Angeles in the spring of 1967. "It has caught on and is growing by leaps and bounds." In addition to attracting more readers than anyone thought possible, the area's radical community newspapers were said to draw from "a vast reservoir of talent and good will in the bohemian community. . . . Artists, writers, photographers, typists, runners [and] street hawkers, all combine to bring into creation these organs of Vox populi, the voice of the people. The effort will grow and expand."[109]

THOUGH THE *LOS ANGELES FREE PRESS* was primarily read by city dwellers, underground rags also flourished in smaller communities, often in close proximity to colleges and universities. The pioneering publication of this type, begun in late 1965 in East Lansing, Michigan, was simply called the *Paper*. Initially it presented itself as merely an alternative to Michigan State University's tepid campus newspaper, the *State News*. In 1965, when it published its first issue, New Left ideas were just beginning to circulate on campus, largely as the result of the loosely organized Committee for Student Rights (CSR), which some seventy-five students formed the previous winter. Before then, Michigan State University (MSU) had never seen a genuine student movement. Within a year, the *Paper* had sharpened and articulated students' grievances, provoked debate, and thrust itself into campus controversies where New Leftists had an indisputable advantage (namely free speech and *in loco parentis* regulations). In addition to stirring political passions at Michigan State, which quickly took on a life of their own, through its membership in the Underground Press Syndicate (UPS), the *Paper* was also said "to plug the East Lansing radical community into radical communities around the country."[110] Although the *Paper* changed in character over the years as some of its writers became Marxists and others turned on to psychedelic drugs, it ran more or less continuously until 1969.

East Lansing in the early 1960s was a rather quaint college town, surrounded by cornfields and run by a conservative political establishment that prohibited the sale of alcohol. MSU, however, was undergoing a rapid transition, from an institute for agriculture and applied science into one of the largest universities in the country. Between 1950 and 1965, its undergraduate enrollment swelled from fifteen thousand to thirty-eight thousand, and it built the biggest residential housing complex in the world.[111] Walter Adams, a noted economist who served as MSU's interim president for nine months in 1969, described MSU in this period as a vast and complex "megaversity" that, like many American universities during the Cold War, was becoming increasingly responsive to the needs of the federal government (particularly the U.S. Agency for International Development). "It is almost impossible," Adams wrote, "to convey a feeling for the immensity, diversity, and complexity of this institution."[112] However, MSU had yet to gain much in the way of academic prestige. Sometimes called "Cow College" or "Moo U" by its detractors, it ran a virtually open admissions policy, and in 1960 only 20 percent of its undergraduates majored in the liberal arts and social sciences.[113] In an effort to bolster its reputation, MSU in the early 1960s began recruiting some of the nation's top-ranked high school students with generous scholarships, glossy brochures, and promises of close mentoring relationships with its faculty. In 1963 it boasted nearly two hundred National Merit Scholars—more than any other school in the country.[114]

Among them was Michael Kindman, a cherubic teenager from Long Island who later became the *Paper*'s founding editor. Initially Kindman was "excited by what was being offered . . . at MSU" and "ready to develop a loyal connection" to the school, but not long after his arrival he began experiencing a nagging sensation that he'd been "hoodwinked." Everywhere he turned, his undergrad experience fell short of his ideal. He gleaned practical newsroom experience from his paying job at the *State News*, but his journalism courses were "unexciting, taught by traditionalist faculty with a heavy commitment to what we have since come to know as 'the myth of objectivity.'" MSU was growing in renown, not for its new emphasis of the humanities, but for its powerhouse football program. Intellectually and culturally, East Lansing struck him as a depressing "backwater."[115] On the perimeter of its splendidly landscaped campus hovered gargantuan new dormitories that seemed sterile and uninspiring. Worse still, students were required to live in these depressing buildings throughout their freshman and sophomore years, during which time an array of housing and curfew regulations fell over their lives like a wet blanket.

By the beginning of his second year, Kindman's reservations about Michigan State had metastasized into a full-blown case of buyer's remorse. Many of his Merit Scholar colleagues likewise felt snookered into attending a mediocre university in sleepy East Lansing when they likely could have attended the school of their choice. "The Honors College program that had been offered to us whiz-kid recruits had turned out to be more hype than opportunity," Kindman later wrote. "Many of us were going increasingly stir-crazy. Our education was working, but not in the way the university might have hoped: the more educated we became, the more frustrated we felt."[116] By this point, MSU had a tiny Young Socialist Club and a small, rather "straitlaced" SDS chapter, which one former member said was "very much a family affair."[117] Nevertheless, throughout this period, clusters of students were gathering and complaining that MSU was a massive and impersonal behemoth and that East Lansing was a cultural Sahara, unappreciative of the arts and lacking in creative ferment. Many of them lived off campus, some were graduate students, and some were members of the Young Socialist Club. Together they listened to folk music and rock and roll, shared their affinities for the arts, and monitored political developments in other parts of the country.[118]

The Berkeley free speech movement, which got under way in the fall of 1965, seemed especially significant to this proto-underground community. Although Berkeley students were eloquent in their defense of free speech, their protests were likewise colored by their dissatisfaction with their university's depersonalized atmosphere: its large lecture classes and remote faculty, emphasis on industrial research and professional training, and depressing maw of bureaucratic red tape.[119] These issues reverberated with MSU students as well. When the rebellion climaxed in December (after nearly eight hundred Berkeley students were arrested during a sit-in) Kindman was invited to a secret off-campus meeting to discuss the "Berkeley situation and its parallels in East Lansing."[120]

Kindman later recounted his attendance at the meeting in nearly mystical terms. "I was aware of stepping into an alternate reality of some kind," he said. The house he visited was "mysterious." Off in the background, someone played the latest album by the folksinger Buffy Sainte-Marie, a Native American songwriter whose politically charged lyrics and pastoral melodies drew inspiration from European madrigals, beat poetry, and the Greenwich Village folk scene. Conversation revolved around the formation of the CSR and its plans to roll back MSU's *in loco parentis* regulations.[121] In the style of SDS, the CSR was extremely democratic; it had no membership requirements, and anyone who attended its meetings was allowed to talk and vote.[122] Some of its members were among the first MSU students to cast themselves as "outsiders" by wearing beards and sandals.[123] Wrote Kindman: "We talked [of] frustrations and strategies and made plans; by the end of the evening my life had been changed forever."[124]

The rest of the year was a blur of protest activity and self-scrutiny. From his perch at the *State News*, where he helped run the editorial page, Kindman championed the CSR and applauded the students' tactics at Berkeley.[125] In March 1965 he journeyed to Alabama to participate in Martin Luther King Jr.'s historic march from Selma to Montgomery; and in the summer he rented an off-campus house with his longtime girlfriend. What passed for leisure time was frequently spent at Spiro's, an off-campus restaurant that doubled as the CSR's unofficial "headquarters." Kindman recalled Spiro's fondly, as a place "where at any time of the day we could find some of our friends to hang out with. At last, an alternative to dorm life and bland, university-authorized activities." Although his grades fell and his career ambitions faded, he was thankful to find himself "deeply enmeshed in a community of like-minded friends, an interesting, diverse, and tolerant gang."[126]

Having made the leap from "liberal Democrat" to "confirmed radical," Kindman's defection from the *State News* seemed almost predictable.[127] The final impetus came in the autumn of 1965, when the paper's directorate issued a writ prohibiting its young journalists from taking leadership roles in any other student organizations. Since Kindman and his roommate, Larry Tate, had already been batting around the idea of starting a weekly alternative to the *State News*, rather than fighting to change the new rule, they simply left to start their own operation. Not everyone who founded the *Paper*, however, was as political as Kindman; Tate recalled that his "political awareness" was at first very low. "We just wanted a voice, we wanted . . . a place to publish, something that belonged to us in this large, not exactly hostile, but un-empathetic environment."[128] Still, the *Paper* would not have been possible without a rising local movement. Its most ardent supporters were students and young faculty who had been involved "in all the campaigns of the previous year."[129]

Another signal that things were changing in East Lansing came in the form of *Zeitgeist*, a local literary magazine that a group of malcontented graduate students launched in September 1965. Some may have found *Zeitgeist* long on hubris; in the prolegomena that accompanied the first issue, the editors explicitly presented themselves as Whitmanesque provocateurs, pitching their barbaric yawps at a complacent and lowbrow citizenry.[130] Nevertheless, the group aimed to attract a critical mass of support from the area's tiny cognoscenti—"lovers of art, architecture, and good books," who "think that tasteful coffee shops [are] important to reflection and conversation and learning" and who "are not afraid to be labeled 'eggheads' or 'beatniks.'"[131] As a quarterly journal that mainly featured poetry, *Zeitgeist*'s agenda differed from the *Paper*'s—but both publications indicated that rumblings of youthful discontent were at last beginning to pierce East Lansing's bland and platitudinous din.

The *Paper*'s inaugural issue, dated December 3, 1965, featured a feisty front-page editorial from Kindman, denouncing the *State News* and describing the *Paper*'s goals and concerns. "We hope to make it possible, even desirable and exciting, to express . . . intelligent thoughts about things of concern to people at Michigan State University," he wrote. "We are interested in politics, in social studies, in the arts, in creative writing, in intelligent commentary, and most of all in presenting all sides of the issues discussed." And in a not-so-subtle dig at the *State News'* so-called "loyalty oath" (which was reprinted on page two) Kindman proclaimed, "Our loyalty is to the practice of imaginative, creative, thoughtful journalism. We hope unabashedly to be a forum for ideas, a center for debate, a champion of the common man, a thorn in the side of the powerful. . . . We hope never to become so sure of our position and so unaware of our real job that we will concentrate merely on putting out a paper. . . . And we intend to do all this in a spirit of editorial independence for which there is hardly a model on campus."[132] This issue also contained commentary by a professor of food science on the looming world hunger crisis, an article critical of MSU's student government, an essay about factional tensions in the CSR, several short poems, and, on the back page, a cryptic interview with Bob Dylan reprinted from the *Los Angeles Free Press*.[133]

In the following months, the *Paper* established itself as a critic of Michigan State, the *State News*, and the great mass of conformist students in and around East Lansing, while at the same time earning its bona fides as a New Left organ—relishing its gadfly role, collapsing the boundaries between advocacy and journalism, and leavening its serious political commentary with sarcastic humor.[134] One provocative article drew a comparison between MSU's supposedly authoritarian administration and the harsh, repressive government of Mississippi, "the symbolic land of darkness in the South."[135] Another controversial essay, published anonymously, lampooned the drunken debauchery of MSU students who traveled to Pasadena, California, to cheer the football team in the Rose Bowl.[136] After widespread negative publicity convinced MSU administrators to reverse its denial of readmission to a graduate-student activist named Paul Schiff, the episode was celebrated as a boon to student radicals, "the first major step toward rearranging power . . . so that the people educating and being educated have some say about how the show is run."[137]

The *Paper* also reported on early protests against the Vietnam War and gave heavy coverage to a campus visit by two SDS leaders.[138] Other pieces railed against bureaucratic bumbledom, curfew restrictions, and bland dormitory life—all issues that resonated with students who grew increasingly frustrated with the way the university "[flexed] its *in loco parentis* muscles with abandon," issuing "fiat after arbitrary fiat."[139] MSU president John A. Hannah, whom some regarded an oafish sort of man, was frequently ridiculed. In April 1966, a mock-sensational headline blared across the front page: "Hannah Revealed to be Palindrome."[140] The following month, the *Paper* debuted a running comic strip called "Land Grant Man," in which "Dr. John Palindrome"—beleaguered by peaceniks, Communists, and free speech advocates—is magically transformed into a powerful superhero (equipped with a helmet, cape, codpiece, and a garden hoe) who declares himself ready to "show those students whose multiversity this really is!!!"[141]

In its early months, the *Paper* also devoted a great deal of space to defending itself in a complicated controversy with the university over whether or not it could be sold on campus (as opposed to being distributed for free). At the time, MSU lacked established guidelines concerning independently operated publications, and it was unclear what campus organization had jurisdiction over the *Paper*. Incensed by MSU's "bureaucratic idiocy," Kindman compared the situation to something out of the *Twilight Zone*—an apt metaphor, since the *Paper* was literally being kept in legal limbo.[142] Although the ensuing negotiations were ludicrously complicated, Kindman and company used their own pages to describe the situation in elaborate detail, thereby turning itself into a news story, and capably demonstrating one of the New Left's contentions: when challenged by students, the university would invariably abuse its authority.[143] "The university didn't know what it was doing because they had never encountered anything like this," Tate recalled.[144] Finally, in the spring of 1966, MSU's Board of Student Publications set up rules by which the *Paper* could lawfully be sold on campus, at which point Kindman ran a petulant editorial proclaiming "Gratitude Will Get Us Nowhere."[145]

Another major event for the *Paper* was its coverage of a scandal that journalist Warren Hinckle uncovered in April 1966 for the left-wing magazine *Ramparts*: as part of its general mission to assist U.S. foreign policy, in the late 1950s MSU established its "Vietnam Project," a major developmental program that doubled as a front for the CIA. One of the project's tasks was to train and assist the "civil service and police network" that was the backbone of Ngo Dinh Diem's corrupt government in South Vietnam; in practice, this amounted to "the supplying of guns and ammunition for city police, the civil guard, palace police, and the dreaded *Sûreté*—South Vietnam's version of the FBI."[146] The last sentence of Hinckle's article doubled as the text of a full-page advertisement that *Ramparts* took out in the *Paper* on April 21, 1966: "What the hell is a university doing buying guns, anyway?"[147]

Meanwhile, the *Paper* regularly celebrated the upswing of activism and cultural energy in East Lansing. One essay noted that during spring break alone, protestors against MSU's Vietnam Project garnered statewide publicity, local antiwar activists had their trespassing convictions overturned by a higher court, pacifist David Dellinger visited campus, and local students and faculty launched the Free University of East Lansing (FUEL)—"an alternative to the drab, automated education of course outlines, credits, multiple-choice exams and IBM cards."[148] In another piece, Kindman credited "*Zeitgeist*, CSR, the campus anarchists, Kewpeeites, *The Paper*, [and] the Free

University" for enlivening the community. ("Kewpeeites" was a nickname for those who hung out at Spiro's, after the disgustingly named "Kewpee Burgers" on the menu.)[149] Whereas Kindman once regretted "doing college . . . in the conservative, teetotaling town of East Lansing," now he exulted that MSU was fast becoming "a reasonably active and almost interesting campus of the '60s."[150] In May 1966 the *Paper* favorably covered a *Zeitgeist*-sponsored happening at Spiro's called "Culture-Fest," at which some 150 students gathered for an evening of poetry, folk and jazz music, and spoken word performances.[151] ("The name 'Culture-Fest' was originally meant to be ironic," *Zeitgeist*'s editors said, "but so many people in our culturally-deprived university took it seriously that we let it stand.")[152] Later that month, the *Paper*'s staff excitedly hosted a visit from Paul Krassner, who had written them an admiring note a few months before.[153] Char Jolles, another of the original staffers at the *Paper*, fondly recalled her experience. "It was very exciting to be in each other's company. We pursued lots of ideas, laughed a lot, and eventually the paper became a countercultural scene."[154]

Of course, East Lansing was hardly the only community witnessing frenetic expressions of New Left and countercultural activity. By early 1966, SDS had 15,000 members in 172 chapters engaged in everything from civil-rights and antipoverty initiatives to antiwar teach-ins and free universities.[155] Meanwhile, garage and psychedelic rock bands were becoming louder and brasher, performance and visual artists started channeling their talents toward political expression, and youth-oriented underground newspapers sprang to life in several other communities. Amidst all this, the *Paper* began fashioning itself as not simply a local initiative, but also as a constitutive element of a national youth awakening. In the final issue of the 1965–66 school year, Kindman boasted that the *Paper* was no longer merely an alternative to the *State News*. Rather, it was now plugged into "a loose alliance between like-thinking people and organizations all over." He continued: "SDS and Paul Krassner and the *Los Angeles Free Press* and the Free University of New York and all the rest see in the *Paper*, presumably, something of what we see in them." Namely:

> a revitalized feeling for people and for the kinds of things people care about. Even if our orientation and tone are a bit more academic than theirs . . . we feel ourselves part of the same movement toward making sense out of things and letting the people decide and actually practicing freedom of expression. That seems to be enough to let us in on a nebulous kind of community that's developing, not quite underground, in this country.[156]

During the summer of 1966, Kindman helped to run an SDS storefront in San Francisco, where he met Thorne Dreyer, an activist from Austin, Texas, with whom he discussed the potential for an expanded network of underground newspapers. Around this same period, he won a small degree of notoriety when he was photographed and quoted in an article in *Time* magazine on the emerging underground press.[157] Even more significantly, while in California, he took his first LSD trip. It was a good one, and when he returned to East Lansing in the fall, Tate said he was in full-tilt "evangelical mode," strongly encouraging others to experiment with acid.[158] Although some at the *Paper* followed his lead, others were ambivalent about drugs, and still others avoided them entirely. In October Kindman wrote "The Newspaper as Art Form," an unusual manifesto in which he blended commentary on the importance of radical newspapers (supposedly influenced by media theorist Marshall McLuhan) with lyrics from the Beatles' mind-bending song "Tomorrow Never Knows." "Being at *The Paper* feels different this year," Kindman announced. "There's a spirit to it, a feeling of community and enlightened consensus about it that proves . . . the value of the 'underground press' as an instrument of communication." This was not Kindman's finest essay—in fact, his opaque and elliptical prose showed telltale signs of his recent plunge into the counterculture—but it addressed the vital role the *Paper* played in East Lansing's underground community. By tapping into "the spirit of the times" and providing an opportunity for "people to participate in a medium of communication among themselves," the *Paper* was said to work "within a context of relevance," to enjoy a "mandate from readers," and to emanate from an "increasingly radical and enlightened community."[159] According to Jolles, suddenly "people began hanging out at *The Paper*. There were so many people there that you couldn't even do the work! So it did become a kind of community."[160] Several years later, two writers for Liberation News Service put the matter more simply: "Recognized as a second campus paper at Michigan State," the *Paper* "helped to build a radical community where none had existed before."[161]

THE FIRST UNDERGROUND NEWSPAPER to pop up below the Mason-Dixon Line was the *Rag*, out of Austin, Texas—easily "the largest center of New Left activism in the American South."[162] According to underground press historian Abe Peck, the *Rag* was also "the first independent undergrounder to represent, even in a small way, the participatory democracy, community organizing, and synthesis of politics and culture that the New Left of the midsixties was trying to develop."[163] Whereas the *Los Angeles Free Press* and the *Paper* were both led by unusually resolute and energetic individuals, the

Rag owed its distinctive style and temperament to a collective known as the "Ragstaff" (or, sometimes, "Ragamuffins"). It was a spirited, quirky, and humorous paper, whose founders pushed the New Left's political agenda even as they embraced the counterculture's zeal for rock music, psychedelics, and personal liberation. Nevertheless, the general trajectory of its early development will seem familiar. The *Rag* was established by youths whose tastes, attitudes, and ideas marked them as outsiders in their own community; in turn, their paper helped to embolden and unify the underground cliques and coteries from which it grew. According to Doug Rossinow, who has written authoritatively on the New Left in Austin, the *Rag* became the main fount of information for hippies and politicos alike, and was "enormously important" to local activists.[164]

This is not to suggest, however, that Austin was any kind of left-wing haven. In fact, right-wing extremism carried the day at the University of Texas (UT), and anyone involved in even the most minor forms of social deviance, whether by supporting labor groups, expressing limited tolerance for homosexuality, or reading "obscene" writers like John Dos Passos, was likely to face grave charges of "pinko-communism."[165] Robert Pardun, a prominent SDS activist who helped to establish the *Rag*, recalled learning about local folkways within a month of moving to Austin from Colorado in the fall of 1963. After he fell into a conversation with a couple of strangers at a local watering hole, the conversation turned to Communism. "I was amazed," Pardun said, "when one of them advocated dropping nuclear bombs on all the major cities in the Soviet Union as a 'pre-emptive strike' . . . and I said something like, 'Wow! That's pretty extreme. You know, Russians are people too.'" For this, Pardun was promptly attacked by one of the men. "As I ran for the street I could hear him yelling 'dirty communist bastard.' I walked to the school infirmary [with a broken finger] wondering if he really thought I was a communist. If so, it didn't take much to be a communist in Texas."[166] As it happens, Pardun may have gotten off easy; another of the *Rag*'s founders later mused, "Hardly a week goes by that some beatnik doesn't get bashed on the head by a beer bottle."[167]

One of the places where young nonconformists found a measure of refuge was in Austin's vibrant music scene. Although countless youths turned to the folk revival of the 1950s and early 1960s as an alterative to mass culture, the historian Alice Echols observes that in "more urban places like Cambridge, Berkeley, and Greenwich Village, the search for authenticity led folk music mavens to seek out obscure records and songbooks. But in Austin authenticity was considerably less hard to come by. Texas was a region still alive with 'real' music, including country and western."[168] Particularly important in this regard was Threadgill's Bar, located on the city's northern rim. The joint's owner, Kenneth Threadgill, was an ex-bootlegger who filled every single slot in his jukebox with records by Jimmie Rodgers, the Mississippi-born yodeler whom many regard as the "father of country music."[169]

For almost two decades, working-class locals had the run of the place, but in 1959 a small group of UT graduate student musicians started showing up; after charming the crowd with their deep enthusiasm for old-time bluegrass and honky-tonk, they began participating in weekly hootenannies.[170] Meanwhile, a folk scene was taking shape around UT. According to cultural historian Barry Shank, in Austin "folksinging quickly became a way of marking one's difference from the student body represented by fraternities, sororities, and football players." Although there weren't many folkies, they were, "by all accounts, intense and active."[171] Most of them lived in an off-campus rooming house known as "the Ghetto," where they frequently held late-night drinking parties. A tumbledown eatery in UT's student union called the Chuck Wagon was their favorite gathering spot; eventually, "beatniks, folksingers, artists and poets" became regular patrons. According to one of its former habitués, "The Chuck Wagon was where the bohemian community of Austin constructed itself—through cheap coffee and intense conversation."[172]

By this time, the gatherings at Threadgill's also changed in character, as more and more UT students and "longhairs" showed up, while some of the bar's "rednecks" apparently began drinking elsewhere.[173] (African Americans, of course, were not allowed there at all.)[174] Nevertheless, according to Shank, "By the winter of 1962–63, musical taste and musical practice were established in Austin as the most significant indicators of cultural difference among the generally white, middle-class students at the University of Texas. The hip sang . . . under the tutelage of older white working men near the edge of the city limits, while the mainstream twisted to Chubby Checker records at parties near campus."[175]

Others found refuge from reactionary local politics by immersing themselves in the study of social-gospel Christianity and existential philosophy. Of course, existentialism was in vogue on other campuses as well; in 1965, a college professor noted the trend in a lengthy *Harper's* article, describing existentialism as "both a mood and a metaphysics" that prized, above all else, "authenticity."[176] But as Rossinow explains, in socially conservative Austin, where "Protestantism was the rule" and Fundamentalism remained "alive and well," the ethics of authenticity had to be explored in "safe" venues, such as the Christian Faith-and-Life Community, a religious center connected to UT, and the University YMCA-YWCA.[177]

Founded in 1952, the Christian Faith-and-Life Community (usually just called "the Community") was a communal experiment that encouraged extracurricular theological study among UT students. Although Protestants dominated, the Community was open to people of all faiths from a variety of nationalities and social backgrounds, and in 1954 it began welcoming African Americans, making it the first place on UT's campus with desegregated residential housing. Its controversial director of curriculum, Joe Matthews, believed that in order to reach a state of "authenticity" and "wholeness" one first had to experience a kind of cataclysmic breakthrough—a rupture with past understandings, a sense of profound humiliation, and a deeply felt immersion in a community. To that end, he adamantly encouraged cultural and political risk taking. While some came to regard this as a pernicious, almost cult-like doctrine, it encouraged intense dialogues about how to make life meaningful, which frequently turned into conversations about vexing social and political issues, such as racism, poverty, and war. Matthews was forced to resign in 1962, but until then, Rossinow writes, the Christian Faith-and-Life Community "served as a medium for communicating existentialist themes that were becoming attractive to many young people in the late 1950s and early 1960s."[178]

Located directly across from UT's campus, the University YMCA-YWCA, or "Y," likewise functioned as an incubator for alternative values (and in fact both institutions attracted overlapping groups of students). Here again, by filtering their yearnings for a more authentic mode of living through Christian liberalism, students safely explored ideas that otherwise might not have been tolerated in such a conservative stronghold. The Y hosted controversial speakers, ran seminars addressing sensitive political issues, organized retreats and conferences where students openly questioned American values, and even ran a study abroad program that sent UT students to Africa, the Soviet Union, and other Eastern Bloc countries. Finally, while the Y was not quite an "activist" organization, Rossinow explains that it was colored with a style of Christian liberalism that emphasized courage and personal responsibility, risk taking, and human fellowship—all of which fused with the civil rights movement's existential imperatives.[179] This kind of melding of private concerns and social troubles also helped to fuel much of the New Left. Looking back upon his undergraduate days at UT, journalist Willie Morris wrote, "These groups, and they were good people, were the repositories of whatever liberalism existed on a conscious level at the University of Texas at that time."[180]

A cluster of about five activists started an SDS chapter at UT in late 1963. Among them was Jeff Shero, a former Army brat whose conservative worldview was ruptured by his confrontations with "southern fascism" after his family moved to rural Texas while he was in high school. Earlier that year, Shero had attended SDS's national convention in Pine Hill, New York, where he was elected to the National Council after pluckily debating Tom Hayden. With the possible exception of the UT's Campus Interracial Committee, Austin lacked an organized Left from which SDS's founders could draw, so they began by recruiting "every alienated person [they] could get of every kind" Shero said, "which was perfect for SDS's kind of politics. That year we had an alliance between the guys that rode motorcycles, the kind of bohemian artist-writer types, the integrationists, the early vegetarian peacenik types, even people who hated fraternities and sororities, which ran the school. So it was an interesting coalition that year."[181]

Perhaps ironically, the vitriolic resistance that southern New Leftists faced may have helped them to forge unusually strong communal bonds. "To go against the government . . . was so out of step with your parent's generation that you were generally disowned," Shero remembered.

> You were an embarrassment to the family, especially if you came from a small town, and in the worst cases, which was often, you didn't go home at Christmas. If you were in college, everyone goes home at Christmas, but we'd sit around and there'd be like twenty-five people who weren't going home. It was like, we'll have our own Christmas here. This is my new family. . . . You were much more bonded . . . than [old-guard SDSers] from the East Coast who were doing something that was in the tradition of their families.[182]

Austin's SDS chapter was consistently offbeat, free spirited, and, if anything, even *more* democratic than the SDS strongholds at Ann Arbor and Swarthmore.[183] Todd Gitlin called them "instinctive anarchists."[184] While the Austin SDS chapter was initially consumed with antiracist activities—integrating a downtown restaurant, registering voters, tutoring poor black schoolchildren, and protesting against a Greek-sponsored "Cowboy Minstrel Show"—it later emerged at the forefront of southern antiwar activity. In April 1965—a time when many Americans were only dimly aware of the conflict in Vietnam—about forty of UT's student rabble-rousers lined the road near President Lyndon Johnson's ranch in Stonewall, Texas, demanding that he "Stop the Bombing and Negotiate."[185] By then, Austin's SDS chapter could boast of being one of the nation's largest, and several of its members would soon become activists of national significance.[186]

By the time the *Rag* came to fruition in the fall of 1966, a diverse bohemian subculture and an organized expression of the New Left was already rooted in Austin. This marks a difference between the *Rag* and its predecessors. Though attuned to the faint rumblings of cultural discontent in their respective communities, neither Kunkin nor Kindman conceived of their papers as adjuncts of a flourishing local movement; in fact, it was just the opposite: the *Freep* and the *Paper* both sought to shake their readers out of their political somnambulism. By contrast, the *Rag* aimed to unify and direct a local youth rebellion that was already under way. The northern underground papers, however, were clearly an inspiration. "What [Michael Kindman] had done [with the *Paper*] was really part of the model for what we did," Dreyer said.[187] The previous spring's ascension of an obnoxious right-wing student named John Economidy to the editorship of UT's campus paper, the *Daily Texan*, was another impetus for the *Rag*.[188]

On October 5, 1966, Dreyer—who, along with Carol Neiman, was among the chief agents in getting the *Rag* going—elaborated on the situation in a letter he wrote to the seven papers that made up the Underground Press Syndicate (UPS), which was trying to bolster the underground press by allowing member papers to freely reprint each other's material. "The Rag sees itself fulfilling several needs," he wrote:

> Most of the student body at the University of Texas can be aptly described as the soggy green masses. Apathy and dullness thrive. However, as a reaction to this a rather notable percentage of the university community has completely disassociated from the Machine. Austin has for several years been the home of a very active and vocal underground. . . .
>
> Point two: Austin is the capital of radical political activity in the South-Southwest. . . . The Austin radical scene has the strongest sense of community of any I have come in contact with; hippies and politicos merge.
>
> And finally . . . This year, after three run-offs, a veritable fascist was elected editor [of the *Daily Texan*]. His campaign platform was essentially to kill the commies and uncover all the dope on campus. Needless to say, there is a great demand for THE RAG. . . . I definitely think the [Underground Press] Syndicate has exciting potential and I want to announce THE RAG's intention to hook up. So send us the UPS Organizer's Handbook, the Secret Initiation Rights, and the Keytto [*sic*] the White John.[189]

In every respect, the whimsical, democratically controlled *Rag* was the antithesis of the *Daily Texan*. "People had job descriptions, but they wanted to get away from traditional terminology and . . . redefine the roles," Pardun recalled.[190] For instance, there was no editor in chief, but rather a "funnel" and a "funnella" (originally Dreyer and Neiman) "who brought letters and inquiries to the staff's attention."[191] Others were listed on the masthead as "Artist-Type People" and "Shitworkers."[192] "Editing was a very communal affair," remembered David Mahler. "Somebody would bring something in, and Thorne would look through it and say 'This is bullshit!' and scratch through a bunch of stuff, and somebody would say 'No, I like it,' and people would argue for days whether we should put something in. It was a free-for-all." Since many Ragstaffers spent virtually all of their time together, he added, they formed such close relationships that "editing decisions were theoretical and personal at the same time."[193] Later, the paper experimented with rotating "issue coordinators" and guarded against the glorification of individuals by using only first names in bylines.[194]

According to Pardun, "The *Rag* was imbedded in a community that provided support and a place to relax and have fun. The staff made collective decisions, and volunteers from the growing movement did much of the layout and pasteup in preparation for printing."[195] But others point out that the paper's hyperdemocratic style didn't guarantee harmonious relations. Mariann Wizard (formerly Vizard) recalled that from the moment people began brainstorming about the *Rag*, there was "something of a power struggle" about how it would be run. While some "would like to have been called an editor . . . and had an editorial structure," others replied "'No, no. We don't want an editor. Editors fuck you up.'" Later on, she said, some people went on "power trips" that could make the *Rag*'s structure "terrible to work within."[196] Predictably, women were more likely to shoulder the most laborious chores—folding and collating, typing articles, and running the Multilith printing machine.[197] "I don't think it was anything we did in a conscious way," Dreyer remembered, "but there's no denying that men [initially] played a stronger role and women tended to do the more mundane jobs."[198]

The *Rag*'s premier issue went on sale on Monday, October 10, 1966. While most Ragstaffers sold their papers in downtown Austin without incident, one of their number, a flamboyant (some said "fearless") SDS leader named George Vizard caused a minor commotion by hawking the *Rag* on UT's West Mall, in violation of a campus ordinance. "Commie propaganda—get it while it's hot!, . . . Page 6 is soaked in LSD—it's a cheap trip. Read about the freaks!!"[199] After a crowd gathered and someone from the office of UT's dean of student life told him to stop, Vizard replied, "Well, sir, I'm not a student here so you can go to hell," at which point sales surged. A while later, Vizard was approached by the chief of campus security, who threatened to arrest him. When Vizard blew him off ("Hell, man, I've been busted before. That doesn't scare me. I'm here to sell papers, not to bull it with you"), a crowd of onlookers cheered him on. Supposedly, 1,500 copies were sold that day.[200]

Initially, the *Rag*'s New Left politics may have been softened by its home-spun charm and proto-psychedelic graphics. Its logo was a cartoon-style drawing of the words "The Rag," with each letter made out of a mélange of humorously sketched reptiles and random counterculture artifacts (including a hookah, a curly-toed boot, and a clarinet). Hand-drawn illustrations on the inside pages were equally hallucinatory. Like just about every other under-ground newspaper, the *Rag* regularly offered a community calendar (called the "Rag Bag"), but its weekly motorcycle column (the "Bent Spokesman") was unique. The first issue included a strange burlesque of Greek-dominated campus life, an exposé attacking Economidy's editorship at the *Daily Texan*, and a critique of *Playboy* magazine—less for its sexism than for its phony and affected presentation of modern sexuality, which ran counter to the New Left's call for authenticity in human relations.[201] Issue number two included an essay on a Dutch anarchist group called the Provos, a look back at UT's short-lived (sixteen days) Student League for Responsible Sexual Freedom, and a skeptical review of an outré Andy Warhol film, *Camp* (which was said to be about as bad as his last release, *Blow Job*)—all material that must have seemed more than faintly scandalous in the capital of Texas.[202]

As the paper began its third month, columnist and printer Larry Freud-iger explained that there was a very good reason the Ragstaff had never pub-lished a mission statement revealing its "principles and philosophy": No one was certain what they were. Such was the paper's style. However, he added that an "empirical analysis" of the first eight issues gave a pretty good idea of what the *Rag* stood for: "Such basic things as free speech, black liberation, sex, the Beatles, student power, consciousness expansion, children, cats, and all the other good things in life."[203] Freudiger's assessment recognized the *Rag*'s coupling of Austin's New Left and bohemian sensibilities.

However, the paper's "Gentle Thursday" celebrations probably best illus-trate how its synthesis of strategic and expressive politics helped to unify Austin's underground community. As countercultural picnics that deliber-ately politicized public space, Gentle Thursdays had much in common with the era's be-ins.[204] Although Shero came up with the idea for Gentle Thursday and pitched it at an SDS meeting, the *Rag* was primarily responsible for pub-licizing and defining the event.[205] Certainly *Rag* readers would not have missed its modernist-flavored full-page spread in the October 31 issue an-nouncing: "This Thursday is Gentle Thursday The Celebration Of Our Belief That There Is Nothing Wrong With Fun."

We Are Asking That On This Particular Thursday Everybody Do Exactly What They Want on gentle thursday bring your dog to campus or a baby or a whole bunch of red balloons on gentle thursday hold a picnic in front of the West Mall Office Building or maybe read poetry to the picnickers and there will be musicians all around the campus leading merry bands of celebrants on gentle thursday you may bring your paintings to the "Y" and they will exhibit them on the sidewalks or maybe you would like to wade in a fountain or sit on one of the Mustangs you might even take flowers to your Math Professor on gentle thursday feel free to fly a kite on the main mall and at the very least wear brightly coloured clothing![206]

For all its pacific charm, the Gentle Thursday flyer was also flavored with a dash of provocation, since the event was timed to coincide with a Greek-sponsored masquerade known as "Eeyore's Birthday Party," which was ritzy and exclusive. By contrast, Gentle Thursday was open to everyone, and some organizers even "hoped to break down the 'us and them' mentality on both sides—the 'freaks' versus the 'frat rats,' the 'straights' versus the 'hippies,' even the 'hippies' versus the 'politicos.'"[207] While there's scant evidence of Greek participation in the picnic, folklorist Glenn W. Jones observes that those who planned the Gentle Thursday revelry—which included folk music, bongo drumming, kite flying, food sharing, chalk drawing, and amicable conversation—signaled their "ideological solidarity with radical politics and bohemian values which were in opposition to dominant structure."[208] This likewise held true for the handful of students who spontaneously joined the picnic. Susan Olan, a UT undergrad who participated in the event, later remarked, "You have to understand that until that moment, people didn't just do things like sit down on the West Mall and talk to other people."[209] But on Gentle Thursday, simply to lounge on the grass was to partake in a "rite of separation from mainstream society." "I swear, what came to be thought of as the Austin community was born that day," Olan added.[210]

After the first Gentle Thursday proved successful, the *Rag* helped SDS to sponsor four more similar events, the next of which, "Flipped Out Week," was an extravaganza in April 1967 that was coordinated with Austin's Spring Mobilization Against the War.[211] Undoubtedly, the *Rag*'s favorable coverage of Gentle Thursday helped the ritual to spread to other states, including Colorado, Iowa, Kentucky, Missouri, New Mexico, and Michigan.[212] In Austin, though, as the city's "oppositional forces" outgrew "the boundaries of face to face community," Gentle Thursdays morphed into larger-scale festivals, at which gently strummed guitars and conversations gave way to psychedelic rock bands and polemical speeches.[213]

In addition to promoting these big events, the *Rag* implicitly endorsed the idea of rock and roll as a community-building force. Album reviews and concert announcements were staples of most underground newspapers, but save for major metropolises like New York, Los Angeles, and San Francisco, few communities gave rise to a music scene as vibrant and distinctive as Austin's. "Throughout the early sixties young people from all regions of Texas had flocked to Austin as a center of cultural possibility, where they could live a bohemian, beatnik, proto-hippie life and mark their own difference from the Texan cultural mainstream through such practices as folk-singing, liberal politics, and drug use," Shank writes.[214] This influx gave rise to venues like the Library, the Chequered Flag, and later, the famous Vulcan Gas Co., each of which booked local rock acts that cultivated followings of offbeat fans. One beloved band was the Conqueroo, a racially mixed group whose complex songs were "written deliberately to flout the conventions of commercial pop music." Meanwhile, the 13th Floor Elevators openly used peyote and LSD and blended proto-psychedelic sounds into their garage rock rave-ups. (The band's trademark was its mysterious-sounding electric jug.) Tary Owens, a veteran of the scene, recalled that the 13th Floor Elevators' shows attracted "a large underground contingent of people—proto-hippies, I don't know what you want to call them—but there were a lot of people that were becoming more and more weird, student drop-outs, artists, writers."[215]

Finally, the *Rag* contributed to Austin's New Left community by functioning as an activist organization in its own right. According to two of its founders, Thorne Dreyer and Victoria Smith, "From the beginning . . . *The Rag* was the common ground of the Austin radical community," since those who worked on the paper were also "among the leaders of confrontations with local authorities" and "at the forefront of local cultural happenings." When SDS held an unauthorized rally protesting Vice President Hubert Humphrey's appearance on campus in April 1967, five of the six students to face disciplinary action were also affiliated with the *Rag*. Here again, the *Rag* "not only reported the news of the New Left community, but was integrally involved in creating the situations out of which the news emerged."

According to Dreyer and Smith,

Austin had always had a large 'underground' scene' . . . lots of radical politicos, ethic folkniks, academic left-libs, peyote freaks and bearded bikers. They were all there, dispersed around the campus area, but there was nothing to pull them together, to give them political direction, to bring them into actions, to give them a sense of common identity. The *Rag* was primarily responsible for bringing together a coherent left-hip scene, and for its first two years it was a prime focus of that community.[216]

By organizing itself as a democratic collective, the *Rag* established a precedent that most subsequent underground newspapers would follow. Although the *Freep* and the *Paper* presented themselves as open forums through which just about anyone could make a claim on the community's attention, by the late 1960s most New Leftists were so scrupulously democratic that they scoffed at the idea of an underground newspaper being owned or controlled by a single individual. But by championing New Left values, challenging local officials and the mainstream media with bravado, and blossoming into the most visible representation of Austin's oppositional culture, the *Rag* followed a familiar pattern: it put down roots in a community that came to regard it as a beautiful and precious thing.

BY THE STANDARDS of the underground press movement, each of these papers was long lasting, although by the late 1960s none of them resembled their original form. The *Free Press* became an astonishing success; according to one of Kunkin's former confidantes, in the early 1970s the paper was grossing around a million dollars per year.[217] Some felt that Kunkin became increasingly profit minded in this period, and much of the goodwill he won with his newspaper coverage was lost after he took to meandering around the Strip in a giant Pontiac convertible that was equipped with a mobile radio telephone. Others were turned off as the *Free Press* increasingly ran notices for X-rated movie theaters and sexually explicit personal ads, which some said threatened to overrun the magazine. After his ill-fated decision to reveal the contact information for scores of undercover narcotics agents, the *Freep* faced a flurry of multimillion-dollar lawsuits for receiving stolen property, obstructing justice, and invasion of privacy. Kunkin was eventually cleared of the criminal charges, but he lost money in settlements and legal fees, and the well-publicized controversy scared off local printers. In an effort to keep the paper afloat, he bought a printing press from Marvin Miller, a pornographer and convicted tax evader, but the press was a lemon. Miller eventually won control of the paper, which he sold to two San Diego businessmen who fired Kunkin in 1973.[218] The *Freep*'s final owner was Larry Flynt, the notorious publisher of *Hustler*, who dissolved the paper in 1978.

At MSU, the New Left and the *Paper* grew in tandem for several years.[219] By the late 1960s, however, the *Paper's* staff became increasingly polarized. Although everyone who contributed to the newssheet shared the New Left's broad goals of ending the Vietnam War and bolstering student power, some among them championed the revolutionary aims of SDS's ultramilitants, while others, like Kindman, became increasingly involved with the psychedelic movement. During the 1966–67 school year, Kindman gradually withdrew from the paper, and in the autumn of 1967 he lost $1,000 of his friends' money while trying to buy a suitcase full of drugs in California. Kindman's final article for the newspaper, datelined November 30, was an incoherent diatribe that simultaneously proclaimed "WE DON'T NEED DRUGS" and "Drugs are beautiful! We should have them!"[220] By the time the *Paper* published its final issue in 1969, Kindman had already moved to the Fort Hill area of Boston, where he became heavily involved in a bizarre cult run by a hypnotic acid freak named Mel Lyman.[221] After many harrowing interactions with members of the "Lyman Family," he fearfully escaped from the group's Kansas farm in the dead of night in March 1973. The ensuing years were difficult ones; he worked on a community newspaper called the *Mendocino Grapevine*, started a construction business that went bankrupt, and in the early 1980s he immersed himself in the gay counterculture. In 1988 he was diagnosed with HIV, and he died from AIDS in 1991.

The *Rag* lasted until 1976. Like the *Paper*, in the late 1960s the staff divided along cultural and political lines, although in Austin the two factions seemed to coexist amiably enough. (One Ragstaffer called the paper "a miracle of functioning anarchy.")[222] In 1969 UT's Board of Regents tried to torpedo the *Rag* with a regulation prohibiting commercial solicitation on campus. In response, David Richards, a local liberal attorney, sued UT in federal court and won a ruling decreeing the regent's ban unconstitutional. The university appealed the federal court's decision all the way up to the U.S. Supreme Court, but its attempt to stifle the newspaper was not productive.[223] Meanwhile, the *Rag* soldiered on. Though the paper was always run as a collective, in subsequent years it even tried to do away with its informal hierarchies. In 1971, the Ragstaff wrote an article unfairly describing the paper's founders as "power-oriented . . . chiefs" who "ran the paper with an authoritarian style that the Indians of today's anarchistic staff would never tolerate"— a sign that the paper was becoming increasingly feminist oriented as well.[224] Like a few other underground newspapers, the *Rag* also began offering free subscriptions to prisoners and servicemen. Eventually, though, it lost its relevance, until finally it "died with a whimper." According to Danny Schweers, who joined the paper in 1971 and stayed until the very end, the *Rag's* demise had several predictable causes: "No money. No energy. No community. . . . Times changed. The Vietnam War ended. The promises of solidarity, revolution, drugs, free love, spiritual ecstasy, and pure nutrition found fewer believers. Most importantly . . . the Rag was no longer perceived as innovative, fresh, on the edge, special. If anything, it was a thing of the past."[225]

3

"Electrical Bananas"

The Underground Press and the Great Banana Hoax of 1967

IN JUNE 1967, journalist Sara Davidson visited New York City to report on a hippie happening in Central Park, a "three-day cosmic love-in." The Beatles' *Sgt. Pepper* record, she said, was "everywhere" that summer; another writer recalls that "snatches of the album drifted out of open windows, faded in and out of consciousness as cars passed by, came in and out of focus in tinny tones from distant transistor radios, the songs hanging in the air like a hologram of bliss."[1] Elsewhere were palpable signs that the "Summer of Love" was something more than just a media phenomenon. In hip enclaves across the land, young men and women grew their hair and costumed themselves in a medley of outrageous fashions: tattered jeans and flannels, Western boots, Benjamin Franklin glasses, Mohican lacings, army jackets, and tie-dyed T-shirts. But especially noteworthy for Davidson was the sight of a young hippie in a wizard hat selling bananas on an East Village corner. They were going for ten cents each, with a three-cent deposit on the skins. "Anyone who heard [folksinger] Donovan sing 'Mellow Yellow' knew why," she remembered. "Smoking banana peels could get you high. Outtaaaaa-sight!"[2]

Davidson was mistaken about the psychoactive potential of banana peels. (Hippies later joked that the only way to trip on a banana peel was by accidentally stepping on one.) But she was far from alone in her confusion. Throughout that spring and summer, the notion that one could get high from smoking "banana joints" circulated widely, first in the underground press, then later in the mainstream media and even among some gullible federal officials. Recipes for "bananadine powder"—the boiled, dried insides of banana peels, rolled in tobacco paper and smoked like marijuana—were frequently reprinted, and some clever entrepreneurs on the West Coast founded their own mail-order company, Mellow Yellow, which sold banana peels all across the country. "I hope to make $100,000 in the next six-months on bananas," boasted Nat Freedland, an editor of the *Los Angeles Free Press* and a partner in the firm.[3] In April 1967, *Time* and *Newsweek* both ran stories about the banana craze during the same week, with the latter magazine claiming the rumors had "touched off a banana-buying boom from the Haight-Ashbury district to Harvard Square."[4] At a festival in Central Park's Sheep Meadow, hippies playfully regarded bananas as sacred totems; they gave a "banana pledge" ("one banana, under Banana, with liberty and justice for all"), signaled to each other with a banana salute ("middle finger, up and bent"), and rallied around a large wooden replica of a banana.[5] Frank Thompson, a Democratic congressman from New Jersey, facetiously proposed the Banana Labeling Act of 1967, which would have put stickers on bananas that said "Caution: Banana Peel Smoking May Be Injurious to Your Health." "From bananas it is a short but shocking step to other fruits," he intoned. "Today the cry is 'burn, banana, burn.' Tomorrow, we may face strawberry smoking, dried apricot inhaling, or prune puffing."[6] But the fad and the humor that surrounded it proved short-lived. On May 26, 1967, the Food and Drug Administration issued a press release indicating that scientific analysis of several banana concoctions failed to produce "detectable quantities of known hallucinogenics."[7] One investigator later recalled, "We took 30 pounds of bananas into the lab, cooked, scraped, and did everything else to them that the underground papers told us to do. But it was a put-on."[8]

Not surprisingly, the Great Banana Hoax of 1967 has failed to gain attention from historians. And it may still be hard for scholars to regard the banana-smoking craze as little more than a curious incident, something to remind us yet again just how puerile hippies could be. But when we examine the fad's mysterious origins and meanings, as well as the mechanisms by which it spread so quickly, we can see in microcosm some of the important accomplishments of the 1960s underground press. The irony is thick; Someone once remarked, "Almost everyone likes bananas, but no one takes them seriously."[9] Yet through the banana rumors, the underground papers helped to carve social spaces (called "scenes") where certain commonalities of taste, style, and behavior were generated, and youths were socialized into whole new ways of thinking and being. Meanwhile, formal networks within the underground press meant that scenes rarely stayed "local" for too long.

Through a coordinated exchange of articles and information, alternative subjectivities that arose in one part of the country could be quickly spread to others, thereby giving youths a sense of generational potency, a feeling that their movement was something more than just the sum of its parts.[10]

BRIEFLY TOUTED AS BRITAIN'S ANSWER to Bob Dylan, the Scottish-born folk balladeer Donovan released the single "Mellow Yellow" in Europe in November 1966, and it was released stateside in January 1967.[11] The short, jazzy song featured a whispered refrain from Paul McCartney, and it contained the lyrics "E-lec-trical banana / Is gonna be a sudden craze / E-lec-trical banana / Is bound to be the very next phase / They call it Mellow Yellow." According to rock critic Jim DeRogatis, "The tune was inspired by the rumor that you could get high smoking dried banana peels."[12] But in fact Donovan's song predated the first documented mention of the banana rumor by several months, and even during its heyday in 1967, the lyric's intended meaning was subject to speculation. When *Newsweek* magazine claimed that "Banana highs were heralded by the British pop singer Donovan," a reader wrote back with a correction.[13] "Donovan is a fan of the Youngbloods, a new rock group out of California," she claimed. "Said group has an [electric] organist . . . by the name of Banana. *That* is where Donovan got [the phrase] electrical banana."[14] Meanwhile, Donovan stoked curiosity about the song by refusing to answer any questions about it. "People asked me all the time," he recalled. In reply, he would simply smile and sing the chorus: "They call me Mellow Yellow."[15] But Donovan eventually confessed that the lyric was a sly reference to a yellow electric vibrator that he saw advertised in the back pages of a magazine—a plausible claim, seeing as double entendres figured in other Donovan songs from the era, most notably "Superlungs" ("She's only fourteen but she knows how to draw").[16]

The true origins of the banana fad are not well known.[17] By some fluke, the first printed reference connecting bananas, drugs, and the avant-garde probably appeared in the quasi-pornographic poetry journal *Fuck You: A Magazine of the Arts*, which was one of the few radical papers of the era that was truly an *underground* publication. Crudely mimeographed onto colorful granatext and wire-stitched by hand, its masthead boasted that it was "EDITED, PUBLISHED & PRINTED BY ED SANDERS AT A SECRET LOCATION IN THE LOWER EAST SIDE, NEW YORK CITY U.S.A."[18] According to poetry critic John Palattella, it "was available just at a small number of stores, hidden behind the counter, and only those in the know could find it."[19] In May 1963, Sanders dedicated Volume 3, Number 5 of *Fuck You* to, among other things, "dope thrill banana rites."[20] The magazine was always full of in-jokes (many of them very crude) but Sanders left no clues as to what this curious turn of phrase may have meant.[21]

In any event, the Great Banana Hoax originated in California in late 1966, the year that Ronald Reagan was elected Governor, Walt Disney died, and the Beach Boys gave up their striped shirts, Pendletons, and surfboards to record *Pet Sounds*, their vaguely psychedelic orchestral-pop masterpiece about lost innocence. This was also when LSD began to garner a great deal of lurid media attention (although paradoxically, the drug was mostly a phenomenon among the hip intelligentsia). While some of the era's most important drug-inspired rock masterpieces were released in 1965 and 1966 (among them, Bob Dylan's *Bringing It All Back Home* and *Highway 61 Revisited* and the Beatles' *Rubber Soul* and *Revolver*), these records generally struck a pre-psychedelic consciousness. As literary professor Nick Bromell put it, "Rock 'n' roll brought psychedelics into popular culture even for the millions of Americans who never knew what marijuana smelled like."[22]

All of which is to say that a certain naïveté about drugs, along with a giddy sense of awe and wonder at their possibilities, probably fueled the first experiments in banana smoking. "Country" Joe McDonald, leader of the Bay Area jug band Country Joe and the Fish, and his drummer, Gary "Chicken" Hirsh, are primarily responsible for setting the hoax in motion. McDonald recalls that while driving to a show at the Kitsilano Theater in Vancouver, Canada, "Our drummer . . . said he had just figured out that banana peels have [chemical] qualities similar to marijuana. His theory was that if you dried out a banana peel and smoked the white pulp on the underside, you would get high. At the time, the band was living on peanut-butter-and-banana sandwiches. All the ingredients were cheap. We were just throwing the peels away, so this sounded like a great idea."[23]

No doubt, Hirsh's suggestion to smoke banana peels sounds peculiar, but it was merely one episode in his long history of experimentation with folk recipes for getting high. Previously, he'd been interested in scotch broom (Cytisus scoparius), a noxious, weedy shrub that's commonly found on California roadsides. In the mid-1960s Hirsh filled dozens of mason jars with scotch broom, carefully labeling each of them according to the location and date that the weed was picked. Sometimes he simply dried out various parts of the plant before he smoked it; other times he cured it in brandy first. But he never got it to work. "I was sure I was just preparing it wrong," he later said. Once he tried getting high by chewing on a nasal-decongestant inhaler; another time he ate a huge amount of the pickling spice mace. Hirsh decided to experiment with bananas after hearing somewhere that they contained trace amounts of a chemical that acted as a "natural tranquilizer." When he recalled that his family had long used bananas as a bedtime relaxant, the idea seemed "almost logical."[24]

So before their performance, Country Joe and the Fish bought some bananas, scraped out the pith inside the peels, and laid it out to dry in the back room of a nearby head shop. Later they smoked the banana peels like joints, according to plan . . . but they also drank from a bottle of water backstage in which someone had "just dissolved a hundred tabs of LSD." When the acid-laced water took its effect, the band members may have attributed their high to the bananas. Or they may have been clowning around. In any event, Country Joe remembers everyone saying, "Man, this shit is really working! I'm getting really ripped! This stuff is incredible!"[25] Hirsh recalls the scene as "hysterically funny."[26] Soon afterward, they returned to the Bay Area to play at a benefit concert for the legalization of marijuana, at which the band passed out hundreds of banana joints and told the crowd that banana peels could get you high.[27] To this day, McDonald says he really believed what he was saying, whereas Hirsh admits he was "pretty stoned most of the time anyway [so] determining the effectiveness of smoking banana skins was pretty tough." Nevertheless, he remembers "just running around telling everyone that it worked. . . . Even if it didn't work, it was great fun."[28]

A few months later, on March 3, 1967, the banana rumor was disseminated in print for the first very first time in the *Berkeley Barb*—one of the earliest, best known, and most influential underground newspapers of the 1960s.[29] Ed Denson, who wrote a regular music column for the *Barb* and also served as Country Joe and the Fish's manager, said that the night before, while "feeling mellow," he lit up a banana joint. He added that he'd been "turned on to bananas" while in Vancouver, and offered a recipe for transforming banana pith into a marijuana-like substance. (In a cheeky reference to the incident described above, he added that the joints could be smoked "with 50 mg. of acid swallowed.")[30] Denson says he always knew the recipe was specious. "I was fully involved in perpetrating the hoax when I wrote that article," he later confessed.[31] But in the very same issue of the *Barb*, an unusual letter to the editor appeared, from someone who reportedly saw an undercover officer from the Berkeley Police Department "lurking in the fresh produce section" of a local grocery store. "I would guess that they have been assigned to observe persons buying large quantities of bananas," the writer claimed. He went on to explain that bananas have psychoactive properties, and he predicted that possession of large amounts of bananas would soon become a criminal offense. The letter was signed "A careful shopper and Co-op member."[32]

We'll probably never know who this "careful shopper" was (Denson says it wasn't him). Possibly someone else at the *Barb* helped to perpetuate the ruse, but more likely, word about bananas had already hit the street. Later in the week, the *San Francisco Chronicle* carried the banner headline "Kicks for Hippies: The Banana Turn-On." "Bananas—the ordinary bananas found in every grocery store—may be the new trend in the psychedelic world," the article proclaimed. The sensationalized piece recounted the "careful shopper's" anonymous letter to the *Barb* and even included a quote from a Berkeley police chief, who denied having undercover cops assigned to any local produce sections. "We've heard about the banana effect but don't believe it," he said.[33] Nevertheless, the story prompted an immediate run on bananas. The day the story broke, McDonald scoured the produce departments at local stores before finally concluding, "you couldn't get a banana in the Bay Area that day."[34] His search was fruitless.

THOSE WHO WOULD DOWNPLAY the counterculture's subversive power typically point out that the youth rebellion was triggered "at least as much by developments in mass culture . . . as changes at the grassroots."[35] That is, because the movement was led by rock stars and celebrity icons, whose messages were transmitted by film, television, and radio, the borders between populist rebellion ("authentic") and commodified trend ("fake") are thought to be impossible to delineate. In this instance, it doesn't take a sleuth to point out that a certain amount of artifice was built into the banana-smoking rumor from the beginning. After all, it was a *hoax*. And although Donovan never intended "Mellow Yellow" as a massive put-on, it is hard to imagine bananas could have captured so much of the countercultural imagination if the song hadn't been soaring through the airwaves.[36] But as *Time* magazine conceded, the banana rumor "quickly passed around the underground through such newspapers as Manhattan's *East Village Other* and the *Berkeley Barb*"—papers whose adversarial outlook and political mission were fairly explicit.[37] Wrote one scholar, "Shattering received cultural patterns—in love and war, in work, in matters of the mind and spirit—was the announced purpose of the underground press."[38]

At the most basic level, papers performed this function by attuning readers to local happenings that helped to define the hip community, including trends, protests, rallies, concerts, and readings. Art Kunkin once described the *Freep* as a "picture frame that fills up each week with what the community is doing."[39] Information about community services—such as free clinics, youth hostels, and food or clothing co-ops—mingled with practical tips and guidelines on how to hitchhike, where to hang out, or what drugs to take (or avoid). Jeff Shero, who after contributing to the *Rag* became editor of a militant New York organ called the *Rat*, said that "hip survival information" was that paper's "most popular feature."[40] In addition to acting as community switchboards, almost all underground newspapers featured book, record, and film reviews, and even advice columns, such as the *Washington Free Press*'s "Dear General Marsbars" (which focused on draft resistance) and the syndicated "Dear Dr. Hip Pocrates," (where Eugene Schoenfeld, an actual doctor, answered questions about health, drugs, and sexuality that the mainstream prints could scarcely have fathomed).[41] As one underground press reader put it in a letter to the editor, "Were it not for the existence of papers like [Detroit's] *Fifth Estate* and its continuous airing of certain issues, its fresh way of looking at movies and the space it provides for news of crucial organizations and where to find them, interest in these matters might wane and be forever lost."[42] Another writer told the staff of Madison, Wisconsin's *Connections*, "While your paper is still young [and] it will probably be some time before it reaches the consistent high quality of the *Barb* or the *Los Angeles Free Press*, I must thank you [for bringing a left-wing viewpoint to the Madison area]." He suggested, however, that the paper "add a section . . . listing the upcoming activities planned by the various hippie and activist groups on campus. I feel this would be a great service to the campus community."[43]

Most underground newspapers ran such listings, but they were more than just community bulletins; they also projected a culture, enhancing identities, affirming social styles, and molding a local avant-garde. As media activist Jerry Rubin explained, "Part of the underground press's role was to . . . define an alternative community and give it a voice and a consciousness and an identity. It did those things pretty well."[44] Underground papers "had a lot to do with keeping people plugged in in that period," another activist recalled.[45] In the spring of 1967, the *East Village Other* (*EVO*) received a letter to the editor from a New Yorker living temporarily in Georgia. "You may not know it," he said, "but your publication is my only escape to the hip scene. . . . You really don't know what it means just to read about . . . the off-the-wall happenings in New York."[46]

By the time of the banana rumors, other local underground papers were likewise well positioned to report on trends that were happening in faraway parts of the country—but this hadn't always been the case. The original undergrounds of the 1960s initially focused attention on their own communities. When Kunkin founded the *Free Press*, he wanted to bring together local poets, artists, and the habitués of the area's coffee houses.[47] Michael Kindman spearheaded the *Paper* "in something of a void," as a "rather limited alternative" to Michigan State University's campus newspaper.[48] Dreyer's announcement for the *Rag* stressed purely local concerns. The *Seed* declared itself "the voice of the Chicago underground."[49] Of the *Barb*, editor Max Scherr said, "We have to be of our own community [by addressing] indigenous issues."[50] Even the *EVO*, which was born in the media capital of the world, trumpeted its provincial mission in its first issue; it would cater "to the new citizenry of the East Village."[51]

As a result, the papers initially grew in relative isolation from the other bohemian enclaves that were taking shape in other regions. Although historians are fond of referring to an overarching "youth community" in the 1960s, before the advent of the underground press, the youth revolt was marked more by fragmentation than cohesion. Local struggles were the primary catalysts for change, and small groups the dominant social unit.[52] News in the underground traveled slowly and fitfully. Head shops and offbeat bookstores typically carried radical papers from out of town, but just as often information spread by word-of-mouth. Returning from a cross-country sojourn in 1966, Kindman recalled feeling like an "ambassador from a developing national counterculture, bringing news of the future back to my provincial homeland."[53]

When a cluster of underground papers banded together to form the Underground Press Syndicate (UPS) in June 1966, however, the radical papers literally multiplied their potential audience. UPS simply facilitated the free exchange of articles, news stories, and reviews among underground papers, and it drew a broad range of New Left, counterculture, and youth-oriented papers into its fold.[54] Walter Bowart, a founder of the *EVO*, and two of his close compatriots, Alan Katzman and John Wilcock, were responsible for getting the Syndicate off the ground. Wilcock says he came up with the name "UPS" while huddled over a typewriter in the paper's Tompkins Square office, drafting a statement announcing that the nation's first wave of underground papers had agreed to begin circulating each other's material. "I commented that my adolescent idols [had] been the papers of the French *maquis*, the underground resistance group whose propaganda leaflets urged continued resistance to the German occupiers. We all agreed that though a little grandiose, it was an appropriate image for a new Fuck Censorship press in a supposedly free society."[55] Certainly UPS arrived at a propitious moment. Within six months, some twenty-five more papers were founded, all of which joined UPS. Collectively, their circulation at the beginning of 1967 was around 250,000, although, as one record executive observed, papers of this type had "a tremendous pass-along readership."[56] "Underground publishing continues to be one of the success stories of the year," Wilcock boasted. "Hardly a day goes by without new papers proliferating."[57]

Despite its formidable name, the "Underground Press Syndicate" wasn't without its problems; it described itself, in a classic oxymoron, as an "anarchistic organization," and later in the decade it was nearly rent asunder in a power struggle.[58] Its staff turned over several times, and its more ambitious goals of linking papers with Telex machines, soliciting national advertising revenue, and assisting in underground press distribution never got very far. There were also allegations of ego-tripping, financial mismanagement, and bad faith, and in March 1968 Wilcock found it necessary to apologize to member papers, declaring, "In short, the whole operation has been thoroughly fucked up."[59] A bit later, when journalist Ethel Romm was researching an article on the underground press, she spoke with several editors who told her UPS was "in limbo."[60] Nevertheless, testimonials from underground writers suggest that UPS coordinated the exchange of papers fairly well. Kindman recalled that membership in UPS "brought immediate benefit to us, in the form of a wealth of interesting articles available for reprinting, as all of the member papers began exchanging copies with one another."[61] Even underground papers overseas joined UPS. The year 1966 saw the birth of Europe's first underground newspaper, *International Times* (*it*), which cofounders Barry Miles and John Hopkins modeled on *EVO* and the *Freep*. "It was wonderful to have my work reprinted across the world, to see something as mundane as a record review appear in a paper from Minneapolis or an essay translated into Dutch or Swedish," Miles recalled.[62] By circulating texts, graphics, and comics from newspapers all across the country, the underground papers were suddenly able to take their readers on a much larger cultural journey than they had originally envisaged.

In addition to linking geographically separated communities, the underground press was also emerging in late 1966 as the youth movement's most important means of internal communication. Unlike most mass media outlets, underground papers frequently encouraged a "horizontal" conversation among their readers. That is, rather than always showcasing the thinking and writing of privileged elites, underground rags typically opened their pages to anyone with the wherewithal to write about something. Kunkin even went so far as to describe his *Free Press* as a "reader-written paper."[63] Editors rarely exercised the discretion that their title implied, for fear of being labeled "elitist" or "professional."[64] As Abe Peck explained, "for an editor to unilaterally spike copy in the underground press was generally seen as an ego trip rather than a reasoned judgment."[65] Although a few notable personalities played key roles in the banana hoax, the most important purveyors of the rumor were ordinary participants in the youth revolt who simply took advantage of their easy access to their community papers.

As *Newsweek* later recounted, underground papers started reprinting the *Barb*'s recipe for Mellow Yellow "[a]lmost before anyone could peel a banana."[66] The hoax made its way to Texas via two newspapers, the Austin *Rag* and Dallas's *Notes from the Underground*. The *Rag* reprinted the "careful shopper's" letter to the *Barb*, as well a giddy piece from the San Francisco *Oracle* that began "Banana Sunshine! The banana is for real," and went on to make a variety of comically pedantic pseudoscientific claims about bananas ("The peel contains arterenol, a sympathomimetic agent that is also found in the human body, in the adrenal meduala [*sic*]").[67] Meanwhile, editors at the Dallas *Notes* smoked bananas themselves to see if the rumor was true and concluded (in print) that it was.[68] A writer for the *Spokane Natural* surveyed several friends who smoked bananas and reported that their experiences ranged widely; a few experienced "no effect or [a] *very* mild effect," whereas others said it was "better than grass-acid-or-DMT."[69] Marvin Garson of the *Village Voice* also smoked a banana joint and reported "it was identical in its effects to about half a joint of second-rate pot." But he predicted that before long, underground pharmacologists would perfect recipes for high-grade banana powder, "and then the fun will begin."[70] Two *EVO* editors fibbed that *they* were the ones who had discovered psychoactive properties in bananas.[71] Abbie Hoffman (still going by "Abbott" at the time) passed along his own personal recipe in the *Worcester Punch*. "Bananas are the new craze," he said. "Mellow Yellow—the word's out."[72] Detroit's *Fifth Estate* reprinted a recipe for Mellow Yellow that first appeared in the *Los Angeles Free Press*. "Yes, banana-powder works," it proclaimed. "Two or three bombers will get you stoned out of your skull. A toke or a joint will give you a beautiful subtle *mellow* high—Makes the universe into a tranquil delight for an hour!" The article also reported that Larry Starin, a twenty-six-year-old California transplant, had perfected a recipe for banana powder and was turning a quick profit selling it in Berkeley. "I'm ashamed to admit I was selling matchboxes of Mellow Yellow for as much as fifteen dollars," he said. Later, Starin marketed his product via advertisements in the *Barb*.[73]

Several papers also ran advertisements from a company called Mellow Yellow, which sold "100% LEGAL, PURE BANANA." "Made by hippies in SF's Haight-Ashbury," who mailed their product "in beautiful psychedelic envelopes," the enterprise was said to be staffed with a lawyer, an accountant, a printer, a wholesaler, and an art director.[74] Elsewhere, merchants sold yellow pipes that were made to resemble bananas and T-shirts emblazoned with the blue logo of the United Fruit Company.[75] Someone also designed a poster that parodied Grant Wood's famous "American Gothic" painting, recasting the staid Iowans as hippies; instead of a pitchfork, the farmer is holding a sign that reads "Up the Establishment," and, in his left hand, a banana with a sticker that says "Mello."[76] Before long, "mellow yellow" was being used by underground press writers as an adjective (a record reviewer for the Washington *Free Press* referred to the "luscious mellow yellowness of the vocals" on Moby Grape's debut album) and as a proper noun (to describe banana powder itself, as well events where people gathered to smoke it. For instance, Berkeley undergrads reportedly gathered on the steps of Sproul Hall for "a mass Mellow Yellow.")[77] Some people even made up banana-themed ditties, such as: "I went shopping at the A & P/ But they didn't have any grass or LSD / So I peeled a banana and got so high / I thought I was actually going to fly."[78]

Most underground papers seemed well aware of their ability to generate excitement; a common cliché was that "while the *New York Times* was reporting history, the alternative press was involved in creating history."[79] Max Scherr, editor of the *Barb*, recalled, "We'd plant small articles in the paper saying 'There's a rumor that something is going to happen on Telegraph Avenue Friday at two o'clock.' So people would show up on Friday at two to see what would happen, someone would say, 'Hey, let's close off the street,' and something *would* happen."[80] But in addition to self-consciously spreading the banana rumor, underground newspapers also reported on how the phenomenon spread across the country with bona fide news stories, which were considerably more revealing than those that appeared in the mainstream press. SDS described the banana fad in its official organ, *New Left Notes*.[81] The *Chicago Seed* reprinted the entire text of the aforementioned speech by Rep. Frank Thompson, who jokingly called for Congress to "move quickly to stop the sinister spread of banana smoking."[82] The *Rag* devoted its front page to the misadventures of two young Texans who may have been the only people ever arrested for possession of dried banana pith. Pulled over while speeding, they were caught trying to hide a pipe and a tin foil wrapper that contained the brown, powdery substance ("It's bananas, sir.") Hauled off to jail, interrogated, and held overnight, they were finally released after a Dallas narcotics officer explained the new banana rumor to the arresting officer.[83]

The hoax also caused a stir during the Gentle Thursday celebrations at the University of Texas. These events being a constant source of aggravation to campus officials, one UT administrator balked when Austin's SDS chapter asked the university to formally sanction one of the Gentle Thursdays. "While there is no objection to approved organizations promoting cordiality, friendship, and gentleness on campus, the University cannot approve the proposed 'Gentle Thursday,'" read an official statement. The reason? Some of the planned activities, including "mellow yellow, en masse, all over campus" were "too vague" and "could not be sanctioned by the University." Naturally, the *Rag* made great sport of UT's obstinacy. "If the Administration's intent is to prohibit a mellow-yellow light-in, one must appreciate their forthrightness in becoming the first official body in the United States to ban banana smoking," said one writer. "If, on the other hand, their objection is to lack of clarity, this certainly represents a revolutionary departure from previous University policy."[84]

The hoopla around electrical bananas probably owed much to the power of suggestion; that is, it seems plausible to someone in a sufficiently receptive state of mind that smoking bananas could cause a mild high or a relaxed disposition. But this scarcely begins to explain the comical, even absurd enthusiasm with which young people touted bananas—to the point where, as mentioned above, a "raggle-taggle mob brandishing a giant 3-foot long mock banana" once snake-danced through New York's Central Park, chanting "Ba-nan-a! Ba-nan-a! Ba-nan-a!" as they were "cheered on by girls wearing banana crowns, while one student, dressed in a yellow slicker, tried to pass himself off as the biggest banana of them all."[85] At a "banana rally" in Washington Square Park in Greenwich Village, someone reportedly sat atop a bronze statue of the famous engineer Alexander Lyman Holley and "sang calypso praise to the banana gods."[86] Even though bananas lacked hallucinogenic properties, they were intoxicating to youths for the ability to bemuse, bewilder, and irritate defenders of the established culture.

First, the simple fact that bananas were legal (and, unlike marijuana, could not plausibly be made illegal) seemed delightful. It is probably not a coincidence that the counterculture took shape at a time when America's marijuana laws were most severe.[87] Sociologists have noted that as drug use rose in the 1960s, "an increasing number of college youth experienced harassment by officials. Such repression led to a delegitimation of institutional authority, radicalizing youth along the way."[88] As a *Fifth Estate* writer observed in December 1966, drug laws against marijuana had the perverse effect of criminalizing the behavior of "thousands of innocent, truth-seeking people who otherwise have no connection with the world of crime."[89] Jerry Rubin said much the same thing in his manifesto *Do It!* "As pot-heads we came face to face with the real world of cops, jails, courts, trials, undercover narcs, paranoia and the war with our parents. An entire generation of flower-smokers has been turned into criminals."[90] Meanwhile, growing legions of people who actually used drugs couldn't help but grimace at the painful contortions of fact and logic that accompanied official statements about them. A *Washington Free Press* writer noted that such governmentspeak was all the more "painful because growing numbers of young people are suffering in prison because of such ignorance."[91]

What's more, in the early 1960s, marijuana was still linked in the public imagination with Mexican immigrants, poor blacks, jazz musicians, and beatniks—minorities and subcultures that seemed threatening to mainstream America.[92] Bananas, on the other hand, were ubiquitous; here youths found a potentially corrupting influence on American life right out in the open. Thus we find the undisguised glee with which many of them greeted the banana rumors. "Do you realize what this means? Do you?" the *Los Angeles Free Press* asked. "Everybody can get high, anytime they want to from now on!—You can light up a banana joint in the street, at the freakout, in public, anywhere, anywhere, wheee!"[93] Abbie Hoffman was likewise enamored. Banana highs were "legal, cheap, and you can blow your mind on the process alone," he said. "Just think of it, United Fruit Company peddles dope!"[94] In his *Voice* column, Marvin Garson jovially wrote about how electrical bananas could be used to taunt the police. If a policeman ever stopped a youth to ask what he or she was smoking, the teen could reply "It's all right, officer, I'm just smoking bananas. *I smoke 'em to get high, you know.*"[95]

So profound was the youth culture's skepticism regarding official pronouncements against drugs that one underground press writer sketched a sophomoric one-act play in response to the FDA's attempts to sink the banana rumors. In it, "Lyndon Straight" encounters his friend "Timothy Hippie," who is lying down in his apartment, smiling pleasantly. Thinking he knows what's up, Straight says, "I thought you didn't have any pot."

"I don't, I'm flying on bananas."

"Oh come on!" Straight replies. "You know what the FDA said about bananas." "I know, but I'm still stoned out of my skull," Hippie says.

At this, Straight turns indignant. "Now do you think a responsible government agency would mislead the American public? . . . Now look, they had this real scientific test with all kinds of equipment." But Straight's remarks fall upon deaf ears. Timothy Hippie is too zonked to follow the conversation or offer a coherent reply; instead he drifts in and out of consciousness, loses track of time, announces that he has "the munchies," and mistakes a nearby pile of bananas for "weird looking snakes."[96]

Also attractive to youths was the degree to which the banana rumors seemed to bypass rational thought. That bananas already held a somewhat indelicate position in American humor and wordplay was one thing; the possibility that they could get you stoned was something else altogether, and hippies delighted at the thought that something so healthy and commonplace could be a source of such worry and bemusement. In fusing avant-gardism and social agitation, Mellow Yellow's champions democratized an impulse extending at least as far back as the lyrical left of the early twentieth century, even as they acted in a "countercultural mode" that "reveled in tangents, metaphors, unresolved contradictions [and] conscious ruptures of logic and reason."[97]

That bananas were deployed to signal a flouting of conventional authority is clear. Said *Newsweek*, "The banana cult may be a way to tease the police."[98] But with the help of underground newspapers, the fad also contributed to an informal process of socialization, as Mellow Yellow smoke-ins brought people into proximity with one another and provided an arena where they could embrace new viewpoints. Ideals that were deeply felt in the New Left may have been communicated to people who were at first simply drawn to the playful camaraderie that fueled the banana hoax. To put it another way, the Great Banana Hoax created a liminal space, a conceptual border area between the counterculture and straight society. In smoking a banana joint, youths could participate in a hippie ritual without undertaking a significant amount of risk. Meanwhile they entered a process where the mundane spaces of everyday life were suddenly transformed into arenas for cultural experimentation.

Underground newspaper coverage of the Great Banana Hoax also reminds us of the frequency with which the expressive, aesthetic radicalism of the hippies meshed with the strategic, political activism characteristic of the New Left. Though there were exceptions at each end of the spectrum, most underground papers were a pastiche of culture *and* politics. Arts, leisure, and lifestyle issues shared the page with hard-boiled political analysis of the Vietnam War, the civil rights movement, and various university reforms. Nevertheless, there were always some New Leftists who looked unfavorably upon the "revolutionary tourism" they perceived among cultural radicals, and it should be no surprise that in the banana fad they perceived the worst excesses of the hippie movement. "Bananas, incense and pointing love rays to the Pentagon have nothing to do with redeeming America," journalist Jack Newfield grumbled.[99] Allen Young, a left-wing journalist who in 1967 was preparing to return to the United States after an extended stay in South America, received two letters from friends who warned him about the banana fad. "Bet you're going to be surprised with this barbarian country of yours," one writer remarked. "For your own sake you must get acquainted with the themes of current debate here, such as banana peel [*sic*], hippies, etc."[100] In 1967 Todd Gitlin wrote a vinegary condemnation of the whole banana craze for Liberation News Service, replete with statistics on banana production versus revenue, unfair land-distribution policies in South America, and the concentrated power of the United Fruit Company. "These circumstances come to mind whenever bananas are flaunted with humor or symbolic meaning, as a means of liberation," he wrote.[101] Other underground journalists railed against the ease with which countercultural symbols morphed into commodified trends. For instance, in June 1967, *EVO* ran a cartoon that showed a police officer using a nightstick to clear the way for a long-haired hippie tycoon. As the cop barks out orders to "make way for the psychedelic merchant," the entrepreneur grins impishly, dreaming of the money he'll make from "leather goods, posters, acid rock, books, head shops, and bananas."[102]

Nevertheless, understanding the underground press's role in the Great Banana Hoax helps us gain a keener appreciation of how these papers functioned in the youth revolt more generally. By acting in confederation, underground newspapers could transform local or regional scenes into national trends, thereby bringing a sense of cohesion and community to the sprawling youth rebellion. In this instance, the antics of West Coast hippies were exported to scattered patches of bohemia all across the country in just a few months. Whether they lived in large cities, suburbs, or in the hinterland, young people forged connections to distant underground scenes through radical newspapers. As one media analyst commented in 1966, the youth-identified journals of the 1960s were, "in a sense, community newspapers, but their communities are socio-political rather than geographic."[103]

Underground newspapers also served as agents of mass recruitment. In self-consciously hyping the banana fad—by eagerly passing along the latest bananadine concoctions, by celebrating Mellow Yellow smoke-ins, and even by providing hip merchants with space to advertise their banana wares—they helped to craft an entry point into the counterculture. Along with many other types of youth-oriented festivities that were discussed in underground newspapers, from Gentle Thursdays to gargantuan rock festivals, Mellow Yellows were relatively harmless (and frequently fun) public ceremonies where people entered a domain of shoulder-to-shoulder sociability and cleared a path for future affiliation. But most importantly, these newspapers gave sanction to thoughts, attitudes, and behaviors that were greatly frowned upon elsewhere. They exemplified a radical culture and articulated a coherent set of values that were an alternative to mainstream ones. They set in motion ideas, trends, fads, and mythologies for youths to emulate, modify, spread, or squash as they saw fit. But this wasn't necessarily a top-down process; one of the underground press's most distinctive features was its democratic nature. Virtually anyone who wanted to make a claim on the attention of the youth movement could do so by penning an article for the local community newspaper. Beginning in the mid-1960s, the underground press was the main public forum for discussion about the meaning and direction of the youth revolt. When UPS was founded, it greatly strengthened the underground papers by allowing them to spread news about events outside of their own communities. With its assistance, underground newspapers functioned as vital institutional bases for radical political and aesthetic communities. In their pages, they replicated the creativity, zaniness, humor—and the other-worldliness—of the youth movement at large.

Postscript

Country Joe and Donovan met on May 10, 1997, in Cleveland, Ohio, at the opening of the Rock and Roll Hall of Fame's first major temporary exhibition, "I Want To Take You Higher: The Psychedelic Era, 1965–1969." John Lennon's "Sgt. Pepper's" jacket, Tom Wolfe's handwritten notes for *The Electric Kool-Aid Acid Test*, a Jimi Hendrix set list—these were just some of five hundred artifacts on display in colorfully painted cabinets. Earlier in the day, both artists had performed some of their hits from the 1960s before a large audience; now they were seated beside one another, signing autographs. According to Donovan, this is when Country Joe leaned in and said, cryptically, "It was me, man."

"What was you?"

"The banana thing."

Donovan says that McDonald proceeded to tell him how he and a few friends from Haight-Ashbury actively plotted "to dupe the gullible media" by spreading the false rumors about banana peels. Said Joe: "We just thought it was a bit of fun, man. Then you released Mellow Yellow the same week, and that was it!"[104]

Country Joe remembers the scene altogether differently. He says that when he met Donovan in Cleveland, he seized the opportunity to ask him a question that had percolated in the back of his mind for many years. Was "Mellow Yellow" about smoking banana peels?

But Donovan proved every bit as elliptical in 1997 as in 1967. According to Country Joe, "He looked at me for a moment and said, 'What do you think?' He wouldn't say anything else."[105]

4

"All the Protest Fit to Print"

The Rise of Liberation News Service

WHETHER THEY HAMMERED OUT PROSE on carbon-ribbon typewriters, pasted articles onto layout sheets with rubber cement, or hawked newspapers on congested street corners, most of those who became involved with the underground press during the late 1960s approached their work with a keen sense of political mission. While on the one hand remaining deeply enmeshed in the cultural stirrings in their own communities, the era's literary demi-mondes also conceived of themselves as crucial social agents who would chart the New Left's progress, champion its goals, and—by establishing an alternative media universe that paralleled that of straight society—meet the Movement's demand for the creation of viable "counterinstitutions." These ideas exerted such force on the imaginations of guerrilla journalists that many of them went about their work in a feverish, euphoric rush. "It was a wonderful and amazing circus," reminisced one such writer. "There was so much to enjoy at one time . . . that we were overstimulated, living in a stunned and prolonged ecstasy."[1]

Even less rhapsodic activists regarded the rise of the underground press as a major accomplishment. After all, New Leftists had long stressed the importance of political *means* as well as ends; that is, rather than working within the left-wing establishment—which was said to be teeming with labor bureaucrats, fence-sitting intellectuals, and out-of-touch politicians—the radical youths of the 1960s set out to build parallel institutions and counter structures embodying their own values.[2] But aside from "free universities" that popped up in many cities (and, later, free medical clinics and various types of co-ops), the New Left's attempt to build alternative institutions at first did not go well. By the mid-1960s, certain social democrats were lampooning the New Left's "go-it-aloneism," and some critics within the Movement began wondering whether it might be better to try to transform existing institutions rather than create new ones.[3] But when hundreds of radical newspapers flowered in every region of the country in 1967 and 1968, they stood in rebuke to those who had downplayed the New Left's potential. As one underground newsman boasted, by launching a media with its own "alternative views, interpretations, and values," the underground press aimed at nothing less than the creation of a "revolutionary consciousness" across the land.[4]

The underground press began expanding dramatically following the formation of the Underground Press Syndicate in 1966. But in late 1967 the radical media was bolstered by a much more elaborate and visionary organization, Liberation News Service (LNS). A kind of radical alternative to the Associated Press, LNS aimed to centralize newsgathering and dissemination in the underground media. From its various headquarters—first in Washington, DC, then in New York City, and then, briefly, a farm in Montague, Massachusetts, as well as Manhattan—LNS regularly sent packets of articles, editorials, photos, and political cartoons to hundreds of college and community newspapers, and even a few radio stations, who were free to print (or broadcast) as much of the material as they liked. As a result, LNS literally reached millions of readers.[5] In 1969, a *New York Times* writer described LNS as "one of the few functional alternatives or counter institutions that The Movement has produced. The two, well-produced, weekly packets of political news and radical analysis that L.N.S. mails to nearly 300 subscribers are a principal pillar of the U.S. underground press."[6] That same year, a *Rolling Stone* reporter observed, "These days . . . the news service's material is carried in virtually every underground paper in the U.S."[7]

This chapter describes how LNS was created and then zeroes in on its coverage of two key events in the New Left's history—a famous antiwar rally at the Pentagon in October 1967 and a rebellion of Columbia University students in April 1968. With this approach we can begin to understand how LNS functioned as a kind of radical lodestar in the late 1960s, supporting, influencing, and inspiring the nation's left-wing press, while strenuously and pugnaciously critiquing the mainstream media. Not every LNS writer shared the same understanding of their journalistic mission, but each agreed that the straight media was unfairly biased in favor of the established culture, and that bourgeois journalists were generally uncomprehending of the ways that they disseminated highly politicized worldviews. In several of their flyers and dispatches, LNS writers favorably quoted Andrew Kopkind, a former reporter for the *Washington Post* and *Time* magazine, who began writing for the commercial left-wing press in the mid-1960s:

> In ways which journalists themselves perceive dimly or not at all, they are bought or compromised, or manipulated into confirming the official lies: Not the little ones, which they delight in exposing, but the big ones, which they do not normally think of as lies, and which they cannot distinguish from the truth.[8]

In a similar vein, *Village Voice* writer Jack Newfield once described mainstream (or "center") values as

> the belief in welfare capitalism, God, the West, Puritanism, the Law, the family, property, the two-party system, and perhaps most crucially . . . the notion that violence is only defensible when employed by the State. I can't think of any White House correspondent, or network television analyst, who doesn't share these values. And at the same time, who doesn't insist he is totally objective.
>
> And it is these assumptions—or prejudices—that prevent publishers and editors from understanding, or even being open to, any new reality that might be an alternative to those assumptions. Potential alternatives are buried deep inside the black liberation movement, the white new left, the counterculture of rock music, long hair, underground newspapers and drugs, as well as in the nonwhite revolutionary movements in the third world. And it is these threatening and unfamiliar social movements that the mass media most systematically misrepresent. And it is their sympathizers who are excluded from positions of real power within media hierarchies.[9]

LNS staffers subscribed to these beliefs exactly. Everything that gave radicals cause for exuberance—the air of experimentation around the rock and drug scenes, the counterculture's promise of magical self-liberation, and the protest culture's anarchic antiauthoritarianism—was far beyond the ken of mainstream journalists. As such, they were said to be incapable of adequately covering the youth rebellion. LNS's writers, however, claimed for themselves a kind of epistemic privilege, arguing that only those who shared their cultural perspectives could truly appreciate what was happening in society.

LNS's freewheeling and controversial cofounders, Marshall Bloom and Raymond Mungo, both left an indelible impression on early LNS, but it bears remembering that outside the context of a rising social movement, their efforts probably would not have amounted to much. As Mungo explained in a spirited manifesto that circulated in early 1968, "Because there is a war in Vietnam, because there is a Stokely Carmichael, because there is an active Resistance, there is also a new audience for independent publications, counter-institutions which can be started anywhere by persons of high competence and serious commitment." "At last," he said triumphantly, "our radical press, disparate and spread-out as it may be, is standing on its own."[10]

"THEY WERE A CURIOUS DUO," one writer said of Marshall Bloom and Ray Mungo, "dope smoking, hip, full of far-out incredulousness, yet terribly concerned about Vietnam, the urban crisis and politics."[11] At times, the two were so inseparable that friends called them "BlooMungo," though each had a formidable personality of his own. According to David Eisenhower (the grandson of former president Dwight D. Eisenhower), who was acquainted with Bloom when they both attended Amherst College, Bloom was known around his alma mater as "a local hero . . . a brilliant and resourceful figure in the early days of campus activism in the Northeast." Gradually, however, Eisenhower concluded that Bloom was also erratic and "desperately confused."[12] Meanwhile, Mungo won notoriety as the impish and inflammatory editor of Boston University's (BU) college newspaper, the *BU News*. In 1967, *College Journalist* magazine featured Mungo in a cover story titled, "The Case of the Angry Young Man from Boston."[13]

Born in 1944, "Mad Marshall" Bloom grew up in a tony neighborhood in Denver, Colorado, the son of the conservative owner of a chain of appliance stores. Evidence suggests his childhood may not have been a happy one. In an undated letter, one of Bloom's older relatives told him, "Up until [age] 8 or 9, your Dad was too busy with business to spend much time with you. . . . [His] business and family [problems] were soothed by regularly hitting the bottle, so during this period, you witnessed and perhaps were party to some unpleasant things involving your dad."[14] Nevertheless, Bloom was popular and precocious in high school. He excelled in his studies, immersed himself in a blizzard of extracurricular activities, and even started his own business—a fireworks stand. During his senior year he edited his high school newspaper, for which he interviewed his hero, Senator Barry Goldwater. Yet those who knew Bloom in Denver also detected "a certain social awkwardness" in his personality, "a lack of grace" and feeling of "ineptitude" that he "could neither hide nor compensate for." Not long after he matriculated into Amherst College in 1962, his mother sent him a letter that ominously referenced what she said was his "*big* problem": Bloom was secretly gay.[15]

While at Amherst, Bloom's politics swerved from right to left. As a freshman he created an organization, called Forum, which helped bring a wider variety of speakers to campus. In the historic summer of 1964 he traveled across the South, where he got arrested at a civil rights demonstration in St. Augustine, Florida, contributed to a liberal newspaper called the *Southern Courier*, and went to Alabama to research his senior thesis, "A Participant Observation Study of the Attitudes of Selma Jews towards Integration." As editor of the *Amherst Student* during his senior year, he doubled the paper's size and expanded its scope to include "issues from the world beyond Amherst: the war in Vietnam, the draft, civil rights [and] the existence of poverty in America."[16] So abrupt and thorough was his defection to the Left that he even received a concerned, handwritten letter from Barry Goldwater. "I'm interested in Marshall Bloom," the senator wrote. "There was a time when a letter on this stationery would have brought him great happiness."[17] In June 1966, Bloom was photographed on the front page of the *New York Times* after organizing a walkout of his own graduation ceremony, in protest of Amherst's decision to award an honorary degree to Secretary of Defense Robert S. McNamara.[18]

The following September, Bloom got a draft deferment by enrolling in the prestigious London School of Economics, where he became president of the school's graduate student association. Not long afterward, he became embroiled in a bitter international controversy. The ruckus began when the head of the University College of Rhodesia, Walter Adams, was appointed the director of the London School of Economics.[19] Student activists charged that Adams was insufficiently committed to academic freedom and denounced him as racist. After several months of grumbling, Bloom and another student, David Adelstein, called for a meeting at a campus theater where they planned to discuss strategies for protesting Adams's appointment. Fearful of what the meeting might lead to, school administrators hastily withdrew permission for the assembly and ordered university janitors to block the theater's doors. "Probably it would have just been a small meeting," a participant later claimed, but outside the theater, "hundreds of students trying to get to classes got caught in the hallway," and amid a chaotic scene of pushing and yelling, someone called for the students to surge past the janitors' locked arms.

At this crucial moment, Marshall grabbed the microphone and tried to restore order, but now it was impossible to hear him above the ruckus. A minute later the doors were stormed, but those of us who had broken through didn't learn for another moment that a porter had collapsed in the assault. I remember coming out of the Old Theater and seeing a man spread out on the floor, the crowd now hushed, and a few minutes later, a doctor appeared and pronounced him dead. The newspapers the next day said he had died from a heart attack.[20]

A torrent of controversy followed the tragedy. After campus administrators suspended Bloom and Adelstein, hundreds of students began an eight-day sit-in strike in the school's main entrance hall in protest, and thousands more students from neighboring schools marched downtown. According to the *London Times*, the demonstrations were "unprecedented in British university history."[21] Another writer said that "England was all but immobilized as the press . . . gave saturation coverage to the sit-in."[22] According to Mungo, the lead editorial of another paper, the *London American*, was headlined "Bloom, Go Home."[23] At one point during the strike, Bloom stood before a massive student assembly to give a speech, but when he approached the microphone, he fell silent, and after a long, awkward pause, "he just started sobbing."[24] Soon thereafter, students narrowly voted to end the sit-in, and eventually the university rescinded Bloom's expulsion. By then, however, Bloom had already decided to return to America to take a position as head of the U.S. Student Press Association (USSPA). One of the first things he did upon his arrival was give a lecture at BU, at the invitation of Ray Mungo, who was then winding up his stormy tenure as editor of the *BU News*.[25]

Mungo hailed from Lawrence, Massachusetts, just downriver from another famous nonconformist, Jack Kerouac. His father worked for a paper mill for thirty years "and loved it."[26] His Roman Catholic parents, he said, were "hardworking, ordinary people." Slight of stature and perhaps a bit nerdy looking, Mungo said he made a point of becoming "the smartest kid in school."[27] In eighth grade, his father suggested he might attend a boys' seminary, but his mother—clearly the more perceptive parent—vetoed the idea ("This boy . . . doesn't know a thing about women," she thundered. "When he's old enough to know about women, he can decide for himself if he wants to be a priest!").[28] She was unable to protect him, however, from being sexually abused by a local priest when he was twelve and thirteen years old. "He took me in the rectory, in the projection booth of the parish auditorium, in the car, anywhere he could and as often as he liked," Mungo later disclosed.[29] In 1963, when he entered BU, Mungo wasn't the least bit political. In fact, the very first day he arrived on campus, he was astonished to observe young socialists openly passing out literature.

"I thought that was illegal!" Mungo explained. "I honestly didn't think people were allowed to be socialists or communists in a public way like that."[30]

Almost immediately, he got turned on to marijuana. "Dope didn't really become an all-American preoccupation until 1966 or 1967," he later joked, "so I was a few years ahead in that department."[31] Meanwhile, he began spending time with "all these cool Jewish kids from New York," whose left-wing views he quietly absorbed. At the end of his junior year, Mungo managed to win the top spot at the *BU News*, which he deliberately packed with what he boasted was "the nation's most pinko editorial board."[32] The following fall, "all hell broke loose. . . . We used the paper as a highly political vehicle," Mungo said. "It was a new crusade each week."[33] According to *Time* magazine, Mungo kept BU "in a constant state of nerves" during the 1966–67 school year.[34] Writing for the *Voice*, media critic Nat Hentoff called Mungo's paper "the most extraordinary, relevant, and campus-shaking newspaper in at least a decade."[35] Others saw it differently. A local tabloid, the *Boston American Record*, ran an editorial suggesting that Mungo be deported to Cuba.[36]

One reason Mungo drew so much attention is because he was among the first notable students to publicly call for President Johnson's impeachment. Harvey Wasserman, a former *Michigan Daily* editor who later helped to establish LNS, recalled meeting Mungo for the first time at a college press conference.

> Ray was up on a panel with key Johnson and Kennedy advisors Walt Rostow, John Roche, and Richard Goodwin, to discuss the war in Vietnam, which was just starting to get bad reviews. Ray gave a brilliant inflammatory speech against LBJ and his bloody hoax, concluding with a demand for [Johnson's] impeachment. The student editors gasped with disbelief. . . .. Goodwin, the Kennedy man, waltzed in: "Now you all know I have strong disagreements with the way the Johnson administration is pursuing the war in Vietnam. But I hardly think any sensible, serious American could endorse the substance or tone of Mr. Mungo's speech. Let's see now, how many of you think the president should be impeached?" Four of us raised our hands. Ray and I looked at each other and became friends.[37]

Later on, when the *BU News* likewise called for Johnson's impeachment, Mungo claimed that the university's president, Harold C. Case, "actually telegrammed every single member of congress . . . to reassure them that the average student at Boston University is not *a fucking maniac* like

Raymond Mungo."[38] Another time, after the local draft board called Mungo for his preinduction physical, some six hundred people "turned out at the gates of the Boston Army Base . . . and watched him stand on the hood of a car, tear up his induction papers and cast them into the frigid coastal wind."[39]

By the time he was twenty-one, the "slight, bespectacled" Mungo had gained "the confidence of being part of something larger than himself." The power of the baby boom generation, the beginning of a global movement against the Vietnam War, and LSD's magical effects "left Mungo self-assured, even cocky."[40] An outstanding student despite the extremely long hours he worked each week at the paper, he was awarded a full scholarship to pursue graduate study in English literature at Harvard and was just about to embark upon an academic career when he met with a peculiar twist of fate: As he put it, "A madman named Marshall Bloom flew into Boston from London one cold April day and put the question to me, did I want to join him in overthrowing the state down in Washington, D.C.?"

The answer was "yes." In the summer of 1967, Mungo set off for DC "to tear down the walls of the rotten imperial city and have fun doing it."[41]

Having been elected general secretary of USSPA by a mail ballot, Bloom's plan was to radicalize the organization, which was tainted by its ties to the National Student Association—an organization that had been surreptitiously funded by the CIA.[42] Tensions arose within USSPA, however, just as soon as Bloom arrived at his post. Though editors voiced specific grievances against Bloom—he was too strident in his denunciation of the National Student Association, unwise in appointing Mungo to become international news director, and reckless in proposing programs that would outrun the group's annual budget[43]—his Jewish Afro, Fu Manchu moustache, and intense personality must have alarmed them as well. Even Bloom's closest friends characterized him as moody, demanding, and manipulative.[44] In his delightful memoir *Famous Long Ago*, Mungo said this about Bloom:

> He has what seems to some people a nervous and high-strung way of carrying himself, forever fleeing to some other engagement or taking notes or dreaming up apocalyptic schemes or speaking at a pace too rapid to imitate. To some this remarkable performance-in-life seems domineering, unstable, and disconcerting, while to those like me, who love him it is simply his way.[45]

At a national student press conference in Minneapolis in August 1967, a coalition of anti-Bloom students managed to rewrite USSPA's bylaws to allow them to elect a new leader. By a 41 to 32 vote, Bloom was, in effect, fired. Someone who later worked with Bloom said that while he was thought to have been dismissed because of his "radical politics and pot-head acid-freak lifestyle," people who were "intimately connected with the incident" mentioned that Bloom's effeminate demeanor was also "a major factor in some people's negative attitudes towards him and in the eventual decision to fire him."[46]

Regardless, after his rebuff, Bloom and several of his allies gathered in a nearby meeting room. Late into the night, over Cokes, coffee, and cigarettes, they talked about forming a new organization, which they wanted to be "mischievous" and "muckraking."[47] The following morning, Bloom passed out a leaflet announcing their plans to launch what was supposed to be called the "New Press Project." "We are all agreed . . . that we must look beyond the major media for accurate reportage on everything from the war in Vietnam to the revolution against oppression in our own ghettos, our own hemisphere, and around the world," he said. The project's "major activity will be an international wire service, so that what happens in Newark or Dar es Salaam can be conveyed on the same day to papers going to press in Seattle or Taos."[48] Later they kicked around other possible names—Radical Press Service, Resistance Press Service, and (more facetiously) the Young Traitors Communications System, the Hip AP, and the Subversive Underground Revolutionary Shortwave Association—until Bloom had the clever idea of forming the "New Media Project," with its organ, the "Liberation News Service." There was no meaningful difference between the two outfits, but the dual titles proved convenient. When raising money or renting equipment, they presented themselves as the straight-sounding New Media Project; to youthful dissidents across the country, they were LNS.[49]

Both names were deceptively grandiose. At the time, the group's total resources consisted of $80 they had rounded up in donations, $20 of which they spent on an ounce of high-grade marijuana they picked up in Ann Arbor on their way home.[50] Once back in Washington, DC, Bloom and Mungo headed straight for the USSPA office, where they "liberated" its office supplies, and then set up shop in a brownstone near DuPont Circle for which they had just signed a twelve-month lease. Mungo later noted the irony that although they felt morally obligated to keep their agreement with the elderly woman who rented them the house (she "had been *so* nice") they spent the next year warring with the phone company, bouncing checks, and taking in several questionable, transient boarders—including a fifteen year old runaway and an escaped mental patient.[51] Today, it is difficult to assess just how committed the two were to LNS. "The reality is we had all just lost our jobs and we needed something to do," Mungo later remarked. "We had already signed a lease on this expensive house . . . and we didn't have any work . . . and so I figured, 'I gotta find some way to make some fucking money!'"[52] But in October 1967—just two months after the USSPA conference—Bloom spun the situation differently, writing to a friend that LNS had "burgeoned into something that was entirely [in] keeping with my wildest dreams the night it was formed."[53]

ALTHOUGH BLOOM'S UNCEREMONIOUS DISMISSAL from USSPA became the immediate impetus for LNS, it was the unbridled growth of countless radical newspapers across the country that made LNS seem necessary. In fact, Bloom later suggested that if he'd better understood what was happening in the United States while he was in London, he'd never have coveted the USSPA position in the first place. "I didn't see then the full and exciting potential for a news service and I was unaware of the renaissance of American journalism represented by the underground papers which are in almost every major and small city in the country," he told a friend in December 1967. "We are only now beginning to have ideas as vast and exciting as this renaissance makes possible."[54] With their proposals for disseminating left-wing news and opinions, hosting workshops and conferences, and establishing a cooperative advertising program, LNS hoped to build connections and alliances between radical papers and, in effect, unify the sprawling underground press movement. Moreover, they aimed to do this in a highly democratic fashion; early letters to new and prospective members emphasized that the scope of LNS's activities would depend upon the ideas, needs, and level of participation of those who joined the group. Even LNS's name, they said, was "negotiable."[55]

At the time, those who had hoped that UPS would unify the underground press were disappointed. By coordinating the free exchange of newspapers and encouraging them to reprint each other's material, UPS played a vital and important role. But by late 1967, UPS still wasn't much more than a shell. Although "headquartered" in the offices of the *East Village Other*, the organization didn't even have its own bank account; its funds simply intermingled with *EVO*'s. Some even regarded UPS as a pseudo-organization whose primary purpose was to "create the *illusion* of a giant, coordinated network of freaky papers, poised for the kill."[56] The Syndicate existed for nearly a year before it got around to hosting its first organizational "pow-wow"—a harum-scarum affair held amid the coastal bluffs of Stinson Beach, California, in March 1967. Thorne Dreyer, who attended on behalf of the *Rag*, complained, "We listened to flipped out diatribes about our own beauty and the coming of a new era."[57] Of UPS's nineteen papers, his was one of only six that sent representatives to the gathering, out of which came a vague and hubristic mission statement that was described as "nothing less than a . . . repeal of Western civilization."[58] The following July, *EVO* editor and UPS cofounder Walter Bowart sent out a bizarre letter to UPS editors, in which he vastly inflated the power of the "Psychedelic Movement," and called for hippies to build an alliance with the Republican Party.[59]

To be sure, some were untroubled by UPS's direction. Throughout the late 1960s, psychedelic millenarians saw little need for finely honed institutions. Others felt that regardless of its deficiencies, UPS remained *symbolically* important. By virtue of its name alone, they said, UPS generated a "sense of national community that new papers could plug into and feel just a little less isolated in their efforts."[60] On the other hand, John Bryan, editor of Los Angeles's *Open City*, was so put off by the Stinson Beach affair that he sent a circular letter calling for UPS to hold another, better-planned meeting. "I feel that it is past time that some kind of a truly effective alternative informational network be established to provide fuller coverage of what's happening in cities outside our own," he wrote.[61] Wayne Hansen, of Boston's *Avatar*, sent a similar letter to UPS editors, acknowledging that relations between several papers had grown testy and calling for UPS to extricate itself from *EVO*'s control. "I hope that everyone will see the importance of all of us coming together and ease the fears of competition from other member newspapers," he said. "Everyone seems to be doing different versions of the same thing. There is no reason for us to feel competitive."[62]

It was amid these fissures and tensions that LNS organized the first movement-wide gathering of the underground press, which they held in Washington, DC, in an abandoned loft on Corcoran Street on October 20, 1967—the day before a massive rally against the Vietnam War was scheduled at the Pentagon.[63] "We saw the meeting as our chance to cement into one movement the independent journals which had sprung up across the country," Mungo recalled.[64] Although turnout far surpassed expectations, the meeting quickly degenerated into a "circus of circa-1967 Movement politics."[65] Bloom arrived wearing scarlet trousers and a Sgt. Pepper jacket and, after ceremoniously burning his draft card, began trying to chair the meeting.[66] Soon thereafter, avant-garde filmmaker Kenneth Anger interrupted him by wandering around the room, insulting people, and spouting paranoid gibberish. Moments later, Bowart addressed the group to underscore the importance of UPS, at which point several others angrily accused him of embezzlement. After that, someone launched into an incongruous poetry reading, thereby prompting what Mungo described as "a lengthy East-West poetry competition between the New York Indian forces of the

EVO and the *San Francisco Oracle* Hari-Krishna heads."[67] One disappointed attendee later recalled, "Chaos reigned; the community of papers that we hoped would develop, did not."[68] Said another: "Periodic attempts to assert leadership, by Marshall, Ray, other LNSers, and delegates from the floor, merely created in their wake new expressions of each person's 'thing' in reaction to the last."[69]

However badly the meeting flopped, LNS's organizers gleaned an important lesson—one that would later have tremendous implications for its history. As Mungo put it, "Our conception of LNS as a 'democratic organization,' owned by those it served, was clearly ridiculous; among those it served were, in fact, men whose very lives were devoted to the principle that no organization, no institution, was desirable."[70] Dorothy Devine, a student reporter from Wellesley College who had high hopes for LNS, said much the same thing: "Marshall and Ray had tried, but failed, to create a democratic, member-directed, organization. Their centralized leadership will probably continue along with their mailed releases. And somehow, having seen the members," she added, "it seems better this way."[71]

THE DAY AFTER THE FAILED MEETING, LNS's small staff of reporters headed for a hugely publicized antiwar rally. It began peaceably at the Lincoln Memorial, where upward of 100,000 citizens mingled on an unseasonably warm afternoon, and ended violently at the steps of the Pentagon, as a phalanx of American soldiers battered hundreds of young demonstrators with billy clubs and rifle butts.[72] More than just a study in contrasts, the "Battle of the Pentagon" also had many of the dreamlike, distorted qualities we associate with the surreal. *Village Voice* reporter Jack Newfield called it "a day of one absurdity piled on another. Reality and fantasy, truth and untruth, were lost in the chaos."[73] Norman Mailer later echoed Newfield in his Pulitzer Prize-winning *Armies of the Night*, where he described the rally as "an ambiguous event whose value or absurdity may not be established for ten or twenty years, or indeed ever."[74] Noting the rally's size and the tremendous range of activity that took place "in many places at once," editors at the pacifist *WIN* magazine doubted that a full and accurate account of the event was even possible.[75]

Of course, none of this prevented New Left partisans from ridiculing the conventional news coverage of the Pentagon demonstration, which they said was factually inaccurate, biased, and inflammatory. According to the left-wing *Guardian*, mainstream news accounts "had to be entirely discarded."[76] The media "created a forest of inaccuracy which would blind the best efforts of an historian," Mailer added.[77] One problem was the lack of television cameras on hand to document the soldiers' brutality. Although that very week large protests in California and Wisconsin had seen considerable violence, no one thought it necessary to offer live coverage of the Pentagon siege.[78] "Network executives explained they ruled out live coverage because they feared that their presence would lead demonstrators to perform for the cameras," historian Melvin Small writes.[79] Demonstrators also complained that the print media exaggerated the unruliness of a few rabble-rousers. "With few exceptions," Small writes, "the media concentrated on the violent and the sensational . . . virtually ignoring the peaceful aspects of the largest Washington antiwar protest to date.[80]

This polarized and confusing situation afforded LNS a perfect opportunity to showcase how its reportage would counter that of the daily press. Although highly critical of the distortions they perceived in major newspapers, LNS could scarcely claim to be a more "objective" alternative. To the contrary, the group avowed its partisanship, maintaining that its own nakedly ideological approach was, at worst, no more disturbing or inconsistent with the canons of contemporary journalism than what they found in the mainstream media. Said one LNSer, "We . . . try for an honest subjectivity that will convey a sense of what it's like to be on our side of the story."[81] A few LNS journalists may even have gone so far as to assume that their own fundamental decency—the righteousness of their cause and the purity of their motivations—bestowed upon them a kind of special insight or angle on "truth" that could not be communicated through the cold arithmetic of facts.

For instance, Mungo once brashly argued that the underground press was important not for its aesthetics, fairness, or professionalism, but because it described the world from a privileged viewpoint. Straight journalists, he said, couldn't even conceive of the ways that their bourgeois lifestyles limited their consciousness.[82] As upholders of conformity and tradition, stuck "in lifelong competition with other men for trifling honors and material goods," salaried journalists could only be expected to represent the world as it appeared to them from their limited cultural perspective. In a crucial passage in *Famous Long Ago*, Mungo argued that professional reporters couldn't write truthfully if they tried, for they had

> compromised their right to truth as well as eight hours of their day. They will write serious accounts of the Chamber of Commerce dinner, the President's press conference, the Thanksgiving football game, millions of facts without even one simple truthful picture of the slavery of Everyman in "this dog-eat-dog world" they inhabit.

By contrast, underground press journalists perceived the truth differently because they inhabited a separate moral and ethical universe—one which most of society would condemn. Mungo has said his world was about "getting up in the morning around 2:00 P.M.":

> Discovering opium. Having sex with someone you just met. And your best friend. Longing for just an inch of honest black soil under your toes where you could raise one honest cucumber. Begging dimes at the airport. . . . Arranging the abortion of a child you're not sure you fathered. Bouncing checks. Getting stoned and meeting Christ. Getting busted for getting stoned. Worrying about tomorrow the day after tomorrow. Splitting to Morocco. Getting all sick and strung out on Demerol. Tiring of your scene and leaving it. Looking for a little sense, peace, or justice among powerful men and generally failing to find them. Looking to score. Playing music everywhere you go. Eating whatever you can get. And writing about everything that happened to you just as it happened.[83]

In short, Mungo championed a kind of standpoint epistemology that later became fashionable with certain anthropologists, feminists, and critical theorists. Truth, he said, is "simply the way you see the world."[84] Although most of LNS's writers attempted to report scrupulously and accurately from a left-wing perspective, the group's coverage of the Pentagon protest veered sharply enough from mainstream accounts that it may be worth considering whether anyone in LNS consciously distorted the facts in an attempt to convey some kind moral, symbolic, or impressionistic truth. Either way, their aggressive coverage of the Battle of the Pentagon was an enormous boon to the organization. Its reports were said to have run in over one hundred newspapers, and Norman Mailer quoted liberally from them in his best-selling account of the demonstration. For countless activists, LNS became the leading source of opinion on what happened there.

An array of swirling tensions had preceded the Pentagon March. First, there had been an escalation of rhetoric in the New Left. Throughout the fall, spokespersons for SDS had boasted of a sea change in the antiwar movement's strategy: it would move "From Protest to Resistance." Similarly, the event's sponsors billed the rally as an opportunity to "Confront the Warmakers." Deploying a military metaphor that would have been anathema to much of the antiwar movement the previous spring, MOBE (National Mobilization Committee to End the War in Vietnam) chairman David Dellinger said that protestors would "shut down the Pentagon" and avowed "there will be no government building left unattacked."[85] In response, President Johnson called upon the National Guard to assist an anxious contingent of military policemen, paratroopers, U.S. marshals, government security guards, and metropolitan police assigned to guard DC, and it was rumored that troops had been put on alert as far away as the Rocky Mountains.[86] Never before in American history had so many troops been necessary to defend the capital city from its own citizens.

The march's organizers knew, however, that they also needed to keep the moderate wing of the peace movement on board, and so they organized a two-part demonstration for October 21. The first half of the rally, designed to attract liberal protestors and their families, was a conventional mass protest at the Lincoln Memorial. The assembly was an "American pastiche," said one observer, made of "older people with graying hair and grim faces, quite at home among the more numerous youngsters of college age," and even "some children, playing among the placards."[87] But in order to tap the new militancy of the youth movement, organizers also secured an unusual permit that actually allowed for what would normally be considered "civil disobedience" at the Pentagon later that afternoon. Accordingly, between about 2 PM and 4 PM, a noisy throng of demonstrators crossed the Arlington Memorial Bridge for a standoff at the U.S. Department of Defense. Here, hippies and radical students predominated.[88]

The Pentagon's North Parking Lot served as the official "cut off" point—the spot where those who wished to avoid any tense confrontations could either turn around, or, if they preferred, view the action at the Pentagon from a safe distance. This was also the area where a group of hippies performed a well-publicized "exorcism" of the Pentagon.[89] Before the exorcism began, though, a contingent of about one thousand radicals broke away from the mass of protestors and dashed through the Virginia woods. Some said they hoped to "storm" the Pentagon, but if this was ever anyone's plan, it was nullified when they reached the top of the steps at the Pentagon Mall, where they found themselves confronted by a stolid line of armed marshals. Several who were present recall the scene as almost unbearably tense. "I was very afraid that the marshals would be provoked into firing tear gas into the crowd which, had it panicked and attempted to flee back down the steps, would almost certainly have trampled people in the surging mass that now poured up the stairs," SDS national secretary Greg Calvert recalled.[90]

As the unprecedented standoff continued, and the warm afternoon turned cooler, both sides sent countermanding signals to one another. Protestors alternately taunted, consoled, and tried to educate the soldiers, who, by turns, displayed stoicism, sympathy, and aggression. At least one hippie famously placed flowers in the barrels of soldiers' rifles.[91] Sometime around 7 PM, joyous chants of "Join Us! Join Us! Join Us!" erupted from the crowd. Elsewhere, angry emotions spilled out. Among the New Leftists who harassed the soldiers were some women who stood before them and opened their blouses; others cursed as they threw wilted flowers at the soldiers. In a gesture of mass defiance, hundreds of young people burned their draft cards right before the soldiers' very eyes—this at a time when draft-card-burning carried something more than a whiff of scandal. "In the gathering dark it looked like a dusting of fireflies over the great shrub of the Mall," Mailer wrote.[92]

The *coup de théâtre* came after midnight, when Pentagon officials summoned the press inside the building for a final briefing, and members of the 82nd Airborne Division—soldiers who had already served tours of duty in Vietnam—replaced the "more frightened reserves" who had been standing guard.[93] At about 2:00 AM, the soldiers aligned themselves into a V-formation and slowly wedged their way into the front ranks of demonstrators. Amidst the shouts of "Move! Move! MOVE!" from the GIs, and cries of "Go limp! Go limp!" from the protestors, one could hear sickening thumps: the sound of billy clubs and rifle butts striking human skulls.[94] As some activists fled the scene, others flooded into the front ranks to take their place, locking arms and bracing themselves. All night long, military vans hauled off the demonstrators to nearby Lorton Prison.

Predictably, LNS's coverage focused on the more militant youths who gathered at the Pentagon. The *Rag*'s Thorne Dreyer wrote what may have been the most widely circulated LNS report to come out of the march, an exuberant, emotional, firsthand account in which he signaled his disregard for journalistic conventions with his lead sentence: "On October 21, 1967," he wrote, "the white left got its shit together." After noting that many had been "dubious" about whether the protest would truly exemplify a new phase of militant resistance, Dreyer rapturously asserted, "A new stage is upon us." The thrust of his article was to emphasize the protest's favorable effects on almost everyone involved. Though he admitted that a few radicals had tried to provoke "violent confrontations" with the GIs, he dismissed their antics as pointless and stupid before vividly describing the ways that other marchers had gently reached out to the soldiers. Here, Dreyer ratcheted up his already sentimental prose by quoting demonstrators at their most maudlin. "We said we're on the same side," Dreyer wrote.

It's those generals [we're against], those officers that make you come out here and stand in the cold and beat on us, when that's not what you really want to do. . . . Look at us. We've got food. Grass—we'd love to turn you on. We're digging each other. And we're doing something that we believe in. Won't you join us?

Describing the scene of thousands of demonstrators spontaneously chanting to the soldiers—"Join Us! Join Us! Join Us!"—Dreyer said, "An amazing magic was created."[95]

By contrast, James Reston of the *New York Times* held that "everybody seemed to have lost in the antiwar siege of the Pentagon this weekend." The march had been taken over, he said, by a "militant minority" of "pugnacious young activists" who personally vilified Lyndon Johnson with placards reading "LBJ the Butcher," and "Johnson's War in Vietnam Makes America Puke." "It is difficult to report publicly on the ugly and vulgar provocation of many of the militants," Reston claimed (perhaps disingenuously). "They spat on some of the soldiers in the front line . . . and goaded them with the most vicious personal slander."[96] Meanwhile, a news account in the *Times* charged that troops and federal marshals had arrested demonstrators "with a minimum of physical force."[97] In the *Washington Post*, Jimmy Breslin maintained that several thousand "troublemakers . . . put a deep gash into the antiwar movement." The worst of them, he said, were "dropout[s] and drifters and rabble," including some who even "went to the bathroom on the side of the Pentagon building." In his view, the protestors were responsible for the violence that was unleashed against them, for they had "turned a demonstration for peace . . . into a sickening, club-swinging mess."[98]

Undoubtedly all of this happened—the goading and taunting of the soldiers as well as the protestor's gentle pleadings for peace and uplifting chants. The mainstream and underground press simply "emplotted" the Battle of the Pentagon differently, emphasizing and ascribing significance to those events that helped them to tell the stories they wished to tell. Theorists who address the ways that narrative structures undergird historical writing can help us to understand how journalists could present such polar accounts. As Hayden White remarked, "most historical sequences can be emplotted in a number of different ways, so as to provide different interpretations of those events and to endow them with different meanings." In certain respects, the competing versions presented by LNS on the one hand and the *New York Times* and *Washington Post* on the other resemble White's characterization of Michelet and Tocqueville's contrasting accounts of the French Revolution. "Neither could be said to have had more command of the 'facts' contained in the record; they simply had different notions of the kind of story that best fitted the facts they knew."[99]

There may, however, be some caveats to this argument. In an unsigned LNS report, Bloom claimed that "two, perhaps three, American military men in the line of troops at the Pentagon took off their helmets, lay down their guns, and joined the demonstrators sitting-in on the Pentagon steps."[100] By contrast, the mainstream press was either unaware of LNS's claim or unwilling to entertain it as a possibility. It simply went unmentioned. Today, it is impossible to know who was correct, although there's no doubt that *rumors* about the defections circulated throughout the crowd in the evening hours. Dreyer even referenced them in his article: when demonstrators heard that a soldier had defected, he wrote, "the reaction was overwhelming. We yelled and cheered and it shook the whole place."[101] But Bloom's account was more definitive. He maintained that one soldier actually managed to get lost in a crowd of demonstrators who helped to conceal him, whereas at least one other fleeing soldier was "quickly apprehended," only to disappear back "into the sea of helmets." In response to a military spokesman's denial that this happened, LNS scoffed, "Even if the defectors cannot be specifically identified by name, rank, and serial number," it was certain that they existed: "The recollection of witnesses is too vivid." Altogether, LNS presented testimony from four activists who claimed to have seen the defections, along with others who offered corroborating testimony of a "helmetless soldier being marched to [a] paddy wagon." Undoubtedly, LNS had a stake in believing that renegade soldiers had dropped their weapons and tried to join the protestors. "From the demonstrators [*sic*] point of view" LNS wrote, "the effectiveness of this campaign was made dramatically clear—beyond all expectations—by the defections." However, even though LNS publicly sought out "additional testimonies from any witnesses," neither side ever proved its case.[102]

The controversy is worth examining, though, in light of the grounds upon which some of the New Left's media activists defended the strategic use of myths. Abbie Hoffman may have been the movement's chief theorist of the ways that mythic personas or events could be used to advance the movement's aspirations, but Mungo also was not completely against fudging the truth on behalf of a noble cause.[103] In 1970 he actually defended an instance where someone planted a false story in the Boston *Avatar*, alleging U.S. atrocities in a Vietnamese village. Of course, it is well known that some American soldiers committed heinous war crimes in Vietnam, but this particular account was a pernicious and inflammatory lie—a terrible affront to every established covenant in journalism.[104] Nevertheless, Mungo maintained that because such things happened elsewhere, the story retained a kind of impressionistic honesty, even if it wasn't photorealistically accurate. He later insisted, however, that the story about GI defections was not a deliberate fabrication. "I remember being absolutely convinced myself that this had happened, although in truth I did not see it," he said. "It just kind of spread like a rumor."[105]

LNS countered the mainstream coverage of the Battle of the Pentagon in several more respects. While the print media emphasized the violence at the protest, rather than the moral and political considerations that propelled some 100,000 citizens to participate in public antiwar activities, LNS offered the full transcript of a speech at the protest by Gary Rader, a special-forces reservist who had burned his draft card the previous spring.[106] And in an effort to counteract reports that soldiers had shown "admirable restraint in the face of extreme provocation," LNS distributed testimony from two anonymous soldiers who witnessed the protestors being treated roughly, and who alleged (perhaps implausibly) that around 40 percent of their fellow servicemen had secretly sympathized with the demonstration.[107] Another LNS mailing presented long quotations from several of the March's attendees that rebutted various aspects of the aboveground press's "slanted" news reports, which were designed to be run as boxes or sidebars in local papers that may have lacked the resources to get appropriate quotes from participants from their own community.[108] Still another piece ridiculed the Pentagon's ludicrous claim that the noxious tear gas that wafted through the air at the demonstration had not been discharged by U.S. soldiers, but rather by the protestors, *against themselves*, in an attempt to discredit the military. (This in spite of the fact that the *Washington Post*'s own reporters "saw military police throw at least three tear gas grenades.")[109]

Finally, Mungo wrote his own first-person account of how he became one of the 647 demonstrators who were arrested at the March. On their way from the so-called "transition" rally in the North Parking Lot, a cluster of the event's prominent personalities, including Dellinger, pediatrician Benjamin Spock, academic Noam Chomsky, and writers Robert Lowell, Norman Mailer, and Dwight Macdonald, approached the Pentagon's right flank, where they confronted a gathering of troops. As Spock was delivering a moving story about having once written a letter to a soldier who opposed the war, only to have the letter returned to him, marked "Verified Deceased," Mungo heard a sergeant give an order: "Push 'em out now."[110] At first, the soldiers gently tapped them with what Dellinger called "symbolic blows," but within a few moments, another group of military men arrived on the scene, "flailing and beating" everyone within their range.[111] Mungo wrote:

> I felt an irresistible force pulling my right leg out of its socket, a billy
> club over my head, and two bodies wrenching my left arm so far

behind my head that I let out what must have been a blood-curdling shout. Seconds before I also lost my glasses, I turned to see Dellinger and Lowell, Chomsky and MacDonald [*sic*], hunched up under the flailing arms of the marshals, and Spock, getting repeatedly kicked in the side, still talking.

With regard to one detail, though, Mungo was either confused or exaggerating. In his memoir, Spock never mentioned being assaulted at the Pentagon rally, nor is the incident mentioned in the secondary literature that has been written about him.[112] Spock was sixty-four years old at the time of the Pentagon rally, and had he really been "repeatedly kicked in the side" by an American serviceman while "still talking" (an image that is difficult to conjure) this likely would have been a major news story.

Later, Mungo describes being hauled off to a nearby military van, where the "black comedy" of the situation became clear: Several of the soldiers who arrested them were actually sympathetic to their cause! Said one, "*We don't have anything to do with the war, you know.*" Another serviceman kindly assured a protestor that he'd take good care of his camera. Meanwhile, from the rear of the bus, a prisoner played the melody of "My Country 'Tis of Thee" on a harmonica. The van traveled to a federal prison in Occoquan, Virginia, a small town some fifteen miles south, where Mungo said he was given a ham sandwich, a cup of coffee, sheets and towels, and— as he was escorted to his cell—a "swift, hard, and utterly unprovoked kick in the ass." The rest of the article is a seriocomic treatment of the jailhouse scene, describing Dellinger cheerfully sipping his coffee, Chomsky fretting about needing to return to his teaching duties at MIT, and Mailer pacing back and forth in the cell. As some prisoners argued over politics, while others shared stories or sat in stoic silence, Mungo recalled thinking "how incredibly mind-blowing it is to be with all these wildly different people who care what it's like to be North Vietnamese and get your skin seared off from fire from the sky."[113] Virtually every theme that LNS developed elsewhere in its coverage—the surprising juxtaposition of brutality and sympathy from the military; the camaraderie, ideological diversity, and savage indignation of the protestors—found expression in Mungo's essay. Meanwhile, Mungo's intimate voice and clear political viewpoint contrasted with the sham objectivity that prevailed in conventional news reports.

LNS's reporting on the Pentagon reveals the crucial elements of the group's riptide strategy for dealing with the shibboleths and inaccuracies they perceived in the conventional media. On the one hand, LNS simply trumpeted its own subjectivity. In contrast to the mainstream print media, which described the antiwar counterculture with varying levels of animus and skepticism, LNS actively championed the New Left's agenda, burnished its image, and stressed its agency. Yet at the very same time, LNS writers presented themselves as more honest than the aboveground reporters. Their argument was simple: although neither side was impartial, only the radicals would admit to their biases. Finally, from their privileged position near the fulcrum of the youth rebellion, LNS claimed that they, rather than trained media professionals, were best equipped to tell the truth. As one LNS writer maintained, "With its scraggly crew of reporters and editors, [an underground newspaper] can hardly amass the facts contained in the big dailies. But they can tell it like it is."[114] Accordingly, LNS frequently claimed that its reporting was more accurate and reliable than what could be found in the mainstream press. A flyer that LNS crafted in the aftermath of the Pentagon Siege underscored this point.

> LIBERATION News Service provides a totally different alternative media for those of us who are fed up with hearing Time magazine, AP, UPI, NY Times, etc., all saying that there were "some 25 to 40,000 demonstrators" when we ourselves saw at least twice that many; hearing them say that "police acted with appropriate restraint" when we saw the guy next to us getting his skull busted just because he had long hair; hearing that we "are only bombing military installations," that we are "sincerely working for peace" and that we are "supporting and defending democratic government in Vietnam" when we see our government destroying a countryside, waging an undeclared war of attrition on helpless women, children and farmers in the name of one totalitarian puppet regime after another, with no sane end in sight . . . IF YOU TOO ARE REALLY UPTIGHT ABOUT ALL THIS, and want to get the truth to as many people as convincingly as the truth can be [told] . . . then we want to help *you*, because if there is going to be any truth and humanity found in today's American Press, it is going to be up to us. . . . the college and under-ground press to print it, and keep printing it till we win or fold.[115]

Certainly LNS was thrilled with its Pentagon coverage. To Bloom, the simple fact that leading underground papers had used "substantial amounts" of LNS copy proved that there was a need for the service. "We have shown already that there are papers [that] want our material and these papers are being read," he told a friend.[116] Mungo put the matter even more triumphantly. "Our version of the weekend was printed, in part or whole, in over one hundred newspapers with a total readership in the vicinity of a million. Not bad, we thought, for our third week."[117]

By February 1968, LNS had installed a new teletype network linking offices in Berkeley, Chicago, and New York City. Telex machines allowed reporters across the globe to file stories from any Western Union office for the price of a phone call. Teletypes were commonplace at the nation's daily newspapers, and all of the establishment news services—the Associated Press, United Press International, and Reuters—used them to distribute their copy. "It was a big deal, a little bit of a thrill even, to have LNS imitate this technology of the straight press," one LNSer remembered.[118] Meanwhile, nearly two hundred newspapers took out subscriptions with the news service at a rate of $15 per month. In return, the papers received mimeographed news packets, mailed twice weekly, often on brightly colored paper, addressing a wide range of issues, including the draft, antiwar activity, Cuba, SDS, the black power movement, and the far-out, acid-drenched wing of the youth movement.[119] Testimonials from several underground editors suggest that if it had not been for LNS, the movement's press would not have flourished as it did. The editor of the Champaign, Illinois, *Walrus* wrote LNS to say it was "essential" that they receive the news service "to do a good job."[120] Peter Werbe, of Detroit's *Fifth Estate*, said his paper used an "extraordinary" amount of LNS material, adding, "We sometimes ask . . . what we used to do for copy before you people started publishing."[121] Jeff Shero, who moved from Austin to launch New York City's *Rat*, told LNS, "Your work has been important to the timelyness [*sic*] of many underground publications. You must live. You must continue."[122]

Around the same time that LNS started operating in Washington, DC, another news service called the Student Communication Network (SCN) established operations in Berkeley and New York. Launched by an ecumenical group of religious organizations called the University Christian Movement, SCN regarded itself as a kind of left-wing alternative to USSPA, and at first Bloom and Mungo regarded them suspiciously. During the first week of 1968, though, they got to meet "the SCN kids" at a weeklong conference in Cleveland, sponsored by the University Christian Movement. The night before the conference ended, Mungo says, the whole group got so stoned in their hotel room that they sang a "beautiful chorus" of "OM's" for about an hour before finally falling asleep. The following morning, they set aside their differences, and SCN resolved to subsume its Berkeley office into LNS.[123] Meanwhile, George Cavalletto, a Columbia University graduate student who had abandoned his studies to become the manager of SCN's East Coast branch, called LNS's headquarters to ask whether they'd like SCN to feed them copy. The answer was an enthusiastic "yes!" "And so we started sending stories down, and very quickly the LNS packets had a lot of articles from us," until eventually his storefront office on upper Broadway began functioning as the New York bureau of LNS.[124] Once again, LNS's timing was propitious: on April 23, 1968, when an SDS protest at Columbia University unexpectedly flared into a major rebellion—during which students seized five buildings and held them for an entire week—LNS could boast of having its own functioning office right around the corner. Better yet, numerous activists who participated in the revolt also doubled as LNS reporters, and some of them were among the 720 people who eventually got arrested. As a result, LNS was able to provide dramatic behind-the-scenes accounts that could not be found in any of the major dailies.

The rebellion was partly fueled by Columbia's arrogant behavior toward the surrounding community. Considering that the university's gorgeous neoclassical buildings rested atop a large hill overlooking some of the most impoverished areas of Harlem, its supposedly liberal administrators might have been mindful of the concerns of its poorest neighbors. Instead, they often treated Harlem's denizens with a toxic mix of suspicion, indifference, and contempt.[125] Worse still, these attitudes were on display as the university expanded geographically in the early 1960s, buying up about one hundred nearby buildings and evicting thousands of residents from their rent-controlled apartments.[126] In 1961, the university secured a generous, long-term lease from New York's park department, allowing it to build a gymnasium in nearby Morningside Park, which was mostly used by Harlem residents. Although Columbia was required to set aside a small portion of the building for use by the general public, no one ever bothered asking Harlemites whether they wanted to give up 2.1 acres of the park in return for limited use of a large concrete gym. Additionally, the building's design literally called for the neighborhood's overwhelmingly African American population to enter through what some said was a back door.[127] By the time work crews finally broke ground at the site, on February 19, 1968, many students and citizens saw the gym as a symbol of Columbia's institutional racism.[128]

Students also grew infuriated with Columbia's ties to a military think tank, the Institute for Defense Analyses (IDA). Although activists frequently described Columbia's connection to the IDA as "secret," this was a bit of an exaggeration; in fact, the IDA noted all of its affiliations in its annual public reports. However, administrators quietly established the partnership without any input from faculty or students, and for several years hardly anyone on campus knew about it. In March 1967, when a team of SDS researchers began exposing Columbia's ties to the military-industrial complex, the IDA's affiliation with Columbia suddenly became a contentious issue.[129] It is not hard to see why: Through its ties to the IDA, the university had made itself complicit in what some said was one of the most unjust wars ever fought.

Finally, in the months leading up the rebellion, local activists were becoming increasingly militant.[130] In March 1968, Columbia SDS elected as its leader Mark Rudd, a brash and charismatic student who championed an aggressive "politics of confrontation" that SDS hard-liners said would help to mobilize other young people.[131] Additionally, Columbia's Student Afro-American Society (SAS), which in previous years had primarily functioned as a support group for isolated black students, had recently begun involving itself in local political issues, and many of its members identified with the Black Power Movement. Meanwhile, at the national level, SDS began calling for student agitators to "connect campus issues with off-campus questions." One of the chief proponents of this idea was SDS officer Carl Davidson, who wrote an influential pamphlet calling for students to rid American campuses of their military ties.[132] Although Davidson was not directly connected to the storm that was brewing at Columbia, this idea proved potent to Morningside Heights' student politicos. As a result of Columbia's encroachment into Harlem and its IDA ties, they could plausibly claim that their own "enlightened" university was actually helping to perpetuate the gravest iniquities of the day, racism and war.

In spite of all this, the Columbia rebellion was not planned in advance. Instead, it grew out of a rally that began at noon on April 23 at the center of campus, at which SDS and SAS distributed a handbill calling for Columbia to disaffiliate from IDA and to revise its procedures for disciplining student demonstrators.[133] Although many leftists were excited to see black and white radicals cooperating at the rally, at first things did not go well. After several speeches, anonymous voices in the crowd began yelling for everyone to march into Columbia's administration building, thereby defying a recent ban on indoor demonstrations. But when they discovered the building's doors had been locked, the group seemed unsure of what to do. Then, while Rudd was in the middle of a speech, several hundred students drifted toward the gym construction site, where they tore down part of a fence, and one student was arrested after scuffling with a police officer. Next, the crowd reassembled on campus, where tensions arose between Rudd and some of the SAS leaders, who perceived him to be acting arrogantly. Desperate to salvage the demonstration and provoke a showdown with the administration, Rudd finally led the group into Hamilton Hall, where they took Dean Henry S. Coleman hostage and began a sit-in. Almost immediately, a steering committee demanded that the university stop construction on the gym, sever its ties to the IDA, and give amnesty to everyone involved with protest.[134] Some sixteen hours later, the African American students decided that the white protestors weren't fully committed to holding the building and asked them to leave. As a result, the whites went on to seize Low Library, and eventually three additional buildings—Avery Hall, Fayerweather Hall, and the Mathematics Building—with the help of hundreds more students. It would be a full week before New York City police finally cleared the buildings in a brutal assault that sent nearly one hundred students to the hospital.[135]

Throughout the weeklong siege, LNS had its own corps of reporters living in the barricaded buildings. Meanwhile, Steve Diamond, a twenty-one-year-old student who planned on a career in journalism, shuffled back and forth between the various buildings and collected each reporter's notes, which he later used to write up LNS's exuberant, six-thousand word, day-by-day account of the events. "Because no one trusted the established media," he recalled, "the students didn't allow any regular reporters in the occupied buildings."[136] By contrast, underground press journalists were welcomed.[137] Although the turmoil at Columbia was front-page news across the country, Ethel Romm, a writer for *Editor & Publisher* magazine, later observed that most of the reportage "was curiously detached, telling the story from the outside." In order to get an insider account of what went on inside the buildings, or "a definitive article" on the massive police raid, she said one needed to turn to the underground press, "that mushrooming group of coast-to-coast weeklies and bi-weeklies now numbering about 125 with a paid circulation of well over a million."[138]

"A new, more fluid style of revolutionary activity on the American campus has been introduced by Columbia University students, black and white, who held physical control of [Columbia] for a week," Diamond's gutsy lead proclaimed.[139] In one sense, this was a prescient statement, since building takeovers soon became much more commonplace on American campuses. His suggestion that the protest had been marked by interracial harmony, however, was pure spin. Although it is true that SAS and SDS had teamed up at the April 23 rally, when Rudd tried to restore order after the protest began unraveling, SAS leader Cicero Wilson chastised him for acting imperiously. "You're not too much better than Columbia," he supposedly said. "You're trying to decide what black people should be doing."[140] Worse still, many whites were humiliated when the African American students asked them to leave Hamilton.[141] Considering the lengths to which New Leftists had tried to win the trust and approval of black militants, another reporter might have been tempted to delve deeper into the schism. Instead, Diamond disposed of it in a few scant sentences, arguing, "Although the split was unwanted in the beginning, it developed into an unexpected source of power," since it ultimately gave white radicals an opportunity to fortify themselves in Low Library, in a show of interracial "solidarity."[142] By skipping so lightly over this angle of the story, Diamond falsely implied that after the initial split, everything was fine between black and white militants.[143]

Diamond also put a gloss on the noontime rally, which, by most accounts, had been a fiasco. The so-called Cox Commission—a fact-finding team that investigated the April uprising, headed by Harvard law professor (and future Watergate prosecutor) Archibald Cox—called it "entirely haphazard," adding, "The crowd had responded to the calls of unknown members rather than its leaders."[144] Similarly, writers for the *Columbia Spectator* said Rudd appeared "bewildered" as demonstrators wandered errantly around the campus.[145] Another writer explained Rudd's predicament more specifically, noting that he "had gone from the sundial [a campus landmark] to storm a locked building; and when that failed, he made a speech to a disappearing crowd; and after that, he watched and goaded while others wrestled with a policeman," before finding himself "back at the sundial again, bickering with a black."[146] But according to Diamond, right up until the seizure of Hamilton, the rally was marked by "momentous energy [that] had been growing since noon," until Rudd reacted "in the beautifully spontaneous fashion [that] characterized the entire rebellion, [and] led the jubilant demonstrators . . . into Hamilton Hall."[147] Elsewhere, Diamond infused his prose with dramatic tones. He routinely referred to the occupied buildings as "fronts," as if the campus were literally a battleground. Columbia's bearded and tousle-haired students, he said, summoned to mind the New Left's favorite *echt*-revolutionary, Che Guevara. Describing a group of radicals lounging about in Kirk's opulent office, he mused, "One could not help but be reminded of the photos of the Sierra Maestra rebels in [Fulgencio] Batista's Royal Havana Palace in 1959."[148] When at one point during the demonstration a student urged the occupiers to modify their demand for amnesty in hopes of reaching a settlement with the administration, Diamond sketched the scene this way:

> John Jacobs, an SDS leader, was pissed. "No concessions, we are here to win. If we do not get total amnesty, all is lost. We are winning now, but we must win the whole war. No concessions." The whole

Mathematics buildings applauded as "j.j." turned and left the room. He had made his point. It was all or nothing.[149]

Although Diamond occasionally mocked some of the demonstrators' opponents, he expended considerably more energy lauding the radicals. The African Americans, he said, were especially confident, disciplined, and fearless. Although it had been rumored that some young men from Harlem had brought guns onto campus, Diamond suggested that the more levelheaded students in Hamilton Hall commanded enough authority to evict them.[150] But the whites, too, behaved methodically and democratically, organizing garbage details to keep the buildings clean, as well as night-watch squads that stayed on the lookout for a possible invasion by police or "jocks." "Here was a community talking, sharing meager food supplies and co-operating," Diamond rhapsodized.[151] In Fayerweather Hall, men and women divvyed up the cooking duties, and in the Math Building, the occupiers bonded with such intimacy that they tore away the "Men" and "Women" signs over the bathrooms and shared a "community toothbrush."[152] Though each hall was the site of "incredibly long and tedious" meetings, "every voice" was heard. When Tom Hayden visited the Math Building, he declined an invitation to address the crowd through a bullhorn; instead, he simply helped to moderate the discussion. According to Diamond, "It was truly a beautiful scene" to see "democracy evolving before 'one's very eyes.'" When describing a major disagreement in the Math Building over what to do when the police came, Diamond was so determined to portray a harmonious scene that his prose nearly turned oxymoronic: "The whole place seemed divided," he said, "yet somehow unified."[153]

Another LNS scribe, Tom Hamilton, finished up the story by describing "The Bust," when approximately one thousand New York City cops broke the students' hold on the occupied buildings in the wee hours of the morning on Tuesday, April 30. By his account, the police behaved like ruffians, randomly assaulting students and even faculty members who had stood outside the buildings. "Many of Columbia's most illustrious professors were clubbed and hit with swinging handcuffs, which were a popular weapon with police," he wrote. A campus rabbi was repeatedly clubbed with a blackjack and then "trampled by a series of policemen." James Shenton, a popular history professor, was likewise "knocked on the ground and repeatedly struck in the back and kicked in the kidneys." According to Hamilton, the "stream of people leaving campus, who had been part of the human barrier to prevent violence . . . looked like refugees from an attack by an army on a civilian population. Men and women of the faculty and students came staggering

[away] . . . many stunned and bleeding." Although New York City police commissioner Howard R. Leary commended his force for handling "a potentially difficult situation without [causing] a single case of serious injury," the LNS report dryly noted that, in fact, eighty-seven students were treated at nearby St. Luke's hospital, while more "serious cases" were taken to Knickerbocker Hospital.[154]

In addition to appearing in numerous underground newspapers, Diamond and Hamilton's report made its way to the San Francisco offices of *Ramparts*, which by then had evolved from a Catholic quarterly, founded in 1962, to become the nation's "first left-of-center commercial magazine," published bimonthly with a circulation approaching 250,000.[155] Bloom was coincidentally in the Bay Area at the time, where he was trying to establish a formal partnership between LNS and *Ramparts*. The deal never came through, but since LNS was the only news service with a full account of the Columbia rebellion, *Ramparts* editor Warren Hinckle put Bloom and others to work for several days, during which they made cuts, revisions, and additions to various aspects of Diamond's story. Diamond's manuscript was virtually unrecognizable in the long essay that resulted, but it preserved his opinions about the odiousness of Columbia's administration, the courage and nobility of the protestors, and the brutality of the police. On June 15, 1968, "The Siege of Columbia" was *Ramparts'* cover story, an exclusive report "compiled . . . with the assistance of staff reporters from Liberation News Service in New York City."[156]

BY THE TIME LNS FINISHED its account, at 5:00 AM the day after the raid, the Columbia uprising had already dominated the front page of the *New York Times* for an entire week. Many aspects of the *Times* coverage generated serious criticisms in the local media, as well as from protesting students, who noted that Arthur "Punch" Sulzberger, the venerable president and publisher of the *Times*, was also a Columbia trustee.[157] On May 2, a group of about eighty students picketed outside Sulzberger's Fifth Avenue home, where they accused him of a conflict of interest and charged that his reporters had generally failed to "understand fundamental aspects of the demonstrators' goals and procedures."[158] Although Diamond acknowledged that he and his LNS compatriots were always running down the *Times*, he says he never thought of his story on the Columbia rebellion as a direct riposte to its coverage. Instead, he said his main goal was to compel other students to take similar actions at their own universities.[159] Still, the *Times* proved itself an able foil to LNS, and by briefly examining its lopsided coverage of the Columbia events, it becomes apparent how easy it was for LNS to suggest that that their own subjectivities were not all that different in kind from those that could be found at the nation's paper of record.

Certainly the *Times* editorial page heaped an unusual amount of abuse on the protestors.[160] Of course, the *Times* editorials always reflected the publisher's opinions, but to those who looked to the paper as a guardian of civil discussion, some of its opinions may have seemed extreme.[161] Others argued that the paper's rants were sadly predictable, given Sulzberger's privileged cultural position; "The *Times* editorials," they said, "grow out of perceptions consistent with [those] of a Columbia trustee."[162] One LNS writer who helped occupy Fayerweather Hall called the editorials "an outrageous lie," noting that the "vast majority" of those with whom he sat in were undergraduate and graduate students who bravely risked their degrees, and even their careers, in trying to force Columbia "to stand for something human and decent."[163]

It was *Voice* reporter Jack Newfield, however, who made the most convincing case against the *Times*. Nearly every story the paper printed about the police bust, he said, "was inept, dishonest, and slanted against the student demonstrators." Even worse, Newfield alleged, "The *Times* itself was unethically implicated in the planning of the police raid," since the police had provided the paper with a detailed copy of their plans for arresting the students, possibly in expectation of a quid pro quo, whereby the police would receive favorable news and editorial coverage in return for their inside information.[164]

The following day, *Times* assistant managing editor Abe Rosenthal "broke with the tradition that insulates editing from reporting" to write a front-page "mood piece" describing the campus after the bust, which critics said oozed with compassion for Kirk, forbearance toward the police, and venom toward the demonstrators.[165] It began this way:

> It was 4:30 in the morning and the president of the university leaned against the wall of the room that had been his office. He passed a hand over his face.
>
> "My God," he said, "how could human beings do a thing like this."

Rosenthal added that desks and chairs in Low had been "smashed," that Kirk's rug was "spattered," and that David Truman, Columbia's provost, seemed dazed as he "wandered . . . back and forth from wrecked room to wrecked room."[166] According to the Cox Commission, however, "There was no substantial vandalism in Low Library."[167] Rosenthal also claimed that some of the arresting policemen "seemed almost fond, in a professional way, of the students," and he described one of them picking up a book from the floor of Kirk's office and musing, "The whole world is in these books; how could they do this to these books?"[168] Finally, Rosenthal minimized the police brutality that marred the arrests. "The first passing mention of the bloody heads of students," one critic observed, "appears in paragraph fifty."[169] According to Tifft and Jones, "Within New York journalism circles, there was talk that [Rosenthal] had purposely assigned himself the Columbia story because Punch was a university trustee."[170]

In an unusual statement, Sulzberger later defended the *Times* reporting, which he insisted was "in no way" influenced or shaped by its editorials. "In the coverage of the Columbia situation" he said, "the *Times* has used its resources to provide full, accurate, and dispassionate coverage." However, the *Times* failed to convey one very important point, on which the *New York Post* and LNS agreed—the violent police assault had played a pivotal role in turning the majority of student opinion against the administration.[171] Indeed, "not until the 23rd paragraph of [the *Times*] lead story were 'charges' of police brutality even mentioned."[172]

On May 1, *Times* reporter Martin Arnold addressed the brutality issue in an unusual, rather schizophrenic article that the paper buried on page 35. Near the top of the piece, Arnold said that no one was "hospitalized" after the police raid (by which he must have meant that no one required *overnight* hospital treatment). Next, he relativized the violence: "To an experienced antiwar or civil rights demonstrator," he observed, the police action "was, for the most part, relatively gentle." The problem, he implied, was that many of the students had been novice protestors who were shocked to see so many helmeted police officers on their campus, and who regarded "pushing by police lines" as "brutality." But just a little later in the article, Arnold injected a different tone into his report, citing numerous specific examples of police violence: students were "pummeled, dragged along concrete steps, kicked, punched, and struck with police saps." Two uniformed policemen deliberately spun a woman into a tree. Cops flung another student to the ground, and "when he tried to get up, they grabbed him and threw him down again. A plainclothesman rushed up and stomped on the fallen man." Elsewhere, plainclothesmen "charged through" a line of faculty and students, "stomping on hands and feet and flinging bodies to the ground," without making any effort to move or arrest them. One student "could hardly see because blood was running down the side of his face." Another *Times* reporter at the scene "was struck on the head by a policeman using handcuffs as brass knuckles," while a *Life* photographer was "punched in the eye by a policeman." Then, when the newsman flashed his press identification, the cop smashed his camera.[173] According to Newfield, Arnold's mollifying lead paragraphs, which were so at odds from what came later, were a necessary concession to his desk editors.[174]

Finally, Newfield reported that despite the protestors' ban on allowing establishment journalists inside any of the occupied buildings, one *Times* writer, John Kifner, had actually gotten inside the Math Building in the hours before the police assault. One might have expected his editors to be pleased. After all, several national magazines, including *Life* and *Look*, offered to pay LNS for its behind-the-barricades photographs—proposals that LNS briefly considered, then rejected.[175] Kifner's editors, however, "inexplicably told him they weren't interested" in having him write a behind-the-scenes account. Instead, they asked him to report on allegations of student vandalism in the Math Building. But many radicals maintained the vandalism wasn't caused by students, but by the police. Later, the *Columbia Daily Spectator* presented testimony from several professors that seemed to establish, beyond any doubt, that their offices were ransacked *after* the buildings had been cleared of the rebelling students.[176]

In an unusual gesture, Sulzberger released a statement in reply to the students who protested the *New York Times* coverage, arguing that it was not a conflict of interest for *Times* executives to serve as university trustees, adding, "It is a cardinal rule of the *Times* . . . that opinions of the publisher, or opinions expressed in editorials, must in no way influence or shape the coverage of this newspaper."[177] This, anyhow, was the public line. According to *Times* historians Susan Tifft and Alex Jones, "Officially the *New York Times* never admitted any error . . . but privately the paper was embarrassed."[178]

EVEN BY THE TIME LNS started operations in the fall of 1967, community papers across the country had already shown enough energy and promise to fire the imaginations of even the most avid New Leftists. Whether through their swirling layouts and rainbow-splashed pages, or, more piercingly, their escalating assaults on American institutions and values, youthful guerilla journalists carved out new territory in the mediascape and won the allegiance of radical multitudes. Part of what made their efforts so attractive initially was the deep attention they paid to the youthful insurgencies that were evolving in their own backyards. Meanwhile, by helping to recycle articles that first appeared in local street-corner newspapers, UPS helped the movement's scribes to command larger audiences than they had ever thought possible.

But LNS played the most pivotal role in transforming the fledgling underground press into the New Left's most significant counterinstitution. By the late 1960s, almost every radical newspaper in the country received LNS copy, and some of the smaller and more amateurish papers leaned so heavily on LNS that without its support they might not have survived. Needless to say, the new media universe that LNS helped to establish was crucial to the New Left's development. It allowed activists to stay informed about events that the mainstream press either ignored or could not understand; it helped to popularize and disseminate a radical framework of values; and because it was uniquely situated at the heart of the New Left rebellion, it provided conceptions of knowledge—perspectives, or "truths"—that helped to counteract the establishment media's coverage.

Ironically, LNS was initially very chaotically run. "As far as we were concerned," Mungo remembered, "we ran on magic. Not democracy, not logic, *magic*. And you know what? We actually believed it."[179] Put another way, LNS emerged as a highly influential force within the movement without ever arriving at a shared understanding of how it should operate, or a strategy under which it could expect to develop and thrive in the coming years. As a result, some of those who joined LNS shortly after it was formed pegged Bloom and Mungo as congenitally disorganized, lacking in commitment, or just plain spaced out. Meanwhile, Bloom's erratic personality further stressed the organization.

Nevertheless, by the vertiginous spring of 1968, LNS's founding members had much to be proud of. Writing to a friend in late 1967, Bloom boasted that LNS was the only media organization to report that although some of the GIs at the Pentagon demonstration behaved like brutes, many others secretly sympathized with the protestors, and some had even deserted their posts. "There are stories which would not happen, anywhere, without us," he said.[180] A few months later, in its coverage of the Columbia rebellion, LNS presented intimate, first-hand accounts that put to shame the ideologically colored reports that appeared in the nation's leading newspaper. Although LNS's coverage was not nearly as detailed or as well written as that of the *New York Times*, by articulating the frustrations of protesting students, and by presenting an unvarnished account of the vicious police assault of April 30, LNS could plausibly argue that its own cub reporters had bested the Brahmins of American journalism; at the very least, they could point to the *Times* coverage to show that the underground press didn't have a monopoly on polemical discourse. As Todd Gitlin later wrote, thanks in large measure to the achievements of the underground press, the Columbia occupation became "a ritual of unmasking. *Of course* Columbia had its seats in the boardrooms of power; *of course*, push comes to shove, they would mow down whatever stood in their way, from ghetto blacks to antiwar students."[181]

For all of these reasons, Liberation News Service was giddy with success in the months after it was founded, even in spite of its internal difficulties.

Many years later, Steve Diamond chuckled, "As that old journalistic hound dog, A. J. Liebling put it, 'Freedom of the press belongs to those who own one.' Right-o, Amigo. And we owned one."[182] In September 1968, Mungo gauged LNS's success in defiant terms. Speaking to a reporter from the *New York Times*, he said flatly: "We've educated a generation that no longer buys or needs daily papers. They believe us, not you."[183]

John Wilcock and his wife at the time, Amber LaMann, in Sheffield, England, in the early 1960s. A legend in underground publishing, the British expatriate Wilcock was affiliated with the *Village Voice*, the *East Village Other*, the Underground Press Syndicate, and other publications. Courtesy of John Wilcock.

BU News editor and LNS cofounder Raymond Mungo being hung in effigy by students at Boston University, ca. 1966. © Peter Simon.

The staff of the *East Village Other* in New York City, January 14, 1966. From left: Dan Rattiner, Walter Bowart, and brothers Allen and Don Katzman. Associated Press.

Local SDS leader George Vizard selling copies of Austin's *Rag* near the University of Texas campus in 1966. On July 23, 1967, Vizard was murdered while working the late-night shift at a convenience store. To this day, many in Austin's radical community think he was killed because of his political activism. At left: his wife, Mariann Vizard (now Mariann Wizard). © Thorne Dreyer.

Boston University episcopal chaplain Jack Smith posing reading a "banned" edition of *Avatar* in the BU Student Union, 1967. (In fact, the paper had only been pulled from Cambridge newsstands.) At right: *BU News* editor Joe Pilati. © Clif Garboden.

Raymond Mungo at his desk in the the "Liberated Zone"—3 Thomas Circle NW, in Washington, DC—in early 1968. © Clif Garboden.

Amherst Student editor and
LNS cofounder Marshall Bloom.
© Peter Simon.

John Walrus, sitting in the office of the *Chicago Seed*, which was also
headquarters for radicals planning to disrupt the 1968 Democratic
National Convention. Getty Images.

James Gurley, guitarist
for Big Brother and
the Holding Company,
reading the *Ann Arbor Sun*,
ca. 1968. © Leni Sinclair.

Street-theater protestors "Gen. Waste More Land" (a.k.a. Tom Dunphy) and "Gen. Hershey Bar" (a.k.a. Calypso Joe) posing with satirical newspapers at anti–Vietnam War protest, April 16, 1969, in Portland, Oregon. © Robert Altman.

Underground press activist, White Panther leader, and one-time manager of the MC-5, John Sinclair served twenty-nine months of a nine-and-a-half- to ten-year prison sentence for passing two joints to an undercover policewoman. In 1972, Michigan's Supreme Court ruled that the Detroit police had entrapped Sinclair and reversed his conviction. Courtesy of Leni Sinclair.

LNSer Allen Young standing before a North Vietnamese flag at the National Mobilization to End the Vietnam War in Washington, DC, November 15, 1969. Getty Images.

Rozzie Melnicoff on the phone in LNS's New York City office, 160 Claremont Avenue. In the background, Sheila Ryan. © David Fenton.

LNS-NY collective sitting down for a meal. From left to right: Mark Feinstein, unidentified (possibly Pete Knobler), Ralph Greenspan, Barbara Feinstein, Nick Gruenberg, Alan Howard (standing), Howie Epstein, Beryl Epstein, unidentified. © David Fenton.

Berkeley Barb publisher Max Scherr in December 1969. The *Barb* was the only newspaper that tried to find anything out about African American teenager Meredith Hunter, "The Kid They Killed at Altamont." © Robert Altman.

Kathy Mulvihill
running LNS's
offset press,
December 9, 1970.
Courtesy of Andy Marx.
Photo by Anne Dockery.

Moe Slotin selling the *Great Speckled Bird* in Atlanta, Georgia. At right, two police officers scrutinize the paper. "Everyone who met Moe loved him," said photographer Carter Tomassi. "In his photo, I'm sure he charmed the two cops into reading the *Bird*." © Carter Tomassi.

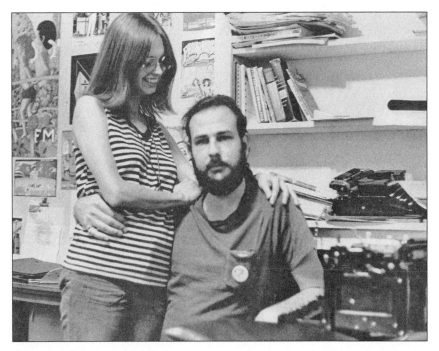

Thorne Dreyer and Victoria Smith, posing in the workspace for Houston's *Space City!* in 1970. The paper's staff endured vandalism, break-ins, and death threats. Courtesy of Thorne Dreyer.

UPS coordinator Thomas King Forcade throws a pie in the face of University of Washington sociology professor Otto N. Larson after testifying before President Richard Nixon's Commission on Obscenity and Pornography in Washington, DC, on May 13, 1970. Associated Press.

Larry Yurdin, at the Alternative Media Conference at Goddard College in Vermont, June 1970. © Mark Goff.

Boston Phoenix publisher Stephen M. Mindich spearheaded the alternative press's break with its underground roots by adding consumer guides and lifestyle features to its editorial mix in the mid-1970s. © Peter Simon.

5

"Either We Have Freedom of the Press . . . or We Don't Have Freedom of the Press"

Thomas King Forcade and the War against Underground Newspapers

As youths increasingly turned their attention to underground newspapers in the late 1960s, so too did local and federal authorities. On November 5, 1968—the very day that a razor-thin margin of voters elected Richard Nixon president—FBI director J. Edgar Hoover sent a memo to FBI offices nationwide instructing his agents to begin making detailed surveys of "New Left–type publications being printed in [their] territories," and to compile information concerning each paper's staff, printer, and advertisers. A few months earlier, agents had been instructed to take whatever actions were required to cause the papers to "fold and cease publication."[1] Though top secret, Hoover's orders were in keeping with his public statements about the New Left. Earlier that year, he had complained about the Movement's "nauseating air of self-righteousness," with which it "criticizes, belittles, [and] mocks." The mood "of anarchism and nihilism" that activists showcased in the nation's underground papers, he said, would inevitably lead to "disrespect for law" and "violence."[2]

As part of its massive counterintelligence program (COINTELPRO), the FBI used infiltrators, provocateurs, wiretaps, forged letters and documents, and smear campaigns against SDS officers and Movement publications. In 1971, after a group of anonymous activists calling themselves the Citizens' Commission to Investigate the FBI broke into a Bureau office in Media, Pennsylvania, and pilfered thousands of documents revealing some of these activities, activists across the country could be heard musing that even in their most cynical imaginations, they never envisioned just how extensive the FBI's campaign against them was. Who would have thought, for instance, that the FBI would go so far as to create two *fake* underground publications—*Armageddon News* (in Indiana) and *Longhorn Tales* (in Texas)—that were meant to promote more moderate (as opposed to radical) viewpoints?[3]

But the FBI was hardly the only group to go after underground newspapers. In many instances, local authorities used existing laws prohibiting drug use, pornography, and unlicensed vending against New Leftists, who were no doubt targeted because of their political activities. Other times, police ransacked underground press offices, stole valuable records, destroyed expensive equipment, or were accused of planting evidence or fabricating charges.[4] More often than not, radicals were vindicated in courtrooms, but the lengthy and expensive trials they faced occupied their time and diverted resources away from their political activities. Furthermore, even though underground newspapers always had the means to draw attention to the harassment they faced, their complaints registered only faintly when compared with the momentous events that streamed from their pages in the late 1960s and early 1970s. Even today, those who are generally aware of the repressive measures that have historically been leveled against American radicals frequently seem unaware of the extent of the efforts to squash the underground press.

This is true despite the important efforts of Thomas King Forcade (pronounced for-SAHD), who in 1968 became the Underground Press Syndicate's national coordinator. Many colleagues and associates remember Forcade as a fascinating bundle of contradictions. He could be flamboyant and provocative in one moment, and mysterious and elusive in the next. He relished political theater and confrontation, even when these tactics were plainly self-sabotaging. He was deeply invested in countercultural politics, yet he also jeopardized his work on the Movement's behalf by recklessly engaging in drug trafficking. But almost everyone agreed he was exceedingly generous (he was sometimes called him "the hippie Robin Hood") and that he had an extreme predilection for newsprint.[5] Rex Weiner, a friend, recalled that Forcade knew publishing "from top to bottom. He could pull into a town and publish a newspaper from scratch. He knew typesetting. He knew layout. He could sell the ads. He knew about printing processes. He knew about ink and paper. . . . He knew all of the printers in the United States. He had a technical knowledge that was thorough and encyclopedic."[6] Journalist Ron Rosenbaum, another friend, characterized him as a "linear—okay, slightly warped—descendent of the American tradition of revolutionary pamphleteer that traces its descent to Tom Paine. Tom Forcade had the pamphleteer's enthusiasm for his craft . . . and the crusader's compulsion to make his vision visible in black and white."[7]

Among his many accomplishments, Forcade transformed UPS from a chaotic and somewhat anemic organization into a legal corporation, designed an underground press directory, and hired Concert Hall Productions to sell advertisements for seventy-nine UPS papers, which (for a time) netted thousands of dollars for the papers each month. Forcade also established a partnership with the Bell & Howell Company, thereby making hundreds of underground newspapers available on microfilm. He also got UPS admittance into the U.S. House and Senate press galleries, but not, despite his best efforts, the White House press corps. According to a friend, after he joined the congressional press corps, "horrified legislators began enforcing the 'Forcade Rule,' requiring a tie on all newspersons in the gallery. Forcade complied by appearing in black tie and black shoes, black pants, black shirt, black frock coat, black cowboy hat and dark sunglasses."[8]

Tom underscored his tremendous enthusiasm for underground newspapers with a furious anger at authorities who would suppress them. And it was always a *personal* anger. Growing up, Forcade was interested in science fiction, airplanes, and drag racing, and at the University of Utah he quickly earned a degree in business administration. If not for underground newspapers, he might have become a civil engineer, like his father. Instead, the vibrant radical newssheets became his lifeline to the New Left, the counterculture, and outlaw culture more generally. After graduating from college in 1966, Forcade moved to right-wing Phoenix, Arizona, where he amassed a huge private collection of radical tabloids from across the country and began publishing his own underground digest, *Orpheus*. In this period he also began helping to run UPS. While there, he claimed to have been the target of some extraordinary acts of intimidation. This is part of the reason he moved to New York, where he became UPS's coordinator, at which point phone calls and letters from young men and women poured in from every region of the country, alleging that they, too, were being hit with various repressive measures. During Forcade's career as a subterranean journalist, editor, and publisher, his outlook and his behavior was so greatly affected by attempts to stultify radical newspapers that it makes sense to examine two topics—Forcade and the war against the underground press—in close proximity.

IN ITS EARLIEST INCARNATION, UPS hardly seemed destined for greatness. Peter Leggieri, a New York artist who worked on the *East Village Other*, remembered that when Walter Bowart and John Wilcock first created the organization, it was "a farce, a big goof. . . . There were just half a dozen papers, and they said, like, 'let's call it a syndicate. For the hell of it.' They did, and it created a little stir, and that was that." In fact, soon after its inception, Wilcock left the United States to begin research for a Frommer's travel guide he wrote, *Mexico on $5 a Day*. While he was away, Leggieri continues, "man, the floodgates opened and all of a sudden there were papers all over the country. I know none of them ever expected it."[9]

Although the rock impresario Bill Graham had allowed *EVO* to move from its cramped Avenue A offices to roomier digs atop the Fillmore East, on Second Avenue, the paper was nevertheless overwhelmed with its responsibilities, and *EVO*'s Bob Rudnick, who was supposed to be keeping watch over UPS, apparently was not up to the task. Wilcock recalls that when he returned to Manhattan in the early spring of 1968, the organization was in "total chaos." "Listen, you'd better take this whole thing back and organize it yourself," Bowart told him.[10]

Right away, Wilcock discovered that UPS was completely broke; as some had predicted at LNS's October 1967 meeting, *EVO* had apparently siphoned off some of UPS's money. In order to underscore that UPS would henceforth be operating with complete independence, Wilcock rented it its own post office box and paid for all its expenses—stationery, mimeographing, and mailing—out of his own pocket. In a circular letter to member papers, he struck a conciliatory tone. "I realize that many of you are very skeptical about UPS by now—with good reason—but let's give it another try," he said. "If I had remained with *EVO*, I would probably have taken over UPS long ago and [I] can honestly say [I] would have made a better job of it than has been done so far. If you've been familiar with my work and my writing the past few years"—on Fleet Stret in London, at the *Village Voice*, and at the *East Village Other*—"you'll probably trust me now; if not, there's not much I can say to convince you."[11]

"But what the Underground Press Syndicate still needed," Wilcock later maintained, "was more coordination," and so he was no doubt relieved—if not also a touch perplexed—when his letter generated an unexpected phone call from one Thomas King Forcade, who was then collecting underground papers while living in Phoenix.[12] Wilcock remembers being pleasantly surprised to hear that Forcade had a business degree. Right away, the two agreed to begin running UPS together (and to guard against anymore rip-offs, they jointly opened a UPS bank account and began countersigning each other's checks).[13] As always, every paper that joined UPS was required to send one copy of each issue they produced to all of the other member papers, each of which could freely reprint whatever they received. "Tom and I agreed that our initial income would come from selling 'UPS subscriptions' for about $25," Wilcock explained. That is, "if *Time* wanted a UPS subscription [to keep abreast of what was happening in the Movement] they would send us $25 and each of the papers would send a copy to *Time* each month."[14] Soon the UPS would also form a loose steering committee made up of Wilcock, the *Rat*'s Jeff Shero, the *Freep*'s Art Kunkin, and LNS's George Cavalletto and Sheila Ryan. For a time, Forcade ran his end of things out of a 1946 Chevrolet school bus, which he reconfigured by tearing out the seats to make room for a desk and a small table; it was fitted with mattresses that were tucked away during working hours. Later, he moved the operation to a large, nondescript stucco building just west of downtown Phoenix.

At the most mundane level, Forcade charged himself with handling "executive tasks" like "opening the mail, rapping with people about the underground, seeing to it that the papers get advertising representation, seeing to it that UPS members get books and records for review, and getting out self-help bulletins" that explained how to apply for copyrights, find the cheapest bulk mailing, deal with distributors, and so forth. But another of his goals was to promote UPS, which he did aggressively. Even when the organization was struggling for survival, he said that one of his tasks was to "sustain the myth of a finely honed media institution that's going to roll over the whole land. I think the day will come," he wrote, "when we'll have a daily underground paper in every city and a weekly in every town."[15]

Around this time, Forcade was also sporadically publishing his own underground magazine, *Orpheus*. Although *Orpheus* mostly consisted of articles reprinted from elsewhere, Forcade made a point of making his mark on the magazine in the most literal way: "One issue featured a bullethole in the middle of a peace sign on the cover—a real bullethole. Forcade took each bundle of the magazines and shot them with a Colt .45 automatic. He designed the entire magazine so the bullethole became an integral part of each page layout."[16] He was also rumored to have soaked some of the magazine's covers with LSD. One time, he assembled an entire issue while on a long road trip through Berkeley, Chicago, and Denver. James Retherford, of Indiana's *Spectator*, recalled Forcade stopping by Bloomington on that trip and showing off his bullet-pierced newspapers. "While I thought that was a cool Dadaist graphic device, I was put off by something about Forcade," he remembered. "I got the sense he was a self-conscious high priest of cool on a pilgrimage, seeking supplicants."[17]

In the style of some of the West Coast papers, *Orpheus* was heavily trippy, but it was also notably celebratory of the underground press scene of which it was a part. "When they stormed the Pentagon," he wrote in one issue, "the underground press people were literally in the forefront. When they took over Columbia, the Liberation News Service and Newsreel people were inside helping and reporting. . . . They are in the communes, a part of rock groups, acting with street theater groups, demonstrating, petitioning, secretly being. The strength of the underground press lies in the people who do not melt away when threatened."[18]

All of this was vintage Forcade: In the style of many New Leftists, he had a penchant for first baiting the authorities, and then becoming indignant at their hostile response. After the U.S. Post Office declined to grant UPS a third-class mail permit for its newsletter, Forcade publicly suggested that "the epithet 'pig' should be broadened to include not only the police uniform but also the post employees uniform."[19] He also alleged that the Phoenix police had raided his home, destroyed his stereo, spilled his files on the floor, and ransacked the UPS library.[20] Another time he claimed that "forty printers" refused to publish *Orpheus*.[21] In yet another article, he maintained that over a yearlong period, the authorities "systematically busted nearly every person on [his] staff" for drug violations and infiltrated his paper with a narcotics agent. After six months, Forcade said, "they set us up. We got off, but it cost us nearly $2,000 in legal fees to do it."[22]

In a January 1969 letter to LNS, Forcade described an even more ominous situation: He said that he and some of his UPS staff took a quick trip to Los Angeles—where *Orpheus* was printed at the time—and when they returned, four of the group discovered they'd all been burglarized at roughly the same time. In each instance, very few if any valuables were stolen. Around this same time, Forcade said he'd also spotted someone peering into his office with binoculars, and he saw a paperboy with a walkie-talkie.[23] When a *Rolling Stone* reporter visited UPS in Phoenix, Forcade told him that UPS had twice been attacked with firebombs. Though no one was hurt in either incident, Forcade responded by strewing wire mesh over the windows, securing the front door with a heavy bar, and formulating an elaborate plan for self-defense. "We don't talk about it," he said, "and we don't seek confrontation, but we're prepared."[24]

In July 1969 Forcade and some of his staff ventured to Ann Arbor, Michigan, to attend a four-day UPS conference that was hosted by a commune called

Trans-Love Energies Unlimited. In the previous year, media activists had hosted two conferences—in Iowa City and in Madison, Wisconsin—that were said to "capture a shift from peace signs to clenched fists," and the summer of 1969 was a time when many people involved with the underground press increasingly believed they were under siege.[25] And the Trans-Love people *especially* felt this way. In April 1967, they'd staged a "Love-In" on Detroit's Belle Isle, which was supposed to be modeled after a peaceful hippie gathering that had taken place in San Francisco almost two months earlier. Instead, belligerent bikers showed up, drunken fights broke out, and at dusk a contingent of police on horseback swarmed upon the revelers with wooden batons.[26] The following year, Trans-Love's commune was firebombed twice, and so the group relocated from Detroit to two huge Victorian houses near the University of Michigan. There they became closely associated with the MC-5, a protopunk band from Detroit that, under Sinclair's influence, championed hedonism, confrontation, and cultural revolution, and whose shows always attracted a heavy police presence.[27] For all these reasons, UPS kept the exact location of its conference a secret until just before it began. Finally, it was revealed that it would take place just a couple miles outside Ann Arbor, atop a hilly farm that had a knoll from which "all avenues of access could be observed." Near the bottom, just off the highway, a member of the countercultural White Panther Party stood guard with a 12-gauge shotgun.[28]

In addition to guarding against intruders, the underground press radicals were also exceedingly wary of the straight press. Don DeMaio, editor of Philadelphia's *Distant Drummer*, recalls that as the meeting was beginning, someone stood up and made a portentous announcement: "We have it on good authority that there's a reporter here working undercover for *Rolling Stone*"— the commercially oriented rock tabloid that Berkeley dropout Jann Wenner founded in 1967. In fact, there was such a person; it was DeMaio.[29] Uneasily, he kept silent about it, apparently with good cause, since a reporter who revealed his association with the *Detroit Free Press* was promptly ejected from the conference. And Richard Goldstein, the *Village Voice*'s pioneering rock critic, felt so unwelcome that he left after the first day. At one point, a disagreement even arose over whether it was wise for UPS to tape-record the proceedings, prompting Wilcock to remark, "Aren't we overdoing the paranoia business? First, we bar the establishment press, and now we can't even cover the meeting ourselves?"[30]

Nevertheless, the group managed to discuss many of the main issues that were roiling the underground press in this period. One focal point was sexism; a group of women's liberationists complained that they were treated shabbily by their colleagues, and despite heavy opposition from the White Panthers, LNS's Shelia Ryan was able to spearhead the passage of a three-point resolution proclaiming: "(1) sexism must be eliminated from underground papers' content and ads, (2) undergrounds should publish articles on women's oppression, [and] (3) women should have full roles in underground papers' staffs."[31] A Berkeley radical explained why roughly forty workers at the *Berkeley Barb* had recently revolted against publisher Max Scherr, who was said to be ludicrously tightfisted despite making about $130,000 annually from his paper.[32]

Others raised the possibility of launching some sort of attack upon Columbia Records, which they lit into for first attempting to co-opt the movement with their ludicrous "But The Man Can't Bust Our Music" advertisement, and then for suddenly canceling its substantial ad buys in the underground press.[33] "The discussion meandered into a heated condemnation of artists and producers who exploit hip themes and life-style without reimbursing the hip community," one participant remarked.[34] Radicals had especially harsh words for *Rolling Stone*, which initially appeared on quarter-folded newsprint with serrated edges and therefore struck some readers as a slightly upscale underground newspaper.[35] From a marketing standpoint, Wenner's approach was both genius and cunning; his magazine was generally favorable toward the cultural and the commodifiable aspects of the youth rebellion—especially rock and roll—while thumbing its nose at New Left political activism.[36] As a result, the magazine was able to lure advertisers and readers that were apprehensive about the Movement's growing militancy.

The conference then took an unexpected turn after attendees got word that representatives from Wayne State University's radical student organ, *The South End*, were holding a nearby press conference to denounce the university's president, William Keast, for suspending publication of the paper.[37] According to one attendee, UPS representatives "expressed shock that a newspaper like their own could be completely suppressed at the exact time that they were meeting to discuss suppression on a national level."[38] At least twenty UPSers, including Forcade, drove eastward toward Detroit to show their solidarity with *The South End*, though by the time they got there, the press conference was over.

The following night, the UPSers' shock gave way to fear and anger. First, two police officers showed up, looking, they said, for a young woman from the *Chicago Seed* who had been picked up a few days earlier on a pot charge. After the radicals told them the woman had already left town, a contingent of perhaps thirty more policemen—equipped with "shotguns, rifles, pistols, bulletproof vests, mace, helmets and face shields"—sneaked up on the farmhouse and surrounded the radicals. According to Forcade, they destroyed a camera, tried to take some film, confiscated several underground papers, broke three doors, and "generally conduct[ed] themselves like oafs."[39] Another conferee alleged that some of the police nervously "unclicked safeties and jammed their shotguns at the heads of people who tried to walk by them. Lives were really hanging on literally trembling fingers. One wrong move and tomorrow there'd be a mass demonstration for the Ann Arbor martyrs."[40] After about thirty minutes, LNS reported, "the gendarmes got ready to leave. One of them flashed a V-sign as he departed. The conference people booed him loudly as they stood watching from the hill."[41]

When the media summit was over, Forcade and his gang journeyed to New York City, where they met with Yippies Abbie Hoffman, Jerry Rubin, Paul Krassner and Stew Albert, along with Marvin Garson (editor of the Bay Area's *Good Times*) and Bob Fass (the WBAI disc jockey whose late night, free-form program, *Radio Unnameable*, was *de rigueur* for Gotham's bohemians).[42] One imagines Forcade mixing easily in such a stimulating crowd, but once again, the revelry and merriment was dampened when word arrived that another of their own had just been throttled by the law: After passing two joints to an undercover policewoman, John Sinclair was sentenced to nine and a half to ten years in prison. Forcade recalled that Sinclair's friends "openly wept when they heard the news."

From all of this—the cascading series of setbacks he'd encountered in Phoenix, the growing rapport he was establishing with plugged-in protest leaders, and a general sense within the New Left that conflict between radicals and authorities was quickly heating up—Forcade reached a clear conclusion: It was time to leave Phoenix and relocate his UPS office to Manhattan "as soon as possible."[43]

AFTER SITUATING UPS IN GROUND-FLOOR OFFICES on West Tenth Street, Forcade announced that, per a resolution from the Ann Arbor conference, he was taking the helm as UPS project coordinator. He was quick to point out, however, that any "major decisions" pertaining to UPS would be put to a vote of the member papers. His official sounding title, he said, was created "purely for the purpose of dealing with title-oriented straight people."[44]

Here he was letting on more than most people grasped, since his position as the head of UPS also provided cover for his stepped-up drug-dealing activity. No one who knew Forcade would have mistaken him for a teetotaling law-and-order type; he kept a heavy canister of nitrous oxide (laughing gas) in the UPS office. But probably only a few were aware of the scope of his operations. According to a legend, Forcade once narrowly escaped imprisonment when he eluded Florida authorities by hiding for almost twenty-four hours in a swamp after he was spotted helping to unload tons of marijuana from a giant sailboat.[45] Wilcock recalls a time when Forcade escorted him to a storeroom on Greenwich Avenue that was "lined from floor to ceiling with . . . bales of weed."[46] Later, Forcade opened up a smoking club in Soho. According to a friend, upon entering it, "first you got eyeballed by a TV camera, then you got buzzed into one room and immediately taken to a little cubicle, like in a whorehouse, so you could not meet any of the other customers. Then a pretty little girl would wheel in a cartful of marijuana and you could take your pick."[47] Weiner remembers that later, when UPS was operating from a giant loft on Seventeenth Street, "a huge, tie-dyed tent sat in the middle . . . and people were just waking up around the middle of the day, crawling out of this tent. There was a rock 'n' roll band living there, and a bunch of really hot babes were walking around. Tom seemed to have the whole place under his control and command."[48]

Still, Forcade continued to impress his colleagues with his phenomenal energy and efficiency. And of all the activities he undertook while running UPS—generating publicity, acquiring advertisers, writing newsletters, and advising the Movement's underground newspapers on things like printing, distribution, copyrights, and permits—he seemed especially interested in documenting the widespread attempts to stifle the under-ground press. In a 1969 essay, he identified the many styles of repressive actions that were wielded against UPS papers. Some subterranean journal-ists were ostensibly busted for obscenity or drugs, when in fact the evi-dence suggests they were politically targeted. Other times, the papers' landlords, printers, distributors or advertisers were intimidated, harassed, boycotted, or otherwise coerced into ceasing to do business with the underground press. Street vendors faced various types of interference, and sometimes papers were physically attacked, usually by firebombs or ran-sacking.[49] The only kind of harassment that Forcade didn't mention is that experienced by those who ran afoul of the U.S. military. By one count, American servicemen, with the help of civilian allies, put out more than two hundred antiwar publications worldwide, although most of these were short-lived mimeographed sheets, rather than full-fledged tabloids.[50] On top of all of this, the FBI flirted with, but ultimately did not pursue, schemes to sabotage underground papers that were so outlandish they sound like something from a James Bond film. One memorandum actu-ally called for the creation of a chemical that emitted the scent of "foul-smelling feces," which could then be sprayed upon bundles of newspapers in order to render them unreadable.[51]

It should be stressed that the underground papers were not victimized by any single, primary law-enforcement agency. Instead, the efforts of the FBI, local police, politicians, and vigilantes were uncoordinated. If anything, this may have made the overall effort to suppress underground papers even more effective, since it meant they could be attacked on multiple fronts, by a range of enemies that were sometimes hard to discern. In 1981, a PEN American Center Report titled *The Campaign Against the Underground Press*, which was based largely on documents obtained under the Freedom of Information Act, as well as materials compiled by Allen Ginsberg (a prominent member of PEN's Freedom to Write Committee), listed hundreds of instances in which authorities went after underground rags. The report found that "the withering of the underground press was not entirely a natural decline. Alternative presses, whether serious journals of adversary politics or countercultural avant-garde papers, were targets of surveillance, harassment, and unlawful search and seizure by U.S. government agencies."[52] In one respect, the study was methodologically flawed, because it frequently took *accusations* of harassment as *evidence* of harassment. Still, the PEN Center's overall conclusions seem irrefutable. While it would be tedious to list all of the instances in which papers appear to have been unfairly targeted, a few choice examples of the various types of crackdowns that Forcade concerned himself with may prove edifying.

First, let it be said that salacious material was commonplace in the underground press. Few young writers in the Movement expressed compunctions about the fact that all seven of George Carlin's "seven dirty words" could be found in many papers. Furthermore, following the lead of the *EVO*—which ran cheesy pinup-style photos of beautiful hippie women in various Lower East Side locations in a regular feature called "Slum Goddess"—underground papers began running photos and montages of naked and half-naked women with increasing frequency in the late 1960s.[53] Meanwhile, sexually explicit classified advertisements, which seemed outrageous in their day, became mainstays of many papers. From a contemporary perspective, the toilet humor, four-letter words, and nudity that prevailed in the subterranean press may seem more childish than shocking. But as historian Beth Bailey reminds us, when this material is recontextualized, we can see how such words and images were alluring to youths who "embraced sex with revolutionary intent, using it not only for pleasure but also for power in a new form of cultural politics that shook the nation." It wasn't just that radicals took an unembarrassed attitude toward sexual experimentation, celebrated a pleasure ethic, and valued authenticity more than they valued conventional notions about sexuality and civility (although that was the case). Sometimes they simply

reveled in making adults uncomfortable. The word "fuck," which was ubiquitous in underground newspapers, "was not polite," Bailey acknowledges.
"But more than anything else, 'fuck' got attention."[54] Radical youths were
also adept at inverting the cultural logic that stifled sexual expression but
justified war—a tactic displayed in the popular slogan "Make Love, Not
War" and in this pithy poem, which appeared in the Omaha, Nebraska,
Asterisk:

> Is it obscene to fuck,
>
> or,
>
> Is it obscene to kill?[55]

The desire to shock and offend bourgeois sensibilities was perhaps most
exemplified, however, in popular underground "comix," which were *intended*
to be objectionable to Middle America. According to one cartoonist, underground comix were spelled with an "x" to imply they were X-rated, or suitable only for an adult readership, but frankly they often seemed aimed at
young males.[56] Again, the *EVO* was pioneering in printing counterculture-
oriented strips like Nancy Kalish's "Gentle's Trip Out," and Bill Beckman's
"Captain High," although Gilbert Shelton's "Fabulous Furry Freak Brothers"
(an iconic strip that chronicled a trio of hippie antiheroes who gave their lives
over to drugs) first appeared in the Austin *Rag*, and Ron Cobb (who has been
called "the dean of underground political cartoonists") got started at the *Los
Angeles Free Press*.[57] But it was in the work of artists such as Robert Crumb,
Robert Williams, and S. Clay Wilson that readers encountered the most crass
and perverse depictions of all types of sexual activity, including group sex,
incest, nonconsensual domination, and even sexual mutilation.

The controversy that underground comix provoked within the Movement was predictable. Some celebrated these strips for subversively injecting "unacceptable" attitudes into the comic-strip medium, and some held
that, ethnographically, they could be appreciated as outgrowths of a new
culture.[58] Others went a touch further: they observed that underground
comix satirized freaks and hippies as much as they did authority figures, and
underscored that they were, in fact, *cartoons*. Essentially, they asked their
critics to lighten up.[59] At the other end of the spectrum, some radicals saw
them as a distraction from worthwhile political causes. They either attacked
the comix for their rank sexism or else turned up their noses in disgust.
"There [has] never been any degree of discontent when the UPS newspapers
used four-letter words or called the police chief a dirty name," one critic
explained. But he said that some anti-Establishment types were genuinely
disturbed by the far-out comix, and he alleged that a few UPS papers went

so far as to cancel their subscriptions to papers that relied too heavily on such material.[60]

Though it is easy to see how ordinary citizens could be angered or threatened by some of this material, all of it was clearly constitutionally protected. As Justice William Brennan wrote in 1957 in *Roth v. the United States* (also known as the *Fanny Hill* case), in order to be declared legally obscene, a work needed to appeal to prurient interests, affront community standards, and be "utterly" without redeeming social value. Underground sheets could be crass and misguided, but since they were always concerned with politics in the broadest sense, and since they reflected the sensibilities of millions of anti-Establishment youths, they ought to have been immune from obscenity charges.[61]

But this was not the case. In July 1969, UPS maintained that twenty-three papers had been charged with, or convicted of, "spurious charges designed to shut them down."[62] Eugene Guerrero, of Atlanta's *Great Speckled Bird*, recalls winning a case that originated from the use of the word "motherfucker" on the cover.[63] Five of the staff of Jackson, Mississippi's, *Kudzu* were likewise arrested for using four letter words and also for referring to LSD.[64] Mike Abrahams and Abe Peck, both of the *Chicago Seed*, were hauled into court on account of an artist's drawing.[65] Dale Herschler, publisher of the *San Diego Door*, was collared for distributing obscene materials because his paper ran a photo of a nude woman, only to have the charges dismissed after a district attorney couldn't produce a single witness who was willing to characterize the offending issue as obscene.[66] Stoney Burns (aka Brent Stein), the frequently targeted publisher of *Dallas Notes*, was likewise arrested for possession of pornography.[67] John Bryan, editor of Los Angeles's *Open City*, was convicted of obscenity for running "a half-page ad for an electronic music group" that an LNS writer claimed was merely "a parody on the use of sex to sell products." Police hauled in students at the Greater Hartford campus of the University of Connecticut for a cartoon that depicted president-elect Richard Nixon as a middle finger.[68] At Pennsylvania State University, state troopers arrested four students affiliated with a tiny paper called *Water Tunnel* and charged them with providing obscene material to minors because they ran a photo of the cover of John Lennon and Yoko Ono's infamous *Two Virgins* record, on which the two artists appear frontally (and posteriorly) nude.[69] John Kois, of Milwaukee's *Kaleidoscope*, was found guilty of two counts of publishing "obscene material": one for a suggestive (that is, not explicit) photo of an interracial couple making love, and another for a poem that contained two four-letter words (both of which also appeared in Allen Ginsberg's *Howl*).[70] By the time Kois won his case on appeal before the U.S. Supreme

Court in 1972, his paper was defunct.[71] Jerry Powers, editor of Miami's *Daily Planet*, told a reporter that although he'd been arrested twenty-nine times for "selling an obscene newspaper," he'd only been convicted once, and that case was currently on appeal. But the "bonds for those arrests totaled between $92,000 and $93,000," he said. "We beat these charges every time but it is enormously expensive."[72]

Forcade and his UPS colleagues were galled by the apparently politically motivated attacks. "If they were really worried about pornography, they would bust the color crotch magazines, but it is obvious that obscenity is only an excuse," he said. "They realize they can't win in the high courts, but their purpose is to bleed the papers with legal costs."[73] That same year, a judge in Vancouver, Canada, who dismissed obscenity charges against the *Georgia Straight* acknowledged that this seemed to be the authorities' intent. "It is common knowledge," he said, "that many publications are being sold in newsstands and so-called grocery stores" that "are full of nothing but obscene material and it has always remained a mystery why [only] some of them are singled out for prosecution."[74]

Police were also accused of selectively prosecuting underground journalists for drug offenses. Of course recreational drugs were immensely popular in the Movement, and perhaps especially so in underground press milieus. (In 1968, the *EVO* ran an unscientific survey purporting that a staggering 98 percent of its readers had smoked marijuana . . . and 19 percent had tried smoking bananas.)[75] Rex Weiner recalls that "paste-up night" at the *EVO* was "frequently carried out on LSD, but most often pot, speed and coke, which various dealers, dropping by between midnight and dawn, donated to the process."[76] Chip Berlet, a cofounder of the College Press Service and a writer for Denver's *Straight Creek Journal*, recalls that although some papers had "no drugs in the office" policies, soft drugs were otherwise "ubiquitous." "What underground journalist," he asked, "didn't engage in manic sweeping and vacuuming in an attempt to remove every last marijuana seed from his or her car, home, or underground newspaper office the night before publishing an article calculated to drive governmental officials to the brink of madness?"[77]

Most undergrounders also actively championed marijuana's legalization. Still, Forcade maintained that drug laws were unfairly applied in the late 1960s, and he estimated (perhaps wildly) that drug-using underground journalists were a hundred times more likely to be arrested than regular drug users.[78] Though he lacked any data to back up his claim, he could point to several editors who were serving hefty prison sentences for marijuana offenses. The most notorious of them was John Sinclair, music editor and columnist for Detroit's *Fifth Estate*, who served twenty-nine months of a nine-and-a-half- to ten-year prison sentence for passing two joints to an undercover agent who had befriended him over a period of six months. In 1972, Michigan's Supreme Court ruled that the Detroit police had entrapped Sinclair, and reversed his conviction. Two justices further opined that Sinclair's sentence was "cruel and unusual punishment in light of the case against him."[79] Later, *Dallas Notes* publisher Stoney Burns was sentenced to ten years and a day for possession of one-tenth of an ounce of marijuana (his first offense), at which point even *Time* magazine was compelled to remark, "The law in Dallas, from all appearances, has been bent on getting Stoney Burns for years."[80]

Sometimes politicians even invited reprisals against underground rags. In August 1968, Chicago mayor Richard Daley appeared before a television camera, jabbed his finger at a copy of the *Rat*, and thundered, "And this, this is the terrorists' guide to Chicago."[81] In Wisconsin, state senator Ernest C. Keppler stood in that state's capitol building and said that *Connections* editor Ann Gordon should be fired as a university teaching assistant simply because some people (him included) held her in poor repute. "Put it this way," he explained to reporters. "Would a prostitute be a proper T.A.? I don't mean to say she's a prostitute, but a person in public employment should have good character. If she doesn't, then she's not effective."[82] Joe Pool, a congressman from Texas, said of the underground press, "These smut sheets are today's Molotov cocktails thrown at respectability and decency in our nation. . . . They encourage depravity and irresponsibility, and they nurture a breakdown in the continued capacity of the government to conduct an orderly and constitutional society."[83] On another occasion he declared, with no trace of irony, "The plan of this Underground Press Syndicate is to take advantage of that part of the First Amendment which protects newspapers and gives them freedom of press."[84]

In other instances, building owners, advertisers, distributors, and printers were all pressured into refusing to do business with radical publications. In California, for instance, local police apparently forced San Diego Periodicals—the local news distributor—to recall the July 1969 issue of *Ramparts* magazine, which contained sordid allegations of racism against a police officer.[85] In other instances, federal authorities were behind some of these obstructions.[86] In early 1969, Thorne Dreyer reported that Austin's *Rag* had "lost several" printers. Later, a COINTELPRO document revealed that at least one of those printers had been visited by San Antonio–based FBI agents.[87] *Freep* editor Art Kunkin maintained that FBI intimidation cost him his printer as well. *Rat* editor Jeff Shero made a similar allegation concerning his paper's landlord.[88] In 1980, declassified FBI documents proved that a Cleveland-based printer provided the Bureau with the names of New Leftists who had asked him to print material that he found "smutty and extremely critical of the United States."[89]

The FBI was probably most effective, though, when it pressured certain large companies to cease advertising in the underground press. As investigative journalist Angus MacKenzie revealed, in January 1969 a San Francisco–based FBI agent sent a memo to the Bureau's offices in Washington, DC, and New York City, alleging that Columbia Records was giving "active aid and comfort to enemies of the United States" in the form of advertising revenue to underground newspapers. The agent then recommended that the FBI should persuade Columbia to advertise elsewhere.[90] According to Marc Knops, of Madison's *Kaleidoscope*, "The bottom fell out of the ad market" when the record companies stopped buying space in underground papers.[91] Eugene Guerrero likewise remembers that Atlanta's *Great Speckled Bird* was "getting full-page ads . . . from Columbia particularly, and Capital," which suddenly stopped appearing.[92] *Berkeley Tribe* business manager Lionel Haines claimed that beginning in late 1969 his paper suddenly began losing about $17,000 per month worth of record-company advertising. "Within months," he remembered, "most of the viable underground papers around the country were crippled. With big national ads going to *Rolling Stone* and the local classifieds going to free shoppers, there was no economic base."[93]

In another instance, an alliance of right-wing politicians and private citizens organized an economic boycott of a printer named William Schanen, of Port Washington, Wisconsin. Schanen, who was fifty-six when the boycott began, was the longtime owner of Port Publications, and in addition to publishing three small weekly community newspapers of his own, he also contracted to print other papers, including Milwaukee's *Kaleidoscope*. At the time, *Kaleidoscope* had a circulation of about fifteen thousand and was typical of many underground publications. One writer characterized it this way:

> It is anti-Establishment in its editorial policy, lashing out in its news columns against what it sees as abuses of authority by police and priests, mayors and magistrates, high school principals and university presidents. It is antiwar and pro-pot. It also sprinkles its pages with four-letter words and occasionally prints drawings and photographs of nude men and women.[94]

In early 1969, a local district attorney freely acknowledged that although the paper probably could not be shut down through legal channels, "civic action" could be used to force Schanen to stop printing it. A few months later, Benjamin Grob—a prominent local businessman who had previously lent his support to senators Joseph McCarthy and Barry Goldwater—sent a letter to some five hundred retailers, organizations, and individuals, alleging that Schanen was publishing "obscene literature for profit." He added that he would no longer advertise in any of Schanen's papers, nor would he patronize anyone who did. "Ladies and gentlemen," he declared, "I am looking for company."[95] Soon, advertisers began closing their accounts, merchants stopped carrying Schanen's papers, and weekly advertising revenue from his flagship paper, *Ozaukee Press*, plummeted by 77 percent. To try to recover some of his losses, Schanen doubled down and began printing many other underground newspapers that were having trouble finding local publishers, including the *Chicago Seed*, the *Indianapolis Free Press*, and a paper from as far away as Omaha, Nebraska, called the *Buffalo Chip*.[96]

Ironically, Schanen was no radical; he was merely liberal, and his contract with *Kaleidoscope* accounted for only a minuscule portion of his business, which had grossed nearly $400,000 in the year before the boycott. Viewed from a self-interested, financial perspective, the circumstances practically demanded that he simply sever all his ties to the underground press. It could have been easily accomplished. But in the tradition of Benjamin Franklin, he believed that printers were obligated to print even those things they found objectionable.[97] "I don't agree with a lot of it," he said of *Kaleidoscope*, "but what are we supposed to do, get rid of everything we don't agree with? There's an issue here that is much larger than Bill Schanen."[98] Another time, Schanen issued a statement that read, "My family and I are dedicated to fighting the boycott. All we can hope for is that the fair minded people who understand our position, who respect the right to the constitutional guarantee of the freedom of the press, and the right of *Kaleidoscope* to this same freedom too, will come to our support. What is happening in Port Huron, Wisconsin, is cruel, punishing and senseless. No American who values his freedom can long ignore the denial of freedom to others."[99] Although Schanen won financial, moral, and editorial support from an alliance of neighbors, the National Newspaper Association, the ACLU, the University of Wisconsin's journalism department, and the neighboring *Milwaukee Journal*, he was eventually forced to sell off two of his three newspapers. Then in February 1971 he died of a heart attack.

In some instances, vigilante groups physically attacked the young men and women who staffed underground newspapers. Victoria Smith, of Houston's *Space City!*, recalls a night in July 1969 when their home/office was hit by a pipe bomb while one of their staffers was inside. "Over the next several months," she says, "we endured break-ins, thefts, tire-slashings, potshots (including a steel arrow fired from a crossbow through the front door) and threats, to both staff members and advertisers."[100] One memorable threat came in the form of a note that read, "The Knights of the Ku Klux Klan Is [*sic*] Watching You." Soon the collective illuminated their yard with floodlights and occasionally kept an armed guard at night, but this was of limited practical value.[101] Between October 1969 and February 1970, an apparently unhinged character kept hanging around the office *Space City!* office; eventually he was discovered to be a Klansman named Mike Lowe.[102]

Other papers experienced similar problems. On May 1, 1968, someone bombed the *Los Angeles Free Press*.[103] The following year, after some of the staff of the *Great Speckled Bird* wrote about their experiences with the first Venceremos Brigade (a group of young radicals who demonstrated their support for the Cuban Revolution by chopping sugarcane alongside Cuban agricultural workers), their office also was firebombed.[104] In California, the collective behind an early 1970s feminist newspaper, *Goodbye to All That*, found a note on their front door that said "You are the Target."[105] The aforementioned *Dallas Notes* editor, Stoney Burns, complained that on three occasions he found his car's tires slashed, and once the car was riddled with bullet holes.[106]

The San Diego *Street Journal* was beset by a particularly harrowing string of attacks. In October 1969 the paper's windows were shot out. Eleven days later, someone smashed the paper's front door and stole 2,500 copies of its most recent edition. Then the paper began receiving bomb threats over the phone. After that, someone ransacked the *Street Journal*'s office, stealing records and wrecking $5,000 worth of equipment. "During this time," former staffer Julie Wittman recalled, "it was impossible to look out of the window without seeing a steady stream of circling cars: police cars, unmarked police cars, sheriff's cars, shore patrol. But no one ever spotted the perpetrators of the vandalism."[107] Meanwhile, local police harassed the paper's street vendors, seized some of their vending machines, and conducted illegal searches. One day, Wittman says, her landlord burst into their building. "'I'm not going to die for you,' he said. 'Get out. I'm not going to die for you.' Someone had called and threatened both him and his family unless he stopped renting us office space." The papers' advertisers received similar threats.[108] In 1970 one of the *Street Journal*'s writers, Lowell Bergman—who later rose to journalistic fame as a producer for CBS's 60 *Minutes* and PBS's *Frontline* (and who was portrayed by Al Pacino in the movie *The Insider*)—helped file a lawsuit against the San Diego police department. But by the time it was ready to be heard, the paper had folded, and most of the plaintiffs had already left town. Later, a member of a local vigilante gang affiliated with the Minutemen claimed responsibility for most of the attacks mentioned above, and said his group had been in league with the local police and the FBI.[109] "We were targets along with a lot of other people," Bergman said.[110]

Perhaps the most common aggravation that underground newspapers faced involved the hassling, detaining, or arrest of their street vendors, even though they were almost always within their rights to sell their newspapers publicly. Street sellers of the *Washington Free Press* were sometimes arrested for jaywalking.[111] Hawkers of the *Spokane Natural* complained they were targeted for loitering, or for selling their papers too boisterously, and one salesman claimed he was held by police for thirty-six hours. He said he was finally released when some from the ACLU called, but no charges were ever filed against him.[112] Two vendors selling San Francisco's *Good Times* were booked for obstructing the sidewalk and being a public nuisance. A seller of the *Berkeley Barb* was charged with disturbing the peace.[113] In Oregon, a salesman of the *Willamette Bridge* was arrested for "interfering with the flow of traffic."[114] In 1970 the *New York Times* reported that San Diego police "continued to arrest sidewalk hawkers of the paper on loitering charges even though . . . a local lawyer for the American Civil Liberties Union has been able to get acquittals by challenging the constitutionality of the arrests."[115] In Dallas, Stoney Burns was arrested for selling his paper without a permit. In fact, no permit was necessary, and these charges were later dropped.[116] Sellers of Mississippi's *Kudzu* were likewise picked up for vagrancy, only to have the charges dismissed.[117] In New Orleans, the *NOLA Express* obtained a restraining order enjoining police from harassing its vendors, but when a federal court fined a police officer $100 for violating the order, a city councilman collected a fund and personally reimbursed him.[118] Harassment of vendors was such a problem in Texas that Houston's *Space City!* and Austin's *Rag* both published guidelines for vendors in the event they were questioned by a police officer, arrested, or detained.[119]

Some underground newsmen may have been targeted for draft evasion. In 1967–68, James Retherford, editor of Indiana's *Spectator*, was indicted on three technical charges relating to the draft. But the case against him was marred by numerous irregularities from the very start, and when he was put on trial on July 10, 1968, prosecutors seemed intent on trying him for sedition—for which he was *not* under indictment. According to Retherford, prosecutors, relying in part on his *Spectator* editorials, unfairly portrayed him as "a revolutionary advocating the violent overthrow of the government, a communist subversive, [and] a seditious traitor."[120] After he was sentenced to six years in prison, a New York advocacy group caught wind of his case, and Leonard Boudin, the celebrated lawyer, agreed to represent him pro bono. The whole complicated matter was finally resolved in October 1969, when a three-judge appeals court unanimously threw out Retherford's conviction and scolded the U.S. attorney for bringing the case in the first place.

Those involved with underground newspapers at military installations faced obvious risks. Generally, these papers portrayed the military as an instrument of American imperialism and kept servicemen abreast of various antiwar activities. A *New York Times* article about Fort Dix, New Jersey's, *Shakedown* explained the army post had an ordinance prohibiting the distribution of anything that was considered "in bad taste, prejudicial to good order or discipline . . . subversive, or otherwise contrary to [its] best interests."[121] As a result, *Shakedown* was literally smuggled into the areas where soldiers frequented, and its staff tried to remain anonymous. Similarly, bundles of the *Ally*, from Berkeley, were hidden in care packages before they were mailed to soldiers in Vietnam, who then redistributed them surreptitiously. A writer for *Aboveground*, which came out of Fort Carson, Colorado, recalls undergoing a harrowing interrogation from military intelligence officers. As it was under way, he realized that his questioners had gotten their information from a provocateur who had earlier tried to goad him into committing murderous arson.[122]

One of the most notable figures in the GI underground press to endure harassment was Roger Priest, an apprentice seaman at the Pentagon who single-handedly put out three issues (one thousand copies apiece) of an inflammatory pamphlet called *OM*. Priest was spied upon by military intelligence agents, arrested, and court-martialed, even though, according to one scholar, he "followed military regulations to the letter in all aspects of his behavior, ensuring that if the brass were going to get rid of him, they could not do it on a technicality."[123] For fourteen alleged violations under the Uniform Code of Military Justice, Priest faced thirty-nine years imprisonment, but ultimately he was merely demoted and given a bad-conduct discharge. One suspects that the whole matter might have been avoided had Priest not provoked L. Mendel Rivers, chairman of the House Armed Services Committee, by sending him a copy of *OM*. Rivers responded by asking Pentagon officials to investigate whether Priest had committed "gross abuse of the constitutional right to free speech."[124]

For all the repression that underground papers faced, in a few instances radicals may have successfully leveraged their influence in the Movement to avoid certain punishments. For instance, *BU News* editor Ray Mungo seemed determined to draw the government's wrath in October 1967 when he perched himself on the hood of a car that was parked near the gates of the Boston Army Base and ripped up his induction papers before a crowd of about six hundred. As historian Michael S. Foley writes, "Despite this flagrant violation of the law, neither the Selective Service nor the Justice Department moved to punish him." "It was an open and shut case," Mungo later admitted. "I expected to be prosecuted . . . but they never prosecuted me. I can only conclude that they didn't want to give me the right to make a martyr of myself."[125] In another instance, *Distant Drummer* editor Don DeMaio ran a letter to the editor that, if read uncharitably, could be taken to advocate the murder of Frank Rizzo, the notorious local police commissioner.[126] DeMaio says that in response, Rizzo pushed Arlen Specter, who was then the city's district attorney, to press charges against him. Ultimately, though, Specter declined, supposedly because he "didn't want a riot over that crummy paper."[127]

It is true, though, that some underground journalists were guilty of very serious crimes. Notably, two *Rat* staffers, Pat Swinton and Jane Alpert, participated in the bombing of government buildings in 1969. When they sought to justify their self-described guerrilla activity by delivering communiqués to LNS and a handful of papers, they were following the custom established by other violent organizations.[128] As Chip Berlet pointed out, the handling of such material from fugitive groups "became such an issue that the UPS newsletter carried an article on the subject" ("Training at one underground newspaper," he added, "included use of small arms").[129] Members of some of the most radical papers, like the *Berkeley Tribe*, had ties to, and were among the chief sources of information about, clandestine groups such as the Weather Underground. In turn, the underground press was the only reliable mouthpiece that such groups had. For years, the New Left's tabloids were sites of lengthy debate about the use of violence by the Left. Many writers offered at least rhetorical support for "armed struggle," though criticisms of violence were just as common.[130] Finally, it bears remembering that the biased reporting and self-justifying rhetoric that was common in underground rags could seem particularly skewed when youths narrated their own persecution. If the claims that federal investigators, sheriffs, business leaders, and politicians made against underground newspapers sometimes seemed paranoid, exaggerated, or conveniently selective, the reverse is also true.

Still, in a country that unequivocally guarantees its citizens the right to express themselves freely, and that generally regards that freedom as one of the most important freedoms in the Bill of Rights, it is striking how swiftly authorities mobilized to try to shut down underground newspapers and how imaginative they proved in their efforts. It is also disturbing that the difficulties that radical journalists encountered were rarely discussed in the Establishment press, which has typically been so vigilant in defense of its own rights.[131] One can only surmise why this was the case. In a 1974 speech, the *Washington Post*'s Bob Woodward put forth the most obvious explanation.

"The underground press was largely right about government sabotage," he acknowledged, "but the country didn't get upset because it was the left that was sabotaged. The country got upset when [in the Watergate Era] the broad political center, with its established institutions, came under attack."

By contrast, Thomas King Forcade carefully monitored the deplorable efforts to suppress underground newspapers, and he fully grasped what was happening. In 1969 he published a survey revealing that 60 percent of all underground newspapers said they were frequently hassled by police.[132] To someone who was so committed to building a sustainable revolutionary press, this came as dispiriting news. "With obscenity busts they get your money, with drug busts they get your people, with intimidation they get your printer, with bombings they get your office, and if you can still manage to somehow get out a sheet, their distribution monopolies and rousts keep it from ever getting to the people," he fumed.[133] But on other occasions, Forcade characterized the underground press as remarkably resilient. "I never write any of them off," he told a reporter in 1969. "You won't see a copy of a paper for six months, maybe, and I'll think about taking it off the [UPS] list, and the very next day, there it is. Underground papers are like algae, the way they cling to life." Another time, he predicted the emergence of radical dailies. "The underground press is crouched like a Panther," he wrote, "dollars and days away from daily publication and thus total domination of the print media. After the underground press goes daily, they'll drop like flies."[134] Sometimes he even seemed to believe that the oppressive measures taken against the underground press could be viewed as an *encouraging* sign, insofar as they meant that people in powerful positions must have truly felt threatened by the new radical media. He presented the underground press as a powerful institution that young people could rally around, and as one that would never buckle or compromise. In fact, the tactics deployed against the underground press may only have emboldened Forcade.

Certainly this seemed the case when he testified before President Nixon's Commission on Obscenity and Pornography, in Washington, DC, on May 13, 1970, and single-handedly transformed what would otherwise have been a small-bore affair into what the *Los Angeles Times* called "one of the most bizarre hearings ever held on the Congressional premises."[135] Like many First Amendment absolutists, Forcade held that constitutional guarantees to free speech mattered most when they protected the rights of citizens to criticize, mock, or belittle people in positions of authority. And at the Capitol Hill hearings, he found himself before a panel that he thought was overwhelmingly deserving of such ridicule. Forcade was dressed completely in black, with a parson's hat pulled low over his head, and his prepared statement was antic and hyperbolic in the extreme. It also may have been adorned with inaccurate or misleading statistics, and some of it was clearly intended for comic value. Still, probably no document from the 1960s better captures the unusual style in which underground press radicals sought to leverage the constitutional protections that were handed down by Madison, Jefferson, and the other Founding Fathers. It is reprinted below in full:

> *The Constitution of the United States of America says, "Congress shall make no law . . . abridging freedom of speech or of the press." This unconstitutional, illegitimate, unlawful, prehistoric, obscene, absurd, Keystone Kommittee had been set up to "recommend advisable, appropriate, effective, and constitutional (??) means to deal effectively with such traffic in obscenity and pornography." To this we say, fuck off, and fuck censorship.*
>
> *This Keystone Kommittee, engaged in a blatant McCarthyesque witch hunt, holding inquisitional "hearings" around the country, is the vanguard of the Brain Police, Mind Monitors, Thought Thugs, {and} Honky Heaven Whores grasping to make thought criminals out of millions of innocent citizens. You ARE 1984, with all that that implies. This phony Kommittee begins with the pornography and obscenity existing in the eyes of the bullshit beholders and ends with total state control of the mind of every man, woman, child, hunchback and midget. What pretentious arrogance to presume, what colossal nerve to attempt to impose your standards on the public, while you jack off in the censorship room. Fuck off, and fuck censorship!*
>
> *Either we have freedom of the press . . . or we don't have freedom of the press.*
>
> *The Underground Press Syndicate has repeatedly encountered your brand of political repression in the thin but transparent guise of obscenity, despite the obvious fact that the primary content of Underground Press Syndicate papers is political and social writing. This becomes even more obvious when underground papers are compared to the millions of tons of specifically salacious and prurient four-color crotch shot magazines which are readily available in the same cities where underground papers are repeatedly busted for "pornography." We know where that's at, and we know where you're coming from. Besides, arousing prurient interest in America IS a socially redeeming value. So fuck off, and fuck censorship.*
>
> *A study of daily newspapers found that 70 percent of the readership did not believe the papers they read. They thought they were lying. In the past 20 years, over 400 establishment dailies have died, while in the past four years, the UPS has gone from nothing to over 6 million readers. A journalism professor in California made a study of his class of 45 students, and found that 42 read the local underground paper. Only 1 read the establishment propaganda organ.*

The head of the American Association of Advertising Agencies warns the straight papers to "get in touch" or they will lose their advertising revenue to the underground press. But {they} can't "get in touch," because they are lackeys of a power structure whose only touch is a Midas touch, which tries to turn war into money, natural resources into money, even whole segments of our population into money.

The Underground Press Syndicate is fighting this, and winning, and you are terrified because we are robbing the power structure of its replacements. You are a dying breed, because young people love the underground press, live it, and know that it speaks the truth. But you walking antiques are constantly trying to stamp out our freedom of the press—uptight Smokey the Bears of the totalitarian forest, rushing around with shotguns and shovels, trying to quench the fires of freedom. But the fire is out of control, and we will not be brought down. America's Children for Breakfast program—youth genocide—is not working. To it we say, fuck off, and fuck censorship.

You politically self-ordained demi-gods have decided to jam two copies of the Reader's Digest into every shithole in America, with your dried-up, perverted, ugly, bland, middle-aged, hypocritic {sic}, jack-off, psychopathic, totalitarian, un sexed, dictatorial, Bank of America, warped, hyena, rancid, muck of your own decaying existence you make me puke green monkey shit.

In opposition to this, our program is liberation—total freedom—and we are totally committed to carrying out this program. A dictatorial structure cannot withstand the absolute power of a media that can turn out half a million people at Woodstock or a million people to sit on Nixon's back porch until the war ends. And we will no more passively accept the suppression of that voice than we will of our bodies.

We are the solution to America's problems. We are revolution, these goddamned papers are our lives, and nobody shall take our lives away with your goddamned laws. We are tomorrow, not you. We are the working model of tomorrow's paleocybernetic culture, soul, life, manifesting love, force, anarchy, euphoria, positive, sensual, communal, abandoned, united, brotherhood, universal, organismic, orgasmic, harmonious, flowing new consciousness media on paper, coming from our lives in the streets. So fuck off, and fuck censorship!

We are in charge of our own lives, and we bear allegiance only to our own Free Nation. We hold your ancient myths of sterile blue laws in utter, scum bag contempt for jamming up the river of human progress, trying to hold back, push back, compartmentalize, ram down our throat your death trip of thought control, the last perversion of Babylon. And the straight media is equally responsible, for they bear the guilt of the crime of silence, the crime of inaction *as they watch and cheer while their media brothers in the underground press go down the drain of lost freedom of the press. They mouth empty words and they are total hypocrites.*

There can be no free country without a free press, and if there is no free country, then there will be no country. There is no difference and no separation between what is happening to the underground press and what is happening to the Black Panthers or any other group which opposes America's last crazed epilepsy. The Underground Press Syndicate has been harrassed {sic} unrelentingly since it was founded in 1966, yet it has grown from just 5 papers and less than 50,000 circulation to over 200 papers and circulation over 6 million. For every paper destroyed by a bust, 10 more have taken its place, and if the message of that is not clear, then you must surely have to learn it by experience.

Congressman Joe Pool, late HUAC chairman, said "The plan of this Underground Press Syndicate is to take advantage of that part of the First Amendment which protects newspapers and gives them freedom of the press." Bob Dylan says, "Without freedom of speech I might be in the swamp." I say, "Write On!"

I do not agree with a word you say, and I will defend to my death my right to say it.

According to a press report, the Commission "sat dumbfounded on a semi-circular rostrum" while Forcade launched his verbal assault. When he was finished, Commissioner Otto N. Larson, a sociology professor at the University of Washington, was incredulous.

"Would you mind explaining to me how we have engaged in 'McCarthyesque witch hunts and inquisitional hearings'?" he asked?

"I think I have material in my box to explain that," Forcade answered, gesturing to large cardboard box in front of him. Then he reached into the box, pulled out a whipped-cream pie, and dumped it on Larson's head.[136]

6

Questioning Who Decides

Participatory Democracy in the Underground Press

SOMETIME IN EARLY 1969, WHILE living in an eleven-room farmhouse in western Massachusetts, Marshall Bloom began writing what appears to be the beginning of a memoir describing his experiences with Liberation News Service. He never finished, and it was never published. In fact, the original manuscript—an eight-page typewritten fragment, located in the Archives and Special Collections Library at Bloom's alma mater, Amherst College— has all the hallmarks of a first draft: false starts are scribbled out by hand, and at several points, Bloom typed alternative turns of phrase over his original prose, which alternates between tones of nostalgia and beleaguered resentment. Had the essay ever been printed, its title, "LIBERATION NEWS SERVICE IS DEAD. LONG LIVE LIBERATION NEWS SERVICE," might have provoked a frisson of recognition in certain circles; it was lifted from a line in an anonymous letter that began circulating throughout the underground press in October 1968 in which Bloom was mercilessly ridiculed.[1] Sadly, Bloom never lived to discover that the letter was actually a forgery, written by the FBI in an attempt to exacerbate tensions within LNS, the underground press, and the New Left.[2]

"I wish I could tell you everything that flashes in my mind when I think about LNS and my life for the past year and a half," Bloom begins. "Much more than it should have been—perhaps that was the problem—LNS and my life were all mixed together."

Nevertheless, Bloom vows to describe his involvement with LNS "in straight [and] coherent order," adding that his narrative may prove "even too embarrassingly candid." His earliest memory connected to LNS, he says, dates back to the blustery afternoon in April 1967 when he stepped off an airplane from London to meet Raymond Mungo at Boston's Logan Airport. At the time, Bloom was preparing to move to Washington, DC, where he would take the helm of the United States Student Press Association, while Mungo, the controversial editor of the *BU News*, had just won a fellowship to begin graduate study at Harvard. The two were already aware of one another's reputations, but this was the first time they met face to face, and for Bloom, it was pure kismet. Within minutes, he "adjusted to this big, brave editorial voice coming from a teeny, short fellow with glasses." Later that evening, Bloom delivered a sparsely attended lecture at Boston University, after which he and Mungo repaired to a tumbledown bar for beers and conversation, where Bloom surprised Mungo. First, he "asked him" to join USSPA, then he "urged him" to accept the offer, and then he practically insisted that Mungo commit to taking the position on the spot. Wrote Bloom: "I didn't then pause on the inherent unfairness [of the fact that] I had my life planned for the next year and was merely asking him to join it; that for him it meant a new plan for the year." Nevertheless, Bloom somehow persuaded Mungo to scratch his graduate plans in order to become USSPA's international news editor.

"Perhaps here is the beginning of my downfall," Bloom reflects, feeling anxious, or perhaps guilty, about having pressured Mungo to upend his plans. Bloom also admits, however, that he was heavily dependent upon Mungo's friendship and assistance. A few months later, when Mungo arrived at the huge brownstone they rented together in Washington, DC, Bloom greeted him "with joy and relief."

Later that night, Mungo returned from a nearby laundromat, disturbed at having seen an elderly homeless woman sleeping uneasily in a chair. "What shall we do?" he asked. Bloom answered immediately: "Run and get her and ask her to sleep here, of course." Moments later, in came "a bedraggled, wet, head-shaking old woman of the streets whose stories came tumbling forth as we offered her a cup of tea in Raymond's room."[3] The next evening, a nervous teenaged runaway showed up at their door, looking for Mungo. Uncertain whether she'd be allowed to stay, she had left her luggage at a nearby hotel. She needn't have worried: that night, she too was welcomed into their "wretched hippy hovel." And so within just two days, without any planning or discussion, they began transforming their home and workplace into a chaotic urban commune. Within months the house became overcrowded. Phones rang at all hours of the day and night, while stereos blasted everything from Bob Dylan and the Rolling Stones to Monteverdi, Bach, and *Walt Disney's Greatest Hits*. Local police responded by stationing a cruiser outside the house.[4]

"I say all of this," Bloom writes, "because in a way it's your business, if you are to know what to think about LNS."[5] That is, Bloom wanted to convey that LNS was begun with an improvisational and ad hoc energy that sometimes seemed willfully irrational. These first few pages of Bloom's memoir also betray his heavy personal investment in the news service, as well as his headlong, occasionally domineering leadership style.

Certainly Bloom was not unique in becoming deeply immersed in his media activism. Others involved with the underground press in the late 1960s worked feverishly, with an exalted sense of mission and purpose, approaching radical journalism as if it were a way of life. But the top-down approach that Bloom took in running LNS contrasted sharply with the egalitarian and anti-elitist sentiments that were elsewhere so pronounced in the Movement. As LNS became an established force, many of those who worked for the news service became increasingly uncomfortable with how it was run. Although Bloom always had a small coterie of followers who were impressed by his vision and energy, others found him manipulative, unreliable, and impulsive. More importantly, the majority of LNS's staff took it as an article of faith that the New Left's organizations should be scrupulously democratic. When Bloom and several others refused to relinquish control of LNS in the summer of 1968, the organization became embroiled in a bitter power struggle that reverberated across the Movement.

Surprisingly, though, the rift in LNS has not received much attention from scholars, and where it has been discussed, it has generally been mischaracterized as a dispute along cultural and political lines, with Bloom and his wild hippie followers clashing with a larger group of dour Marxists over their contrasting values and lifestyles.[6] In fact, this is only part of the story. The battle for control over the news service was also a contest between two different understandings of what was meant by "participatory democracy." By reexamining the conflagration within LNS—and by framing the matter within its broader historical context—we can do more than just correct the distortions in previous accounts. We can also better understand just how thoroughly the New Left's print culture became imbued with democratic values.

Under Bloom's leadership, LNS claimed to meet the Movement's democratic litmus test by distributing virtually any left-wing or youth-oriented articles that came over the transom, regardless of their ideological content or quality. Here the group was following a precedent established by SDS, in effect making it their editorial policy *not to edit*. However, another faction in LNS rejected the idea that the group was behaving democratically. In their understanding—which also harkened back to SDS—it was essential that LNS should be run as some kind of a collective, in which large groups made decisions, staff positions rotated, and resources were pooled together. Their assumption was that the New Left's media should do more than disseminate alternative viewpoints (as important as this was). It was also meant to draw people into its fold, build a democracy of participation on the Left, and show-case the Movement's superior, egalitarian values. According to one radical newsman, underground papers doubled as "laboratories" in the late 1960s, testing the New Left's theories about collective organization.[7] "If [a] paper is run democratically," said another, "it becomes a community and involves people in ways [that] few other areas of society would allow."[8]

AMONG THOSE WHO CALLED FOR decentralized leadership within LNS was Allen Young, who left a promising job at the *Washington Post* to join the rad-ical news service in December 1967, when he was twenty-six years old. By then, Young already had a long history of involvement in left-wing causes. He'd grown up on a chicken farm in the Catskill Mountains, and both of his parents remained loyal members of the Communist Party throughout most of the 1950s. In his childhood he was proud of his parents' support for the labor and civil rights struggles, and he greatly enjoyed the special camarade-rie he found with other red-diaper babies. Once when he was very young, he and a friend hid behind a hedge of bushes and squirted random passersby with water pistols. "But when a black woman walked by, we didn't squirt, instinctively protecting her. Later, we had a long discussion about what was the right thing to do: show our belief in equality by squirting the black woman the same way we squirted white people, or refrain from squirting because we understood the unfairness of racism."[9]

Eventually, though, Young concluded that he had been "essentially indoc-trinated into left-wing dogma" during his childhood. After arriving at Columbia University in 1958, he took a course with C. Wright Mills, expanded his circle of friends, and opened himself up to a wider range of left-wing viewpoints. Meanwhile, he was much impressed with the energy and promise of the Cuban Revolution, and in the middle of his undergraduate career he began learning Spanish in preparation for a career as a foreign cor-respondent in Latin America. "There was no magic moment that turned me into a New Leftist," he later remarked. It "was a gradual process that led me to change my views. I like to say that I began to think for myself."[10]

Like Bloom and Mungo, Young had dabbled in journalism while in high school, and by his senior year he became editor-in-chief of his college newspaper, the *Columbia Daily Spectator*, where he was "able to mix journalism and activism for the first time" primarily by supporting a left-wing campus organization called ACTION. (One of the group's notable protests was against a civil defense test in 1961, during which New Yorkers were legally required to "take cover" at the sound of air raid sirens. Instead, as the sirens' warbling tones blared across Columbia's campus, hundreds of students flooded into Low Memorial Plaza.) Upon finishing his undergraduate degree, he studied for a year at Stanford, worked briefly as a reporter for a small newspaper in Middletown, New York, and then matriculated into Columbia University's prestigious Graduate School of Journalism. Ironically, although Young understood the importance of writing professional, balanced news stories, through his training he began perceiving all of the ways that less principled reporters could get away with distorting the news to make it fit their viewpoints.[11]

From 1964 to 1967, Young lived in Brazil and Chile under fellowships from the Fulbright Program and the Inter-American Press Association, during which time he freelanced for major American newspapers, including the *Christian Science Monitor* and the *New York Times*. Meanwhile, he kept tabs on the developing New Left by subscribing to SDS's newsletter, *New Left Notes*, and through his steady correspondence with friends, including history graduate student Eric Foner. In January 1967, a correspondent on the West Coast wrote to say, "I think that you will find the US to have changed a great deal since you were last here—that is, the youth have begun to change a great deal."[12] The following month, another letter writer told him: "America is on the verge of a politico-cultural revolution."[13] Still, Young was unprepared for the madcap scene he discovered when he visited San Francisco's Haight-Ashbury district during the famous "Summer of Love." Like many hippies, Young enjoyed smoking marijuana, and he was strenuously opposed to the Vietnam War, but he was scarcely interested in "dropping out." To the contrary, he still dreamed of a high-powered career at a major American newspaper. When he interviewed at the *Washington Post* with managing editor Benjamin Bradlee (later famous for overseeing Bob Woodward and Carl Bernstein's Watergate coverage), he was careful to keep his left-wing political beliefs under wraps, save for one slip: he said he was interested in the civil rights movement.

As Young recalls, Bradlee "responded sharply with a question: 'You aren't one of those activists, are you?' I lied, saying that of course I wasn't, and got the job."[14]

Though thrilled to be launching his career at the *Post*, where he was assigned the nighttime police beat, Young felt conflicted in several important ways.

First, he resented the fact that he was trained "to pay serious attention to a murder if the victim was white, and not to worry too much about it if the victim is black." And while Young regarded the *Post* as a rather conservative paper, he was surprised to learn that the cops he worked with thought it was scandalously left-wing. Jokingly, they called it the "*L Street Pravda*." Another complication was that Young was secretly gay at the time, and as a result he regretted having to spend so much time in the newsroom and the police precinct; the first struck him as a "boys club," and the latter was a "highly macho environment." But probably his biggest frustration lay in the fact that as a working journalist, he was prohibited from taking an active role in the antiwar activity that was happening right before his eyes. One night Young accompanied Foner and several friends to a screening of *The Battle of Algiers*, Gillo Pontecorvo's masterful portrayal of the Franco-Algerian conflict. "I was very moved by that film," Young recalled. "Maybe it was a little romantic on my part, since I wasn't in any danger the way [Ali la Pointe] was in that movie, but the commitment of the young Algerian revolutionaries struck me kind of deeply, and I thought 'this is something I care about, my opposition to the Vietnam War, and here I am at the *Washington Post* doing the night police beat.'"

Around the same time, Young came to know several local underground press writers at the *Washington Free Press* and LNS. Though Bloom and Mungo struck him as "committed and intelligent," right away he noticed that they were both "more involved with the counterculture than [he] was."[15] Another time, he put the matter more sharply: the time he spent with the duo, he proclaimed, was "far too chaotic for my way of thinking."[16] Nevertheless, given all the dissonance Young was experiencing as a radical gay journalist at the *Washington Post*, LNS struck him as the better bet. The following month, he made what was "probably the biggest single decision of [his] life," and torpedoed his professional journalism career by resigning his position at the *Post* and migrating to LNS's new headquarters—a shabby, three-story office building at 3 Thomas Circle, which they shared with several other movement groups, nicknaming it the "Liberated Zone."[17]

AROUND THIS TIME, LNS and the underground press began receiving attention from both the mainstream media and from municipal and federal authorities.[18] After the *New York Times* ran an article on the Liberated Zone, Rep. John R. Rarick, of Louisiana, entered the story into the *Congressional Record*. "Mr. Speaker," he proclaimed "the American Cong now blatantly announce revolutionary headquarters in our Nation's Capital."[19] In response, LNS promptly ordered two thousand black-and-orange lapel buttons that read: "I AM THE AMERICAN CONG."[20]

It was in some ways an inapt metaphor, since Bloom and Mungo had always insisted that LNS would never become a mouthpiece for anyone— not for SDS, the hippies, the Black Panthers, and certainly not for the Vietcong.[21] In fact, the group prided itself in its willingness to distribute a broad spectrum of radical viewpoints. "We'd print any kind of crazy shit that anybody sent us," Mungo remembered.[22] Wasserman said much the same. "Our idea of editorial selection was, if you were committed enough to type an article and put it in the mail, and we knew who you were, that should be good enough. . . . We believed in participatory democracy."[23] Elsewhere, he elaborated: "We had unlimited copy space and for me at least the one thing that made the news service valuable was our freedom to print anything that happened to fall into our hands. We had a lot of misses, but then, who were we to judge?"[24] LNS also welcomed feedback from underground newspapers. In a December 1967 letter, Mungo told subscribers, "We didn't envision LNS as entirely 'our thing,' a news service whose ideas and inspirations come entirely from us, [rather] we think it will operate best when it reflects the consciousness of many people around the country."[25]

Although LNS won acclaim for its excellent coverage of the Battle of the Pentagon and the Columbia rebellion, its news packets were more typically filled with a wide assortment of dispatches from across the country. Sometimes printed on colored paper, articles of purely regional interest ran alongside analyses of movement-wide trends, while serious essays intermingled with whimsical pieces. Once, as a prank, Mungo and LNSer Marc Sommer falsely reported that in the redneck town of St. Rouet, Arkansas, the editor of an underground newspaper called *Fuckoff* had been tarred and feathered by a gang of angry yokels. In fact, no such editor, paper, or town even existed.[26] An article describing Secretary of State Dean Rusk's evasive testimony before the Senate Foreign Relations Committee in March 1968 began this way: "Dean Rusk sang and danced for some ten hours in the last two days. Some of his most popular routines were 'The Common Danger to Us All,' 'The Yellow-Peril Polka,' . . . and that old, old standby of the Johnson Administration, 'Tell Me Lies.'"[27]

Meanwhile, life and work in the Liberated Zone carried on at a dizzying pace. Although it was located just six blocks from the White House, the building served as the nerve center of the local New Left. Plumes of marijuana smoke drifted out of the windows, psychedelic and political posters lined the walls, the teletype machine spat out "infernal clatter" at all hours, mail poured in from everywhere, and, as Mungo later described, "everything was happening too fast." Staffers worked furiously "trying to keep up with the insurrection in colleges, ghettoes, and hip communities all at the same time," and soon LNS began producing three hefty mailings per week.[28] Despite LNS being hugely influential in the world of the underground press, its office remained disordered. Even Mungo regarded his position at LNS as "a big comedown" from his previous perch at the *BU News*, which, despite its radicalism, was still a serious, professional-looking newspaper. "But all of a sudden," he remembered, he was "reduced to living like a gypsy in this crappy commune turning out this *crappiest* of crappy looking mimeographed flyers."[29] Then again, it could also seem thrilling to dance at the counterculture's Dionysian edge, taking drugs and running on karma, comedy, and chaos. "While I was typing rock-and-roll lyrics in the margins of the mailings," Wasserman wrote, "Marshall was holding the operation together with mirrors in a way that would put Jay Gould to shame. He got money from nowhere, sent it somewhere else, and two days later equipment would arrive. Magic!!"[30] "A lot of what was done at the news service was done on acid, not just marijuana," he added. "You know, Marshall used to walk around the office naked."[31]

Others doubted whether LNS could continue functioning amid such chaos. When Bloom asked his friend John Diamante to join LNS, Diamante was forthright about his reservations. Exhausted and in debt from having recently worked "full-tilt" as a reporter for the *Southern Courier*, he said he'd become cautious about "where [his] energy goes," and he basically told Bloom that he didn't think LNS was up to the task it set for itself. If the news service was truly going to rival mainstream media organizations, he said, it would need to create self-sustaining projects, build hundreds of contacts across the country, and recruit a reliable, top-notch staff; this, in turn, would require legal backing, business savvy, "thousands of form letters and individually crafted notes," and countless hours of steadfast work. "To return to an old theme," Diamante wrote, "this is not to be accomplished by people flying up and down the stairs, losing telephone numbers, misplacing their cool, or becoming myopic about where people(s) are headed."[32]

Others shared similar concerns. One was Sheila Ryan, a reporter for the *Washington Free Press* who began writing pieces for LNS in early 1968 after serving a harrowing six-month jail sentence for having sat in at the White House.[33] Although hardly a cookie-cutter conformist, by the wild standards set by Bloom and Mungo, Ryan may have seemed culturally conservative. She had attended Catholic University, where she'd only rarely smoked marijuana ("because we didn't have that much time to"), and she always knew that eventually she wanted to become a wife and a mother. Meanwhile, having steeped herself in the civil rights movement, Ryan was impressed with that struggle's emphasis on democratic participation and consensus building. Her idea of a good leader, she said, was one "who would facilitate the democratic process and really allow people to come together and refine their ideas, and help the best ideas . . . emerge."[34] By contrast, she perceived an altogether different approach at LNS, whereby people clustered sycophantically around Bloom. Too often, the group's accomplishments could be traced to a single individual's inspiration, rather than the whole group's collective effort.

Young was also increasingly frustrated with LNS. Although happy to have freed himself from the strictures that the *Post* imposed on his politics and lifestyle, he was no cultural anarchist. Moreover, after abandoning such a promising professional career in order to devote himself to the New Left, he was sometimes annoyed by Bloom and Mungo's irresponsibility. By way of example, he recalls that shortly after Martin Luther King Jr. was assassinated, Bloom, Mungo, and several others foolishly ventured into downtown Washington, DC, in a black Cadillac hearse that Bloom had leased—this in spite of the fact that the whole group was stoned and in possession of marijuana, and authorities had just imposed a citywide curfew in an effort to quell the large-scale rioting that had recently occurred. After police stopped the hearse at a routine checkpoint, the entire group was arrested for violating the curfew, and Mungo and another LNSer, Marty Jezer, were charged with narcotics possession.[35] Young laments that as Mungo narrates the story in *Famous Long Ago*, the whole escapade sounds "groovy . . . very exciting and lots of fun." But that very night, he said, "we were supposed to get a packet out! And I remember being left alone in the office to do all the grunt-work."[36]

It was in this context that some began questioning Bloom's leadership and holding discussions about the possibility of moving LNS's headquarters from Washington, DC, to New York City. Though Bloom had been instrumental in getting LNS off the ground, some claimed that by early 1968 it was Young who was "greatly responsible for keeping LNS together."[37] Others observed that during the Columbia rebellion, LNS had effectively been headquartered in New York anyhow. In fact, as LNS's biggest story of the year was unfolding in Morningside Heights, Bloom and Mungo were in the midst of a month-long sojourn across the country. Though they had claimed the trip was necessary in order to build connections with various underground newspapers, not everyone agreed that that was the best use of their energies, and some suspected that they had something else on their agenda: a vacation. Certainly Mungo was feeling burned out. Just before he left, he dashed a note to John Wilcock, bemoaning the situation in DC ("Riots are bloody serious, man") and proclaiming, "I may soon leave D.C. and LNS."[38] True enough, later that spring, he and LNS poetry editor Verandah Porche began making plans to start a commune in rural Vermont.

Meanwhile, Mungo and Young began having conversations about Bloom's recent behavior with Cavalletto, who was managing the New York office. "What Ray and Allen told me," Cavalletto remembered, "was that Marshall—who was sort of the administrator, the day-to-day guy—sort of worked by inspiration. He was a charismatic kind of guy but he was very disorganized, and I think he had mood swings, and so he'd get depressed."[39] However close Bloom and Mungo were, many years later, Mungo confessed that there were times when he found Bloom "impossible to bear except for short periods of time. . . . He brooked no opposition whatsoever. If you didn't want to do what Marshall wanted to do, there was no room for compromise."[40]

One fight Bloom did lose, though, was over whether or not LNS should relocate to New York. Though he badly wanted to stay in DC, he was almost entirely without support. Young, Cavalletto, and others successfully argued that by moving to Manhattan, LNS would be situating itself within a hub of left-wing activity, where they could tap into a wealth of resources—more people, more energy, and more philanthropists to donate badly needed funds. As an added enticement, Cavalletto had managed to find a 1,700-square-foot office at 160 Claremont Avenue. Formerly a Chinese restaurant, the space was horribly rundown, but it was cheap—only $200 per month—and when it was finally decided that LNS should move there, he personally signed the lease, and, with the help of Colin Connery, a carpenter who had been involved with Student Communications Network, led a major effort to refurbish the place. Over the course of about a month, dozens of volunteers laid a cement floor, installed wiring, and built new walls, which they splashed with vivid chartreuse and fuchsia paints. "Everybody dug into their pockets" to finance the renovations, Cavalletto remembered.[41]

On the eve of the move, Young dashed off an optimistic note to Bloom. "I really think we can create a good team of people in NY," he said. Young also hinted that with the transition, however, Bloom should prepare for his stewardship over LNS to begin to wane. "I have given some thought to a natural division of labor, since you have been sort of a 'wheel' in LNS-WASH . . . and George has been sort of a wheel at LNS-NY," he remarked. "Hopefully we can overcome our problems of hierarchy and mistrust through division of labor and mutual confidence." Although Young closed his letter by saying, "I do not and did not hold any ill will toward you personally," not everyone in LNS was so convinced of this.[42] Wasserman later speculated that the move to New York was a sort of set-up. "The heavies were waiting for us," he said. "Allen Young was in charge of the takeover."[43]

THE MOVE TO MANHATTAN only exacerbated tensions within LNS. Just a day or two before the New York staff was scheduled to drive to DC to pick up the equipment, Bloom phoned Cavalletto and tried to call the whole thing off; LNS still owed $2,150 on its offset press, he said, and the woman from whom they had bought it would not let it leave town until it was fully paid for. Cavalletto was livid: "I've spent a month, a whole crew of us, twelve, fifteen people fixing up the office," he recalled. "I said 'Marshall, how come you didn't tell me before, what the hell?'"[44] But if anything, Bloom's attempt to stall the move only hardened Cavalletto's determination to see it through, and he quickly managed to raise the necessary money, thanks in part to a loan from his mother. Then, on the drive to New York, Mungo allegedly launched into a lengthy tirade against Bloom, describing him as "compulsively authoritarian" and even suggesting that it might be desirable for him to leave the organization.[45] According to Ryan, Mungo's characterization of Bloom was "scandalously negative."[46]

In *Famous Long Ago*, Mungo never admits to betraying Bloom in this way; in fact, he implies that the idea never could have occurred to him. Forcing Bloom out of LNS, he said, would have been "like kicking Mickey Mantle off the Yankees."[47] Bloom later wrote an accusatory letter to Mungo, however, in which he proclaimed, "I can quite accept that there was a period in which you were absolutely convinced that I could get along with no-one and for the survival of LNS should leave."[48] Probably his hunch was correct. Many years later, Mungo wistfully remarked that although Bloom "was an intensely brilliant genius and a wonderful guy" who he "really loved," he was also "so incredibly mentally ill. And if you know anything about psychotics, they're hard to be around. They wear you out, basically."[49] As Mungo and Porche began solidifying their plans to relocate to Vermont, they reached a decision: Bloom would not be invited to join them.

Once LNS became ensconced in New York, however, Mungo rose to Bloom's defense, no doubt because he was turned off by the ugliness of the confrontation that developed between what he called "the Vulgar Marxists (all of the New York people except Allen Young) and the Virtuous Caucus (all of the Washington people except Steve Diamond)."[50] By his account, the Marxists began trying to purge Bloom from LNS in an "unfair, inhumane, and ruthless" manner. To Bloom's face, he says, people "snapped" and "shouted" at him; behind his back, they raised pernicious questions suggesting he was a "thief," a "sex pervert," and a "compulsive liar." Underlying it all, he alleges, was an ideological dispute. The Marxists craved control of LNS "because they wanted to do a news service that was substantially different from the one Marshall had created, a news service which would be more serious, more militant, more straight, edited and managed by a collective and not an individual."[51] Wasserman said something similar: "They were the politicos (our name for them), we the insufficiently militants (theirs for us)."

> Debate, which carried on for about two weeks and often went on for as long as eight hours straight, ran through Cadres, Lenin, Marcuse, Cuba, North Vietnam, Algeria, democratic centrism, Russia, participatory democracy, Haiti, the Panthers, our parents, bourgeois democracy, Mr. LSD, LBJ, the sanitation department, John Stuart Mill, Bugs Bunny, and the people's struggle to off Porky Pig. The walls shook with college rhetoric.[52]

The Vulgar Marxists denied, however, that the feud had much to do with politics, or that they held any great animus toward the counterculture. To the contrary, they claimed that "personal liberation" was an "integral part of the revolutionary process in twentieth-century America" and that LNS should promote the Movement's cultural politics through "poetry, graphics, photography and joy in media."[53] According to Thorne Dreyer, a few of the Vulgar Marxists "probably did just as many psychedelic drugs" as the Virtuous Caucus, and almost everyone in LNS was heavily into rock and roll.[54] Ryan added that many of the Vulgar Marxists lived and ate together and fostered a "very vibrant sense of community, interdependence, and mutual aid."[55] Their goal was not to turn LNS into a sectarian group that would push some hard or narrow ideological line, but rather to rescue the ailing news service, improve its quality, and transform the staff into a smoothly running collective. "One of the principles I had early on," Cavalletto said, "was that the people who did the work should make the decisions."[56] Young echoed this sentiment, adding, "Some of the people that were in Ray and Marshall's court, quite frankly, didn't really do a lot."[57] According to Ryan, the attempt to democratize LNS was both ideological and practical. By mid-1968, LNS had obviously grown into a major operation, requiring the sustained effort of at least a dozen full-time workers. "And the question," she said, "was how do you get a lot of people to work really hard on something for no material reward?"[58] To the Vulgar Marxists—some of whom also belonged to SDS—the answer seemed obvious: LNS's own staff should help make the decisions that affected their workplace lives.

Shortly after the move to New York, the newly combined LNS staff gathered for two exasperating all-night meetings. By then, Cavalletto was already running LNS's financial operations, but the Bloom faction controlled the New Media Project's board of directors. The Marxists were a larger group, but many among them were fresh arrivals to LNS, whereas the Caucus was more experienced and (they claimed) better connected through bonds of loyalty and friendship.[59] The first night, Young explained that he found Bloom impossible to work with and said that he wished he would leave. He stopped short, however, of asking the entire staff to vote on whether or not Bloom should formally be made to resign, since they had not yet learned, through their own, wearying experience, just how difficult he could be. After these meetings, Young left New York for a two-month trip overseas, where he visited London and the Soviet Union and reported on the World Youth Festival in Sofia, Bulgaria. While he was away, he dashed off a note to Cavalletto, apologizing for having to leave at such a stressful moment, and underscoring his hope that LNS could flourish as a harmonious and smoothly functioning community—albeit one that might not include Bloom. Young wrote, "LNS is increasingly relevant and important. . . . We need to create among ourselves good political consciousness, as well as bonds of trust and love. I am very excited about the possibility of building such bonds and doing imaginative radical work. . . . Let this letter be another reaffirmation of solidarity, and cooperation, regardless of the 'Bloom Problem.'"[60]

As July turned to August, the Movement braced itself for the bloody spectacle that many predicted would erupt at the Democratic National Convention in Chicago. Meanwhile, in New York City, the weather was hot and sticky, and tensions in New York's hip community were rising, in part because of the growing schism between the Virtuous Caucus and the Vulgar Marxists.[61] Both factions "met in secret, night after night," Mungo wrote, "and both devised lurid fantasies against the other, and both found the members of the other group to be base fellows. In short, our few weeks in New York virtually halted all the ongoing research and news gathering of the organization, and whipped one and all into a frenzy of personal fury and protective loyalty."[62] Wasserman recalls one tense, crowded, late-night meeting in LNS's basement office, when Mungo stood up to deliver a speech:

"Now I've worked with Marshall a year, and there are times when it's been really rough. But that Bloom, you know, he's got magic. It comes from somewhere, and that's what LNS is, magic."

"Booooom," Wasserman exclaimed. "They hit the ceiling. Sheila [Ryan] screamed that they had magic too, dammit."[63]

There was a moment in early August, however, when it seemed as if the two warring factions might have arrived at the beginnings of a rapprochement. In an unexpected turnaround, Bloom and several others announced that they would agree to restructure LNS's board of directors so that it would include all of the news service's full-time workers. Had they followed through, this would have effectively turned control of LNS over to the Marxists, who for a time seemed pleased to have "made some progress in making LNS more democratic and better able to function."[64] But the Virtuous Caucus wasn't acting in good faith. Around this same time, at one of the their secret meetings, Bloom put forth a daring proposal: "I think we should just take the whole news service out from under them," he said, "and move it up to a farm in the country, maybe somewhere in Western Massachusetts."[65]

IN CERTAIN RESPECTS, the tensions that plagued LNS in 1968 resembled those that had dogged SDS a few years earlier. As even the Vulgar Marxists conceded, everyone initially understood that when LNS was founded, it was primarily Bloom and Mungo's operation. They were the ones with the moxie to establish the news service at a time when few thought it would succeed, and whether through hard work, fortuitous timing, or "magic," they quickly turned it into a pillar in the underground press, guiding and inspiring countless radical papers across the country and greatly amplifying the power of the underground press. Bloom, especially, had worked to establish a culture within LNS that was nearly as frenetic as his own personality ("LNS and my life were all mixed together"). Founded by a small clique of friends, the news service attracted the participation of a wider range of writers, editors, and photographers who—however talented and enthusiastic—didn't always share the same temperaments and ideologies of its founders. The personality clash between Young and BlooMungo is a case in point. "The difference between Allen and me struck me in a phrase," Mungo later wrote. "[He] sees the revolution as 'the people' all working together, I see it as 'the people' all *not* working together."[66]

When they weren't at each other's throats, both sides in the LNS dispute must have recognized that they were enmeshed in a difficult situation.

The comparison to SDS, however, can only be extended so far. A few years earlier, the "old guard" in SDS quickly relinquished the reins to its newer members. True, some of them grumbled that the tenderfoots who surged into their organization had unsettled their "we-happy-few mystique," but by then the old guarders had already committed themselves to egalitarianism.[67] Having spent years soliciting broader membership participation, they could hardly deny newcomers a say about how SDS should be run. By contrast, Bloom and Mungo were unconvincing as participatory democrats. Neither seems to have studied the New Left's early theorists, nor did they have firsthand involvement with SDS's political culture.[68] Instead, they both became educated and politicized in their college newsrooms, where they had labored to win the high prestige editorships of their campus papers.

Nevertheless, as they began drumming up enthusiasm for LNS in 1967, Bloom and Mungo offered subscribing newspapers some say in determining how the news service should function. The depth of their sincerity, though, is hard to gauge. Given their early accomplishments and famously refulgent personalities, they may have been sensitive to charges of elitism. In a December 1967 letter to subscribers, Mungo seemed at pains to persuade his readers that, far from being remote or cliquish, LNS was actually an open and accessible organization, determined to build connections between the nation's far-flung media activists.

> Those of you who were at the October 20 LNS-UPS meeting in Washington will remember how difficult it seemed to gather a national cooperative in those few hours, but the need for our union and the circumstances to achieve it are much greater now. . . . So what we need is you—your consciousness, your ideals and your information on what has happened, what you are doing, and what will follow. If we have your influence on our minds, we will have your influence on the minds of our brother editors, and on the joint LNS-UPS readership of something like four million. . . . In the next few weeks . . . we will be proposing gentle gatherings of like souls around the country to discuss how we can help each other, strengthen our impact, [and] alter the future of this long, too long, America. . . . So write, telephone, concentrate, inform, advise, criticize, suggest, love, meet, coalesce everywhere you can . . . and struggle.[69]

Meanwhile, under Bloom's influence, LNS continually prided itself in its ideological diversity and its eagerness to showcase a broad spectrum of left-wing viewpoints. In November 1967, an LNS writer boasted that its staff "might be considered a microcosm of the peace-and-liberation movement in the U.S. . . . Our views range from pacifist to insurrectionary, our heads from grassy to austere, our sexual habits from asceticism to insatiability. All have unambiguously rejected the two pounds of fetid owlshit in a pound bag that is contemporary America."[70] To an interviewer, Bloom once explained that although LNS was consistently left-wing, it gave voice to "many views and debates within the movement concerning tactics and goals."[71]

By using only minimal discretion in determining what types of material it would distribute, LNS initially fashioned an editorial policy similar to that of most underground publications. As one radical writer put it, "If you had something to say, if you were doing something you wanted to show the world, you just walked into your local underground paper, and more frequently than not your message was circulated."[72] The statement also applied to countless irregularly published leaflets and fly-by-night operations. In May 1967, SDS activists at Temple University launched a newsletter called *Dialogue* by announcing, "We invite and eagerly accept any and all articles from students at Temple who believe they have something to say."[73] A few months later, at the New School in New York City, students founded *Granpa*, an "open-ended, non-restrictive underground newspaper," in which they boasted, "we ain't got no editor [and] we ain't got no standard editorial policy."[74] Peter Shapiro remembered that San Francisco State University's *Open Process*, for which he wrote film reviews, functioned "like a lot of underground papers" because it imposed "no discipline whatsoever on the writers. You could sit down and say anything that came into your goddamn head, and you could go on for five pages, and every word of it would be printed. Any editor who dared to suggest that it should be changed was [considered] a counter-revolutionary."[75] Meanwhile, a few papers that refused to turn their pages over to the Movement's rank and file, such as Madison, Wisconsin's *Connections*, recognized they were anomalous. As that paper's coeditor, Robert Gabriner, remarked, "Other outlets on the left . . . have seldom rejected material. We have rejected quite a bit and our concept of media permits our staff to scrutinize, tear apart, and reassemble much of what we accept—we are demanding quality."[76]

When it came to the actual operations and management of radical newspapers, however, Bloom and Mungo seemed wary about the potential hazards of *too much* democratic participation. To some degree, their caution may have resulted from their experience working near the *Washington Free Press*, which rented office space two floors below LNS in the Liberated Zone. Although many LNSers had close and friendly relations with that paper's staff, Mungo had a low opinion of their work, describing the paper as "a bi-weekly specializing in lurid colors, wretched typography, and anguished struggles with the politics of communal living."[77] As he recalls, the paper literally had a policy whereby "anyone who walked through the door was allowed a vote" in determining how it should be run. Accordingly, "they would have these endless, torturous meetings that would go on for twelve hours, and anyone—some kid, fifteen years old who had just gotten off a bus from Ohio—by the very next day, he had the same voting power as the editor-in-chief, and other people who had been there a very long time!"[78] Other papers carried their egalitarianism to similar extremes. Eugene Guerrero, one of the founders of the *Great Speckled Bird* in Atlanta, Georgia, recalled that the entire staff sometimes congregated for long and tedious meetings simply "to try to decide whether we'd cut a paragraph out of a story or not."[79] In an effort to steer clear of any similar hang-ups, LNS's founders simply gave Bloom carte blanche to make crucial decisions about the organization's strategy, fundraising, and operations.

No doubt this was Bloom's preference as well. As Mungo described it, Bloom "had always handled LNS as a personal cause."[80] Accordingly, he was sometimes demanding and manipulative. He was "completely capable of interspersing long, heartfelt compliments of your work with totally outrageous demands on your life without changing facial expression," Wasserman remembered.[81] Paul Millman, an LNS writer affiliated with the Vulgar Marxists, added, "Marshall created intense relationships immediately. [He] was brilliant, I think, at sizing up a person and either finding their vulnerable points, or their seductive points."[82] After observing LNS up close in Washington, DC, and then working briefly with Bloom in New York, Sheila Ryan puzzled over why LNS's founding members so willingly ceded control of the news service to Bloom, before finally concluding that they'd embraced a kind of "tribal mentality," in which Bloom was their "chief." When Bloom sometimes boasted, hatched outrageous schemes, or made irrational decisions, Ryan says "that just contributed" to his reputation as a "magical, mystical" personality.[83]

This type of top-down (or "tribal") model wasn't unheard of in the underground press. In the most extreme case, a dangerous acidhead named Mel Lyman ran Boston's *Avatar* that way, before finally turning the paper into a bona fide cult. Meanwhile, a few owner-editors who got involved with the underground press when it was just beginning, such as Art Kunkin of the *Los Angeles Free Press* and Max Scherr of the *Berkeley Barb,* ran their influential newspapers hierarchically.[84] In other instances, papers that experimented with collective approaches later became dominated by whoever was most talented, experienced, or assertive. For example, when Jeff Shero founded the *Rat* in 1968, he had not planned on listing any job titles or descriptions on the masthead. However, according to Millman, Shero later proclaimed that if the paper was to raise money and be successful, it needed some clear and centralized authority. "And Jeff wanted, needed, and thought it correct that *he* be the editor."[85] However, the great majority of those involved with the underground press in the late 1960s believed that it was "logically absurd for a paper that preache[d] egalitarianism to have a boss."[86]

SDS did much to encourage this line of thought. In addition to wanting to democratize the larger society, the organization labored to build a democracy of participation in the Movement. From the very beginning, SDS officers welcomed disputations of their own ideas and proposals, and stressed the importance of group-centered leadership. In 1966, SDS abolished its offices of president and vice president in favor of having three national secretaries.

Assistant National Secretary Steve Halliwell explained the logic behind SDS's antileader mentality to a student who had just drafted an overly bureaucratic charter for a campus chapter of SDS:

> The one thing that frankly distresses me in your Declaration is the emphasis on titles and whatnot. . . . It is very important that maximum flexibility be maintained among the leaders of a chapter so that people coming in do not feel like less than the leaders—otherwise you get people dependent on a few people and they don't develop the self-sustaining energies that radicals must have if they are to challenge the system. Participatory democracy only works if everyone has a sense of equal participation in the system.[87]

Since it was virtually a consensus in SDS that no individual member should have a high public profile or play a dominating role in determining institutional policy, SDS's rank and file tried to rein in charismatic and talented individuals. One writer contributing to *New Left Notes* even called for SDS's leaders to confine themselves to administrative work and to refrain from ever telling others what to do.[88] A popular pastime at SDS meetings and conventions, another writer observed, was "throwing stones at national officers suspected of misuse of power."[89] According to Dick Flacks, SDS's "commitment to participatory democracy created strong resistance to self-perpetuating leadership groups." Even informal leaders, he said, "felt, and were made to feel, that they should limit their attempts to influence the organization's development."[90]

LNS's Vulgar Marxists may have shared a similar distrust of leaders; at the very least, they regarded the Virtuous Caucus's resistance to their efforts to democratize LNS as an affront to the New Left's fundamental values. It would be "ironic," they wrote, "if a news service for a movement devoted to democracy allowed itself to be ruled by a person whose only claim was that he was one of the co-founders and had corporate power in the eyes of the state." If the Bloom faction was allowed to maintain its grip on LNS, they said, the entire Movement would be forced to rely on a news service that "was based on the antithesis of its principles."[91]

It is doubtful, though, that those in the Virtuous Caucus ever thought of themselves as antidemocratic. "No-one votes 'no' to democracy," they once said in a statement. Instead, they stressed that the Marxist's attempt to "democratize" LNS (delegitimizing quotation marks in original) was nothing more than a power grab.[92] As they saw it, LNS was in danger of being hijacked by a group of heavily ideological "Johnny-come-latelies," none of whom shared their own imaginative vision of where LNS should be headed.[93] No

doubt, given their notoriety, personal loyalties, and general cocksureness—
implied by their belief in "magic"—the possibility that they might lose control of LNS provoked considerable indignation. To be overtaken by a group
of humorless politicos would have been the unkindest cut of all. As Diamond
later observed, everyone in the Virtuous Caucus, "but mainly Marshall, had
been basing a whole identity around LNS."[94] And yet, in spite of this, the
news service really was slipping away. In the New Left cosmology, "magic"
was no match for democracy. If the majority of those who worked at LNS
wanted some say in determining how it should be run, they would have the
underground press's sympathies behind them.

BUT TO SWIPE LIBERATION NEWS SERVICE right out from under its own staff
and move the whole operation to a farm? It was a radical and far-fetched
vision, especially considering that this was several years before the heyday of
the back-to-the-land movement, when Americans formed thousands of rural
communes across the country.[95] But like many of the hippies who would soon
begin fleeing to countryside havens, Bloom was animated by dueling feelings
of political powerlessness and grandiosity. Initially, he had considered LNS to
be an "ever growing, left-wing competitor to AP-UPI," but now he wanted
it to become "a whole, new revolutionary idea," resting on the premise that
"revolutionaries [should] live the life they advocate." By this, he simply
meant that LNSers ought to carve out a more enjoyable, bucolic existence,
where their work would be "more personally liberating" than in the stuffy
confines of a basement office.[96] By its "very essence," Bloom argued, LNS
should "signify the New Age, a new way for journalists, artists, and photographers to share, grow, and create together."[97] With modern technology—
telephones, telex machines, decent roads, and assistance from the United
States Postal Service—he was convinced that LNS could flourish even on a
remote farm. However, he also argued, rather apocalyptically, that white radicals would soon need to escape the nation's cities anyhow. As the Movement
intensified, he imagined urban centers becoming sites of guerilla combat,
either between black revolutionaries and the state or between black-power
militants and white vigilantes. In either case, white city dwellers would be
caught in the crosshairs. "But insofar as the cities will be a viable place for
radical action," he wrote, "country support will be a vital thing: a place for
quick refuge and getaway, [and] a place to grow food for the city guerilas."[98]
    On August 10, 1968, Bloom, Mungo, and Wasserman gathered to pass
motions knocking Allen Young off LNS's board of directors, and establishing that LNS's new address—to which the post office would soon be delivering all of their mail—would be a PO box in Montague, Massachusetts.[99]

"Something *had* to be done," Mungo later wrote, "for to leave bad enough alone meant simply that Marshall, Sluggo [Harvey Wasserman], Craig [Spratt], Lazarus [Quan], and all the people who had made LNS what it was would be stripped of any role within the news service and just go looking for a whole new life. . . . The Vulgar Marxists had imported a sizable group of people to help them run the news service, and we couldn't expect our little band to long survive in an atmosphere of hostility and rejection . . . from their own co-workers." The only solution, he claimed, "was to move the news service . . . out of New York, to some place, any place, where we could be ourselves again, and where George Cavalletto didn't own the lease on the building."

This was essentially the logic behind the Great Newspaper Heist—a "burn scheme" that the Virtuous Caucus ran on the Vulgar Marxists in order to relocate LNS to the country. In *Famous Long Ago*, Mungo describes their heist of the news service as "crazy, harebrained, funny, challenging, and heavy—in short in the best tradition of Church Street and Thomas Circle."[100] Relocating the news service was largely Bloom and Mungo's idea, but Steve Diamond played a crucial role in executing the plan. A few months earlier, while having breakfast at a local Chock full o' Nuts, Diamond had noticed a short item in the *New York Times* indicating that the Beatles' film *Magical Mystery Tour*—a critically panned psychedelic "documentary"—had been pulled from its scheduled broadcast on network television.[101] Knowing that New York's rock aficionados would rush to see *any* Beatles movie, no matter how bad, Diamond whimsically called the Beatles' New York office to ask if he could show it at a local theater as part of an LNS fund-raiser. To his astonishment, he was invited to come and talk about the proposal; the very next day he found himself sitting across from Nat Weiss, one of the Beatles' lawyers, in a plush office overlooking Times Square. After a short conversation, Weiss instructed his assistant to dial up George Harrison.

"I took a deep breath," Diamond recalled, until finally, a familiar voice poured out of a speakerphone: "Hullo, this is George."

"Nat Weiss here. George, I'm sitting here with Steve Diamond from an underground press group called Liberation News Service . . . and he's wondering about showing the movie for a benefit . . ."

"Liberation News Service? Oh, I know those blokes . . ." Harrison said. "They're good chaps, sure, let them have it."[102]

Soon thereafter Diamond rented space for LNS to show the U.S. premier of *Magical Mystery Tour* at the Fillmore East, the popular club owned by rock promoter Bill Graham. In return for $1,000 to rent the theater, LNS could keep whatever box-office receipts they could generate from two showings of the film. Since Diamond was mistakenly thought to be neutral in the LNS imbroglio, he was charged with handling publicity and collecting advance ticket sales, which he deposited in a Polish-American bank on the Lower East Side. But Diamond was acting as a double agent; he actually sympathized with the Virtuous Caucus, and as revenue began accumulating, he and Bloom made several surreptitious trips to New England in search of a farm, until finally they found one that struck their fancy—a forty-acre plot of land near Amherst, upon which rested a large 150-year-old farmhouse and a barn. Although Diamond told the LNS collective that "advertising costs were higher than expected, ticket sales were lagging, and the benefit was in bad shape," tickets actually sold briskly enough that Diamond was able to funnel $5,000 to Bloom, who used it to make a down payment on the $25,000 farm.[103]

The benefit screening of *Magical Mystery Tour*, Diamond recalls, was a "smash." Both showings sold out, generating another $6,000. Instead of storing the money in the Fillmore's safe, as he was supposed to do, Diamond wrapped the greenbacks into tinfoil bricks and stashed them in a friend's freezer. Meanwhile, as most of the Vulgar Marxists were enjoying the film, the Virtuous Caucus was busily preparing to evacuate the Claremont office. Even though he knew what was going on uptown, Wasserman coolly attended the benefit, where he observed that the Marxists were completely unaware of being scammed; everyone was "very friendly," he recalled.[104] The very next morning—a Sunday—the Caucus and about twenty of their allies rented a large truck with a hydraulic lift and, in a feverish rush of mischievous energy, cleaned out the entire office. "It wasn't a theft in legal terms," Mungo later maintained, "but it was an extraordinarily frantic moving-party."[105] In addition to taking the $4,000 printing press and collator (to which the New Yorkers had contributed $2,150), addressograph, desks, and file cabinets, they took LNS's Rolodex, $180 in cash meant for payroll, notes off bulletin boards, and—in an attempt to prevent the New York crew from running LNS in their absence—every single copy of LNS's mailing list. "We were smartly thinking, 'they won't be able to get out an issue for a while,'" chuckled Mungo. "It would have been very difficult for them to reconstitute the entire mailing list, which was huge." Although Mungo and Porche did not originally plan on assisting in the actual heist, Bloom was adamant that their "good karma" was required, and he badgered them into joining in the activity. Once all the equipment was loaded onto the truck, Wasserman jammed Duco Cement into the front door lock.

Ironically, late Sunday morning, rather than the dead of night, was the most convenient time for the heist. Since the Marxists generally thought of themselves as "workers," Mungo explained, they typically took Sunday off. "But that was exactly the opposite of us," he elaborated. "We [were willing to work] twenty-four hours a day, any day, we worked on Christmas, so part of our joke, part of our aesthetic, part of our culture, was that . . . Sunday wasn't any different than any other day."[106] However, it was also important to the Caucus that they not be thought of as thieves, but rather as LNS's legitimate titleholders. As Bloom supposedly remarked, "Only criminals move furniture in the dark."[107] By emptying the office in broad daylight, they hoped to generate the impression that they were *taking* the new service, rather than *stealing* it.

When Cavalletto discovered that LNS's equipment was missing on Sunday evening, he immediately called Diamond, exclaiming, "We've been robbed!" Diamond professed shock, but reassured Cavelletto that at least the LNS money was safe, and would soon be available in the form of a cashier's check. In fact, at that very moment, Diamond was preparing to flee to New England, and the $6,000 had already been turned over to his girlfriend, Cathy Hutchinson, who was about to deposit it in an Amherst bank.

The following morning, one of LNS's New Yorkers discovered that Bloom had arranged for LNS's mail to be forwarded to a PO box in Montague. That explained a lot, but it didn't tell them precisely where Bloom was living or where the press was. By phoning the post office and pretending to be Bloom's sister, desperate to convey the news of a family tragedy, Ryan persuaded them to release the actual address of Bloom's farm. Later that day, the post office gave the Marxists something equally precious—LNS's mailing list. Although everyone had assumed the post office had distributed news packet No. 99 a few days earlier, none of the mailings had actually been delivered, because several members of Up Against the Wall, Motherfucker, a Lower East Side anarchist collective, had stuffed copies of one of their own broadsides into LNS's envelopes; in so doing, they caused the news packets to be in violation of LNS's postal permit, and so all four hundred of them were returned to 160 Claremont. As a result, LNS-NY was soon able to reestablish communication with their subscribers.

Although they were determined to retrieve the news service, the New Yorkers found themselves in a bind. They reasoned that filing criminal complaints against Bloom and his cohorts was out of the question, because they had always held that the legal issues regarding LNS's corporate structure and ownership were largely irrelevant.[108] Besides, as revolutionaries dedicated to overthrowing the state, they could scarcely appeal to authorities to resolve a Movement dispute. Nor were they about to capitulate and allow Bloom, who they disliked intensely, to run LNS from a remote farm, where they expected (not unreasonably) that the news service would wither away.[109] That left one choice: they would go up to Montague and simply take the news service back, by force if necessary.

Sometime around eight o'clock that night, a hastily arranged posse of nearly thirty angry radicals—including LNS staffers, writers for *Rat*, members of the Newsreel collective (who were owed some of the benefit's proceeds), Columbia SDS members, and a local, multiracial rock band called the Children of God—crammed into four large vehicles and set off for western Massachusetts. The Virtuous Caucus later charged that these non-LNSers were recruited as "muscle," whereas the Vulgar Marxists claimed that they wanted to assemble a group that symbolically represented a broad range of Movement opinion. Either way, at least some of them were in a vengeful mood. "Everybody, I mean the entire staff, we were just outraged," Dreyer remembered. "So everybody piled in cars and went looking for them. . . . At that point, we were all confrontational and figured it had to be dealt with."[110] Having done so much to establish LNS's New York office, Cavalletto remembers being livid. "They took everything, all the addresses, they took absolutely everything, because in the collective meetings, they hadn't won the vote."[111] Ryan, though, does not recall the New York crew departing for Montague with very much bloodlust. "I think my feeling is we were gonna catch 'em by surprise, and we were going to tell them the truth: that this was a bad thing to have done, and you need to give us some stuff back. But I don't feel as if people were enraged or wanted to hurt Marshall or do anything really, *really* bad."[112]

That night, Mungo and Porche paid a friendly visit to Bloom at the farm. Around midnight, just as they were about to leave, the caravan's rumbling engines and shining headlights pierced the countryside's ink-black darkness. Several of the New Yorkers took Mungo's car keys and ushered the two back inside. "Lights flashed everywhere as car after car pulled into the farm driveway," Mungo later wrote. "Each of the invaders was carrying something—sticks, mostly, though one had a knife and a beanbrained fellow named Tom [Hamilton] was waving a metal rod wildly in the air. Very few words needed to be said, it was absolutely evident that we were hostages now."[113] Later, Diamond and Hutchinson pulled up, and they too were promptly taken captive.

In subsequent statements, both sides in the rift tried to cast the other in the harshest possible light. According to LNS-Mass, the New Yorkers were brutally violent, beating up Bloom, destroying things throughout the farmhouse, and frightening them with threats of worse things to come. LNS-NY admitted engaging in some minimal amount of violence, but mostly they emphasized how nefariously Bloom's group had behaved in the lead-up to the confrontation, and they insisted that none of the hostages had been hurt.[114] Nevertheless, through close attention to the available primary sources, one can gather a rudimentary sense of what happened that night.

The New Yorkers' primary concern was to retrieve the printing press, which was being stored in a neighbor's barn—but only Bloom knew its exact whereabouts, and even after he was assaulted and bleeding from the nose, he refused to divulge its location. By LNS-NY's account, "one LNS member became enraged at Marshall's arrogance and slapped him twice: Marshall's nose bled briefly."[115] Mungo described a much more harrowing scene: "Now Marshall was bleeding, scarlet rivers running down from his face across his chest and down his legs. Now Marshall was naked and limp. Now his body itself was being tossed, banged against a wall, kicked to the floor."[116]

Of all the New Yorkers, Hamilton was said to have been particularly menacing, smashing someone's guitar and violently swinging his metal rod just inches above the heads of his captives, causing them to scream in terror. Even the LNS-NY crew admitted that Hamilton had "flipped out, . . . talked about torturing members of Marshall's group," and "generally acted like a fascist."[117] Others dismantled the telephone to prevent the hostages from calling the police and traipsed through the farmhouse, rifling through people's possessions and scooping up LNS's corporate documents and the deed to the farm. At one point, two of Bloom's crew, Bill Lewis and Steve Marsden, drove up in an Avis rental truck, which the Marxists mistakenly thought was carrying the press. When one of them rushed the truck, he was knocked over by the moving vehicle and suffered a few cracked ribs. Surprisingly, though, there were also some moments during the night when the mood lightened considerably. At one point, members of the Children of God even brought out their guitars and sang songs.[118] "It was an odd situation," Millman remembered, "because I think we thought we would go up there, they would capitulate, and we would leave. After all, we had more numbers and we were more *manly*, if you will. We were *tough*. And they didn't [capitulate]."[119]

However, LNS-NY did manage to seize a $6,000 cashier's check from Bloom's group. Precisely how they procured it is unclear. By one account, Marshall was dragged into a separate room, after which the captives heard a loud and terrible ruckus. Wrote Mungo, "We couldn't tell whether the noises from the living room were legitimate homicide or a staged melodrama of flying furniture and the like, but from what we had just witnessed, we couldn't risk it."[120] At that point, Hutchinson pulled out the check, which had been made out to her, and endorsed it "payable to Liberation News Service." But according to LNS-NY, Diamond was repentant from the very beginning.

"During the night, some of us had a long talk with Steve Diamond," they said, at which point he readily admitted to embezzling the benefit funds and "revealed that there was a $6,000 cashier's check on the premises. . . . Steve seemed genuinely eager to extricate himself from the entire mess, and to relieve himself of any further responsibility for the money."[121] At about 4 AM, Diamond produced the phone number of the person who was storing the offset press, and Cavalletto rang the barn's owner at his home. By LNS-NY's account, the woman who answered the phone *asked* to speak to Bloom; according to LNS-Mass, Bloom had to be "hustled" to the phone by two "brawny longhairs," at which point Cavalletto ordered him to "tell her to give us the press."[122] Either way, Bloom held fast. "Don't be alarmed," he reportedly said. "They came with sticks. If they try to bother you, call the police. Don't let them have the press."[123]

By about 6:00 AM, as the sky began to lighten, everyone was thoroughly exhausted, and the New York faction finally declared that they would return home and simply get a new offset press in order to continue running LNS from Claremont Avenue. According to LNS-Mass, after the "muscle" had left, Bloom even tried to reconnect with the remaining LNSers, giving them a tour of the farm and arguing that it was the best place from which LNS could serve the Movement, until he happened to spot Cavalletto and Ryan "rummaging through his suitcases," at which point he sprinted back to the farmhouse as they scrambled into their truck. Just as they fired up the engine, Diamond and Marsden grabbed the vehicle's side and briefly held on as it pulled away, before falling onto the dirt road.[124] Cavalletto, however, remembers differently. After most of his crew had left, he said, Bloom's group "suddenly realized they outnumbered us . . . and they attacked us!" As they tried to escape, Cavalletto fought back after someone literally grabbed hold of his arm and tried to yank him from the moving truck. "It was like a movie, an action film," he recalled. "I don't know what would have happened to me if they'd got me out."[125]

THERE WERE NOW TWO GROUPS printing LNS news packets, each proclaiming to be the *real* LNS and casting the other as an ersatz version. Immediately, both sides took their case to the left-wing and underground media. "The crucial question," Dreyer told a *New York Times* reporter, "is who will establish legitimacy with the movement."[126] Bloom held that the ugly confrontation at the farm only called attention to the temperamental and ideological differences coloring the two groups. According to a *Village Voice* reporter, Bloom had said that the original heist "was done with style, a sense of humor, and a certain élan."[127] Mungo likewise took mischievous glee in helping to pilfer the news service. "It was to be the ultimate defeat for Allen Young," he crowed. "[He'd] be in *Bulgaria* at some kind of *conference* when the roof fell on him!"[128]

By contrast, the Marxists portrayed the robbery as a thuggish betrayal of the Movement and all it stood for. When Bloom's group canceled the $6,000 check and pressed kidnapping charges against the thirteen New Yorkers—supposedly a capital offense in Massachusetts—LNS-NY railed against them for cravenly turning to the authorities.[129] "This is Bloom's moral problem, not ours," Cavalletto told an *East Village Other* reporter.[130] *New Left Notes* printed an angry polemic—unsigned, but obviously written by someone from LNS-NY—describing how LNS had received "a quick, well-placed kick in the balls from Marshall Bloom." "This is probably the first time that Movement people have been charged with capital crimes by 'brothers' in the Movement," the author noted. And yet LNS-NY declared they would not bring legally well-founded countercharges of embezzlement against Bloom's group. "Corporate and criminal laws," they maintained, "are the kind of bull-shit to be used as cover and pressure on the Man, not as weapons against each other."[131]

Though not entirely without support, few in the underground press were favorable toward LNS-Mass. By insisting that the news service should con-form to the founders' original vision, rather than evolving into a worker-controlled collective, they seemed antidemocratic. By then taking the news service to a distant farm and building a commune around it, they struck some as cliquish and self-absorbed. And when they signed criminal complaints against their erstwhile colleagues, they triggered angry responses from those who questioned their revolutionary commitment. According to Dreyer and Smith, "most of the New Left and a large percentage of the underground papers boycotted the Massachusetts group, especially because of the kidnap-ping charges."[132] "We were the outlaws of the Movement," Diamond remem-bered.[133] Even Bloom later recognized that in most underground circles the move to a farm was "infamous."[134]

Angry letters that poured into Montague underscored the point. "Dear Acid Heads," began one. "You guys are farting around with a million dollar idea. This is too big to go down the drain."[135] "What the fuck are you people trying to prove," asked another correspondent, "moving up there to the woods of Massachusetts when the news . . . is 99% in the cities?"

> And if you take yourselves to be radical organizers as well as newsmen,
> who are you trying to organize besides assorted rabbits, horses, and
> bumble-bees? Doing your own thing and dropping out and moving to

the country is a groovy idea, but I think that the more serious of us who are working for a real revolution in this country feel that the work is with the people, in day to day contact. . . . Not only are you general fuck-ups, but you're traitors to everything which we all . . . are working for.[136]

From Detroit, *Fifth Estate* editor Peter Werbe wrote, "Our staff feels that all criminal charges must be dropped against the New York people. . . . Revolutionaries do not use the courts of the ruling class to settle their disputes and especially do not make use of the repressive apparatus of the State to punish fellow revolutionaries no matter how heinous their alleged crime."[137] Marc Sommer, who had worked for LNS when it was headquartered in Washington, DC, told Bloom, "I can't believe that the clash necessitated making off with all of the equipment, lying, calling in the pigs, [and] setting up a bunch of ridiculous legal charges."[138] Another writer, who actually sympathized with LNS-Mass, nevertheless told Bloom, "I really think you oughta drop the nap charges . . . that just ain't a-gonna ride well with too many people, y'know?"[139] Someone else advised, "As for your move into the idyllic countryside . . . don't get too pretentious about it!"[140] From London, an LNS correspondent expressed disappointment with both sides in the dispute, though he may have been targeting Bloom when he said, "Serious radicals and revolutionaries, the people who are putting their futures and their necks on the line, don't want to deal with nitwits."[141]

Realizing they'd overplayed their hand, LNS-Mass tried to persuade authorities to drop all criminal complaints against LNS-NY. Their entreaties were not completely successful, but the kidnapping charges were eventually reduced to disturbing the peace, and everyone got off lightly (although the Franklin County judge infuriated the five female defendants by fining them only $25, while each of the men got $50 fines). The $6,000 check was frozen in an Amherst bank, and soon the State of Massachusetts and lawyers began gobbling most of it up to cover various legal fees. For a time, LNS-NY and LNS-Mass both printed their own news packets, but the New York collective proved a hardier, more determined lot. In late September, they told subscribers that their staff had bonded through their shared adversity. "For the most part, people are digging each other and are really excited about the work they are doing," they said. "We are working 12 hours a day, often at a level of high tension, getting no salaries, eating communal spaghetti dinners; but still having time to engage ourselves in the sensory and erotic pleasures we all hold so dear, and [ironically] managing to wander off to our farm which we are renting in upstate New York!"[142]

Although some felt that the Claremont Avenue office churned out too much overheated rhetoric in the late 1960s, according to media critic Nat Hentoff, LNS speedily became more polished and sophisticated, and by the early 1970s, it helped to foster a sense of community among the nation's "amorphous, not-so-New Left." "I have seldom picked up an underground newspaper that lacks a sizable number of LNS credit-lines," Hentoff noted.[143] And while Mungo had stereotyped LNS's New York collective as humorless politicos in *Famous Long Ago*, the group published a slew of material favorable to the youth culture, personal liberation, and feminism.[144] "Ironically, what they did in New York in the years after the split was not far a-field from what we'd have done, had we stayed," Wasserman said. "And they were better organized and in the long run, they were able to survive."[145]

By contrast, LNS-Mass produced only a few dozen more news packets before a combination of entropy, torpor, and the cold winter all conspired to kill the operation. As it happened, running the news service from an isolated farm proved every bit as challenging as one might have expected. For one, the group's offset press—nicknamed "Little Johnnie"—fell into disrepair, and during cold snaps its inkwells froze up. Meanwhile, the local stationery store stopped extending them supplies on credit, farm animals began overrunning the barn where the press was stored, and the group spent considerable time attending to chores necessary for their own survival, including chopping wood and raising foodstuffs. Steve Diamond became the editor of LNS-Mass, but he especially grew estranged from the sectarian warfare and abrasive militancy that characterized some of the late 1960s New Left. "The main reason I wanted to stop printing Liberation News Service," he later said, was because the group "didn't have anything more to say, other than perhaps get some land, get your people together, and see what happens."[146] Elsewhere, he wrote, "Although we had no idea what the future held in store, living . . . on the land as an organic communal family had to take precedence to pumping out the latest political blat from far flung regions of the country."[147]

In an undated letter, Bloom likewise second-guessed whether moving LNS to a countryside outpost was such a good idea after all. "The news service is, of course, quite a drag," he said. There "is not the naïve joy there was in the beginning." He also acknowledged having hurt some of his old colleagues by moving to Montague, and observed that he'd earned "a certain amount of hostility from not-too-distant friends."[148] Certainly he was wounded by this: in his unfinished memoir, he complained that the unsigned *New Left Notes* article condemning him was "so ludicrously inaccurate that it seemed hopeless to correct it." When he was last in Washington, DC, he said, Mike Spiegel and Cathy Wilkerson, two of his old friends from SDS, refused to even speak to him.[149] To Mungo, he wrote a letter complaining about all the bad press LNS-Mass received after the heist, adding, "it is difficult to survive all this. if [*sic*] I seem to be reaching out for help it is because help is needed."[150]

Then there was the despicable FBI forgery. As one of the Bureau's functionaries explained in an internal memo in the fall of 1968, "The New Left press has contained considerable charges and countercharges" concerning the newspaper heist and the midnight raid on the farm. "We are attempting to use this situation to further split the New Left." To this end, someone from the FBI's New York office drafted a letter that purported to be a missive from a former LNS staffer.[151] Titled ". . . . . And Who Got the Cookie Jar?," the author drew attention to Bloom's apparent mental instability, declaring he "has always been a bit of a nut" and skewering him for making hysterical accusations, ripping off the Movement, and destroying LNS.[152] Wasserman remembered that the letter, which was reprinted in some Movement papers, "dug into Marshall like a dagger."[153]

Despite all this, Bloom sometimes seemed to enjoy Montague's pastoral simplicity, especially after such a stressful period. "Life is so much less complicated and troubled here, you have no idea," he wrote to Abe Peck, editor of the *Chicago Seed*. "No need for bread allowances for [the] subway, plastic submarine [sandwiches], rent, parking tickets. It is infinitely cheaper and we live better."[154] In another letter, he said he enjoyed the challenges of eking out a Spartan existence on the farm. Chopping wood, discarding useless electric gadgets, buying fresh milk from a local farmer, salvaging material from a local garbage dump, and finding inventive ways to scrimp and save—all of this appealed to his new sensibility.[155] In early 1969 he began talking about plans to create a magazine out of the ashes of LNS, which he would call the *Journal of the New Age.*

Still, Bloom never stopped having wild mood swings. He frequently complained of being lonely, and it must have pained him that even though he'd hoped the farm would become a place for exploring "meaningful, liberated human relationships," he never came to terms with his own homosexuality, choosing instead to remain basically celibate. Apparently, he never even told his closest friends that he was gay. In early 1969 he wrote to Mungo from California with big news concerning his friend Lis Meisner, a friend since his grad school days in London: "Lis and I are getting married in August on the farm and hope to soon have BABIES. The orgy after the wedding will be something you and yours will NEVER forget."[156]

But the wedding never happened. In 1973, Allen Young, who by then was devoting much of his energy toward the Gay Liberation Movement, described the trip as Bloom's "last ditch unsuccessful attempt to make a go of it romantically and sexually with a woman friend."[157] Another problem Bloom faced was that although his draft board had awarded him conscientious-objector status in March 1969, he was still expected to perform a two-year stint at the Denver General Hospital—an entirely unappealing prospect, perhaps in part because the job would have put him in closer proximity to his parents, with whom he never was able to resolve a drawn-out generational feud.[158] This, too, must have been hard. On October 21, 1969, he sent them an effusive letter, apologizing for not always being "properly grateful" and for taking "too much for granted." With tremendous warmth, Bloom reminisced about a recent time they shared when he and his father worked together in a garden while his mother looked on: "We have so few joys together we must cherish those we have," he said. "I wish I could be different for you, I really do, but I know that you love me just as I am and that's an awfully good feeling. Love, Marsh."[159]

Ten days later—on November 1, 1969, at age twenty-five—Bloom committed suicide. He had run a vacuum hose from the exhaust pipe of his car through the vent window. He left no note of explanation, just a last will and testament providing instructions for the disposition of his meager possessions, to which he added an expression of love for his parents and his friends, and a brief apology: "I am sorry about all this."[160]

THANKS LARGELY TO *FAMOUS LONG AGO*, a certain lore surrounds Liberation News Service, at least in its earliest incarnation. It is not hard to see why—Mungo's vivid characterizations, witty asides, and frequently confessional prose make for delightful reading, and the dust-up between the Virtuous Caucus and the Vulgar Marxists—replete with secret meetings, double agents, and daring acts of thievery and sabotage—contain many elements of a classic cloak-and-dagger story. Warmly reviewed by Jack Newfield in the *New York Times*, the book sold scores of thousands of copies (and was optioned for a feature film).[161]

In some respects, though, *Famous Long Ago* seems unreliable. For instance, while Marshall Bloom is faithfully portrayed as an eccentric, Mungo skips lightly over some of the more troublesome aspects of his personality, as well as his poor mental health. Nor does he give evidence of having seriously grappled with the perspectives of some of the Vulgar Marxists, who argued that in order for LNS to survive, it would need to build a democratic culture. Finally, one wonders whether the Marxists were every bit as dull and doctrinaire as Mungo suggests. Given the neo-Thoreauvian direction in which he and Bloom were heading, lots of people probably struck them that way.

Although the LNSers who remained in New York certainly shared deep political commitments and an intense seriousness of purpose, they were not all of the same mind about Movement issues, and in addition to their lengthy meetings and workdays, they enjoyed "fabulous dinners," recreational pot smoking, movie nights, romantic couplings, weekend excursions to their upstate farm, and "late night boogies" at their communal apartments.[162]

When supplemented by a wider range of primary sources, however, Mungo's memoir can help us to appreciate how fully the underground press became saturated with the ideas about democratic participation that SDS had nurtured just a few years earlier. In addition to publicly calling for the democratization of society, New Leftists built a large network of alternative media institutions that were meant to showcase their democratic values. One way of doing this—and this was the tack taken by Bloom and Mungo—was by making their resources available to the community. Just as most underground newspapers opened their pages to whoever wanted to put their left-wing views into circulation, LNS initially postured itself as a "national clearinghouse" that would shower the nation's hip communities with texts and graphics.[163] In this way, the news service could claim to be meeting the Movement's democratic demands: Its dispatches would reflect the range of Movement ideologies and opinions, and whatever use individual newspapers made of that material would be to their preference.

Another approach (and the two were not mutually exclusive) was to run the underground newspapers communally, without an editor or a boss. Instead, the entire staff made editorial decisions, and everyone was encouraged to become involved in all aspects of newspaper production. To the Vulgar Marxists, as well as the vast majority of radical news people in the late 1960s, this seemed perfectly appropriate. Here they may have been guided by a generalized fear of the corruption of power that was commonplace in the New Left, but more specific considerations were at work as well: the belief that radicals ought to live the values they wanted to see enacted in the larger society, and the hope that participatory democracy would be attractive enough to lure people into demanding but fulfilling Movement activities.

When LNS broke wide open at the end of the summer of 1968, it wasn't the only New Left media organization to have experienced a fierce internal power struggle. Two months earlier, a faction of the Boston *Avatar* published a "news-oriented" issue that wasn't to the liking of that paper's mystical leader, Mel Lyman. In response, Lyman directed a group of his followers to steal some thirty-five thousand copies of the paper, which they sold as scrap paper for a pittance.[164] Nevertheless, the LNS feud proved something of a bellwether. In the following years, staffs grew restless or revolted at several leading papers that had traditional management structures.[165] With the advent of radical feminism in the late 1960s, many women began railing against the crude sexism and ugly male chauvinism on display in many papers, and in February 1970 a women's collective famously seized permanent control of the *Rat*.[166] According to a *Rolling Stone* journalist who toured the country in 1969 to take stock of the New Left's media infrastructure, "Who's in charge of making decisions is a very large topic at the moment for nearly every underground paper."[167] That same year, Dreyer and Smith noted that the trend in the underground press was toward encouraging democratic participation. "Most papers are trying to create a democratic work situation and decision-making process," they wrote.

> Often staffers are listed alphabetically or in random order as part of an attempt to avoid establishing hierarchies of power. Trying to work collectively is always a struggle—we are all so corrupted by the ego-tripping ethic of capitalism. Staff conflicts are often great, tensions sometimes run high on layout night, but people gradually develop the ability to work together, sharing responsibility for policy, beginning to purge themselves of the need to give or take orders.[168]

In this way, the underground newspapers of the late 1960s were zeitgeist touchstones by which radicals could measure the purity of their commitments to interdependence, power-sharing, and self-rule. In addition to serving some of the same functions as radical papers in other eras—building an adversary culture and trying to countervail the distortions and shibboleths that spilled forth from the mainstream media—most of the New Left's journalists behaved as unblinkered democrats, determined to usher a spirit of mutuality into their Movement. At the same time that they used their newspapers as platforms to espouse their viewpoints, they transformed the papers into egalitarian communities in their own right. Perhaps there is an irony in this. Just like Marshall Bloom, most of those who worked in the underground press in the late 1960s saw to it that their activism and their lives were all mixed together.

7

"From Underground to Everywhere"

Alternative Media Trends since the Sixties

IN THE 1977 HOLLYWOOD FILM *Between the Lines*, directed by Joan Micklin Silver, the colorful, tightly knit, and idealistic staff of a formerly "underground" newspaper, the *Back Bay Mainline*, finds itself in flux. Although the paper was once known for its muckraking bravado, in this postpsychedelic era of oversized collars, flared trousers, and feathered hair, its main selling point seems to be its randy back-page sex ads. Harry (played by John Heard), the staff's ace reporter, once won a journalism award for exposing corruption in local nursing homes, but now he's stuck covering nightlife and fashion trends and is thinking about quitting. Another writer—this one a superannuated beatnik named Michael (Stephen Collins)—finally does decide to jump ship, but not until he's landed a blockbuster contract to write a book called *The Death of the Counterculture*.

Meanwhile, the whole gang is distressed about rumors that a mercenary publishing mogul named Roy Walsh (Lane Smith) is ready to swoop in and buy the paper. When this finally happens, Walsh plays to type, summoning his new employees to a meeting and telling them they'll need to water down whatever is left of their crusading zeal in order to make the paper more profitable. No hard feelings, he implies. He's just speaking "pragmatically" about facts "we all have to live with." At this point, the staff's tenderhearted receptionist rises to quit.

"I know the *Mainline* means a good business deal to you and a lot of money," she tells the new owner. "But to a lot of us, it *means something*. A lot of us want to work for the *Mainline* and not some . . . *communications empire.*"

The *Back Bay Mainline* never really existed; it sprang from the imagination of screenwriter Fred Barron, who had previously worked for two honest-to-goodness papers of considerable regional clout: the Boston *Phoenix* and the *Real Paper* (both of which were technically established in 1972 but actually originated several years earlier). The transformations Barron depicted in his script, however, were drawn from life. All across America in the 1970s, "alternative newspapers"—with their circulation strategies, reader surveys, polished layouts, expanded arts coverage, and upscale demographics—bid a hearty farewell to the Sixties. Although the crusading and rabble-rousing sentiments that colored the underground papers were not lost completely, henceforth they would be tempered and muted.

It is hard to pinpoint when the transformation was complete, but 1978 seems like a good marker. That was the year that Calvin Trillin, then writing for the *New Yorker*, published a lengthy account of the first annual meeting of the National Association of Newsweeklies, which was held in Seattle. According to Trillin, the group's name was a bit of a misnomer; it sounded too much "like the managing editor of *Time* meeting the managing editor of *Newsweek* for lunch to talk about why their covers so often turn out to have the same person on them."[1] In fact, the meeting was attended exclusively by feisty alternative newspapers that had either evolved from the underground press or were founded in the 1960s or early 1970s as commercially oriented news-sheets. These latter papers, like the *San Francisco Bay Guardian*, the *Chicago Reader*, and the *Maine Times*, were all solidly left-wing, and they often privileged first-person (nonobjective) reporting, but they didn't see themselves as appendages to a social movement. Whereas the underground press was driven by young men and women who saw themselves as activists first and journalists second, these alternative papers made newsgathering and analysis their chief priority. In fact, a majority of them were even reluctant to call themselves "alternative" because "alternative" sounded too much like "underground"—and these papers badly wanted to distance themselves from the angry epithets and clamorous rhetoric that once sullied the radical press.[2]

They had good reason for doing so. As the Sixties drew to a close, perceptive readers of underground newspapers would have found it increasingly difficult to maintain that the New Left was still a rising social movement. In the summer of 1969, SDS—the most powerful student organization in American history—destroyed itself in a paroxysm of factional infighting between Weatherman, an obnoxious clique of ultramilitants who drew their name from a Bob Dylan lyric, and the Progressive Labor Party, an equally unpleasant, doctrinaire neo-Marxist organization. SDS's final convention, at the Chicago Coliseum, was a farrago of rhetoric, recriminations, and orotund pronouncements.

"I remember reading about it in the newspapers," said Jim Jacobs, who had worked in SDS's Radical Education Project, "and just feeling terrible, because I wasn't there. Helpless because an organization I'd spent two years totally into, reading every fucking line of *New Left Notes*, every word, really believing this was going to be *the* organization of the seventies, [was] being smashed to bits."[3]

Meanwhile, a dark (even sinister) mood snaked throughout the counter-culture. This was the period when Charles Manson and his acid-gobbling followers left a string of butchered corpses across Southern California, the Hell's Angels terrorized concert-goers at Altamont, and the Weathermen swarmed through Chicago's Gold Coast with bricks and bats, attacking fancy cars and storefront windows. On March 6, 1970, three members of that group blew themselves up in a West Village townhouse when they accidentally detonated a bomb made up of dynamite and roofing nails. It had been intended for use against American servicemen and their dates at an upcoming dance at Fort Dix, New Jersey.

As a result of all this negativity and violence, to say nothing of the cumulative effect of so much else that transpired in the late Sixties—urban riots, police crackdowns, political assassinations, the daily killing of civilians in Vietnam, and the pointless deaths of thousands of American soldiers—counterjournalists turned increasingly angry, cynical, and insular. Increasingly desperate for *the* correct revolutionary formula, some underground journalists became increasingly enamored with Marxism-Leninism and third-world liberation struggles, and as a result began diluting the distinctive, regional flavor of their newspapers. Soon, the radical newssheets were said to have become so rigid that, according to one aficionado, "You couldn't tell the *Rat* from the *Guardian* from the *San Francisco Express Times*."[4] In late 1970, the staff of Boston's *Old Mole* published a self-critical editorial in which they admitted feeling pressured to inject the words "imperialist" and "capitalism" into every sentence, lest they be "accused of insufficient zeal."[5]

This is not to suggest that underground newspapers didn't find other ways of hastening their own demise. The collective organizational structure of some newspapers proved taxing to work within, leading to burnout and fatigue. The New Left's extreme antielitism and distrust of authority figures led the staffs at some underground newspapers to refrain from demanding quality from their writers. And because of the male chauvinism that ran rampant in the underground press, women's talents were frequently under-utilized; eventually, fissures between men and women tore some papers apart.

As it became increasingly apparent that underground sex ads were attracting a new subset of readers, some in the underground press even began establishing raunchy, apolitical pornzines that siphoned ad revenue and street sales from the politically oriented papers. For instance, Marvin Grafton, formerly of the *Rat*, went on to start *Pleasure*; Joel Fabrikant, of *EVO*, published *Kiss*; and the staff behind the political *New York Free Press* began publishing a sister paper, the *New York Review of Sex*.[6] Finally, while assuming their own righteousness, some of the New Left's scribes may have blurred the lines between advocacy journalism and outright propaganda. And when they slipped from righteousness into self-righteousness—something that's not so hard to do—they subjected their political opponents to scurrilous and dehumanizing rhetoric and isolated themselves even further from the principled Left.

In addition to wanting to distance themselves from all of this, the alternative journalists who gathered in Seattle would have been more than a little turned off by the bacchanalian and in some cases downright frightening behavior that presided at earlier left-wing media conferences. Surely the most notorious such event, sponsored by the Alternative Media Project, was held at Vermont's Goddard College in 1970. Some 1,700 people showed up (which was seven hundred more than organizers expected) to hear such speakers as *Realist* founder Paul Krassner, Yippie Jerry Rubin, cartoonist Gilbert Shelton, underground medical advice columnist Dr. Eugene Schoenfeld, and acid guru Baba Ram Dass (formerly known as Richard Alpert). Some fondly remember the conference's good vibes; "People had these big smiles and you could just smell the acid coming out of their skin," recalled Peter Wolf, a Boston DJ who was then just launching his career with the J. Geils Band.[7] But there was much unpleasantness as well. One woman reported she'd been raped in her dorm room, and at one of the workshops, a man had to be forcibly ejected after he brandished a gun and joked about "killing people." When some men had the idea of videotaping a "love-in" near a swimming hole in the woods, a group of outraged feminists quashed their plan.[8] Rubin angrily declared that someone had stolen $500 from his girlfriend's wallet and demanded the conference goers take up a collection to help compensate for the loss. At one point, a group of radicals even had to be talked out of vandalizing the college's lovely library with graffiti.

"As the conference wore on," someone reported, "the confrontations kept coming: women vs. men; homosexuals vs. men [*sic*]; hippies vs. revolutionaries; political people vs. cultural people; blacks vs. whites [though few blacks attended]; electronic media people vs. printed media people; people who continue to work for commercial enterprises vs. people who've dropped out."[9] Afterwards, conference organizers were billed for $859 worth of missing bed sheets, towels, pillows, and blankets.[10]

Three years later, representatives from fifty-three left-wing papers attended a three-day retreat in Boulder, Colorado, which was hosted by Denver's *Straight Creek Journal*. According to Stephen Foehr, a conference organizer, one of their goals was to help the papers present a more mature image of themselves. "We are the second generation alternative press as opposed to the first generation underground press," he remarked. "The second generation is trying to establish itself on a more stable footing by dropping the rhetoric and getting involved in their communities at the neighborhood level."[11] But it appears they were only partially successful. According to Calvin Trillin:

> Survivors of the Boulder meeting who made it to Seattle remember it as being so dominated by the rhetoric of the period—angry speeches by women about to form their own caucus, philosophical arguments pitting people committed to keeping their bodies free of all chemicals against people who had too many chemicals in their bodies to put up much of an argument, long discussions about whether the true goal of journalism was overthrow of the government or getting one's head together—that those few conferees who wanted to exchange information on how to put out a newspaper had to sneak off to the coffee shop for informal discussions.[12]

By contrast, in Seattle, almost everyone was chiefly concerned with the practical problems associated with newspaper publishing—marketing strategies, distribution problems, business models, and so forth. At one point, Trillin says, "the proprietor of an underground news service"—almost certainly Thomas King Forcade—showed up with a friend. Though no one at the conference would have known it, by then, Forcade had become a very wealthy man. In addition to his drug-smuggling activities, he had gone on to found *High Times*, a lifestyle magazine for pot smokers that quickly blossomed into a multimillion-dollar enterprise.[13] According to Trillin, Forcade and his pal appeared at the trade-association meeting looking "like a retired punk rocker and his manager." They stayed only very briefly, then "quietly took their leave—like a couple of massage parlor operators who had rushed over to work the largest convention in town without having first bothered to find out that it was a conference of Lutheran liturgists." Later, conferees jokingly referred to them as "the two gentlemen in costume."[14]

Nearly six months later, on November 1, 1978, Forcade committed suicide using a small, pearl-handled pistol. It didn't have anything to do with alternative journalism, per se; in the preceding months, he had shown signs of increasing mental instability, which may have been exacerbated by two horrible events: his best friend had recently died in a plane crash while carrying contraband from Colombia to Florida, and another friend was discovered to be a police informer.[15] For some of those who knew him, Forcade's passing was yet another sign that the nation's protest ethic and hippie culture had petered out almost completely. "The '80s would have killed Tom if he didn't kill himself," a friend remarked.[16]

THE *VILLAGE VOICE*, ESTABLISHED IN 1955, actually predated the underground press, and a handful of others successful alt-weeklies, like the *San Francisco Bay Guardian* (1966) and the *Maine Times* (1968), were launched while the New Left was still on the upswing.[17] For the most part, radicals sneered at these more liberally oriented tabloids, which covered the cultural ferment of the 1960s but were generally apprehensive about left-wing militancy. In 1969, the *Village Voice* was subjected to a particularly rococo expression of disdain from lefty journalist Kirkpatrick Sale, who characterized the storied tabloid as a paper for "bo-libs"—those who were "Bohemian, not hip, yip, digger or beat" and "liberal, not radical, revolutionary, love-cultured or anarchistic. . . . [The *Voice*] speaks to those whose revolutions have become doubts, whose hatreds have become merely distrusts, whose passions have become tempered interests." In his final kiss-off, he told the paper, "You've come a long way, baby, but you got stuck there."[18]

But most alternative newspapers came about in the early 1970s. At least one such rag, Boston's *Real Paper*, had an egalitarian working structure mirroring that of many underground papers that preceded it, but the typical alt-weekly was organized hierarchically.[19] And since alternative tabloids did not align themselves with the youth rebellion to the same extent that underground newspapers had, collectively, they proved harder to define. In 1979 *Time* magazine observed that although the alternative press was well established, its papers varied widely in size: at one end, there were outfits like the aforementioned *Straight Creek Journal*, which could claim a circulation of only 5,500; at the other extreme, the *Voice* boasted a circulation of about 170,000. And while the great majority of these papers served metropolitan areas, a small handful of them were suburban, rural, or statewide, and one—the *Maui Sun*—could even be described as literally "insular."[20]

The main reason they all became known as "alternative" is because they positioned themselves against the daily newspapers. And of course this was in an era before commercial dailies faced competition from the Internet, cable television, or satellite radio. "Nobody else [was] using free circulation, running personal ads, writing seriously about the Clash and Funkadelic, telling kids about local bands, covering the independent film scene, writing frankly about sex, [or] printing cuss words," remembers Richard Karpel, currently the executive director of the Association of Alternative Newsweeklies (AAN). "So back then we were '*the* alternative.'"[21]

By setting themselves on sounder economic footing than the underground papers, and by making quality journalism their top priority, the alt-weeklies also usually managed to pursue a wider variety of stories and feature more substantial reporting than the subterranean press. In his 1981 book, *A Trumpet to Arms: Alternative Media in America*, former *Berkeley Barb* editor David Armstrong described how some alt-weeklies had begun to exert a powerful liberal influence in their communities. In Northern California, for instance, the *Mendocino Grapevine* helped to spur reforms in the state's housing code, which had previously been unfavorable to migrant homesteaders who'd built environmentally sound cabins that used solar power, wind turbines, and compost privies. In nearby San Francisco, the *Bay Guardian* helped drive a local movement against high-rise buildings, which were straining the city's finances in ways that many citizens barely understood.[22] With writers like Arthur Bell, Richard Goldstein, and others, the *Village Voice* was often exceptional in its coverage of issues of concern to gays (though the paper also occasionally found ways of rankling gay activists). According to a journalism professor, by the late 1980s the *Voice* was a chief source of reliable information about AIDS, "even as it held up a mirror to the grief, anxiety, and fury that raged through the [gay] community. For several years, and working right up until his death in 1994, Robert Massa was the best AIDS reporter in the country."[23] In the 1980s the paper also began publishing an annual Queer Issue that provided rich coverage of the LGBT (lesbian, gay, bisexual, and transgender) community.

Other stories that emerged from the alternative press proved rather sensational. In 1990, the *Chicago Reader*'s John Conroy uncovered allegations that since as far back as 1972, local police had been torturing African Americans with hideous beatings, suffocations, mock execution, and electric shocks, in order to coerce confessions. Ultimately, the startling claims were found to be credible; in 2000, Illinois governor George Ryan put a moratorium on executions in his state, and in 2003 he cleared its death row.[24] (In June 2010, former Chicago police lieutenant John Burge was convicted on federal charges of lying about abusing suspects in a 2003 civil lawsuit.) In Phoenix, the *New Times* published articles that led to the twenty-three-count federal indictment of Arizona's governor, Fife Symington, in 1997, and the paper broke numerous stories concerning the law-enforcement abuses of Maricopa County's ludicrous sheriff, Joe Arpaio.[25] In 2001, the *Boston Phoenix*'s Kristen Lombardi revealed how archdiocesan officials had covered up allegations that a priest had been sexually molesting young children. A full year later, the *Boston Globe* picked up the story, and with its superior resources the paper was able to obtain previously secret legal documents that led to the resignation of Boston's archbishop, Cardinal Law.[26] In 2005, Nigel Jaquiss, a reporter for Portland, Oregon's, alt-weekly *Willamette Week*, won a Pulitzer Prize for revealing that about thirty years earlier, Oregon's governor, Neil Goldschmidt, had sexually abused his family's fourteen-year-old babysitter.[27]

In some cases, alternative journalists had to practically insist that they be allowed to pursue such work-intensive, and long-winded, exposés. According to Clif Garboden, an alt-press veteran with the *Boston Phoenix* who got his start at Ray Mungo's *BU News*, "While publishers in the early '80s were busily coming up with 'lifestyle' concepts for the 'me generation,' the staffs were devoting equal energy to thwarting the accompanying artificiality."[28] David Carr, formerly of the *Twin Cities Reader* and *Washington City Paper*, said something similar: "We did those big narrative heaves because we liked doing them. The interest in those ambitious news features mostly came from the staffs, as opposed to readers, although occasionally they could land with big impact."[29]

Alt-weeklies have also provided havens for writers whose experimental brio was less welcome in the daily papers. Here they were probably less influenced by underground press journalism than by the New Journalists of the 1960s and 1970s, who were more artful in their application of literary techniques to nonfiction reporting.[30] Even if most alt-weekly journalists couldn't write as well as Tom Wolfe, Gay Talese, or Joan Didion, they *wanted* to, and at a time when the public seemingly had a greater appetite for long-form journalism and thought than it does today, alternative newspapers were more conducive to their aspirations than the daily ones.

"We make no assignments, have no deadlines, and make no promises to run any stories," boasted Bob Roth, the *Chicago Reader*'s founding editor, in a 1980 interview. "We want writers to have the time and freedom to find stories they care about and can write with a point of view."[31] In a 1985 radio interview on WBEZ, Roth elaborated: "As a lot of readers in this town have discovered, 'professional' is a code word. . . . 'Professional' publications are closed to newcomers because they've got their regulars. One of the things the *Reader* has always been proudest of is that we're open to names we have never heard of, people we never met, people who don't have a reputation."[32] For a time, it was even the paper's policy to read every submission from the slush pile *twice* before deciding it was unworthy for publication, just in case they were in a bad mood the first time or were subconsciously prejudiced because the piece in question came from an amateur. "Basically, what we settled on is an approach that rejects two of the most important underpinnings of the ways both dailies in Chicago operate," Roth said:

> One is we've totally rejected the "objectivity" that they think they're bringing to their work. . . . The alternative papers believe that the only way you can write anything that's truly worth reading is if it's interpretive, if it's subjective, if it's got a point of view. . . . Then number two, [we believe] that daily newspapers all over the country display a ridiculously narrow sense of newsworthiness. We, on the other hand . . . try to find something that's broader. That's why you'll find the *Reader* with amazing frequency writing about topics that dailies wouldn't give a moment's consideration to, because newsworthiness to them means the mayor's press conference, it means the NCAA championship game, it means Linda Evans and whoever it is, Joan Collins—Linda Evans and Joan Collins, that's who it is today.[33]

"There used to be such a bright white line between the weeklies and dailies in terms of voice," adds Carr. The alt-weeklies, he said, were some of the best places to find "a primacy of the importance of narrative and story-telling. And yes, fact was important, but it could be rendered in somewhat musical ways, where the prose would dance and be animated by a point of view."[34] *New Yorker* staff writer Susan Orlean, who launched her career at *Willamette Week* and later wrote for the *Boston Phoenix*, is a good example of a writer who profited from the freedom she found in the alternative press. In a 2003 interview, she remarked, "I do think having started my career writing longer-form stories that relied heavily on execution—and not just on concept—was a perfect opportunity to train for the kind of work I like most. I like finding stories that are not obvious, [like] the oblique examination of popular culture and subcultures."[35]

It was the alternative papers' impressive financial success, throughout most of the 1970s, 1980s, and 1990s, that allowed them to publish such daring and ambitious news features. In 1971, the *Chicago Reader*'s founders established a template that was eventually followed by all the other alt-weeklies: instead of charging for their paper and slowly winning over readers, they began with a large free circulation and set corresponding advertising rates. Initially the *Reader* lost money, but eventually it became very profitable, and before long, across the country, alt-weeklies could be picked up for free, whether from sidewalk distribution boxes or from stacks near the entrances of bookstores, record stores, supermarkets, and cafés.[36] By circulating in this way, and by providing imaginative and comprehensive listings of what was happening around town, along with consumer reviews and aggressive coverage of the arts (especially rock and roll), the papers attracted a younger demographic that proved tantalizing to advertisers.

A typical alt-weekly ran ads for appliances, stereos, futons, escorts, and tattoo parlors, and had a thick classifieds section. Jim Larkin, who helped found the *Phoenix New Times* and later became CEO of Village Voice Media, remarked, "When the *Chicago Reader* started to get wind in their sails, that was pretty important, because they really understood free circulation, and . . . free circulation is really a hallmark of the alternative press."[37]

As closely held companies, most alt-weeklies do not reveal information about their finances, but according to one media consultant, by the very late 1980s some papers were making "20 or 30 percent profits before taxes on revenue of $1 million or more," and the AAN, which consisted of thirty papers when it was founded in 1978, had expanded to seventy-six members by 1991, with a combined circulation of four million.[38] That same year, *Forbes* ran a story headlined "Boom Times for New Times," referring to New Times, Inc., the parent company of a national chain of alt-weeklies. But as *Mediaweek* pointed out, the alt-weeklies' success was accompanied by the complaint that "as the papers have begun to make money, the people who run them have taken to behaving like bottom-line-obsessed" CEOs. Labor-versus-management quarrels had recently surfaced at the *Voice* and *SF Weekly*, and some feared "the coming corporatization of the medium," as chains like New Times and the Atlanta-based Creative Loafing began acquiring more newspapers. Others worried that the alt-weeklies were either growing stale, or else turning away from their advocacy roles.[39]

Such hand wringing was hardly unusual. From the early 1970s until the mid-1990s, mainstream press reports described the alternative press as constantly stumbling toward maturity and seeking to sever its ties to the gritty underground press that preceded it. Nearly twenty-five years worth of headlines tell the tale: "Press for Youths Seeks New Image" (1973), "The Alternative Press Goes Straight" (1974), "Up From Underground" (1976), "Berkeley [*Barb*] Gaining Respectability and Readers" (1979), "Underground Papers Come Up on Top" (1980), "Transition in 'Alternative' Press Focus of Meeting" (1984), "Is Success Spoiling the Alternative Press?" (1987), "Alternative Weeklies on the Rise," (1989), "Alternative Weeklies Are Gaining Respect— and Readers" (1989), "The Alternative Press Grows Up" (1991), and finally, "Established Alternatives" (1995).[40] In 1994 the *Washington Post*'s Richard

Leiby found it richly ironic that the AAN's annual convention, hosted in Boston by the *Phoenix*, had been such a bland, clean-cut, middle-of-the-road affair. "If someone had sparked a big fat joint . . . then passed it over to me," Leiby joked, "maybe I'd believe for a stoned moment that I was attending a convention of the nation's most unruly, eccentric and savagely unpredictable counterculture newspaper editors."[41]

In fairness, some conference goers probably agreed that that event was especially establishment-oriented, insofar as AT&T sponsored one of its panels, and ABC's Cokie Roberts delivered the keynote address. But a greater irony may lie in the fact that sixteen years after AAN was founded in Seattle, some were apparently still expecting its trade association meetings to bear some resemblance to a late-1960s SDS conference, even though editors and publishers of alternative papers had already gone to such lengths to highlight their respectability. In a 1982 book about business culture, Paul Solman and Thomas Friedman (a different writer than the foreign affairs columnist for the *New York Times*) pointed out that in 1976 Boston's *Real Paper* produced a paradigmatic brochure with which they sought to attract advertisers. It was headlined, "THEY DON'T THROW ROCKS ANYMORE."

> On the cover was a photo of student demonstrators breaking windows in Harvard Square during the Harvard student strike in 1969. The next page had a photo of a couple in their mid-twenties, lounging on an expensive couch, and playing backgammon as their cat looked on. At their feet, a copy of *The Real Paper* and a volume of Robert Frost's poetry. The headline on this page read, 'BUT THEY'RE STILL DOING THINGS THEIR WAY.[42]

Especially during the 1990s, the business model the alternatives established yielded gangbusters results. In the very same period that daily papers were losing readers (especially younger ones), the free newsweeklies dramatically boosted their circulation (from about 2.7 million in 1989 to 7.6 million in 2000), and they continued to do well with the coveted 18–34 demographic. Alt-weeklies also finally began drawing a bit of national advertising in the 1990s.[43] But this was also a time of consternation in the industry, as corporate parents swallowed up some of the independent papers. In 2003, the U.S Justice Department rebuked New Times Media (which owned eleven papers) and Village Voice Media (which owned six) when the two companies swapped assets and closed newspapers in each other's markets (in L.A. and Cleveland). But the prime example of what alt-press traditionalists lament as the corporatization of their industry was the 2006 merger of the New Times and Village Voice chains, after which the new company took the name Village

Voice Media. Many in the alt-press industry fretted about the merger. The *San Francisco Bay Guardian*—owned by Bruce Brugmann, who was then in the process of suing the New Times owners—editorialized that it "could bring more homogeneity into the last bastion of irreverence and print muck-raking," and expressed fear that even the storied *Village Voice* would be forced to adhere to a New Times–driven "cookie cutter" content formula.[44]

In addition to sharing similar designs, and occasionally even some non-local content, papers that belong to the Arizona-based Village Voice Media all claim to prize hard reporting over commentary, and they strive to appear nonideological. As a result, the supposedly "alternative" papers in cities as distinct as Denver, Houston, Los Angeles, and Seattle are thought by some to be virtually indistinguishable. In 2003, a journalist who assayed the papers at an AAN regional meeting complained they all "looked the same—same format, same fonts, same columns complaining about the local daily, same sex-advice, same five-thousand-word hole for the cover story."[45]

Others agree that a trend toward homogenization was already under way, even before the big merger, and they hold that it was largely voluntary. Russ Smith, who founded three alternative papers, including the *New York Press*, recalls that "In the mid-late 90s, there was a hue and cry among the independent weeklies about New Times . . . publishing 'cookie-cutter' McWeeklies." But at the very same time, he says, many (perhaps most) of the tabloids that groused about homogeneity were all running the same syndicated sex advice column (Dan Savage's "Savage Love"), the same astrology column (Rob Brezsny's "Free Will Astrology"), and the same left-wing political cartoons (by Tom Tomorrow and Ted Rall). Furthermore, he says,

> These independent papers, coasting editorially, would act in lockstep, not in collusion but because of a confluence of leaky imaginations. So, for example, in the election of '96, the endorsements of Bill Clinton were nearly unanimous among those papers that endorsed; if an "alt" filmmaker like [Quentin] Tarrantino or Michael Moore . . . had a new movie out, you could be sure that it'd be a cover subject for most of these weeklies. . . . Even as publishers had ever bulging wallets, they stayed true to the safe lefty editorial content, and just churned it out, while real editors . . . like [New Times executive editor] Mike Lacey, the evil Cookie Cutter Monster, actually encouraged original and daring reporting in his "chain" papers.[46]

But some hold that the papers *are* different, if for no other reason than that they exist in markets that differ widely by size and draw from different talent pools. Others maintain that if the cookie-cutter metaphor is accurate (as applied to Village Voice Media's papers), "then they make a great-tasting cookie."[47] It may also be the case that the whole debate is not nearly as important as it might have been, say, thirty years ago. "I think the fear of homogenization of media overall is ludicrous, in the current context," says David Carr. "If you define the media broadly," to include the Internet, "there's never been more sources of information, and there's just been an explosion of voices—a jailbreak in terms of who can publish and who can gain attention."[48] Left-wing magazines like the *Nation*, *Mother Jones*, the *Progressive*, and the socialist-minded *In These Times* continue to play some of the same roles as alt-weeklies (though they may be more associated with investigative journalism and strong opinions than humorous or sprightly writing).

Furthermore, according to *Slate*'s Jack Shafer, who formerly edited the *Washington City Paper* and *SF Weekly*, "Since the beginning of the alt-newspaper boom, there's been a steady migration of really talented people to daily papers. I don't subscribe to the notion that there remains this huge gap between what the alt papers did and what the daily papers do; that gap has narrowed." Besides, he adds, unlike the underground papers of the Sixties— which never betrayed any anxiety over their libel liability—the free city weeklies all have libel insurance. "And the minute you've got libel insurance, you've got a fucking suit and tie on, I'm sorry!"[49]

Changes at the *Village Voice*, though, have been dramatic. According to one insider, by the end of 2008 the paper was operating with about half of the staff it had before it was acquired by the New Times chain, and several of its star writers were either laid off or resigned; the legendary Nat Hentoff, whose first byline appeared in the *Voice* in 1958, was fired.[50] In 2009 the paper even discontinued its syndicated cartoons, another mainstay of most alt-weeklies. According Larkin, the downsizing was necessary in the face of declining classified ad revenue, which had gone to Craigslist and social networking sites like Match.com. "The *Village Voice* lost 15 million [dollars] in classifieds in seven years," he said.

> The reason we ended up with it is because it was ready to close down when we took it over. Because we made the adjustments we needed to make, the *Village Voice* is alive and now it's back on its feet and doing well. [Until then] no one wanted to pay the piper, no one wanted to face the problem, no one wanted to face the union, no one wanted to face the fact that there were a bunch of old writers there who hadn't *done anything* for a long time, [who] were pulling down big salaries. No one wanted to face the fact that the paper was maintained and put out by interns, in many cases unpaid. You can't operate that way. The *Voice* was overstaffed.[51]

Others may be more sentimental about the paper, which, after all, has a prized reputation. By fusing an ebullient curiosity for the arts with an unembarrassed attitude toward sex, by pursuing a left-wing political agenda, and by granting tremendous liberties to its columnists and investigative reporters, the *Voice* helped to pioneer modern alternative journalism. Today, some of its loyal readers hope that its veterans might exert a spectral influence at 36 Cooper Square.

Afterword

IF OFFSET PUBLISHING made the underground press possible, desktop publishing in the 1980s led to an explosion in the publication of "zines" (said to derive from the term "fanzine"). The first zines are thought to date from the 1930s, when science-fiction fans circulated obsessive letters and commentary about the books and comics they devoured; in the 1970s, punk rock's DIY (do-it-yourself) ethos fed the production of amateur magazines devoted to underground bands and culture. One such magazine, New York's *Punk*, caught Forcade's attention not long after it first started coming out in 1976. According to John Holmstrom, one of *Punk*'s cofounders, Forcade gave them printing advice, set them up with a distributor, and generally took them under his wing. He thought they represented "the next big wave in underground publishing."[1]

But the defiantly amateur, noncommercial, homemade pamphlets or chapbooks that emerged in the 1980s were quirkier and more idiosyncratic than the sci-fi or punk mags that preceded them. Usually composed by individuals rather than groups or collectives, they addressed topics including (but hardly limited to) radical politics, feminism, the suburbs, vegetarianism, low-wage vocations, religion, poetry and literature, travel, technology, gadgets, pop culture, drugs, kinky sex, UFOs, and serial killers. Zines can sometimes be found at offbeat book and record stores, and for a spell in the 1990s, large chains like Tower Records and Barnes & Noble carried a handful of sporadically published titles.[2] But the vast majority of them circulate through the mail.[3] Though it is impossible to know their readership, in 1997 media scholar Stephen Duncombe estimated that somewhere between 500,000 and 750,000 youths were in regular contact with zines.[4]

In a few instances, like-minded zinesters have formed leagues or collectives. One such group—the Cambridge-based Small Press Alliance, which arose in the mid-1980s—was merely practically minded. One of its founders,

Rob Chalfen, recalls that some of its twenty or so members were so quirky and idiosyncratic that they bristled at the group's name; the SPA sounded too much like a Sixties throwback, whereas they wanted to showcase their individualism.[5] Then in the 1990s, the feminist-punk movement Riot Grrrl spawned thousands of zines that circulated in a carefully cultivated distribution network. Collectively, their zines promoted inter-movement communication and helped to build group solidarity, and in this way they served a function not unlike that of the underground newspapers of yore. "In the shadows of the dominant culture, zines and underground culture mark out a *free space*," Duncombe writes, "within which to imagine and experiment with new and idealistic ways of thinking, communicating, and being." In their content, form, and organization, "[they] constitute an alternative ideal of how human relations, creation, and consumption could be organized."[6]

More consequentially, some of what's happening in the left-wing blogosphere can likewise be compared to the Sixties underground press. If offset printing and desktop publishing have lowered the barriers of entry into journalism and created new means for personal expression, the Internet has completely revolutionized the public sphere. As the cliché holds, nowadays freedom of the press belongs to anyone with a laptop computer and an Internet connection. "Never before," writes Matt Welch, "have so many passionate outsiders—hundreds of thousands, at minimum—stormed the ramparts of professional journalism."[7]

By many accounts, the so-called netroots—a loose coalition of activist bloggers—took shape in response to the Florida election recount of 2000, when many grassroots activists concluded that the Democratic Party establishment lacked the stomach for a knock-down, drag-out brawl with Republicans over how the contested ballots ought to be counted.[8] Afterward, the highly polarizing Bush administration provided the (mostly) younger bloggers ample opportunity to hone their skills at political mud wrestling.[9] Although it's obvious that the established media continues to take the lion's share of the responsibility for defining the borders of permissible debate in the United States, no one who surveys the early history of the Web can afford to overlook the roles played by citizen-journalists and activist bloggers.

In 2002, at the one hundredth birthday party of former U.S. senator Strom Thurmond, former senate majority leader Trent Lott was videotaped suggesting that he wished Thurmond had won his 1948 bid for the presidency on the segregationist States' Rights Democratic Party ticket. The mainstream press overlooked his contemptible comments, but after howls of protest from the blogosphere, newspaper and television reporters picked up the story, setting in motion a chain of events that led to Lott's resignation as majority whip. In the 2004 election, the liberal political action committee MoveOn.org demonstrated the Internet's power to bring like-minded people together, and although he didn't win the Democratic primaries, presidential candidate Howard Dean found new ways of harnessing the Web's loose structure; his influence on political campaigning in the United States will be lasting.[10] And while the 2008 election will always be historic because it made Barack Obama president, it should also be remembered as a watershed election in which the Beltway media was frequently outmaneuvered or humbled by the liberal blogosphere.[11] By one account, the netroots have already become "the most significant mass movement in U.S. politics since the rise of the Christian right" in the early 1980s.[12]

Given how quickly and thoroughly our media environment is changing, it is dangerous to say too much about where we might be headed. The Project for Excellence in American Journalism's annual report for 2009, *The State of the News Media*, is bracing: it describes plunging newspaper revenues, papers either falling into bankruptcy or losing most of their values, a speedy audience migration to the Internet, and a lack of consensus (or even many very good ideas) about how to create revenue streams that will support the newsgathering and reporting that is so essential in a democracy.[13] No one knows when it will happen, but eventually—in five years, or maybe ten, or sometime after that—printed daily newspapers of any type will either become rare in the United States, or they will cease to exist altogether.

But one prediction is safe: never again will we see anything like the underground press of the Sixties. One reason is that the technology that spawned the underground press is practically obsolete; it is simply no longer exciting or cost-efficient to transfer inked images to cheap paper. Another reason is that the movement that fueled the growth of underground newspapers is likewise extinct. Of course, the Sixties remain a force in American popular culture; so momentous were that decade's events that even subsequent generations have come of age in its afterglow. But the underground press had a specific raison d'être: it was created to bring tidings of the youth rebellion to cities and campuses across America and to help build a mass movement. And for all of its shortcomings—aesthetic, intellectual, and even sometimes moral—this is something it did remarkably well.

In some cases, the underground papers that emerged from the subcultural stirrings in local communities were anodynes for the socially aggrieved; in other instances, they were much more intoxicating. Whether they advanced the hard-boiled analysis of SDS, Herbert Marcuse, Noam Chomsky, or Huey Newton, or championed the new liberated lifestyles associated with Woodstock (again, two styles of radicalism that were not always mutually exclusive), the radical newssheets became the mediums through which youths transmitted their unfiltered arguments and ideas and popularized their rebellion. After years of stressing the importance of building "counterinstitutions" (most of which, frankly, didn't amount to much), the underground press became the New Left's greatest organizational achievement. In this way, they were inspiring and stimulating. "The most valuable thing about the underground press," Abbie Hoffman once remarked, "is that it's there. It is a visible manifestation of an alternative culture. It helps to create a national identity."[14] And because of the underground papers' extraordinary inclusiveness—their openness to writers and staffers of varying persuasions and capabilities, and their decentralized operating structures—they helped to frame social relations within the Movement.

Of course, none of this came easily. In early 1967, a woman from Madison, Wisconsin, wrote to *WIN* magazine asking for advice for how to go about starting an underground newspaper.[15] "As far as 'problems,' we have many," confessed *WIN*'s editor, Gwen Reyes.

> We are continually deluged with bills we cannot pay and needed improvements we cannot make. Also, when dealing with so much volunteer help, we cannot expect people to show up as regularly as they might if they were paid staffworkers. *Time* becomes a major factor, and we usually finish each issue just under the wire. . . . This time pressure also results in frazzled nerves and occasional mistakes getting printed. Things are seldom proof-read sufficiently, and we are extremely fortunate not to have more errors in our copy. Also, just getting ten or fifteen people together at one time for an editorial meeting is difficult when most of them have other jobs and responsibilities. And then there's correspondence, rejections, late nights, worry, frustration.

Even after all this, though, she stressed that their work still seemed worthwhile and fulfilling. "I hope that all these minute points will not dissuade you in your attempt to organize a paper," she concluded. There remained "countless joys in publishing a finished product of love-labor, especially an underground paper which attempts so strenuously . . . to communicate with kindred minds and perhaps convert a few not-so-kindred ones."[16]

Certainly the era's street-corner newspapers loom large in the memories of many Sixties veterans. In the spring of 1969, Jesse Kornbluth, a former salesman of Boston's *Avatar*, penned a beautiful elegy for the decade, in which he listed "Sgt. Peppers, stoned sex, Country Joe & the Fish, the Love-Ins, and the beautiful newspapers" as things he would miss most about the era. In his estimation, underground newspapers ranked alongside exciting innovations in rock and roll and bountiful supplies of marijuana as essential ingredients in the New Left rebellion; they were what had made "a national though disorganized 'youth movement' possible." He also understood that the papers were significant even beyond the quality and reach of the ideas they disseminated. "The point was that these toys were our own," he crowed, "and everything worked."[17]

The democratic sensibilities that Sixties youths brought to journalism, though, not only persist, but also have already taken on a life of their own. And, barring some dystopian future, they are likely to endure in some fashion or another. With the proliferation of new tools for gathering, recording, and transmitting news, we are going to continue to see a collapsing of private space and a diffusion of power around knowledge and information. For left-wingers in America today, the Internet holds such tremendous promise and opportunity. But much of what the liberal blogosphere is already credited with—democratizing the media, rapidly circulating information, influencing the agenda of the mainstream press, and building communities among like-minded groups—was accomplished on a smaller scale nearly forty years ago by the brash and saucy, threadbare papers of the underground press.

Notes

Note on Sources

1. Quoted in John Kronenberger, "What's Black and White and Pink and Green and Dirty and Read All Over?" *Look*, October 1, 1968, 22. In 1973, an employee for Bell and Howell, which microfilmed the underground papers and sold them to libraries, said something similar. "Ten and 20 years from now, scholars will look at these microfilm copies and see how things have evolved." Quoted in Clark DeLeon, "Underground Press Alive and Well in 300 Cities," *Philadelphia Inquirer*, May 14, 1973.
2. Dickstein, *Gates of Eden*, 132.
3. Ryan, *Civic Wars*, 13.

Introduction

1. The Rolling Stones' tour manager at that time, Sam Cutler, admitted he provided the Angels with $500 worth of beer. But various parties disagree about whether the beer was given freely, perhaps in order to placate the Angels, or whether it was in return for a pledge from the Angels to guard the stage or provide some other form of security.
2. See Nicholas von Hoffman, "Violence at Altamont," *Washington Post and Times-Herald*, January 2, 1970. The quote originally appeared in *Rolling Stone* magazine.
3. See Robert Christgau, "The Rolling Stones: Can't Get No Satisfaction," in Christgau, *Any Old Way*.
4. *Rolling Stone*, which was then located in the Bay Area but was national in scope, likewise provided thorough and outstanding coverage of the Altamont fiasco. See epecially The Editors, "Let it Bleed," *Rolling Stone*, January 21, 1970, 18–38; John Burks, "In the Aftermath of Altamont," *Rolling Stone*, February 7, 1970, 7–8.
5. George Paul Csicsery, "Stones Concert Ends It: America Now Up for Grabs," *Berkeley Tribe*, December 12–19, 1969, 1, 5.
6. Detroit Annie, "You Always Get What You Want," *Berkeley Tribe*, December 12–19, 1969, 5. Another local underground newspaper, the *Berkeley Barb*, wrote about Altamont in only slightly more muted tones. It distinguished itself, however, with an

exclusive cover story on Meredith Hunter. Although other papers mentioned Hunter's name, the *Barb* was the only one that went to any effort to find out about him. See "The Kind They Killed At Altamont," *Berkeley Barb*, December 19–24, 1969, 1, 5–6, 13, 17.

7. Beginning in 1965, the *Examiner* worked under a joint operating agreement with the *San Francisco Chronicle*, in which the *Chronicle* published in the mornings and the *Examiner* in the evenings. The two papers jointly published a Sunday edition.

8. William O'Brien, "300,000 Jam Rock Concert," *San Francisco Examiner*, December 6, 1969.

9. Jim Weed, "300,000 Say It with Music," *San Francisco Examiner*, December 7, 1969. The last bit, referencing the Jefferson Airplane's youth-culture anthem, was a particularly ludicrous distortion, seeing as how one of the Hell's Angels had knocked one of that group's singers, Marty Balin, completely unconscious during the first song of their set.

10. "Rock Festival's Magnetic Draw," *San Francisco Examiner*, December 9, 1969. Speaking of youths, they wrote, "Rock and roll . . . appeals powerfully to their ache of inhibited and unreleased energy. It produces exaltation. The resulting experience . . . had elements of frenzy typical of primitive religions. Those who write, promote and play hard rock are its priests and Pied Pipers."

11. Louis Menand, "It Took A Village: How the *Voice* Changed Journalism." *New Yorker*, January 5, 2008, 44.

12. It is impossible to measure precisely the scope of the underground press at any one time in the late 1960s. Some papers were well established and had paid circulations in the tens of thousands, while others were short lived and irregularly published. In 1972 Laurence Leamer estimated that underground newspapers had a paid circulation of 1.5 million and a readership many times that number. But when talking about the underground press's total circulation, there has never been a consensus about what types of publications ought to be tallied. Leamer's figure of 1.5 million includes only those papers in the Underground Press Syndicate, whereas others might include mimeographed high school papers or counterculture-flavored rock magazines that were not part of UPS, like *Cheetah* and *Rolling Stone*. Underground-press historian Abe Peck holds that "by the highwater mark of protest," in 1969, "at least five hundred papers served communities and constituencies *worldwide*" (emphasis added). Journalist Ethel Romm identified roughly 150 "underground" and "Movement" papers in the United States in 1969, but she said that number was still on the upswing and by 1970 had become "uncountable." She estimated the underground press's combined circulation (not readership) to be about two million. See Leamer, *Paper Revolutionaries*; Peck, *Uncovering the Sixties*, xv; Romm, *Open Conspiracy*, 17.

13. Here my thinking is influenced by Goodwyn, *Populist Moment*, vii–xxiv.

14. See McAdam, *Freedom Summer*, 17–19.

15. James Miller, *Democracy is in the Streets*; Gitlin, *The Sixties*.

16. See McMillian, "You Didn't Have to Be There."

17. These points have been put forth in Breines, "Whose New Left?"; Hunt, "When Did the Sixties Happen?"; Isserman, "Not-So-Dark-and-Bloody"; Wiener, "New Left as History."

18. Since the late 1990s, numerous books have described the New Left from a local or regional perspective, and several have used the methods and approaches of social

history. See Foley, *Confronting the War Machine*; Frost, *Interracial Movement of the Poor*; Hunt, *The Turning*; Lieberman, *Prairie Power*; McBride, "Fault Lines of Mass Culture"; McMillian and Buhle, *New Left Revisited*; Michel, *Struggle for a Better South*; Monhollon, *This is America?*; Rossinow, *Politics of Authenticity*; Wynkoop, *Dissent in the Heartland*.

19. Abe Peck, foreword to Wachsberger, *Voices from the Underground*, 1:xix.

20. There were, however, a few exceptions. From 1962 to 1965, outré poet Ed Sanders published a crude journal called *Fuck You: A Magazine of the Arts*, which circulated surreptitiously until he was arrested on obscenity charges. Later he was acquitted. (I briefly discuss *Fuck You* in chapter 3.) Many GI-produced underground newspapers also operated covertly, and in the early 1970s, fugitives in the Weather Underground secretly disseminated a short-lived underground newspaper called *Osawatomie*.

21. Bob Cummings, "Can You Dig It?" *Georgia Straight*, August 16–22, 1968, reprinted in Pauls and Campbell, *Georgia Straight*, 22.

22. In the 1960s, one could also purchase an easy-to-use power mimeograph machine for a few hundred dollars. Mimeo sheets, however, were often of such poor quality that most underground papers preferred to use the photo-offset method.

23. John Burks, "The Underground Press: A Special Report," *Rolling Stone*, October 4, 1969, 17.

24. Gwen Reyes to Julie Weiner, February 2, 1967, *Connections* Records (1967–68), Wisconsin State Historical Society, Madison, WI, Box 1. Henceforth, this collection will be abbreviated "WSHS."

25. John Wilcock, "How to Start Your Own Newspaper," *Other Scenes* 9 (n.d., ca. 1967): 14.

26. Armstrong, *Trumpet to Arms*, 16.

27. See Hodgson, *America in Our Time*, 139–40.

28. Hunter Thompson, "The Ultimate Freeloader," *Distant Drummer*, November 1967, 6.

29. Responding to the specious objectivity that characterized most news reporting, New Journalists sometimes become personally involved with the stories they covered, and they frequently drew from the techniques of literary fiction in their reporting. Valuable collections of New Journalism include Wolfe and Johnson, *The New Journalism*; Nicolaus Mills, *The New Journalism*.

30. Joan Didion and John Gregory Dune, "Alicia and the Underground Press," *Saturday Evening Post*, January 13, 1968, 14.

31. Thorne Dreyer and Victoria Smith, "The Movement and the New Media," Liberation News Service packet 144, March 1, 1969, 21.

32. Tocqueville, *Democracy in America*, 474.

33. Allen Ginsberg to Thomas Fleming, January 30, 1970, PEN American Center Records, Rare Books and Special Collections Library, Princeton University, Box 96, Folder 7. Henceforth, this collection will be abbreviated "PEN Center." In another context, former *Nation* editor Victor Navasky made the point, which is too easily forgotten, that "it is part of the ideology of the center to deny that it has an ideology." See Navasky, *A Matter of Opinion*, 269.

34. Dreyer and Smith, "The Movement and the New Media," 25.

35. Gitlin, "Underground Press and Its Cave-in," 21.

36. This was the opinion of Marshall Bloom, cofounder of Liberation News Service (LNS). See Marshall Bloom to Dan Bernstein, n.d., Marshall Bloom Papers, Box 8, Folder 23, Amherst College Archives and Special Collections, Amherst, MA. (Henceforth, this

collection will be abbreviated "MBP.") See also Marshall Bloom to Marty [Peretz] December 16, 1967, MBP, Box 8, Folder 23.

37. Miles adds that he was also received warmly when he visited the *Los Angeles Free Press*. "We tried our best to reciprocate," he said, "but we were sometimes overwhelmed by the sheer numbers of visitors to Swinging London, all of whom wanted to meet the Beatles." However impertinent their requests, they had good reason for asking. Miles's paper ran out of the basement of the famous Indica Bookshop, which is where John Lennon famously picked up a copy of Timothy Leary's guidebook to LSD, *The Psychedelic Experience*, in 1966. *IT* also sometimes received financial support from the Beatles. See Barry Miles, "Notes from Underground," foreword to Bizot, *Free Press*, 6–7.

38. See Gregory Calvert, interview by Ron Grele, July 1–3, 1987, Student Movements of the 1960s, Columbia University Oral History Research Office, New York, 292. (Henceforth, this collection will be abbreviated "Columbia.") See also Jon Wiener, interview by Ron Grele, April 26, 1988 and May 6, 1988, Columbia, 46.

39. A good textbook-style survey of the gay and feminist press can be found in Streitmatter, *Voices of Revolution*, 238–74.

40. Leamer writes, "Only the crudest shorthand . . . allows one even to talk about *the* politically radical and *the* culturally radical papers. This cross-pollenization [sic] has studded the landscape with hybrids that defy categorization." Leamer, *Paper Revolutionaries*, 61. See also Armstrong, *Trumpet to Arms*, 44–45.

41. For an analysis of the New Left's countercultural turn in the late 1960s, see Rossinow, "New Left in the Counterculture." For a description of the politicization of many countercultural newspapers, see John Leo, "Politics Now the Focus of the Underground Press," *New York Times*, September 4, 1968.

42. This understanding of the New Left draws varying degrees of support from Breines, "Whose New Left?"; Echols, "We Gotta Get Out of This Place"; Calvert, *Democracy from the Heart*; Sayres et al., *Sixties Without Apology*; McBride, "Death City Radicals."

43. Van Gosse describes the New Left as a "movement of movements," not limited to youths, that encompassed "all of the struggles for fundamental change from the early 1950s roughly to 1975." Although this broad definition allows him to trace influences and draw connections among a diverse assortment of groups, I think it's a flawed definition. The climate of left-wing opinion in the late 1960s and early 1970s was quite different from that which appeared in the 1950s, and (let's face it) very few activists of color ever called themselves New Leftists. Nor did very many middle-aged adults. See Gosse, *Rethinking the New Left*, 4–8; Rossinow, "New Left in the Counterculture," 109n1. I take this all up in more detail in McMillian, "Locating the New Left."

44. See, for instance, Robin Morgan, "Goodbye to All That."

45. Of course, feminists and African American radicals both had their own radical organs. In 1970, a collective of women's liberationists took over the *Rat*, a rabidly sexist underground newspaper in New York City. In roughly this same period, feminists launched publications like Berkeley's *It Ain't Me Babe*, Washington, DC's *off our backs*, and Boston's *No More Fun and Games*. Meanwhile, women's consciousness-raising (or "CR") contributed to the body of writing that anchored political theory and cultural studies in women's concrete life experiences, and in 1972, Gloria Steinem popularized an individualistic feminist vision when she helped establish *Ms.* magazine. By contrast, the leading black radical newspapers of the 1960s were organs of larger organizations.

During the black power movement's heyday, the Nation of Islam's paper, *Muhammad Speaks*, claimed a circulation approaching 300,000, making it one of the largest weekly newspapers in the United States. In April 1967, the Black Panther Party began publishing the *Black Panther*, which eventually reached a circulation of about 85,000. Finally, artists and intellectuals associated with the black arts movement promoted black cultural nationalism in poetry, fiction, and journalism.

46. See Breines, "Whose New Left?" 528; Isserman, "Not-So-Dark and Bloody," 991.

Chapter 1

1. Thomas R. Brooks., "Voice of the New Campus 'Underclass,'" *New York Times Magazine*, November 7, 1965, 25; Robert Pardun, e-mail to author, February 17, 2004; Cathy Wilkerson, e-mail to author, February 16, 2004.

2. Newfield, *Prophetic Minority*, 117–18.

3. SDS's most comprehensive biographer, Kirkpatrick Sale, made a similar observation when he called SDS's new $300 multilith printing press—which at the time was housed at its first headquarters, in New York City's East Village—"the organization's proudest symbol of becomingness." See Sale, *SDS*, 73.

4. Raskin, *Out of the Whale*, 120. By 1969, even "shotguns" may have seemed a little tame to some members of the Weatherman faction of SDS, who advocated "revolutionary wall painting" ("RWP" for short). Suggested slogans included: "PEOPLE'S WAR," "OFF THE PIG," "OFF THE LANDLORDS," "REVOLUTION NOW," "BRING THE WAR HOME," and "VC RUN IT." See *Fire!*, "Draw Your Conclusions on the Wall," November 21, 1969, 14.

5. Major works with this narrative arc include Gitlin, *The Sixties*; James Miller, *Democracy Is in the Streets*; Sale, *SDS*. See also Perlstein, "Who Owns the Sixties?"

6. See, for instance, Peck, *Uncovering the Sixties*, 11–13, 22.

7. C. Wright Mills, *Sociological Imagination*, 226.

8. For information concerning the FBI's illegal operations against SDS, see Cunningham, *There's Something Happening Here*, 167–80.

9. An alternative would be to trace SDS's origins all the way back to the first collegiate radical movement in the United States, the Intercollegiate Socialist Society, which was founded in 1905. That group renamed itself the League for Industrial Democracy in 1921, and throughout the 1920s and 1930s it promoted American socialism through lectures by Jack London, Norman Thomas, and Harry Laidler, as well as through its monthly journal, *Labor Age*. Its student arm was the Student League for Industrial Democracy. After World War Two, the League for Industrial Democracy grew wary of radical socialism and became largely inactive. In 1960, the Student League for Industrial Democracy morphed into SDS, and Al Haber was SDS's first president. Although Haber personally recruited some of SDS's early leaders and organized an impressive conference on student radicalism at the University of Michigan, the group remained basically unknown on American campuses during the 1961–62 school year. Accordingly, most scholars and the great majority of SDS veterans date the group's origins to the drafting of the Port Huron Statement. As SDS national secretary Jim Monsonis explained in 1962, "SDS truly became a movement and an organization at the [Port Huron] convention." See Jim Monsonis, *SDS Membership Bulletin*, September 30 1962,

1, SDS Records, Reel 34, Series 4A, No. 19. See also Sale, *SDS*, 673–93; and James Miller, *Democracy Is in the Streets*, 29.

10. See Tom Hayden and Dick Flacks, "The Port Huron Statement at 40," *The Nation*, (August 5–12, 2002), 18–21. Literary scholar John Downton Hazlett argues that by conflating their personal experiences with those of the so-called "Sixties Generation," the manifesto's authors established a template and reference point for many future memoirists. See Hazlett, *My Generation*, 40–49.

11. Allen Smith, "Present at the Creation." For scholars characterizing the Port Huron Statement as a watershed in the history of the American left, see Sale, *SDS*, 49–51; James Miller, *Democracy Is in the Streets*," 13–14; Isserman, *If I Had a Hammer*, 213–14.

12. Smith, 341. See also Gosse, "Movement of Movements," 279–84. Works by journalists that discussed the Port Huron Statement in the mid 1960s include Fred Powledge, "The New Student Left: Movement Represents Serious Activists in Drive for Changes," *New York Times*, March 15, 1965; Jack Newfield, "The Student Left: Idealism and Action," *Nation*, November 8, 1965, 330–33.

13. For some SDS veterans, the Port Huron Statement seems to have elicited an unusual combination of excitement and tedium. For instance, Todd Gitlin once recalled being "absolutely enraptured" when he read a draft of the document, "thinking, 'My God, this is what I feel.'" But elsewhere he said he found its "programmatic particulars" to be so dull that he didn't finish reading it (see Isserman, *If I Had a Hammer*, 214, and Gitlin, *The Sixties*, 101). Similarly, SDSer Cathy Wilkerson recalled finding parts of the manifesto "very powerful and inspiring," whereas other parts struck her as "boring." See Cathy Wilkerson, interview by Ron Grele, February 17, 1985, Columbia, 26.

14. SDS, "Port Huron Statement," as quoted in James Miller, *Democracy Is in the Streets*, 329. All subsequent quotations from the Port Huron Statement come from Miller's book.

15. Ibid., 374.

16. Ibid., 329.

17. SDS printed some twenty thousand copies of the Port Huron Statement between 1962 and 1964, and another twenty thousand by the end of 1966. (See Allen Smith, "Present at the Creation," 360.)

18. The phrase belongs to Ella Baker (see Baker, "Bigger than a Hamburger," in Carson et al., *Eyes on the Prize*, 121).

19. See James Miller, *Democracy is in the Streets*, esp. 145–47.

20. Echols, *Shaky Ground*, 72.

21. SDS, "Port Huron Statement," 333.

22. This was true until the very late 1960s, anyhow. The Weatherman faction of SDS (which did not exactly enjoy good standing in the New Left) frequently adhered to the Leninist notion of "democratic centralism"—a political framework that allows for vigorous debate within an organization, but also requires members of that organization to publicly adhere to whatever decisions the majority reaches, regardless of their private beliefs. The Marxist group Progressive Labor, which infiltrated SDS in the late 1960s, also adhered to democratic centralism.

23. As quoted in Klatch, *A Generation Divided*, 25.

24. Barbara Haber, interview by Bret Eynon, September 1978, Contemporary History Project (The New Left in Ann Arbor), University of Michigan, 4–5. Henceforth this collection will be abbreviated as CHP.

25. SDS, "Port Huron Statement," 329; emphasis added.

26. As quoted in Klatch, *A Generation Divided*, 24.

27. Frithjof Bergmann, interview by Bret Eynon, June 18, 1978, CHP 5.

28. Gitlin, *Whole World Is Watching*, 135; Flacks, "Making History vs. Making Life," 139.

29. Richard Flacks, interview by Bret Eynon, September 25, 1978, CHP, 14.

30. Jeremy Brecher, interview by Bret Eynon, September 20, 1983, Columbia, 13.

31. Brecher interview, 12.

32. Elise Boulding, interview by Bret Eynon, November 1978, CHP, 4.

33. Peter Dilorenzi, interview by Bret Eynon, May 31, 1979, CHP, 4.

34. Barry Bluestone, interview by Bret Eynon, August 1978, CHP, 3.

35. Brecher interview, 14.

36. Haber interview, 11.

37. Bluestone interview, 7.

38. Sara Evans argues that women were socialized into taking secondary roles in SDS because they weren't accustomed to making and aggressively defending forceful arguments. See Evans, *Personal Politics*, 115, 166.

39. Wilkerson interview, 19.

40. Kitty Cone, as quoted in Gottlieb, *Do You Believe in Magic?* 144.

41. Alan Haber and Barbara Jacobs to "friends," December 15, 1962, SDS Records, Reel 2, Series 2A, No. 1.

42. Sale, *SDS*, 78–80.

43. Sale, *SDS*, 74.

44. See Mickey Flacks, interview by Bret Eynon, September 25, 1978, CHP, 6–7; Bluestone interview, 7.

45. Sale, *SDS*, 81.

46. Ibid., 78–81.

47. Tom Hayden to "SDS executive committee, others," n.d., ca. Spring 1962, SDS Records, Reel 1, Series 1, No. 6.

48. Arthur Waskow to Paul Booth, August 2, 1965, SDS Records, Reel 5, Series 2A, No. 42.

49. Clark Kissinger to Paul Potter, January 31, 1965, SDS Records, Reel 4, Series 2A, No. 29. See also Ken McEldowney to Jim McDougall and George Brosi, July 7, 1965, SDS Records, Reel 14, Series 2A, No. 69.

50. Richard Chase, "The New Campus Magazines," *Harper's*, October 1961, 170.

51. Tom Hayden used both forms; SDSer Betty Garman Robinson recalled that Hayden's dramatic letters describing the Student Nonviolent Coordinating Committee's activities in the Deep South were "the reason [she] went into SDS," quoted in Polletta, *Endless Meeting*, 125.

52. Quite a few internal newsletters came and went during SDS's history. Some were specific to SDS projects, such as the Economic Research and Action Project newsletter, the Peace and Research Education Project newsletter, and the Vietnam Summer newsletter. There was also a *Membership Bulletin* and a *Discussion Bulletin*, which were later combined into the *SDS Bulletin*. *New Era* and *Caw* were two of SDS's very short-lived magazines. Some of SDS's older members founded the *Radicals in the Professions* newsletter, which later changed its name to *Something Else*. SDS's biggest publication in terms of size and circulation was its tabloid newspaper, *New Left Notes*, which briefly

morphed into *The Fire Next Time* and then just *Fire!* In addition to all this, dozens of individual SDS chapters published their own newsletters.

53. As editor of the *SDS Bulletin*, Jeff Shero frequently reprinted articles or essays that first appeared elsewhere. "We just lift these articles, rarely getting permission from the publisher," he told one friend. See Jeff Shero to Gideon Sjoberg, August 18, 1965, SDS Records, Reel 5, Series 2A, No. 35. Shero later changed his name to Jeff Shero Nightbyrd, and then simply to Jeff Nightbyrd. In this book he is referred to by his original surname.

54. See Becky Miller to "Steve," n.d., SDS Records, Reel 5, Series 2A, No. 38.

55. Max added, "I have repeatedly asked not to have my communications to the [SDS National Council] printed unless I say they are for publication." Despite his annoyance, however, he concluded his letter on a humorous note: "Let me warn you editors of *New Left Notes* that if you print any more of my correspondence without authorization, I shall send you a letter which I guarantee will involve you in an obscenity suit. Should you decline to print such a letter I will hold you up before the scorn of the National Council for selling out to the misguided Victorian morality of the Postal Establishment." See Steve Max, "Angry Letter," *New Left Notes*, March 11, 1966, 4.

56. This discussion draws from the minutes of the SDS National Council Meeting, June 16, 1964, taken by Helen Garvy, SDS Records, Reel 3, Series 2A, No. 10.

57. Don McKelvey to Donna G. Hayes, December 10, 1962, SDS Records, Reel 3, Series 2A, No. 21. The *Membership Bulletin* featured reports from SDS presidents, updates on chapter activity and projects, notices of upcoming events, and suggested reading material. However, like the *DB*, it also welcomed feedback and participation from the SDS rank and file. See *SDS Membership Bulletin*, September 30, 1962, 1, in SDS Records, Reel 34, Series 4A, No. 19.

58. Sale, *SDS*, 78.

59. The Student Peace Union flourished from 1960 to 1962, cosponsoring several marches on Washington, DC, and attracting some 3,500 members. Unlike SDS, the Student Peace Union was shaped by Old Left ideas, and concentrated its energies on a single "issue"—nuclear arms control. It collapsed in 1964, just as SDS was gaining momentum.

60. Editor's Note, *SDS Discussion Bulletin*, Spring 1964, n.p., SDS Records, Reel 5, Series 2A, No. 40.

61. Don McKelvey to R. M. Glee, November 17, 1962, SDS Records, Reel 3, Series 2A, No. 21.

62. Helen Garvy, interview by author.

63. Helen Garvy, "From the Editor," *SDS Bulletin*, October 1964, 2, in SDS Records Reel 35, Series 4A, No. 35.

62. Don McKelvey to Donna G. Hayes, December 10, 1962, SDS Records, Reel 3, Series 2A, No. 21; Don McKelvey to Allan Tobin, November 23, 1962, SDS Records, Reel 3, Series 2A, No. 21; Dickie Magidoff to Helen [Garvy] and Clark [Kissinger], January 19, 1965, SDS Records, Reel 3, Series 2A, No. 23.

65. This process has since been described by literary scholars as "freewriting" (or, sometimes, "focused freewriting"). See Peter Elbow, *Writing With Power: Techniques for Mastering the Writing Process* (New York: Oxford University Press, 1981), 213–20.

66. Don McKelvey to Dayton Pruitt, n.d., in SDS Records, Reel 3, Series 2A, No. 21.

67. Don McKelvey to Dennis Kelly, May 15, 1964, in SDS Records, Reel 5, Series 2A, No. 38.

68. Don McKelvey to Edwin Kahn, January 10, 1963, in SDS Records, Reel 3, Series 2A, No. 21.

69. Helen Garvy, "From the Editor," *SDS Bulletin*, October 1964, 2, SDS Records, Reel 35, Series 4A, No. 35.

70. This idea may have been inculcated in SDS early on. In 1960 Al Haber had a brief but warm correspondence with William F. Buckley, the conservative editor of *National Review*, after he asked Buckley if he could distribute some spare copies of *National Review* throughout SDS. Although he didn't expect Buckley's magazine to win many converts, Haber said "I do think . . . that it is valuable for our members to come into contact with views sharply counter to our own." See Alan Haber to William F. Buckley, July 8, 1960, SDS Records, Reel 1, Series 1, No. 10.

71. Don McKelvey to Gerald Knight, December 2, 1963, SDS Records, Reel 8, Series 2A, No. 93.

72. Don McKelvey to Murray L. Katcher, January 26, 1964, SDS Records, Box 6, WSHS.

73. Don McKelvey to Erik Johnson, March 29, 1964, SDS Records, Reel 4, Series 2A, No. 35.

74. Don McKelvey to "Kim and Pete," May 10, 1964, SDS Records, Reel 5, Series 2A, No. 38.

75. Jeff Shero to Mike Davis, August 10, 1965, SDS Records, Reel 28, Series 3, No. 108.

76. Jeff Shero to Jeremy Brecher, August 3, 1965, SDS Records, Reel 28, Series 3, No. 108. One SDSer was more caustic about the problem of quality control in SDS writings: "It doesn't seem to me that we have to prove we don't red bait by serving as a supermarket for the materials of the left in an indiscriminate way." See David Smith to "Friends," August 24, 1965, SDS Records, Reel 3, Series 2A, No. 23.

77. *SDS Membership Bulletin*, January-February 1963, n.p., SDS Records Reel 35, Series 4A, No. 19.

78. *SDS Membership Bulletin*, November-December 1964, n.p., SDS Records, Reel 35, Series 4A, No. 19.

79. "Convention," *SDS Membership Bulletin*, March-April 1963, 1, 3, SDS Records, Reel 35, Series 4A, No. 19.

80. Don McKelvey, to "Worklist," October 23, 1968, SDS Records, Reel 5, Series 2A, No. 48.

81. Helen Garvy, to "Paul Potter, Ken, Sharon, Carol, Rennie, Todd, Booth, Dickie, Rich, Vernon, Nick, Larry, Bob, Lee, Dick, Tom, Carl," October 15, 1964, SDS Records, Reel 5, Series 2A, No. 35.

82. See Richard Armstrong, "The Explosive Revival of the Far Left," *Saturday Evening Post*, May 8 1965, 27–32; Brooks, "New Campus 'Underclass,'" 25; Andrew Kopkind, "Of, By and For the Poor," *The New Republic*, June 19, 1965, 15–19; Jack Newfield "Student Left: Idealism and Action," *The Nation*, November 8, 1965, 330–33; Powledge, "New Student Left"; *Newsweek*, "The Activists—Protesting Too Much?" March 22, 1965, 48–54.

83. Polletta, *Endless Meeting*, 138.

84. Jim Russell to Helen Garvy, October 30, 1965, SDS Records, Box 34, WSHS.

85. Jeremy Brecher, "Some Notes on the 1965 SDS Convention," n.d., SDS Records, Reel 3, Series 2A, No. 14.

86. Newfield, *A Prophetic Minority*, 120; Sale, *SDS*, 204–7.

87. Greg Calvert, interview by Ron Grele, July 1–3, 1987, Columbia, 158.

88. Paul Booth to Vernon Eagle, September 28, 1965, SDS Records, Reel 19, Series 3, No. 1. This was a form letter, apparently sent to SDS benefactors, in advance of an upcoming SDS conference at the University of Illinois in Champaign-Urbana. Booth's quip about "the model SDS personality" was undoubtedly in reference to Tom Hayden, who wrote a master's thesis on C. Wright Mills while at the University of Michigan. See Hayden, "Radical Nomad."

89. It is true, however, that more nonstudents were coming to SDS. According to an SDS membership survey in March 1966, only about 40 percent of SDSers were registered undergrads; another 25 percent were graduate students, and 10 percent of members were in high school. As Sale points out, while on the one hand this means that 75 percent of SDSers were operating in an academic setting, there was still a significant "campus–off campus split" in SDS. See Sale, *SDS*, 271–72.

90. Steve Max, "From Port Huron to Maplehurst," *National Guardian* [ca. summer 1965], fragment, SDS Records, WSHS.

91. Pardun, *Prairie Radical*, 115–16.

92. Dick Shortt to Robert Pardun, August 5, 1965, SDS Records, Reel 6, Series 2A, No. 35.

93. Ken McEldowney to Jim McDougall and George Brosi, July 7, 1965, SDS Records, Reel 6, Series 2A, No. 69.

94. Pardun, *Prairie Radical*, 119.

95. Jeff Shero to "Comrades," August 3, 1965, SDS Records, Reel 28, Series 3, No. 108.

96. Polletta, *Endless Meeting*, 145.

97. Carol McEldowney to SDS N.O., November 7, 1965, SDS Records, Reel 19, Series 3, No. 1.

98. Scott Pittman to Worklist Recipients, October 19, 1965, SDS Records, Reel 19, Series 3, No. 1; David Stamps to Jeff Shero, November 15, 1965, SDS Records, Reel 28, Series 3, No. 108. Balanced against this, however, was at least one highly approving letter from a new SDS member who called the new *Bulletin* "one of the finest publications I've seen on the left." See J. M. Wagner to SDS, November 18, 1965, SDS Records, Reel 21, Series 3, No. 18.

99. Sale, *SDS*, 273.

100. Ibid., 273.

101. "Not With My Life You Don't!!" *A Georgia Student Handbook*, Georgetown SDS, Fall 1968, SDS Records, Reel 22, Series 3, No. 26; Todd Gitlin, "President's Report," *SDS Bulletin*, December 1963, SDS Records, Reel 35, Series 4A, No. 19. Emphasis in original.

102. In an undated letter [ca. 1966–67] an SDSer attributed the phrase to activist and historian Staughton Lynd. See Bill Hartzog to Greg Calvert, n.d., SDS Records, Reel 21, Series 3, No. 11.

Chapter 2

1. Crowley, *Rights of Passage*, 61.

2. *Time*, "Underground Alliance," July 29, 1966, 57.

3. These were among the first six underground newspapers; the others were Detroit's *Fifth Estate*, San Francisco's *Oracle*, and Lower Manhattan's *EVO*. Founded by eighteen-year-old Harvey Ovshinsky, the *Fifth Estate* was by far the most amateurish of these amateur papers. The *Oracle* and the *EVO* reached considerably larger audiences, but initially they were better known for their colorful psychedelic graphics and zestful espousals of the countercultural cosmology.

4. Jeff Shero Nightbyrd, as quoted in Lieberman, *Prairie Power*, 86.

5. George Orwell, "Introduction," in Orwell and Reynolds, *British Pamphleteers*, 15.

6. Streitmatter, *Voices of Revolution*, 55. The first types of radical newspapers also championed unpopular issues that later won broad acceptance. Jacksonian Era labor-movement papers called for shorter workdays, tax-funded schools, an end to debtors' prisons, and the right of workers to organize. The abolitionist press, of course, crusaded on behalf of the struggle against slavery. And in the aftermath of the Civil War, Elizabeth Cady Stanton and Susan B. Anthony published the *Revolution*, the first newspaper devoted to women's rights, in which they denounced sexual exploitation at home and in the workplace, and called for equal pay for equal work.

7. Graham, *Yours for the Revolution*, x, 15.

8. Stansell, *American Moderns*, 166–75.

9. See J. Glenn Gray, "Salvation on the Campus: Why Existentialism is Capturing the Students," *Harper's*, May 1965, 53–59.

10. *Dissent*, "A Word to Our Readers," Winter 1954, 6–7.

11. Abrams, "From Madness to Dysentery," 435.

12. McAuliffe, *Great American Newspaper*, 13.

13. McAuliffe, *Great American Newspaper*, 3; Frankfort, *The Voice*, 32.

14. Judy Feiffer, as quoted in Manso, *Mailer*, 222.

15. Wolf and Fancher, *Village Voice Reader*, 5.

16. Stokes, *Village Voice Anthology*, 8.

17. Ibid., 8–9.

18. McAuliffe, *Great American Newspaper*, 20.

19. The *Village Voice*'s forerunners were *Quill's Weekly* and *Bruno's Bohemia* (in the 1920s) and *Caricature* (in the 1950s). Other publications that were somewhat in sync with the Village's avant-garde climate were *New Masses* (which had its heyday in the 1930s) and the left-wing daily newspaper *PM* (which expired in 1948). The *Village Voice*'s only direct competition in the 1950s was a shopper paper called the *Villager*.

20. Mailer, *Advertisements*, 278.

21. Mailer, *Advertisements*, 325.

22. Mailer, *Advertisements*, 317. Most of Mailer's readers would have recognized the concepts of hip and square from the literature of the beat generation; in lay terms, "squares" were dull conformists, and "hipsters" were edgy, sensual wanderers looking for "kicks." But in Mailer's evolving understanding, "hip" was less an adjective than a comprehensive philosophy, which he later articulated in his 1959 essay "The White Negro." Hipsters, Mailer said, were "the American existentialist[s]" whose subconscious minds were supposedly awhirl with the threat of meaningless death (whether caused by fascism, nuclear war, or a "soul-destroying conformity"). But out of this despair arose an almost intuitive self-awareness, an unharnessed id, and an idealization of society's "outlaws"—beatniks, juvenile delinquents, and (supposedly) African Americans. The

philosophy of Hip, Mailer later said, "offered an antidote to other people's habits, other people's defeats, boredom, quiet desperation, and muted icy self-destroying rage," and had the potential to usher in a "modern revolution." See Mailer, *Advertisements*, 337–58.

23. Peck, *Uncovering the Sixties*, 11.

24. Krassner, *Confessions*, 13, 45.

25. Ken Kesey, "Introduction," in Krassner, *Best of the Realist*, 5.

26. Krassner helped Bruce write his autobiography. See Bruce, *How to Talk Dirty*.

27. Krassner, *Best of the Realist*, 6; Boskin, *Rebellious Laughter*, 73.

28. Krassner, *Best of the Realist*, 102.

29. Krassner, *Confessions*, 51, 92–95.

30. Leamer, *Paper Revolutionaries*, 24.

31. In 1967 Krassner pulled off a Swiftian satire that was gross and tasteless even by the counterculture's loosest standards, when he printed what he falsely claimed was "an unpublished excerpt" from a recent book on John F. Kennedy's assassination in which Lyndon Johnson was said to have been spotted copulating with Kennedy's neck wound as the deceased president was being flown from Dallas to Washington on Air Force One. See Krassner, *Best of the Realist*, 190–93; Peck, *Uncovering the Sixties*, 62–63. In 1968, feminist Robin Morgan skewered Krassner's sexism in her famous polemic, "Goodbye to All That."

32. Thorne Dreyer and Victoria Smith, "The Movement and the New Media," Liberation News Service packet 144, March 1, 1969, 3.

33. Krassner, *Best of the Realist*, 2.

34. Gruen, *New Bohemia*, 6–7.

35. Jacoby, *Last Intellectuals*, 21, 115.

36. See McBride, "Death City Radicals"; Hayden, *Trial*, 158–65.

37. Brick, *Age of Contradiction*, 11.

38. Richard Flacks, e-mail to author, September 4, 2004. Prior to the late 1950s, most paperbacks were of the pulp variety, and they were sold in supermarkets and drugstores.

39. Richard Flacks interview, 4.

40. Jim O'Brien, "Memories of the Student Movement and the New Left in the United States," unpublished manuscript in author's possession, 28. Another offbeat hangout in Madison was the University of Wisconsin's student union, which had a bar called the Rathskeller that sold 3.2 percent beer.

41. Paul Buhle, interview by Bret Eynon and Ron Grele, 1985, Columbia, 36.

42. See McBride, "On the Fault Lines," 122.

43. Renata Adler, "Fly Trans-Love Airways," *New Yorker*, February 25, 1967, 122; emphasis added.

44. Jerry Hopkins, "Los Angeles Scene," *Rolling Stone*, June 22, 1968, 11.

45. McBride, "On the Fault Lines," 124.

46. Art Kunkin, "One Year of the Free Press," *Los Angeles Free Press*, July 23, 1965, 6.

47. Lionel Rolfe and Dennis Koran, "Freeping Out," *Los Angeles Reader*, June 19, 1981, 5.

48. William Murray, "The L.A. Free Press is Rich," *Esquire*, June 1970, 54.

49. As quoted in Peck, *Uncovering the Sixties*, 22.

50. Maynard, *Venice West*, 20; Lipton, *Holy Barbarians*.

51. Land, *Active Radio*, 66; Tom Nolan, "The Free Press Costs 15 Cents," *West*, October 12, 1966, 40.

52. Richard Stone, "Hip Papers: The Underground Press Succeeds by Intriguing the Rebels and Squares," *Wall Street Journal*, March 4, 1968.

53. Lionel Rolfe, "Art Kunkin: Mystic in Paradise," http://www.dabelly.com/columns/bohemian33.htm.

54. Rolfe, *Literary L.A*, 27.

55. See Peck, *Uncovering the Sixties*, 25. Kunkin's own personal investment was said to be just $15. See Nolan, "Free Press Costs," 40; and McBride, "On the Fault Lines," 124.

56. Quoted in Peck, *Uncovering the Sixties*, 21.

57. Murray, "Free Press is Rich," 54.

58. Phyllis Patterson, interview by author, September 7, 2004.

59. See *Los Angeles Free Press*, May 23, 1964, 1.

60. Nolan, "Free Press Costs," 40.

61. Art Kunkin, "Dear Reader," *Los Angeles Free Press*, May 25, 1964, 2; emphasis in original.

62. Seymour Stern, "Puritanism Scores Victory: All Woman Jury Finds Ken Anger's Anti-Fascist Film 'Obscene,'" *Los Angeles Free Press*, May 25, 1964, 1. Michael Getz, manager of Los Angeles's Cinema Theater, was convicted of "lewd exhibition" for screening *Scorpio Rising* on March 7, 1964. Later the California Supreme Court overturned the obscenity verdict.

63. "Noted Singer Refuses to Pay Taxes that Go for War Preparation," *Los Angeles Free Press*, May 25, 1964, C.

64. Quoted in Nolan, "Free Press Costs," 40.

65. Safford Chamberlain, "Death of a Jazzer: an Obituary" *Los Angeles Free Press*, May 25, 1964, 5; Jimmy Garrett, "Black Future," *Los Angeles Free Press*, May 25, 1964, 5. See also May, *Golden State, Golden Youth*, 156–59.

66. Art Kunkin, "Why We Appear," *Los Angeles Free Press*, July 30, 1964, 2–3.

67. McBride, "Death City Radicals," 110, 115.

68. Nolan, "Free Press Costs," 40.

69. Rolfe, *Literary L.A.*, 18.

70. McBride, "On the Fault Lines," 135.

71. Adler, "Fly Trans-Love," 20.

72. McBride, "Death City Radicals," 115; Rolfe, *Literary L.A.*, 18.

73. Kunkin underscored this point in an article he wrote to mark the paper's one-year anniversary. See Kunkin, "One Year," 3.

74. McBride, "Death City Radicals," 115.

75. Rolfe and Koran, "Freeping Out," 5. See also Hal Draper, "The Mind of Clark Kerr," *Los Angeles Free Press*, November 5, 1964, 1–3; Harry J. Coffey, "Berkeley Report," *Los Angeles Free Press*, December 11, 1964, 3; Mario Savio, "Savio on Free Speech: Issues Behind the Student Protest," *Los Angeles Free Press*, January 1, 1965, 1, 3; Bea Rechnitz, "Report from Berkeley," *Los Angeles Free Press*, January 1 1965, 3.

76. Peck, *Uncovering the Sixties*, 27.

77. May, *Golden State, Golden Youth*, 56.

78. Johnson, Sears, and McConahay, "Black Invisibility," 698, 700.

79. Peck, *Uncovering the Sixties*, 27. See also Dori Schaffer, "Bank of America vs. Core: A Duel of Accusations," *Los Angeles Free Press*, July 30, 1964, 1, 3, 4, 6; Jim Blanchfield, "Ghetto Vote Drive," *Los Angeles Free Press*, August 20, 1964, 1, 6; L. M. Meriwether, "Citizen's Council Opponents Convicted," *Los Angeles Free Press*, October 29, 1964, 4; Irvan O'Connell, "Keep Your Eyes on the Prize," *Los Angeles Free Press*, November 12, 1964, 1, 3; Phil L. Snyder, "Will Prop. 14 Survive? The Conflict with the Constitution," *Los Angeles Free Press*, January 8, 1965, 1, 3. Although voters supported Proposition 14 by a two-to-one margin, California's Supreme Court struck it down in 1967.

80. As quoted in Peck, *Uncovering the Sixties*, 27.

81. Art Kunkin, "The Negroes Have Voted!" *Los Angeles Free Press*, August 29, 1965, 1.

82. As quoted in Peck, *Uncovering the Sixties*, 26.

83. Black perspectives on the Watts rebellion were put forth in Bob Freeman, "Core Leader Observes Ghetto Fighting," *Los Angeles Free Press*, August 20, 1965, 1–2; Herb Porter, "Attorney Analyzes Causes of Watts Demonstrations," *Los Angeles Free Press*, August 20, 1965, 4, 5; *Los Angeles Free Press*, "Documented Case-Studies of Police Malpractice," August 27, 1965, 6; *Los Angeles Free Press*, "Los Angeles Groups Comment on Riots," August 27, 1965, 7; *Los Angeles Free Press*, "Discussion Unlimited: Public Hearing Gets Eyewitness Testimony from Watts," October 1, 1965, 2–3.

84. Freeman, "Core Leader Observes," 2.

85. Murray, "Free Press is Rich," 56.

86. Kunkin, as quoted in Murray, "Free Press is Rich," 56.

87. McBride, "On the Fault Lines," 36.

88. During Hollywood's golden age, of course, fancy restaurants and boutiques lined the street, but by the late 1950s they had lost their luster. See Adler, "Fly Trans-Love," 117. See also, Domenic Priore, *Riot on Sunset Strip: Rock 'n' Roll's Last Stand in Hollywood* (London: Jawbone, 2007).

89. Mike Fessier, Jr., "Sunset Boulevard's New Bohemia," *Los Angeles Magazine* (December 1965), 34.

90. McBride, "On the Fault Lines," 206–8.

91. Adler, "Fly Trans-Love," 118; Jerry Farber, "Big Mike at Ben Frank's," *Los Angeles Free Press*, January 7, 1966, 6. A writer for *Los Angeles* magazine advised, "If you want to be inconspicuous" at Ben Franks, "come dressed as a Hopi Indian or the Jolly Green Giant." See Fessier, "Sunset Boulevard's New Bohemia," 39.

92. *Time*, "Sunset Along the Strip," December 2, 1966, 69. See also *Look*, "California Fashion: Dressing for the Strip," June 28, 1966, 74–75; *Newsweek*, "The Teenagers," March 21, 1965, 75.

93. One such event, held at an "aerospace hall" (presumably an airplane hangar) near the Strip, billed itself as a "Lysergic A-Go-Go," and promised "a spectacular of light, color, sound, and motion." See *Los Angeles Free Press*, "Lysergic A-Go-Go," November 19, 1965, 1.

94. Adler, "Fly Trans-Love," 117.

95. Paul J. Robbins, "The Strip is a Bummer?" *Los Angeles Free Press*, January 4, 1966, 6–7.

96. Jerry Farber, "Making It: On the Strip," *Los Angeles Free Press*, December 24, 1966, 6.

97. Anthony Bernhard and Edgar Z. Friedenberg, "The Sunset Strip," *New York Review of Books*, March 9, 1967, http://www.nybooks.com/articles/archives/1967/mar/09/

the-sunset-strip/. A *Life* writer opined, "The police are panicked about the whole scene, they don't know what to do. Crime is up along the Strip. One real-estate owner had a couch in the lobby of his apartment house stolen five times in as many months, even after he bolted it to the cement floor. . . . There was the night a half-drunk member of some motorcycle club threw a coffee cup at a speeding motorcycle policeman from an outdoor eatery place. Twelve cops descended on the place and couldn't find anybody to arrest." See Roger Vaughan, "The Mad New Scene on Sunset Strip," *Life*, August 26, 1966, 82–83.

98. As quoted in Bernhard and Friedenberg, "Sunset Strip."

99. Art Berman, "Shut-downs of Teen-Age Clubs Demanded by Businesses," *Los Angeles Times*, November 15, 1966, 4.

100. Bernhard and Friedenberg, "Sunset Strip."

101. As quoted in Bernhard and Friedenberg, "Sunset Strip."

102. McBride, "Death City Radicals," 117.

103. McBride, "On the Fault Lines," 229.

104. One pair of letter writers from the Sunset Strip Association told the *Freep*, "Although we do not necessarily agree with your conclusions as to the cause and effect of the recent Sunset Strip disturbances, we . . . want you to know that we consider your reportage in the finest journalistic tradition. Of all the local press . . . we found your coverage the most comprehensive." Fred Rosenberg and Shelly Davis, letter to the editor, *Los Angeles Free Press*, November 25, 1966, 4.

105. Over chiming guitars, the lyrics marvel at the sight of "a thousand people in the streets," but caution, "Paranoia strikes deep . . . Step out of line, the man come and take you away" (Buffalo Springfield, "For What It's Worth/Do I Have to Come Right Out and Say It," Atco 45–6459).

106. McBride, "On the Fault Lines," 233–49.

107. At one point during the interview, Kunkin flicked his checkbook toward the reporter who was interviewing him. "Here," he announced, "we've got exactly $110 in the bank, and that's all. . . . We can't even afford a readership survey to find out who reads the paper." See Nolan, "Free Press Costs," 39.

108. *Los Angles Underground*, "Underground Phenomenon," April 23–May 7, 1967, 1. These numbers are admittedly hard to verify; newspapers commonly claim more readers than they actually have, and reports about the *Freep*'s circulation in this period are inconsistent. As noted above, Kunkin professed to have "close to 9,000" readers in an interview that ran in the *Los Angeles Times' West* magazine on October 2, 1966; but in April 1967 the *Los Angeles Underground*'s reported that six months prior (that is, in October, 1966) the *Free Press*'s circulation was 17,000. Either way, the paper's growth after the Strip riots was phenomenal. See Nolan, "Free Press Costs," 40; *Los Angles Underground*, "Underground Phenomenon," 1.

109. *Los Angles Underground*, "Underground Phenomenon," 5.

110. Wachsberger, "A Tradition Continues: East Lansing's Underground Press, 1965-Present," in Wachsberger, *Voices from the Underground*, 234.

111. Heineman, *Campus Wars*, 20. MSU was founded as the Agricultural College of the State of Michigan, and it was the prototype for nearly seventy land-grant colleges established under the 1862 Morrill Act. It was upgraded from a college to a university in 1955.

112. Adams, *The Test*, 18–19. See also Lowen, *Cold War University*.

113. Heineman, *Campus Wars*, 20.

114. Kindman, "My Odyssey," 369–70.

115. Kindman, "My Odyssey," 370–71.

116. Kindman, "My Odyssey," 371. See also Michael Kindman, "Merit Program Still Confused," *Paper*, May 5, 1966, 7.

117. Heineman, *Campus Wars*, 85–86. Both groups were so insignificant that when the *State News* published a lengthy "Historical Outline of Radicalism at MSU" in 1969, the Young Socialist Club wasn't mentioned, and SDS did not appear until the narrative reached 1966. Marion Nowack, "Historical Outline of Radicalism at MSU," *State News*, April 22, 1969, 6–7.

118. Nowack, "Historical Outline," 6; Kindman, "My Odyssey," 371–72.

119. Among the lasting images of the free speech movement was that of a student wearing a cardboard sign that read: "I am a UC student. Please do not bend, fold, spindle, or mutilate me." (The phrase refers to a warning that was commonly found on computer punch cards, also known as Hollerith cards or IBM cards. Now obsolete, the cards were widely used for data input, processing, and storage.) See Bloom and Breines, *Takin' It to the Streets*, 93–94.

120. Kindman, "My Odyssey," 371.

121. Later the CSR would lobby for library improvements, and the group once picketed a local apartment complex known to discriminate against African Americans.

122. John Millhone, "MSU's 'Schiff Affair,' An Echo of Berkeley?" *Detroit Free Press*, December 19, 1965, 2-B.

123. In a letter to the editor of the *State News*, a student wrote a humorous poem with the lines: "Oh! CSR, those crazy beards / Just simply have to go." Daniel L. Cobb, letter to the editor, *State News*, February 17, 1965. Apparently, some in the CSR were defensive about the ribbing they took for their nonconformist appearance. A writer for the CSR's newsletter, *Logos*, contended that "the issue is not beards and sandals vs. madras and cranberry, but what role we students are willing to assume in the campus society today. . . . In contrast to the 'beatniks' of the 1950s, today's 'rebels' no longer aim to escape from society, but to transform it into a better one." *Logos*, Summer 1965, 1, Student Protest Files (1965–71), Michigan State University Archives and Historical Collections, Conrad Hall, East Lansing, Michigan.

124. Kindman, "My Odyssey," 371.

125. See Michael Kindman, "Why I'm in CSR," *State News*, February 17, 1965; Michael Kindman, "Schiff Case May Be A Second 'Berkeley,'" *State News*, October 14, 1965.

126. Kindman, "My Odyssey," 372; Michael Kindman, "Zeitgiest: or, How We Learned to Stop Worrying and Keep our Cool," *Paper*, April 7, 1966, 2.

127. Kindman, "My Odyssey," 372.

128. Larry Tate, interview by author, March 4, 2005.

129. Kindman, "My Odyssey," 373. A writer for the University of Michigan's campus newspaper, the *Michigan Daily*, likewise noted that by the fall of 1965, MSU students were "starting to question policies . . . as they started to question policies here [at the University of Michigan] long ago." J. Russell Gaines, "MSU—Painful Political Maturing," *Michigan Daily*, November 20, 1965.

130. The issue was framed with an epigram from Walt Whitman's "Song of Myself": "I too am not a bit tamed—I too am untranslatable, / I sound my barbaric yawp over the roofs

of the world." See "Why *Zeitgeist*? Or: Prolegomena to Any Future Journals of Ideas and the Arts and a Modest Proposal for Ending the Famine in East Lansing," *Zeitgeist* 1 (September 1965): 4.

131. "Why Zeitgeist," 10.

132. Michael Kindman, "As We Begin: A Loyalty Oath," *Paper*, December 3, 1965, 1.

133. Georg A. Borgstrom, "Food in History and the Future," *Paper*, December 3, 1965, 3; William Pritchard, "Student Government—Up from the Sandbox," *Paper*, December 3, 1965, 4; David Freedman, "Committee for Student Revolution?" *Paper*, December 3, 1965, 5; Marshall Rosenthal, "Three Interviews with Bob Dylan," *Paper*, December 3, 1965, 8.

134. "Paul Krassner was our culture here," Larry Tate remembered. See Tate interview.

135. Michael Kindman, "MSU—The Closed Society," *Paper*, December 10, 1965, 2.

136. [Steve Badrich], "The Children's Crusade: *The Paper* Looks at the Rose Bowl," *Paper*, January 20, 1966, 1.

137. Michael Kindman, "Schiff is Back, But Not Forgotten," *Paper*, January 20, 1966, 2. Schiff had been president of the Young Socialist Club, a member of the steering committee of the Committee on Vietnam, an active member of the CSR, and editor in chief of its official newsletter, *Logos*. By the spring of 1965 he had nearly earned a master's degree in economics, but he decided he wanted to earn an MA in the history department as well. Although the history department had approved his application, MSU's registrar denied his application for readmission in June 1965. The following month, Schiff won the support of the American Association of University Professors and Lansing's branch of the American Civil Liberties Union. In an affidavit on Schiff's behalf, MSU professor Russ Allen described a meeting with MSU vice president John Fuzak, during which Fuzak admitted that Schiff's campus political activity led to his nonreadmission. When a federal court ordered MSU to specify its charges against Schiff and schedule a hearing on the matter, the *State News'* faculty advisor, Louis Berman, prohibited the paper from printing material relating to the hearing, at which point four of its editors resigned. Although their departures were not covered in the *State News*, the University of Michigan's paper, the *Michigan Daily*, gave the fiasco extensive coverage. Schiff was later allowed to enroll for the 1966 winter term. See Charles Larrowe, "The Schiff Case: A Chronology," December 8, 1965, in "Schiff, Paul—Legal Documents," Special Collections Library, Michigan State University; John Millhone, "MSU's 'Schiff Affair,' An Echo of Berkeley?" *Detroit Free Press*, December 19, 1965, 1; J. Russell Gaines, "MSU—Painful Political Maturing," *Michigan Daily*, November 20, 1965.

138. Laurence Tate, "All's Fair in Love and Peace," *Paper*, December 10, 1965, 1, 6.

139. Some of the university's regulations prohibited students from sitting on the floor while waiting in line for dinner, banned card playing in campus grills, and required unmarried pregnant students to leave campus after the first trimester. See Robert Bao and Pat Grauer, "The Sixties at MSU," *MSU Alumni Magazine*, January 1974, 9. See also Doug Lackey, "Why They Lock You Up at Night," *Paper*, January 27, 1966, 7; Denise R. Ivanovitch, "One Day in the Life of 413522," *Paper*, May 26, 1966, 8.

140. Larry Tate and S.P.B., "Palindrome Revelations Rock Campus," *Paper*, April 14, 1966, 1.

141. The Lounge, "Land Grant Man," *Paper*, May 26, 1966, 1. Kindman later described Hannah as "an easy mark, a Michigan farmboy made good, whose only doctorate was an honorary degree in poultry science, and whose ideas for building a great university seemed to come mainly from the world of corporate development." Kindman, "My Odyssey," 380. Surprisingly, Hannah never discussed the *Paper* or his contretemps with student radicals in his autobiography. See Hannah, *A Memoir*.

142. "You Won't Believe This But . . ." *Paper*, March 3, 1966, 1.

143. The *Paper*'s negotiations with the university were ludicrously complicated. At first, the *Paper* seemed to have the authority to sell issues on campus, owing to a "special dispensation" it received from the Student Board. At the time, this seemed an important victory, since earlier the in the year the Board had interfered with the CSR's attempts to distribute its flyers and petitions on campus property. In reality, the Student Board was simply trying to do the *Paper* a favor, on account of the fact that the Board of Student Publications—an entirely separate organization, made up of students, faculty, and administrators (also called the "pub board")—lacked established guidelines for independently operated student publications, and even seemed unsure about its jurisdiction. But by ruling on this matter, the Student Board stretched the limits of its own authority, and so in February 1966 the *Paper* was called before the Student Judiciary— yet another organization—for apparently unauthorized activities: selling issues outright (instead of accepting "contributions") and generating advertising revenue. The *Paper* responded with a mimeographed flyer ridiculing the university and pleading its case to the public. Two weeks later, the *Paper* was back in business, operating temporarily under the auspices of the Student Board (only this time officially) since by now the pub board was claiming it had no authority over the matter, and MSU's administration was unable to immediately create a set of guidelines under which the *Paper* could exist. See *Paper*, "You Won't Believe This, But . . ." March 3, 1966, 1, 8.

144. Tate interview.

145. Kindman, "My Odyssey," 376.

146. Warren Hinckle, "The University on the Make," *Ramparts*, April 1966, 14.

147. *Ramparts* advertisement, *Paper*, April 21, 1966, 4.

148. Michael Kindman, "The Rites/Rights of Spring," *Paper*, April 7, 1966, 1, 6; Brad Lang, "FUEL: The Torch is Passed," *Paper*, April 7, 1966, 6.

149. Incidentally, one of the diner's regulars was Richard Ford, the celebrated novelist and short-story writer. Spiro's "made me feel I was at a better college," Ford remembered, "since I felt sort of New York-ish rather than Moo-U-ish." Richard Ford to author, January 23, 2005.

150. Kindman, "My Odyssey," 371; Michael, Kindman, "Zeitgeist: or, How We Learned to Stop Worrying and Keep Our Cool," *Paper*, April 7, 1966, 2.

151. Greg Hill, "The Culture-Vultures," *Paper*, May 5, 1966, 4.

152. *Zeitgeist*, "Poetry and Truth, or Musings from the Sad American Night & Goodbye to All That . . . or Whatever Happened to the Beat Generation," April 1966, 12.

153. Larry Tate, "Paul Krassner at MSU: Illusion or Realist?" *Paper*, May 12, 1966, 1. Krassner's visit led to a considerable controversy after the *Paper* printed, on the front page, a small photograph of him holding his infamous "Fuck Communism" poster above a caption that posited several other more "suitable" slogans: "Make love communism, sleep communism, ball communism, meaningful relationship communism, beautiful

experience communism, do it communism, want to come up to my room and have a cup of coffee communism . . ." The *State News* deemed the issue "vulgar and inappropriate," a member of the Board of Student Publications called it "prurient," and the *Paper*'s publisher—the *Ingham County News*—promptly quit doing business with them. See *Paper*, "Here We Go Again!!" May 19, 1966, 1; *Paper*, "What We're Up Against," May 22, 1967, 7.

154. Jolles, interview by author, March 16, 2005.

155. Sale, *SDS*, 664.

156. Michael Kindman, "It's Been A Gas!" *Paper*, May 26, 1966, 2. "Let the People Decide" was an SDS slogan.

157. *Time*, "Underground Alliance," July 29, 1966, 57.

158. Tate interview.

159. Michael Kindman, "The Newspaper as Art Form," *Paper*, October 13, 1966, 2.

160. Jolles interview.

161. Dreyer and Smith, "Movement and New Media," 17.

162. Rossinow, *Politics of Authenticity*, 10.

163. Peck, *Uncovering the Sixties*, 58.

164. Rossinow, *Politics of Authenticity*, 260–61.

165. Rossinow, *Politics of Authenticity*, 26–28.

166. Pardun, *Prairie Radical*, 22–23. See also Robert Pardun, "It Wasn't Hard To Be a Communist in Texas," in Janes, *No Apologies*, 51.

167. Thorne Dreyer, as quoted in Peck, *Uncovering the Sixties*, 59.

168. Echols, *Scars of Sweet Paradise*, 53.

169. Janis Joplin, who sang at Threadgill's in the early 1960s before she was famous, remembered him affectionately: "He was old, a great big man with a beer belly and white hair combed back on top of his head. He'd be dishin' out Polish sausages and hard-boiled eggs and Grand Prizes and Lone Stars," and sometimes at the end of the night the bar's remaining customers would coax him into yodeling his favorite Rodgers tunes. "He'd close the bar down, and then walk out front, and he'd lay his hands across his big fat belly, which was covered with a bar apron . . . and lean his head back and sing, just sing like a bird. . . . God he was fantastic!" As quoted in Echols, *Scars of Sweet Paradise*, 55–56.

170. Among them was Bill Malone, who later became an authority on the history of country music.

171. Shank, *Dissonant Identities*, 40–41.

172. Jones, "Gentle Thursday," 39.

173. Echols, *Scars of Sweet Paradise*, 56.

174. Mance Lipscomb, a highly respected African American bluesman, broke the color line at Threadgill's in 1966.

175. Shank, *Dissonant Identities*, 42.

176. Gray, "Salvation on the Campus," 56.

177. Rossinow, *Politics of Authenticity*, 54.

178. Rossinow, *Politics of Authenticity*, 82.

179. See Rossinow, *Politics of Authenticity*, 85–114.

180. Morris, *North Toward Home*, 171.

181. As quoted in Lieberman, *Prairie Power*, 77. As noted in chapter 1, Shero went on to edit the *SDS Bulletin*.

182. As quoted in Lieberman, *Prairie Power*, 88.

183. In the summer of 1964, Austin SDSer Charlie Smith earned himself a small place in movement lore when he arrived at an SDS convention in upstate New York on his Honda 250 motorcycle and introduced himself by thunderously proclaiming: "I'm half-horse and half-alligator! I'm a Marxist-Leninist-Gandhian-anarchist-pacifist community organizer from *Texas*!" See Jones, "Gentle Thursday," 18.

184. Gitlin, *The Sixties*, 186. Gitlin was not referring specifically to the Austin SDS chapter, but to the "prairie power" faction of SDS, of which the Austinites were a part.

185. Pardun, *Prairie Radical*, 105–7. Johnson was at the ranch at the time, trying to escape the twenty thousand protestors who descended upon Washington, DC, for the SDS-sponsored protest described in chapter 1.

186. Several Austinites were already prominent in SDS; Robb and Dorothy Burlage and Casey Hayden had all attended the Port Huron Conference in June 1962. Later, Shero became SDS's vice president in 1965–66, before founding one of New York's most important underground newspapers, the *Rat*; Robert Pardun was SDS's education secretary in 1967–68; Thorne Dreyer was a notable figure in the underground press, writing for LNS and helping to establish Houston's *Space City!* Charlie Smith joined SDS's National Council in 1964.

187. Thorne Dreyer, interview by author, April 23, 2005.

188. Olan, "The Rag," 40. According to a former *Daily Texan* writer, after Economidy was elected editor "he made a grand entrance into the newspaper office wearing an Air Force ROTC uniform and carrying a makeshift swagger stick," which he banged on the rim of a table as he announced: "General John is HERE!" Kaye Northcott, "Gen. John Economidy: The First 100 Days," *Rag*, October 10, 1966, 1.

189. Thorne Dreyer to the *East Village Other*, *Los Angeles Free Press*, *Berkeley Barb*, *Fifth Estate*, *Paper*, *Sanity*, and *Peace News*, October 5, 1966, unpublished letter in author's possession. The last phrase is a dry reference to the fact that in 1966 many of Austin's restrooms were still segregated.

190. Pardun, *Prairie Radical*, 162.

191. Rossinow, *Politics of Authenticity*, 260.

192. *Rag*, October 10, 1966, 2; *Rag*, "August 17, 1966," 3; the *Rag* issue dated "August 17, 1966" is in error; it should have been dated "October 17, 1966."

193. David Mahler, as quoted in Olan, "The Rag," 81.

194. Although this was supposed to help the paper to seem more democratic, one former staffer observed that it may have also "reinforced the [staff's] conceit—those who knew, knew, and those who didn't, wouldn't." Security considerations may have also played a role in the decision not to use anyone's surname. See Danny N. Schweers, "The Community and *The Rag*," in Janes, *No Apologies*, 219.

195. Pardun, *Prairie Radical*, 162–63.

196. As quoted in Olan, "The Rag," 52–53.

197. Rossinow, *Politics of Authenticity*, 260.

198. Dreyer interview.

199. Dreyer and Smith, "Movement and New Media," 26.

200. George Vizard, "Ragamuffins Face Fuzz," *Rag*, August 17, 1966, 1, 4–5, 16, 18. See also "Off Campus Paper Sells Out First Day," *Daily Texan*, October 11, 1966, 1. Vizard was murdered on July 23, 1967, and his killer was arrested in 1980 and later convicted.

Police maintained that Vizard was shot in a robbery, but several Austin activists, then and now, believe the murder was politically motivated. See Kelly Fero, *The Zani Murders* (Austin: Texas Monthly Press, 1990).

201. Carol Neiman, "The Truth (beep) Is on Page," *Rag*, October 10, 1966, 1–10; Kay Northcott, "Gen. John Economidy: The First 100 Days," *Rag*, October 10, 1966, 1–4; Jeff Shero, "Playboy's Tinseled Seductress," *Rag*, October 10, 1966, 4, 7, 8. Ironically, Shero later worked for pornographer Larry Flynt.

202. Anthony Howe, "Provos: The Dutch Anarchists," *Rag*, October 17, 1966, 3, 8, 9; Gary Chason, "Sexual Freedom League: The Naked Truth," *Rag*, October 17, 1966, 1, 4, 7, 17; Thorne Dreyer, "High Camp Brings Down," *Rag*, October 17, 1966, 12–13.

203. Larry Freudiger, "Grassroots Sociology: The Great Headline Fiasco, or, Who Are the Brain Police?" *Rag*, December 5, 1966, 5.

204. Be-ins happened in many cities in the late 1960s, but the first major one took place in San Francisco's Golden Gate Park on January 14, 1967. Also called "A Gathering of the Tribes," it was designed to promote communion and cooperation between political radicals and acidheads.

205. Austin SDS proclaimed, "This will be no SDS function but a circus for everyone." See Glenn W. Jones, "Gentle Thursday: An SDS Circus in Austin, Texas, 1966–1969," in Tischler, *Sights on the Sixties*, 76.

206. "This Thursday is Gentle Thursday," *Rag*, October 31, 1966, 4.

207. Pardun, *Prairie Radical*, 162.

208. Jones, "SDS Circus," 76.

209. Susan Torian Olan, "Blood Debts," in Janes, *No Apologies*, 20.

210. Jones, "SDS Circus," 76.

211. Thorne Dreyer, "Flipped Out Week," *Rag*, April 10, 1967, 1; Gary Thiher, "Gentle Thursday as Revolution," *Rag*, April 24, 1967, 10.

212. Sale, *SDS*, 327.

213. Jones, "Gentle Thursday: Revolutionary Pastoralism," 90–102.

214. Shank, *Dissonant Identities*, 49.

215. Quoted in ibid., 48.

216. Dreyer and Smith, "Movement and New Media," 26.

217. See Rolfe and Koran, "Freeping Out," 1.

218. Peck, *Uncovering the Sixties*, 191; Rolfe and Koran, "Freeping Out," 6. In the ensuing years, Kunkin seemingly became addlepated, studying alchemy and proselytizing for a mystical religious organization called Way of the Magus. In a 2003 interview, he boasted of having secret knowledge of an ancient reincarnation ritual. See Lionel Rolfe, "Art Kunkin: Mystic in Paradise," http://www.bigmagic.com/pages/blackj/column83e.html.

219. MSU-SDS organized around everything from the high cost of textbooks to anti-draft activity (and in 1968 they hoodwinked the university into allowing SDS to hold its national convention on campus) while the *Paper*'s circulation swelled to about 15,000. Margaret Hackett, interview by author, February 4, 2005.

220. Michael Kindman, "The Dove Has Torn Her Wing," *Paper*, November 30, 1967, 3.

221. For more on Lyman, see Felton, Green, and Dalton, *Mindfuckers*, 155–224.

222. "Rag History," *Rag*, October 10, 1971, n.p.

223. Richards, *Once Upon a Time*, 125–35.

224. "Rag History," n.p. As Rossinow observes, "in Texas, of course, the cowboys and not the Indians were usually cast as heroes." Rossinow, *Politics of Authenticity*, 260.

225. Schweers, "Community and *The Rag*," 233. From September 1 through 4, 2005, many former Ragstaffers gathered in Austin to celebrate the thirty-ninth anniversary of the founding of the paper. See Cheryl Smith, "Everything Old is New Again: A Texan's in the White House, We're in a Quagmire War—and *The Rag* returns to Austin," *Austin Chronicle*, September 2, 2005, http://www.austinchronicle.com/gyrobase/Redirect.html/issues/dispatch/2005–09–02/pols/feature3.html.

Chapter 3

1. Sara Davidson, *Loose Change*, 143; James Miller, *Flowers in the Dustbin*, 259–60.

2. Sara Davidson, *Loose Change*, 143.

3. Zane Maitland, "A Hippie Non-Happening," *San Francisco Chronicle*, n.d., n.p. Fragment in Peter Stafford Papers (1960–71), Box 2, Rare Book and Manuscripts Library, Columbia University, New York City. Henceforth, this collection will be abbreviated "PSP."

4. *Time*, "Tripping on Banana Peels," April 7, 1967, 52; *Newsweek*, "Mellow Yellow," April 10, 1967, 93.

5. "Human Be-In Covers Meadow, baffles cops," *New Left Notes*, April 10, 1967,1; McNeill, *Moving Through Here*, 9.

6. Frank Thompson, "Recently Launched U.S. Food and Drug Administration Investigation of Banana Peel Smoking," *Seed*, n.p., n.d, Fragment in PSP, Box 2.

7. Food and Drug Administration Press Release, May 26, 1967, http://countryjoe.com/banana.htm.

8. J. J. Kane, "Banana Appeal," *High Times*, September 1978, 57.

9. Jenkins, *Bananas*, xiii.

10. Going further, the banana craze complicates the popular notion that the counterculture was so market-friendly, co-optable, and nonthreatening to the established values of capitalism that it lacked any oppositional significance at all. Although the banana fad was never linked to any specific political objectives, it was certainly meant to confound the sensibilities of the established order ("freaking out the squares") and it was never without political overtones. Repressive drug laws and the lies they were based upon, misguided corporate values of efficiency, hierarchy, and rationalization, and indeed a whole society's failure of imagination—these were some of the problems that New Leftists perceived in the 1960s, and they go a long way toward explaining why people smoked bananas. In so doing, countercultural youths fashioned a stronger community, in which dissident viewpoints could circulate. Additionally, smoking bananas could also be fun; in the counterculture cosmology, this was no small thing. See Rossinow, "Revolution Is About Our Lives."

11. The song also appeared as the title track on Donovan's album *Mellow Yellow*, which was released in February 1967.

12. DeRogatis, *Kaleidoscope Eyes*, 59. Also see Feigelson, *Underground Revolution*, 24; Gitlin, *The Sixties*, 212; Perry, *Haight-Ashbury*, 82; Taylor, *Twenty Years Ago Today*, 116; John Wolfe, "Positively Queen Jane Approximately," *Distant Drummer*, November 1967, 9.

13. *Newsweek*, "Mellow Yellow," April 10, 1967, 93.

14. Anne-Katherine Britt, letter to the editor, *Newsweek*, May 1, 1967, 7.

15. Donovan Leitch, e-mail to author, January 28, 2003.

16. Donovan Leitch, e-mail to author, January 28, 2003; DeRogatis, 59. Donovan's memory notwithstanding, I have another theory for where he got the inspiration for the song. In the winter of 1965, underground cartoonist Spain Rodriguez began working on an adult, comic tabloid magazine called *Zodiac Mindwarp*, which was published in early 1966. The vulgar cartoon on the cover depicts a curvy woman lying in the supine position, about to be molested by a man holding a large yellow banana emblazoned with the distinctive General Electric logo and the words "Electro-Banana." This magazine did not circulate widely, but it was likely published well before Donovan penned his lyric about electrical bananas. See Rosenkranz, *Rebel Visions*, 43–44.

17. I told the story for the first time in a shorter and less academic version of this chapter. See McMillian, "Electrical Bananas."

18. See Clay and Phillips, *Secret Location*, 166–68.

19. Palattella, "Poetry Was the Rage," 35.

20. *Fuck You: A Magazine of the Arts*, May 1963, 2.

21. After I asked Sanders about this, he sent me this curt reply: "There is absolutely nothing relating to the hippie capitalist phenomenon known as bananadine [in] the reference in the May '63 issue of the magazine." Ed Sanders, e-mail to author, August 23, 2003.

22. Bromell, *Tomorrow Never Knows*, 61.

23. Joe McDonald, "The Banana Affair," http://www.countryjoe.com/banana.htm.

24. Gary Hirsh, e-mail to author, July 13, 2003. Hirsh was no doubt an eccentric, but he probably wasn't alone. In 1967 one underground press writer maintained that "there are, indeed, folks working their way through the produce department, logically and orderly looking for new ways to turn on." See Jerry Hopkins, "Making It," *Los Angeles Free Press*, March 17, 1967, 16. Eugene Schoenfeld, a medical doctor who wrote a syndicated advice column for underground newspapers, adds, "There was so much interest in ways of getting high that people tried anything they heard about." Eugene Schoenfeld, e-mail to author, July 22, 2003. Finally, Hirsh was not the only person to experiment with mace; Paul Krassner once printed a testimonial from someone who ate "two full teaspoons" of mace. Two hours later, he claims he saw "funny bright lights" and heard "wobbly nonsensical voices." See Krassner, *Magic Mushrooms*, 205.

25. McDonald, "Banana Affair."

26. Gary Hirsh, e-mail to author, July 13, 2003.

27. McDonald, "Banana Affair."

28. Joe McDonald, e-mail to author, July 9, 2003; Gary Hirsh, e-mail to author, July 13, 2003.

29. John Burks, "The Underground Press: A Special Report," *Rolling Stone*, October 4, 1969, 27.

30. Ed Denson, "The Folk Scene," *Berkeley Barb*, March 3, 1967, 6.

31. Ed Denson, e-mail to author, August 28, 2003. In some of his later writings, Denson went by the *nom de plume* "Banana Ed."

32. Anonymous, letter to the editor, *Berkeley Barb*, March 3, 1967, 11.

33. Don Wegars, "Kicks for Hippies: The Banana Turn-On," *San Francisco Chronicle*, March 4, 1967. Although the *Chronicle* article on the banana rumor is dated only one day after the *Barb* articles, the *Barb* was a weekly newspaper. Presumably, the issue dated March 3, 1967, had actually hit the streets near the end of April.

34. McDonald, "Banana Affair." *Business Week* magazine later published an article on the banana industry with the punny title "Yes, They Sell More Bananas" (July 8, 1967, 90–94).

35. Frank, *Conquest of Cool*, 8.

36. Others may have made a connection between the banana rumors and another rock production of the era: the Velvet Underground's first record, *The Velvet Underground & Nico* (sometimes called "the banana album"). In the original packaging, designed by Andy Warhol, the record sleeve featured a banana with a stick-on peel that could be pulled away to reveal the bare fruit underneath. The album was released in March 1967, but the image was designed in May 1966, and it has no direct correlation to the banana hoax. However, the banana fad may have given the Velvet's cover an ironic tinge, since their dark, protopunk image and sound is frequently characterized as a conscious reaction *against* the excesses of West Coast hippiedom. See Bourdon, *Warhol*, 236; DeRogatis, *Kaleidoscope Eyes*, 44–46; Perry, *Haight-Ashbury*, 56–57.

37. "Tripping on Banana Peels," *Time*, April 7, 1967, 52.

38. Armstrong, *Trumpet to Arms*, 46.

39. As quoted in Burks, "Underground Press," 18.

40. Burks, "Underground Press," 25.

41. "General Marsbars" was a pun on Gen. Lewis B. Hershey, the beleaguered director of the U.S. Selective Service from 1948 to 1970. See also Schoenfeld, *Dear Doctor Hip Pocrates*.

42. *Fifth Estate* (Detroit), "Subscription Sadie," May 15–31, 1967, 6.

43. Thomas W. Burrows to *Connections*, March 8, 1967, *Connections* Records, WSHS, Box 1.

44. As quoted in Peck, *Uncovering the Sixties*, 21.

45. Peter Shapiro, interview by Ron Grele, April 11, 1984, Columbia, 121.

46. Robert Bulow, letter to the editor, *East Village Other*, April 1, 1967, n.p.

47. See Peck, *Uncovering the Sixties*, 21.

48. Michael Kindman, "The Newspaper as Art Form," *Paper*, October 13, 1966, 2.

49. *Chicago Seed*, July 21–August 4, 1967, 3.

50. Quoted in Michael Lydon, "The Word Gets Out," *Esquire*, September 1967, 111.

51. Quoted in Leamer, *Paper Revolutionaries*, 36.

52. See Flacks, *Making History*, 165.

53. Kindman, "My Odyssey," 378.

54. Fred Hoffman, "The Underground and the Establishment," *PROVO*, July 16–31, 1967, 7.

55. As quoted in Steve Long, "Underground Reunion: Where Have All the Writers Gone?" *Alternative Media*, July-August 1976, 24. The more common version of the story of how UPS got its name—which I'm certain is apocryphal—holds that Bowart offhandedly mentioned his plan to help start a federation of underground papers to a reporter for *Time* magazine. When the reporter asked what it would be called, Bowart said he looked up and saw a United Parcel Service truck whiz past his window, and said,

"We're . . . ah . . . UPS—the Underground Press Syndicate." See Peck, *Uncovering the Sixties*, 39; Armstrong, *Trumpet to Arms*, 59.

56. *Business Week*, "Admen Groove on Underground," April 12, 1969, 86.

57. John Wilcock, "Big Success Story," *Other Scenes*, May 1967, 7.

58. Underground Press Syndicate, "What is U.P.S.?" John Wilcock Papers (1967–71), Box 1, Rare Book and Manuscript Library, Columbia University, New York City. Henceforth, this archival collection will be abbreviated "JWP."

59. John Wilcock to UPS members, March 7, 1968, *Connections* Records (1967–68), Box 1, WSHS.

60. Ethel Romm to John Wilcock, October 15, 1968, JWP, Box 1.

61. Kindman, "My Odyssey," 378–79. See also Abbott, "Karl and Groucho."

62. Miles, in Bizot, *Free Press*, 7.

63. Quoted in Edward P. Morgan, *The '60s Experience*, 206.

64. Langer, "Notes for Next Time," 113.

65. Peck, *Uncovering the Sixties*, 137.

66. *Newsweek*, "Mellow Yellow," April 10, 1967, 93.

67. *Rag*, "Pick Your Load: Banana or Toad?" March 27, 1967, 4.

68. *Notes from the Underground* (Dallas), March 29, 1967.

69. The Herbalist [pseud.], "Things (Legal) to Smoke and Get You High," *Spokane Natural*, June 26, 1967, 6.

70. Marvin Garson, "Electrical Banana—Very Now Craze," *Village Voice*, March 16, 1967, 5.

71. Kane's account of their "discovery" sounds more than a little implausible. "*EVO* editor Allen Katzman and Walter Bowart were sitting around on an idle afternoon perusing a copy of *Morning of the Magicians*, a then-popular paean to the joys of LSD. Discovering that acid worked its magic by releasing a potent cranial fluid called seratonin [it does not], they wondered aloud and in concert whether any natural substances contained that selfsame fluid. They thought they found just the substance [in bananas]." Kane goes on to explain that bananas are "actually rich in *serotin*, not *seratonin*, as the Banana Hoax architects believed." Kane, "Banana Appeal," 60.

72. Abbott Hoffman, "Hallucinations from the Real World," *Worcester Punch*, June 1967, 12.

73. *Fifth Estate*, "Looks Like Mellow Yellow," April 15–30, 1967, 6.

74. *Oracle*, March 1967, 5; *Berkeley Barb*, "Mellow Yellow Makes Fine Fellow," March 24, 1967, 3. At least two other companies also sold banana powder through the mail—Bizarre Bazaar, in Hollywood, and the Electrical Banana Co., in Seattle.

75. *Time*, "Tripping on Banana Peels," April 7, 1967, 52. These items are on display at the International Banana Club Museum in Altadena, California.

76. Reproduced in Yanker, *Prop Art*, 225.

77. *Washington Free Press*, "Moby Grape," September 3, 1967, 15; *Fifth Estate*, "Looks Like Mellow Yellow," April 15–30, 1967, 6.

78. *IN New York*, "Underground Uprising," n.p., fragment, PSC, Box 2. Writer Sol Weinstein—not normally associated with the counterculture—penned lyrics to another banana song that appeared in the "Letters" section of *Playboy* magazine (to the tune of the Chiquita jingle):

> I'm a Chiquita Banana and I've come to say:
> Bananas are exciting in a brand-new way

So don't waste 'em in a pie—ai!

Use bananas to get high—ai!

Oh, how great it really feels!

So smoke one with your baby and I'll guarantee

That either now or later

You will both end up swinging naked

In the refrigerator—ai! ai! ai! ai!

Playboy, October 1967, 11.

79. Abe Peck, foreword to Wachsberger, *Voices from the Underground*, xix. See also Feigelson, *Underground Revolution*, 126.

80. As quoted in Armstrong, *Trumpet to Arms*, 46.

81. *New Left Notes*, "Human Be-In Covers Meadow, Baffles Cops," April 10, 1967, 1.

82. Frank Thompson, *Chicago Seed*, n.p.

83. Jeff Shero, "Dallas Police Jail Banana Users," *Rag*, March 27, 1967, 1. Legend has it that this article caught the eye of Norman Mailer, who found it so amusing that he recommended it be reprinted in the *Village Voice*. See Lovell, "Stoney Burns and Dallas *Notes*," 65.

84. Dennis Fitzgerald, "Gentle Thursday Banned at U-T," *Rag*, April 10, 1967, 1.

85. *Time*, "Tripping on Banana Peels," April 7, 1967, 52.

86. Fragment (probably the *Village Voice*), April 6, 1967, PSC, Box 2.

87. Eric Schlosser, "The U.S. Bucks a Trend on Marijuana Laws," *New York Times*, June 1, 2003.

88. Klatch, *Generation Divided*, 156. See also Mankoff and Flacks, "Changing Social Base," 54–67. Left-wing journalist Andrew Kopkind echoed this point as well: "Not for nothing," he wrote, "has the *Wall Street Journal* . . . questioned the wisdom of anti-marijuana laws. Apart from any inherent injustice, enforcement is turning an entire class of pre-elite kids against established authority." Kopkind, *Thirty Years' Wars*, 153.

89. Lemar, "Narco Bust Set," *Fifth Estate*, December 15–30, 1966, 1. (Lemar is both a pseudonym and an abbreviation standing for "legalize marijuana.")

90. Rubin, *Do It!* 100.

91. Bill Blum, "Harassed Grass," *Washington Free Press*, July 21, 1967, 1.

92. Schlosser, "U.S. Bucks a Trend," 5.

93. *Fifth Estate*, "Looks Like Mellow Yellow," April 15–30, 1967, 6.

94. Hoffman, *Best of Abbie Hoffman*, 12.

95. Garson, "Electrical Banana," 5; emphasis in original.

96. Bill Blum, "The Banana Gap," *Washington Free Press*, June 10, 1967, 10.

97. Peter Braunstein, "Historicizing the American Counterculture of the 1960s and 1970s," in Braunstein and Doyle, 13. *New Left Notes'* account of the Central Park Be-In underscored just this point: "Television news crews with their cameras, batteries, cables and Clean Cut Young Men . . . appeared especially turned on by the Banana Deity and its parading followers. See *New Left Notes*, "Human Be-In Covers Meadow, Baffles Cops," April 10, 1967, 1.

98. *Newsweek*, "Mellow Yellow," April 10, 1967, 93.

99. Jack Newfield, "One Cheer for the Hippies," *Nation*, June 26, 1967, 809.

100. [Illegible] to Allen Young, May 26, 1967, Allen Young Papers (1962–94), Box 2, WSHS.

101. Todd Gitlin, "Children of the Middle-Class," *Rag*, December 19, 1967. Gitlin later described this essay as "moralistic" and "very puritanical." Todd Gitlin, interview with Bret Eynon, September 16, 1978, CHP, 18. Elsewhere, Gitlin told a humorous story of how he once he spotted a woman who was dancing in a Chicago park while wearing a Chiquita sticker on her forehead. When he "sourly" quizzed her about the political economy of Latin America, she harrumphed, "Oh, don't be so hung up on United Fruit!" See Gitlin, *The Sixties*, 212.

102. Spain Rodriguez, cartoon, *East Village Other*, June 3, 1967, 2.

103. Peter Bart, "Bohemian Newspapers Spread Across Country," *New York Times*, August 1, 1966.

104. Donovan Leitch, e-mail to author, July 7, 2003.

105. McDonald, "Banana Affair."

Chapter 4

1. Kornbluth, "No Fire Exit," 94–95.

2. Brienes, *Community and Organization*, 52–53.

3. See Newfield, *Prophetic Minority*, 186; Breines, *Community and Organization*, 89–90. Newfield attributes the phrase "go-it-aloneism" to Irving Howe, the founding editor of *Dissent* magazine. Breines cites Todd Gitlin as a prominent New Leftist who called for activists to work within existing institutions.

4. Harvey Stone, "Papers and Politics," n.d., *Connections* Records, Box 1, WSHS.

5. Of course, it is impossible to determine precisely how many people read various LNS articles during its fourteen-year history. LNS typically overestimated its readership by combining the circulations of all the publications that subscribed to the service and assuming that underground newspapers passed through several hands. In 1968, they issued a press release boasting that the "estimated American readership and listening audience of LNS member publications is now over 5,000,000." See LNS, "What is Liberation News Service?" n.d., MBP, Box 8, Folder 44. Around this same time, though, Bloom confessed, "I don't think of ours as a mass audience of whatever it is figure we spin off." See Marshall Bloom to Jim Aronson, n.d., MBP, Box 8, Folder 24.

6. Peter Babcox, "Meet the Women Of the Revolution, 1969," *New York Times*, February 1969.

7. John Burks, "The Underground Press: A Special Report," *Rolling Stone*, October 4, 1969, 22.

8. See "Prospectus—The New Media Project," November 25, 1967, MBP, Box 8, Folder 32; Allen Young, "*Post* Reporter Defects to *Free Press*," *Washington Free Press*, December 31, 1967, 7

9. Quoted in Navasky, *Matter of Opinion*, 270.

10. Ray Mungo, "The Movement and Its Media," *Radicals in the Professions Newsletter*, January 1968, 2–3. In speaking of an active "Resistance," Mungo was referring to a national antidraft organization by that name, to which he belonged.

11. Leamer, *Paper Revolutionaries*, 46.

12. David Eisenhower, "In Memory of Campus Activism," *New York Times*, April 30, 1973. Though several commentators recoiled from Eisenhower's suggestion that Bloom's alienation in the late 1960s was related to the counterculture's shortcomings and

failures, none of them contradicted his characterization of Bloom's reputation or personality. See Robert S. Nathan, and Howard Blum, "Some Other Memories of Marshall Bloom," *New York Times*, May 19, 1973; Judith Coburn, letter to the editor, *New York Times*, May 30, 1973; Allen Young, "Marshall Bloom: Gay Brother," *Fag Rag* 5, Summer 1973, 6–7, reprinted in Wachsberger, *Voices from the Underground*, 59–60.

13. Jim Foudy, "The Case of the Angry Young Man from Boston," *College Journalist* 4, n.d, 4–5.

14. Anonymous to Marshall Bloom, n.d. MBP, Box 1, Folder, 7.

15. Hillel Goldberg, "The Anatomy of a Suicide," *Intermountain Jewish News Literary Supplement*, May 16, 1986, 3.

16. Elliott Isenberg, "The Fable of Marshall Bloom," *Amherst Student*, March 16, 1972, 4.

17. According to Goldberg, Bloom's typewritten reply oscillated "between insult and friendship." Gracelessly referencing Goldwater's humiliating defeat in the presidential election of 1964, Bloom wrote, "Goldwater has fallen. I should have known even then [in high school], that my character type, my makeup, was not that of a conservative." See Goldberg, "Anatomy of a Suicide," 1, 3.

18. John H. Fenton, "Twenty Amherst Seniors Walk Out to Protest McNamara Degree," *New York Times*, June 4, 1966. Claiming that he'd demonstrated his patriotism through his extensive volunteer activities, Bloom said the protest did not express "any hatred of college or country, but rather opposition to honoring the leader of the war effort in Vietnam." However, he is misidentified in the article as "Paul B. Bloom." See "Correction," *New York Times*, June 5, 1966, 18.

19. This was not the same Walter Adams who briefly served as president of MSU, mentioned in chapter 2.

20. Isenberg, "Fable of Marshall Bloom," 5. A post mortem examination on the porter supposedly indicated that he had a heart condition from which he could have died at any time.

21. Quoted in Schechter, *News Dissector*, 52. See also Granger W. Blair, "Student Protest in London Goes On," *New York Times*, May 16, 1967, 11.

22. Goldberg, "Anatomy of a Suicide," 9.

23. Quoted in Mungo, *Famous Long Ago*, 26.

24. Isenberg, "Fable of Marshall Bloom," 5.

25. "Leader of British Student Revolt Speaks on Student Politics Tomorrow," *BU News*, April 26, 1967, 1.

26. Mungo, *Beyond the Revolution*, 7.

27. Mungo, *Famous Long Ago*, 2.

28. Mungo, *Beyond the Revolution*, 8–9.

29. Ray Mungo, "The Pope Is Toast," May 26, 2010, *The Rag Blog*, http://theragblog. blogspot.com/2010/05/ray-mungo-pope-is-toast.html. Mungo adds that the man who molested him escaped punishment: He was "simply transferred to another parish, where he continued to 'work with' budding youths. Eventually he died, still a holy pastor to his newly hormonal flock."

30. Ray Mungo, interview with author, March 25, 2005.

31. Mungo, *Famous Long Ago*, 3.

32. Quoted in Foudy, "Angry Young Man," 4.

33. Mungo interview.

34. *Time*, "All the News That's Fit to Protest," March 22, 1968, 67.

35. Quoted in Foudy, "Angry Young Man," 5.

36. Mungo, *Beyond the Revolution*, 23.

37. Wasserman, "Joys of Liberation News Service," 55. See also Mungo, *Famous Long Ago*, 85–86.

38. Mungo interview. See also "High Crime," *New York Times*, February 23, 1967.

39. Foley, *Confronting the War Machine*, 158–59.

40. Peck, *Uncovering the Sixties*, 72.

41. Mungo, *Famous Long Ago*, 4.

42. See Sol Stern, "NSA and the CIA," *Ramparts*, March 1967, 29–38.

43. Austin C. Wehrwein, "Student Editor Ferment," *Christian Science Monitor*, September 21, 1967, 12.

44. See Goldberg, "Anatomy of a Suicide," 2; Wasserman, 52; Mungo interview.

45. Mungo, *Famous Long Ago*, 27.

46. Young, "Marshall Bloom: Gay Brother," 60.

47. Lowell B. Wiltbank, "New Media Project Is Born from Rift in Student Press," *Pace College Press*, October 4, 1967, 6.

48. Marshall Bloom, "The New Press Project," n.d., MBP, Box 8, Folder 45.

49. In a mailing to new and prospective members, the group's founders noted that they'd changed from another proposed name, "Resistance Press Service" because "resistance" was used by several other groups, and besides, "after resistance has been successful, comes LIBERATION." Additionally, Mungo argued, "LIBERATION would have more meaning in the third world." See LNS to "College Members of LIBERATION News Service," September 26, 1967, *Underground Newspaper Microfilm Collection, 1963–1973*, Reel 3, No. 10.

50. Marshall Bloom to I. F. Stone, n.d., MBP, Box 8, Folder 23. Bloom added, "Since then, of course, we have gone through saving from each of our home banks. . . . Hardly dropped-out hippies, we are working harder than ever."

51. Mungo, *Beyond the Revolution*, 22–23.

52. Mungo interview.

53. Marshall Bloom to David, October 3, 1967, MBP, Box 8, Folder 22.

54. Marshall Bloom to Mike Kars, December 17, 1967, MBP, Box 8, Folder 23. To another friend, Bloom boasted he was "now a real part of a rapidly growing American 'underground.' . . . You would be surprised at the changes in the US and the vastness of the movement now." See Marshall Bloom to Elliott Blinder, n.d., MBP, Box 8, Folder 23.

55. LNS to "College Members of LIBERATION News Service," September 26, 1967, *Underground Newspaper Collection*, Reel 3, No. 10.

56. Thorne Dreyer and Victoria Smith, "The Movement and the New Media," Liberation News Service packet 144, March 1, 1969, 15; emphasis added.

57. Thorne Dreyer, "Radical Media Conference," Liberation News Service packet 123, December 5, 1968, 28.

58. See Peck, *Uncovering the Sixties*, 45.

59. Walter H. Bowart to "Editors of the Underground Press Syndicate," June 15, 1967, *Connections* Records (1967–68), Box 1, WSHS.

60. Dreyer and Smith, "Movement and the New Media," 15.

61. John Bryan to "friends" [UPS editors] July 31, 1967, *Connections* Records (1967–68), Box 1, WSHS.

62. Wayne Hansen, to "EDITORS OF UPS," July 26, 1967, *Connections* Records (1967–68), Box 1, WSHS.

63. The meeting was originally scheduled to take place at the Institute of Policy Studies, a left-wing think tank on New Hampshire Avenue.

64. Mungo, *Famous Long Ago*, 18.

65. Leamer, *Paper Revolutionaries*, 46.

66. Dorothy Devine, "Radicals Start News Service," *Wellesley News*, November 2, 1967, 4. There are some very minor discrepancies between Devine's account of this meeting and Mungo's in *Famous Long Ago*. For instance, Mungo has Bloom burning his draft card *after* the meeting became a fracas, whereas Devine says he did it to open the meeting.

67. Mungo, *Famous Long Ago*, 18–19.

68. Michael Grossman, "Underground Press Joins Theater of the Absurd," *Washington Free Press*, November 23, 1967, 5.

69. Devine, "Radicals Start News Service," 4.

70. Mungo, *Famous Long Ago*, 19. The following December, Mungo sent LNS subscribers a note professing, "We didn't envision LNS as entirely 'our thing,' a news service whose ideas and inspirations come entirely from us." However, he added, "those of you who were at the October 20 LNS-UPS meeting in Washington will remember how difficult it seemed to gather a national cooperative in those few hours, but the need for our union and the circumstances to achieve it are much greater now [as a result of repression against underground papers and the increasing radicalism of the New Left]." As a result, LNS called for continued feedback from members, as well as smaller, "gentle gatherings of like souls around the country to discuss how we can help each other." Raymond Mungo to "friends," December 19, 1967, *Underground Newspaper Collection*, Reel 3, No. 10.

71. Devine, "Radicals Start News Service," 4.

72. Predictably, estimates of the number of protestors varied. March organizers claimed that upwards of 200,000 assembled at the Lincoln Memorial, while the police and the military contended there were no more than 55,000 demonstrators. See Clinton, ed., *Loyal Opposition*, 34; William Chapman, "55,000 Rally against War; GI's Repel Pentagon Charge," *Washington Post*, October 22, 1967.

73. Jack Newfield, "Pentagon Day: Flight over the Cuckoo's Nest," *Village Voice*, October 26, 1967, 40.

74. Mailer, *Armies of the Night*, 53.

75. *WIN*, "Mobilization! October 21," October 30, 1967, 5.

76. Quoted in Small, *Covering Dissent*, 73.

77. Quoted in ibid., 74.

78. The day before the Pentagon march, some ten thousand radicals—many equipped with army-surplus helmets and trashcan shields—introduced "mobile tactics" to the New Left when they engaged in a six-hour melee with police that temporarily shut down the Oakland Induction Center. Earlier in the week, at the University of Wisconsin, riot police viciously evicted students who had been occupying a campus building that was hosting a recruiter from Dow Chemical Company, the maker of Agent Orange and napalm. This marked the first time that tear gas had been used on a major campus,

79. Small, *Covering Dissent*, 74. Small notes that Todd Gitlin raised the possibility that network brass also might have caved to governmental pressure to stay away from the protest. See Gitlin, *Whole World is Watching*, 228n53.

80. Small, *Covering Dissent*, 80.

81. Kip Shaw, quoted in John Kronenberger, "What's Black and White and Pink and Green and Dirty and Read All Over?" *Look*, October 1, 1968, 22.

82. Another time, Mungo put the matter more sharply, arguing that "American journalists lead a moronic lifestyle and most American newspapers pander to a simplicity that would be charming and amusing were it not so dangerous." See Austin C. Wehrwein, "Student Editors Plan New Aggressiveness," *Chronicle of Higher Education*, September 13, 1967, 8.

83. Mungo, *Famous Long Ago*, 76–77.

84. Ibid., 76. Readers should be advised, though, that Mungo has since expressed considerable bemusement that scholars would ever scrutinize what he now describes as musings ("just some crazy shit I wrote when I was very young and stoned to the tits"). Ray Mungo, e-mail to author, April 20, 2005.

85. "Leaders Divided on Aims of March," *Washington Post*, October 20, 1967; Mailer, *Armies of the Night*, 234.

86. See Gregory Calvert, interview by Ron Grele, July 1–3, 1987, Columbia, 244.

87. Bruce Jackson, "The Battle of the Pentagon," *Atlantic Monthly*, January 1968, 35.

88. See Small, *Covering Dissent*, 73.

89. See Hoffman, *Best of Abbie Hoffman*, 14–35.

90. Calvert, *Democracy from the Heart*, 248–49. See also Cathy Wilkerson, "Victory or Defeat?" *Washington Free Press*, Pentagon Special, n.d., 9.

91. According to Bruce Schulman, the photo has since become a "stock image" in American history textbooks, although ironically, most of these books ignore the connections between the New Left and counterculture that the image depicts. See Schulman, "Out of the Streets," 1531.

92. Mailer, *Armies of the Night*, 262. This was the "largest mass draft card burning in the history of the protest against the Vietnam War." See Ferber and Lynd, *Resistance*, 136.

93. Mailer, *Armies of the Night*, 272.

94. Edward Jacobs, "To the Pentagon and Away to Jail," *Village Voice*, October 26, 1967, 5.

95. Thorne Dreyer, "No Longer a Neat Little Game," *Washington Free Press*, Pentagon Special, n.d., 8. Many of the earliest LNS news packets are difficult to find, and some of those available in the *Underground Newspaper Collection* were originally printed on dark paper, thereby making it difficult to photocopy them. As a result, my analysis of LNS's Pentagon coverage largely rests on articles that appeared in a special issue of the *Washington Free Press*, which leaned heavily on LNS for copy.

96. James Reston, "Everyone Is a Loser," *New York Times*, October 23, 1967.

97. Ben A. Franklin, "War Protestors Defying Deadline Seized in Capital," *New York Times*, October 23, 1967.

98. Jimmy Breslin, "Quiet Rally Turns Vicious," *Washington Post*, October 22, 1967.

99. White, *Tropics of Discourse*, 85.

100. *Washington Free Press*, "Two G.I.'s Defect at Pentagon," Pentagon Special, n.d., 7.

101. Dreyer, "Neat Little Game," 8.

102. *Washington Free Press*, "Two G.I.'s Defect at Pentagon," Pentagon Special, n.d., 7. Even movement veterans clash over this question. In a 1987 oral history interview, former SDS national secretary Greg Calvert claimed to have witnessed one of the defections from his perch on a balustrade (see Calvert interview, 50). However, two writers who were extremely sympathetic to the antiwar movement, Michael Ferber and Staughton Lynd, described the defections as a "movement legend." See Ferber and Lynd, *Resistance*, 137.

103. Hazlett, *My Generation*, 51. Hazlett briefly compares Mungo's sense of myth with Hoffman's (225).

104. A moment later in the text, Mungo tells his readers that he knows he's said an extreme thing ("OK, I can see some of your faces that I'm not going to get away with it that easily"), and he confesses that he shares some of their ethical concerns ("I'm not saying it would be okay to broadcast a false rumor"). He maintains, however, that the news media's preoccupation with facts can actually distort the underlying truth of an event. Ultimately, his maxim was "Tell the truth, brothers, and let the facts fall where they may." Mungo, *Famous Long Ago*, 76. Again, Mungo cautions scholars not to read too deeply into his youthful musings.

105. Mungo interview. Dreyer said much the same thing: although he never witnessed any defections himself, he recalls speaking with, and believing, several demonstrators who claimed to have seen them firsthand (Thorne Dreyer, interview by author, April 23, 2005). Allen Young, a journalist who joined LNS not long after the Pentagon March, also echoes Dreyer and Mungo: "I can't say I spoke to any of the [defecting] soldiers, but I spoke to numerous eyewitnesses who saw it happen," he said. Allen Young, interview with author, March 11, 2005.

106. Rader described how his training in the Green Berets had dulled his personality and made him "accustomed to the idea of killing." By becoming a pacifist, Rader said, he faced up to ten years on prison. According to LNS, Rader's remarks "may have been instrumental in the defections of two, and perhaps three, soldiers." Gary Rader, untitled speech, Liberation News Service, n.d., *Underground Newspaper Collection*, Reel 3, No. 10.

107. "Two GI's Speak," Liberation News Service, n.d., *Underground Newspaper Collection on Microfilm*, Reel 3, No. 10.

108. "Upholding Law and Order in Washington," Liberation News Service, n.d., *Underground Newspaper Microfilm Collection*, Reel 3, No. 10. The original handwritten copies of this testimony survive in the MBP, Box 9, Folder 33.

109. Elliot Blinder, "Tear Gas Controversy," Liberation News Service (n.d.), *Underground Newspaper Collection on Microfilm*, Reel 3, no. 10; "55,000 Rally Against War; GIs Repel Pentagon Charge," *Washington Post*, October 22, 1967.

110. Raymond Mungo, "Zany Notables," *Washington Free Press*, Pentagon Special, n.d., 11.

111. Dellinger, *Yale to Jail*, 306.

112. See Benjamin Spock, *Spock on Spock: A Memoir of Growing Up with the Century* (New York: Pantheon, 1989); Lynn Z. Bloom, *Doctor Spock: Biography of a Conservative Radical* (Indianapolis: Bobbs-Merrill, 1972); Michael S. Foley, ed., *Dear Dr. Spock: Letters about the Vietnam War to America's Favorite Baby Doctor* (New York: New York University Press, 2005); Thomas Maier, *Dr. Spock: An American Life* (New York: Harcourt Brace, 1998).

113. Mungo, "Zany Notables," 12.

114. Allen Young, "Post Reporter Defects to the Free Press," *Washington Free Press*, December 31, 1967, 7. To be precise, Young was referring to the "scraggly crew" of just one particular paper, the *Washington Free Press*, with which he was briefly affiliated. Clearly, though, his comment has wider application.

115. Liberation News Service, "Liberation News Service (Speaks) Freaks Out. . . . . Again," n.d., *Underground Newspaper Collection*, Reel 13, No. 10.

116. Marshall Bloom to Dan Bernstein, n.d., MBP, Box 8, Folder 23.

117. Mungo, *Famous Long Ago*, 21.

118. Allen Young, e-mail to author, June 26 2005.

119. See Sheila Ryan, "A Kind of Justice," Liberation News Service packet 27, January 1968, 12; Harvey Wasserman, "'Crazy' Indian Quits Navy," Liberation News Service packet 27, January 1968, 11; Mark Sommer, "Don't Pray for Peace: You're in the Army Now," Liberation News Service packet 42, February 1968, 15; Allen Young, "SDS National Council Meeting," Liberation News Service packet 24, January 3, 1967, 3; Todd Gitlin, "Mightier than the Sword (But the Machine-Gun? . . .)," Liberation News Service packet 36, February 1968, 2; James Petras, "The Politics of Looting and Looting as Politics," Liberation News Service packet 16, December 1967, 2; Leroi Jones, "the black poet faces the bastard justice of America," Liberation News Service packet 32, January 1968, 24; Mike Lucas, "The Evil Weed Struck Down Once More," Liberation News Service packet 24, January 1967, 3; Jerry Rubin, "What the Revolution is All About," Liberation News Service packet 26, January 10, 1968, n.p.

120. Ron Luucas to LNS, n.d., MBP, Box 8, Folder 21.

121. Peter Werbe to Marshall Bloom, April 24, 1968, MBP, Box 8, Folder 21.

122. Jeff Shero to "dear brothers," May 7, 1968, MBP, Box 8, Folder 22.

123. Mungo, *Famous Long Ago*, 55–56.

124. George Cavalletto, interview with author, July 28, 2003; Mungo, *Famous Long Ago*, 139–40.

125. One student who enrolled at Columbia in 1962 recalls a university dean standing before incoming freshmen to warn them: "Whatever you do, don't go into Harlem, and especially don't go wearing a Columbia sweatshirt." See David Glibert, interview by Ron Grele, January 16, 1985, Columbia, 29.

126. Neighborhood organizations charged Columbia with treating its nonstudent tenants ruthlessly and with breaking a compact concerning its future acquisitions. According to a fact-finding team that investigated the Columbia rebellion, "A number of spokesmen made public, condescending remarks as to the irrelevance of community needs when placed in opposition to those of Columbia." See Cox, *Crisis at Columbia*, 37; Kahn, *Battle for Morningside Heights*, 87–88; Peter Millones, "Gym Controversy Began in Late 50's," *New York Times*, April 26, 1968.

127. In fairness to Columbia's planners, they probably designed the rear door entrance with the convenience of Harlem's residents in mind. The gym was to be built on a steep, rocky hill, whereby Columbia students would enter the upper-level from Morningside Drive, and Harlemites would enter through a lower level door nearer to where they lived. Accordingly, the "back door" nomenclature that was used during the controversy ("No More *Gym Crow*") may have been unfair—it was more like a "lower level door." I thank Allen Young for pointing this out after he read an early draft of this chapter.

128. Although Columbia started working on the gym, as a result of the protests it was never finished at the Morningside Park location; instead, it was built on Columbia's campus.

129. Avorn, *Up Against the Ivy*, 15.

130. In May 1965, students disrupted a Naval Reserve Officers Training Corps awards ceremony; beginning in 1967, SDS began interfering with CIA, U.S. Marine, and Dow Chemical Company recruitment on campus; in February 1968, a raucous demonstration against the gym led to the arrest of a dozen students; the following month, SDS defied a ban on indoor demonstrations by tromping through Low Library with placards and a bullhorn, denouncing the IDA. Finally, on April 9, 1968, at a memorial to honor the memory of Rev. Martin Luther King Jr., Columbia SDS's newly elected chairman, Mark Rudd, burst onto the stage, called Columbia's administrators "racists," and denounced the proceedings as sham. See Cox, *Crisis at Columbia*, 63–74.

131. See Rudd, "Columbia: Notes," 290–312. The phrase "politics of confrontation" belongs to Jeremy Varon; see Varon, *Bringing the War Home*, 26.

132. See Carl Davidson, "New Radicals," 323–24. See also Kahn, *Battle for Morningside Heights*, 76–77.

133. Specifically, the handbill said that those who opposed "Columbia's unjust policies" should not be disciplined, and that six students who had been placed on disciplinary probation for leading an indoor demonstration the previous month should receive a public hearing, "with full rights of due process." Curiously, although SDS and SAS jointly organized the rally, the gymnasium was not mentioned. See Cox, *Crisis at Columbia*, 100.

134. These were their main demands, anyhow. They also called for the administration to drop criminal charges against the student who had just been arrested at the gym construction site, withdraw a ban on indoor demonstrations, and rescind the probations against six student leaders who had organized an unauthorized demonstration against the IDA a month earlier.

135. See Cox, *Crisis at Columbia*, 99–142.

136. Steve Diamond, e-mail to author, June 12, 2005.

137. In addition to LNS, writers from a new newspaper, the *Rat*, provided detailed coverage of the April uprising. According to Peck, "Columbia made . . . [the] *Rat* the underground press's hottest publication." The cover of its May 3–16 issue pictured a Nazi helmet covering Low Library's granite dome, under the banner, "Heil Columbia." Inside, readers could find "liberated documents" from Grayson Kirk's office, which revealed some of Columbia's business partnerships. See Peck, *Uncovering the Sixties*, 93–94.

138. Ethel Grodzins Romm, "You Go Underground for 'Inside' Report," *Editor & Publisher*, May 11, 1968, 12.

139. Steve Diamond et al., "Columbia: The Revolution is Now," Liberation News Service packet 70, April 30, 1968, 1.

140. Avorn, *Up Against the Ivy*, 47.

141. See Kahn, *Battle for Morningside Heights*, 145.

142. Diamond et al., "Revolution is Now," 1, 4.

143. By contrast, the *New York Times* reported that many SDSers were "deeply troubled over their relationship to the Negro students and Harlem residents who ejected them from Hamilton Hall." One student seemed disturbed because he failed to measure up to the

blacks' high radical standard. "We just didn't have the same commitment," he said. "Some of the blacks were actually willing to die. It made me wonder what my commitment really was, and it frightened me." Another *Times* article quoted a member of SAS distancing himself from SDS. "Our organization is in liaison with the community and not with leftist white radicals," he said. See *New York Times*, "Columbia Closes Campus After Disorders," April 25, 1968; Steven V. Roberts, "Sit-In Spectrum Has A Wide Range," *New York Times*, April 25, 1968.

144. Cox, *Crisis at Columbia*, 102.

145. Avorn, "Up Agianst the Ivy," 46.

146. Kahn, *Battle for Morningside Heights*, 126.

147. Diamond et al., "Revolution is Now," 3.

148. Ibid., 3–4. In contrast, a writer for the *New York Times* dismissed the students' pretences, describing Rudd as "given to quoting revolutionary slogans he picked up on a recent trip to Cuba." See Roberts, "Sit-In Spectrum."

149. Diamond et al., "Revolution is Now," 11. Jacobs later joined Weatherman, an ultra-militant offshoot of SDS. After three members of Weatherman died while making bombs on March 6, 1970, Jacobs was expelled from the group. He eventually moved to Vancouver, Canada, where he died in 1997.

150. Ibid., 4.

151. Ibid., 4, 10.

152. Ibid., 10.

153. Ibid., 9.

154. Hamilton was more accurate than Leary. According to the Cox Commission, "Eighty-seven persons . . . obtained treatment at St. Luke's," and fifteen more went to Knickerbocker hospital. (One police officer also required treatment there.) "The character of the injuries ranged from heavy bruises and scalp lacerations to sprains and severe fright," along with two bone fractures. Cox, *Crisis at Columbia*, 142.

155. *Ramparts*, "Apologia," June 15, 1968, 1.

156. *Ramparts*, "The Siege of Columbia: An Exclusive Report," June 15, 1968, 27–39.

157. Additionally, Abe Rosenthal, the paper's assistant managing editor, was said to be an "ardent alumnus" of Columbia College. See Sale, *SDS*, 442.

158. Sylvan Fox, "Columbia Study of Crisis Ordered by Faculty Unit," *New York Times*, May 2, 1968, 52. Another group of placard-bearing students rallied outside the home of William Paley, the president of CBS, who was also a Columbia trustee. The students alleged that CBS's editorials had been biased in favor of the police and that *Face the Nation*, CBS's flagship Sunday morning news program, gave Kirk half an hour of airtime without extending equal consideration to his critics. See Tom Hamilton and Allen Young, "Columbia: The Students Stick With It," Liberation News Service packet 71, May 3, 1968, 6.

159. Steve Diamond, e-mail to author, June 12, 2005.

160. One splenetic essay, titled "Hoodlumism at Columbia," railed against "the degrading spectacle" of students exalting "irresponsibility over reason," as well as the "intolerably undemocratic nature of dictatorial student minorities . . . who undermine academic freedom and the free society itself by resorting to such junta methods." Another editorial alleged that SDS had "substituted dictatorship by temper tantrum for undergraduate democracy," and seemed to endorse Kirk's eventual decision to clear the buildings by force. "Control of the campus cannot be turned over to student juntas operating in

defiance of every consideration of academic discipline and democratic rule." See *New York Times*, "Hoodlumism at Columbia," April 25, 1968; *New York Times*, "Citadel of Reason," April 29, 1968.

161. Meanwhile, both editorials skimmed over the causes of the protest. The first of the two actually said, "The question is not whether all of Columbia's past actions have been sound, either academically or in relation to the community," before adding that Columbia's actions had at least provoked "constructive debate among Columbia's own faculty and administration." Of course, from the protestors' perspective, this was the most pernicious sort of liberal claptrap. The university had already steamrolled over the objections of local political leaders who opposed the gym, and its spokesmen insisted that longstanding legal commitments prohibited Columbia from abandoning or significantly revising the project. Without the protests, the gym would have been built; because of the protests, it wasn't. See *New York Times*, "Hoodlumism at Columbia"; Cox, *Crisis at Columbia*, 87–89.

162. Fox, "Columbia Study."

163. Allen Young, "Columbia Eyewitness: Cultural Revolution," Liberation News Service packet 73, May 13, 1968, 11.

164. Although the police assault happened in the early morning hours on April 30, that day's late edition of the *Times* carried a full report of the raid, most of which had actually been written several hours before it took place: "Only a few facts had to be added when reporters called in the actual details." Moreover, at around 1:00 AM. on April 30—just an hour before the police action began—Newfield says he spotted *Times* assistant managing editor Abe Rosenthal "emerg[ing] from a secret meeting of top police brass." Slightly embarrassed, Rosenthal "claimed he did not know if a police raid on the students was imminent." This was almost certainly untrue; later, Rosenthal admitted that in a lapse of judgment he had actually ridden uptown to the bust in a police car. See Jack Newfield, "Pre-Fitting the News At the Paper of Record," *Village Voice*, May 9, 1968, 7. See also Newfield, *Somebody's Gotta Tell It*, 226. Rosenthal later acknowledged that letting himself be chauffeured by the police was not "the most brilliant [decision] in the world." See Tifft and Jones, *The Trust*, 439.

165. Gitlin, *The Sixties*, 308.

166. A. M. Rosenthal, "Combat and Compassion at Columbia," *New York Times*, May 1, 1968.

167. Quoted in Newfield, *Somebody's Gotta Tell It*, 226.

168. Rosenthal, "Combat and Compassion." Murray Kempton, a writer for the *New York Post*, found this last quote so improbable that he essentially called Rosenthal a fabulist: "I recall thinking that Rosenthal's sense of theater had led him over the brink with that last touch," he wrote. The "dramatist has to be careful in the assignment of the appropriate sentiment to the appropriate character." Quoted in Newfield, *Somebody's Gotta Tell It*, 226.

169. Lemisch, "2.5 Cheers," 189.

170. Tifft and Jones, *The Trust*, 226–27. The passage is also quoted in Newfield, *Somebody's Gotta Tell It*, 225–26.

171. Newfield characterizes the *Post*'s coverage in "Pre-Fitting the News," 8; Margi Werner, "Columbia Eyewitness: Radicalization at the Sundial," Liberation News Service packet 73, May 13, 1968, 6.

172. Newfield, "Pre-Fitting the News," 8.

173. Martin Arnold, "Lindsay Orders Report on Police," *New York Times*, May 1, 1968, 35.

174. Newfield, "Pre-Fitting the News," 8. According to a writer for *Look* magazine, "When the *New York Times* all but ignored the injuries inflicted by police during last spring's Columbia University insurrection, a number of impartial observers had to agree that the underground suspicions [of mainstream media bias] had been somewhat vindicated." See Kronenberger, "Black and White," 22.

175. Peck, *Uncovering the Sixties*, 92; Diamond, e-mail to author, June 12, 2005.

176. According to the *Spectator*, a "large, dripping ink splatter on the wall of one professor's office became a favorite subject for press photographers covering the aftermath of the occupations." However, three math professors said that stain wasn't there when they came to the building at 7 AM on April 30, and the only other people who had access to the building between then and the time the ink appeared were photographers and policemen. Kenneth Clark, the famous psychologist, even claimed to have witnessed what he believes were plainclothes police officers breaking furniture in Fayerweather Hall. See Avorn, "Up Against the Ivy," 190, 201–2. See also John Kifner, "Many Thousands in Damage Reported," *New York Times*, May 1, 1968.

177. Quoted in Fox, "Columbia Study."

178. Tifft and Jones, *The Trust*, 440.

179. Mungo interview.

180. Marshall Bloom to Dan Bernstein, n.d., MBP, Box 8, Folder 23.

181. Gitlin, *The Sixties*, 309.

182. Diamond, e-mail to author, June 12, 2005.

183. Quoted in John Leo, "Politics Now the Focus of the Underground Press," *New York Times*, September 4, 1968, 95.

Chapter 5

1. J. Edgar Hoover to all FBI offices, November 5, 1968; J. Edgar Hoover to Albany, N.Y., field office, July 8, 1968, both quoted in Streitmatter, *Voices of Revolution*, 215.

2. J. Edgar Hoover, "Violence in American Society," reprinted in *Teaspoon and Door*, May 24, 1968, 10. Concomittant to this, in late 1968, a CIA analyst who worked in Project Resistance (essentially a domestic spying program), filed this inelegantly written memo:

   > A modern phenomenon which has evolved in the last three or four years is the vast growth of the Underground Press. Underground means of mass communication utilized to avoid suppression by legal authority and/or attribution is not new to this age, but its volume is and the apparent freedom and ease in which filth, slanderous and libelous statements, and what appear to be almost treasonous anti-establishment propaganda is allowed to circulate is difficult to rationalize.

   Since the CIA was not supposed to spy on American citizens, many of its suggestions for sabotaging the underground press were likely passed off to the FBI. See Angus MacKenzie, "Sabotaging the Dissident Press," *Columbia Journalism Review*, March/April 1981, 60.

3. Rips, "Dissident Voices," 71. In one issue of *Armageddon News*, the FBI agents who posed as anonymous Indiana University students pretended to lament that

dissatisfaction with the Vietnam War was "being used by a few to seize the university and strike at the heart of the democratic system." Agents who reviewed the publication were unimpressed. "The next issue . . . and subsequent material must contain a more sophisticated approach with regards to the situation at Indiana University and in relation to the broad protest movement in this country." See *Armageddon News*, October 25, 1968, 1; FBI Memorandum, October 11, 1968, PEN Records, Box 89, Folder 2.

4. David K. Shipler, "'Underground' Press Coverage Shifts From Rock, Sex and Drugs to Politics," *New York Times*, March 7, 1973, 45.

5. Wilcock, "Manhattan Memories."

6. Rex Weiner, interviewed by John Holmstrom, "Agent of Chaos," *High Times*, October 1988, 86.

7. Ron Rosenbaum, "The Secret Life of Tommy Rotten: The Mysterious Man Behind D.O.A.," *Punk*, April 1981, 24.

8. Chip Berlet, "Alternative News Service in the U.S.—Part II," *Alternative Journalism Revue*, January-February, 1976, 17.

9. Quoted in John Burks, "The Underground Press: A Special Report," *Rolling Stone*, October 4, 1969, 15.

10. John Wilcock, "Manhattan Memories," unpublished manuscript in author's possession.

11. John Wilcock to UPS members, March 7, 1968, *Connections* Records (1967–68), Box 1, WSHS.

12. Wilcock, "Manhattan Memories."

13. In a circular letter to all the UPS members, Wilcock ruefully admitted that "*EVO* has used UPS funds for its own purposes and rendered no accounting of such funds." See John Wilcock to UPS members, March 7, 1968, *Connections* Records (1967–68), Box 1, WSHS.

14. John Wilcock, e-mail to author, January 19, 2009.

15. Burks, "Underground Press," 17.

16. John Holmstrom, "The Ultimate Hippie,"*High Times*, October 1989, 36.

17. James Retherford, e-mail to author, September 4 2009.

18. Quoted in Wilcock, "Manhattan Memories."

19. Tom Forcade, "From UPS," Liberation News Service packet 135, January 30, 1969, 9.

20. Holmstrom, "Ultimate Hippie," 36–37.

21. Burks, "Underground Press," 17.

22. Thomas King Forcade, "Write On!" *East Village Other*, November 19, 1969, 5.

23. Tom Forcade, "From UPS," Liberation News Service packet 135, January 30, 1969, 9.

24. Burks, "Underground Press," 15.

25. Peck, "Underground to Alternative," 157. See also Thorne Dreyer, "Radical Media Conference," Liberation News Service packet 123, December 5, 1968, 27–28.

26. See Hale, "White Panthers," 134.

27. See Hale, "White Panthers."

28. Don DeMaio, untitled sidebar, *Rolling Stone*, October 4, 1969, 19.

29. Don DeMaio, interview with author, June 5, 2009.

30. Quoted in DeMaio, sidebar, *Rolling Stone*.

31. See Pelz, "Fall of the Underground Press," 61.

32. See *Time*, "The Tribe is Restless," July 18, 1969, 46.

33. The infamous ad in question pictured a group of forlorn hippies sitting in a jail cell, surrounded by protest signs and LPs, alongside the tagline: "But The Man can't bust our music." This ham-fisted attempt to cash in on the protest culture was widely ridiculed. Radicals bruited about various responses, including the systematic "liberating" (read: stealing) of Columbia's records from stores, and a sit-in at its company headquarters. But instead of these approaches, they agreed that John Sinclair should write a full-page essay that would run in all UPS papers, calling on musicians and artists to pressure Columbia into changing its policy. As it happened, Sinclair's piece ecstatically praised the underground press, but he never mentioned Columbia Records. See *Rat*, "Underground Press Conference, + r.p.m.," July 24–August 7, 1969, 7; John Sinclair, "Underground Press Syndicate," John Wilcock Papers (1967–71), Rare Books and Manuscripts Library, Columbia University, Box 1, Folder 6.

34. Walt Crowley, "RPM," *Helix* (Seattle) 8, no. 9, ca. summer 1969, 8.

35. Later, Wenner disputed the characterization. "When we started out," he said, "we really had the idea that we were gonna be different from the underground papers. Their reporting was sloppy, their layout was ugly, [and] they [espoused] radical sandbox politics. We didn't want to look like them, sound like them, or be like them." Jann Wenner, interview with author, June 25, 2009.

36. See Atkin, "Over-the-Counter Culture," 191. One of my former students wrote an excellent honors thesis that addressed *Rolling Stone*'s cultural politics. See Ages, "Gather No Moss."

37. *The South End* had previously been known as the *Daily Collegian*, until it was commandeered by black-power militants, who began carrying the front page motto: "One Class-Conscious Worker is Worth 100 Students." See Georgakas and Surkin, *Detroit, I Do Mind Dying*, 54–55, 59, 57.

38. Don DeMaio, "South End Stopped," *Distant Drummer*, July 17, 1969, 5.

39. Peter Rabbit [Forcade], "UPS Odyssey," *Rebirth* (Vol. 1, No. 5), n.d.,3.

40. Demaio, "South End Stopped," 14; *Rat*, "Underground Press Conference + r.p.m.," July 24–August 7, 1969, 7; *Berkeley Tribe*, "U.P.S. and Downs," July 25–31, 1969, 14.

41. Liberation News Service, "Media Conference Raided by Shotgun-Toting Pigs," Liberation News Service packet 179, July 19, 1969, 17.

42. Marc Fisher, "Voice of the Cabal: Bob Fass and the Slow Fade of Countercultural Radio," *New Yorker*, December 4, 2006, 58–65.

43. Rabbit [Forcade], 3.

44. "Underground Press Syndicate," undated pamphlet, JWP, Box 3, Folder 7.

45. See Wilcock, "Manhattan Memories"; Goldman, "Living and Dying," 4–12.

46. Wilcock, "Manhattan Memories."

47. A. J.Weberman, interview with author, June 28, 2008.

48. Weiner, "Agent of Chaos," 41.

49. Forcade, "Write On!" 5.

50. See Haines, "G.I. Resistance."

51. See Rips, *Campaign against the Underground Press*, 82.

52. Rips, *Campaign against the Underground Press*, 45. To some, the PEN Center's findings did not come as a great shock. In 1975 and 1976, the Senate Select Committee on Intelligence, headed by Frank Church (D-ID), revealed many of the tactics the government used in its attempt to destroy New Left and civil rights organizations. It docu-

mented numerous instances in which intelligence-community operatives overlooked or violated existing laws, and concluded that the government's "harassment of innocent citizens engaged in lawful forms of political expression did serious injury to the First Amendment guarantee of freedom of speech and the right of the people to assemble peaceably and to petition the government for redress of grievances." Senate Select Committee to Study Governmental Operations with Respect to Intelligence Activities, *Intelligence Activities and the Rights of Americans*, Book 2, Final Report of the Select Committee to Study Governmental Operations With Respect to Intelligence Activities, 94th Cong., 2nd sess., 1976.

53. This seemed to help sales. In late 1969, John Wilcock remarked that six months prior, some newsstands hadn't wanted to sell his underground paper, *Other Scenes*, because it had nude pictures inside. "Now," he said, "they don't want me unless I put a nude on the cover." See Barry Farrell, "For the Only Freak in Ohio," *Life*, November 21, 1969, 32B.

54. Bailey, *Sex in the Heartland*, 163.

55. John Sieler, quoted in Bailey, *Sex in the Heartland*, 156. This notion was refined in Herbert Marcuse's *Essay on Liberation*, in which he held that "obscenity is a moral concept in the verbal arsenal of the Establishment, which abuses the term by applying it, not to expressions of its own morality but to those of another. Obscene is not the picture of a naked woman who exposes her pubic hair but that of a fully clad general who exposes his medals rewarded in a war of aggression" (8).

56. Jack Jackson, quoted in Pilcher, *Erotic Comics*, 148. Others hold that the meaning of the spelling of "comix" was not so specific, and that it was simply meant to signify a difference from mainstream comics (whether of the DC or Marvel variety, or those from the Sunday funny pages). It is also necessary to add that although some of the era's comix were published in comic-book form—and therefore could be said to be technically independent of underground rags—underground newspapers and underground comic books always shared the same distribution networks and readerships.

57. Quoted in Armstrong, *Trumpet to Arms*, 85.

58. Paul Buhle, "Komix Kountermedia," *Leviathan*, July/August, 1969, 13–17.

59. James Leed, "Underground Comics," *Druid Free Press*, November 12–19, 1968, 13.

60. G. Mason, "Sick, Sick Comics," *National Insider*, December 15, 1968, reprinted in *Extra!* December 24–January 7, 1969, 10.

61. A federal judge explained this point when he threw out an obscenity indictment against New Orleans's *NOLA Express*. According to the Supreme Court, material needs to be evaluated in its entirety before one can judge whether or not it is obscene. "A casual glance at the issue of *NOLA Express* included in the indictment shows that by no reasonable standard can the newspaper as a whole be held outside the protection of the First Amendment," he ruled. See *Times-Picayune*, "Federal Judge Kills Indictment on Obscenity," September 2, 1970, 6.

62. Eric Morgenthaler, "Stopping the Presses: Underground Papers Hit by Official Curbs," *Wall Street Journal*, July 7, 1969, 1.

63. Eugene Guerrero, interview by Ron Grele, November 10, 1984, Columbia, 86. A writer for the Jackson, Mississippi, *Kudzu* reported that the *Great Speckled Bird* was busted for using the same word that "Mayor Daley shouted at Senator Abraham Ribicoff during the Democratic National Convention." See *Kudzu*, "The Man Shoots the Bird," January 14, 1969, 5.

64. See *Great Speckled Bird*, January 13, 1969, 4.

65. Mike Abrahams, "Quasi-Criminal Rap," *Chicago Seed* 3, no. 6, 2.

66. *San Diego Door*, "Door Wins Fight for Freedom of Press," August 14, 1969, 3.

67. Morgenthaler, "Stopping the Presses." While Burns was being arrested, police also seized two tons of papers, along with Burns's typewriters, camera, and several personal items, and placed it all in protective custody.

68. Thorne Dreyer, "Law Harasses Underground Papers," *San Diego Teaspoon Door*, January 17–30, 1969, 1.

69. Burks, "Underground Press," 32. Other papers faced similar prosecutions. In April 1969, a Canadian interviewer asked Lennon, "Do you realize there are underground papers all throughout the States [that] have had obscenity raps thrown at them because they've published the picture of you and Yoko on the cover?" Lennon answered, "I know there's a lot of that been going on," and added, sensibly, that the *Two Virgins* cover wasn't nearly as obscene as the "obscenity [that's] in people's minds." See Fred Latremouille and Dan McLeod, "Lennon, Lenin," *Georgia Straight*, April 4–10, 1969, 8.

70. Tom Paine [pseud.], "Radical Press: More Hassle," *East Village Other*, January 31, 1969, 5.

71. See Hagle, "Do They Have To?" 1045.

72. Quoted in Agis Salpukas, "Underground Papers Are Thriving on Campuses and in Cities Across Nation," *New York Times*, April 5, 1970, 58.

73. Forcade, "Write On!" 5.

74. *Helix* (Seattle), "Straight Ruled Straight," vol. 10, no. 1, Fall 1969, 5.

75. *East Village Other*, "Black Market Research," n.d., ca. summer 1968, reprinted in Rips, *Campaign Against the Underground Press*, 101.

76. Rex Weiner, interview by author, February 10, 2009.

77. Berlet, "Sex, Drugs," 66.

78. Forcade, "Write On!" *East Village Other* (November 19, 1969), 5.

79. Agis Salpukas, "Freed Poet Hails Michigan Ruling," *New York Times*, March 12, 1972.

80. *Time*, "Getting Stoney Burns," November 25, 1974, p. 20. Texas was the last state to count possession of grass as a felony, and the extra day was added to Burns's sentence because under Texas law a judge could not probate a sentence of more than ten years. The UPS participated in a campaign on Burn's behalf, and ultimately his sentence was commuted after he served only nineteen days in jail.

81. *East Village Other*, "Rat On!" November 19, 1969, 5.

82. Jim O'Brien, "Connections Editor Unfit, Says Boy Scout," *Distant Drummer*, March 27–April 2, 1969, 12. Gordon is now a distinguished professor of American history.

83. Robert E. Baskin, "Underground Press a Tool of 'Traitors,' Pool Asserts," *Dallas Morning News*, November 7, 1967.

84. Quoted in Thorne Dreyer and Victoria Smith, "The Movement and the New Media," Liberation News Service packet 144, March 1, 1969. See also Marshall Bloom, "HUAC Confronts Underground Press," *Dallas Notes From Underground*, September 1–15, 1967, 7.

85. *San Diego Free Press*, "Which Brain Police had *Ramparts* Thrown off Local Newsstands?" June 27–July 11, 1969, 3. *Ramparts* was a glossy monthly magazine, not an underground newspaper; but no doubt its readership overlapped with that of many underground rags.

86. Rips, "Campaign Against the Underground Press," 97.

87. Thorne Dreyer, "Law Harasses Underground Papers," *Worcester Punch*, February, 1969, 12; Chip Berlet, "COINTELPRO," *Alternative Media*, Fall, 1978, 11, as cited in Rips, "Campaign Against the Underground Press," 97.

88. Forcade, "Write On!" 5.

89. Rips, "Campaign Against the Underground Press," 98.

90. Of course, no one at UPS knew of the FBI memo. But a UPS advertising report from 1971 (wildly) alleged that "when Nixon was inaugurated, he immediately traded a let-up in anti-trust heat on NBC, CBS and ABC for drastic curtailment of advertising in the underground press." Presumably the author (almost certainly Forcade) believed the same type of pressure could be used against record companies. See UPS Bulletin, "Advertising Report," October 21, 1971, n.p.; Clive Davis, who was then president of Columbia, did not respond to a request to be interviewed for this book.

91. Quoted in MacKenzie, "Sabotaging the Dissident Press," 62.

92. Eugene Guerrero, interview by Ron Grele, November 10, 1984, Columbia, 90. Around the same time, *Rolling Stone* magazine began attracting a considerable amount of advertising from Columbia; see Draper, *Rolling Stone Magazine*, 18. Jann Wenner, however, doubts this had anything to do with the FBI. In his view, *Rolling Stone* proved attractive to record executives because he was able to make a persuasive sales pitch. "I told them, it comes down to two things," he said. "Support *Rolling Stone*, because it's about your industry and it's about our lives. And *Rolling Stone* is the way to reach people who buy the most records! Other newspapers [including the underground papers] weren't covering it, there weren't other [music] magazines, [rock] wasn't on television, there was no internet, obviously no MTV. So here's another way to get to your fans. Pretty simple." Wenner interview.

93. Quoted in Armstrong, *Trumpet to Arms*, 175.

94. Lawrence Lorenz, "Does a Printer Have the Right to Print What He Chooses?" *Grassroots Editor* 10, no. 6, November-December, 1969, 8–11; reprinted in Howard Rusk Long, *Main Street Militants*, 139–40.

95. "Obscenity Debate Hurts Publisher," *New York Times*, August 10, 1969.

96. This type of arrangement was not unusual; in various periods, the *Washington Free Press* was printed in New York; Atlanta's *Great Speckled Bird* was printed in Alabama, Austin's *Rag* was printed in San Antonio; and Bloomington, Indiana's, *Spectator* was printed in both Kentucky and Ohio.

97. Franklin wrote, "It is unreasonable to imagine Printers approve of every thing they print, and to censure them on any particular thing accordingly; since in the way of their Business they print such great variety of things opposite and contradictory. It is like-wise as unreasonable what some assert, That Printers ought not to print any Thing but what they approve; since if all of that Business should make such a Resolution, and abide by it, an End would thereby be put to Free Writing, and the World would after-wards have nothing to read but what happen'd to be the Opinions of Printers." See Benjamin Franklin, "An Apology for Printers," 1731.

98. John Pekkanen, "The Obstinacy of Bill Schanen," *Life*, September 26, 1969, 59.

99. *Indianapolis Free Press*, "Free the Press," n.d., ca. spring 1969, 17.

100. Victoria Smith, "*Space City!* From Opposition to Organizational Collapse," in Wachs-berger, ed., *Voices from the Underground*, 171. See also *Rag*, "Space City News Bombed," July 31, 1969, 4.

101. Dreyer interview.

102. Victoria Smith, "Lowe Down," *Space City!* June 1, 1971, reprinted in Waschsberger, *Voices from the Underground*, 178–80. The *Space City!* crew confirmed Lowe was a Klansman when one of their photographers, posing as a right-wing minister, snapped a photo of Lowe dressed in full regalia.

103. *Our Daily Bread* (Minneapolis), "Free Press Bombed," May 17–19, 1968, 2; *Good Morning Teaspoon*, "Los Angeles Free Press Bombed," May 8, 1968, 3.

104. Guerrero interview, 86.

105. Juliet Wittman, "Law & Disorder," *Westword*, January 4, 1984, 10. Wittman's first-person essay does an extraordinary job of detailing the harassment the *Street Journal* faced and its devastating effectivness.

106. *Dallas Notes*, "*Notes* Editor's Car Shot Fulla Holes," Feb 19–March 4, 1969, 4.

107. Wittman, "Law & Disorder," 9.

108. Ibid.

109. Rips, "Campaign Against the Underground Press," 130–34.

110. Quoted in David E. Kaplan, "The Good Old Bad Days," *U.S. News and World Report*, January 9, 2006, 22–23. The *San Diego Door* (formerly the *Teaspoon Door*) suffered similar harassment. See *Teaspoon Door*, "Our Moral Defense," January 17, 1969, 4; *San Diego Door*, "*Door* Trial July 31," June 19–July 2, 1969, 1; *San Diego Door*, "*Door* Wins Fight For Freedom of the Press," August 14, 1969, 2–4, 16.

111. Claudia Dreifus, "Newsreal," *East Village Other*, July 2, 1969, 6.

112. Russ Nobbs, "Confessions of a Smut Peddler," *Spokane Natural*, July 5–18, 1968, 2; *Spokane Natural*, "Untitled," July 7, 1967, 7.

113. *Berkeley Barb*, "Vendors Vamped," November 7–13, 1968, 4.

114. Glen Swift, "Busted! . . . For Selling on the Stick," *FRINS*, March 9, 1970, 5.

115. Agis Salpukas, "Underground Papers Are Thriving on Campuses and in Cities across Nation," *New York Times*, April 5, 1970.

116. *Notes From the Underground*, "*Notes* Busted For Selling At Stone Mall," August 1–14, 1967, 1.

117. *Rat*, "Mississippi Underground!?" November 1–14, 1968, 2.

118. *Times-Picayune*, "Officer's Fine Will Be Paid," May 4, 1970, 12.

119. *Rag*, "Snip 'n' Save," July 25, 1968, 7.

120. James Retherford, "Events Timeline, 67–68," unpublished document in author's possession.

121. Ronald Sullivan, "Fort Dix Soldiers Publish Newspaper Opposing War," *New York Times*, April 5, 1969, 3.

122. Haines, "Soldiers Against the War in Vietnam: The Story of *Aboveground*," in Wachsberger, ed., *Voices from the Underground*, 181–82.

123. Ostertag, *People's Movements*, 133–34. Priest could, however, be very inflammatory. In one issue he observed "If Spiro Agnew jumped (or was pushed) from the spire of the Empire State Building, and was caught by a favorable crosswind, he would hit 34th St. at a velocity of 281.6 feet per second." See *OM*, "The Best of the Worst," May 1, 1969, quoted in Ostertag, *People's Movements*, 134.

124. Quoted in *Time*, "Priest's Progress," May 11, 1970, 78. See also Cortright, *Soldiers in Revolt*, 107.

125. Quoted in Foley, *Confronting the War Machine*, 159.

126. In June 2009, DeMaio said he'd been wrong to print the letter. "It's not something I can defend now," he said. "But back then we had the idea that if someone had something to say, we should print it." Don DeMaio, interview with author, June 5, 2009.

127. Quoted in Dreyer, "Law Harasses Underground Papers," n.p.

128. See Alpert, *Growing Up Underground*.

129. Berlet, "Sex, Drugs," 67; Gabrielle Schang, "How To Handle Communiques," *Alternative Journalism Revue*, May-April 1976, 4–6.

130. See Varon, *Bringing the War Home*.

131. Quoted in Armstrong, *Trumpet to Arms*, 158.

132. Burks, "Underground Press," 17.

133. Forcade, "Write On!" *East Village Other*, November 11, 1969, 5.

134. Quoted in Armstrong, *Trumpet to Arms*, 60.

135. Jules Witcover, "Well, At Least It Wasn't a Danish," *Los Angeles Times*, May 14, 1970.

136. "Witness Presents Pornography Commissioner With a Pie (in the Face)," *New York Times*, May 14, 1970.

Chapter 6

1. Marshall Bloom, "LIBERATION NEWS SERVICE IS DEAD. LONG LIVE LIBERATION NEWS SERVICE," n.d., MBP, Box 8, Folder 46, 1–3.

2. FBI, ". . . . . And Who Got the Cookie Jar?" Political Research Associates Library and Archive, Somerville, Massachusetts. Henceforth this archival collection will be abbreviated as "PRA Library." Reprinted in Wachsberger, *Voices from the Underground*, 61.

3. The troubled woman ended up staying at Bloom and Mungo's house for about a month before they finally committed her to a mental hospital. See Mungo, *Famous Long Ago*, 92.

4. Mungo, *Famous Long Ago*, 26.

5. Bloom, "NEWS SERVICE IS DEAD," 4.

6. In *Famous Long Ago*, Mungo describes those who called for a democratic internal structure in LNS as "Vulgar Marxists" who saw "everything—music, the planets, sex, love, *everything*—in limited *political* terms." Laurence Leamer similarly describes the contretemps in LNS as an episode in a larger movement-wide conflict between hippies ("heads") and politicos ("fists"). Abe Peck presents a more rounded perspective, though he too describes the LNS schism as being between "Marxists" and "freaks." See Mungo, *Famous Long Ago*, 188–89; Leamer, *Paper Revolutionaries*, 46–47, 49; Peck, *Uncovering the Sixties*, 122–25.

7. Daniel Ben-Horin, "Journalism as a Way of Life," *Nation*, February 19, 1973, 242.

8. Harvey Stone, "Papers and Politics," n.d., *Connections* Records (1967–68), Box 1, WSHS.

9. Young, "Red Diaper Baby," 26.

10. Ibid., 27.

11. Allen Young, "Journalism," unpublished manuscript in author's possession.

12. "Donald" to Allen Young, January 15, 1967, AYP, Box 2

13. Eric Levine to Allen Young, February 3, 1967, AYP, Box 2.

14. Young, "Journalism."

15. Young, interview by author, March 11, 2005.

16. Young, "Journalism."

17. Young interview.

18. The media attention, at least, must have been amusing to the LNSers. First, a *New York Times* article on the Pentagon protest misidentified the *Berkeley Barb* as "an underground leaflet published in Brookville, Ohio." Two weeks later a *Newsweek* writer claimed that one unheralded result of the Pentagon march was "a merger of two far-out networks, the Underground Press Syndicate, which offers psychedelic recipes and pot poetry, and Liberation News Service, which promotes New Left causes." Obviously, this was incorrect: as we've seen, Bloom and Mungo's attempt to unify the underground press was a fiasco. There was certainly no "merger" between UPS and LNS, and contrary to what the report implied, the two organizations blurred, rather than encapsulated, distinctions between hippies and politicos. See John Herbers, "Youths Dominate Capital Throng," *New York Times*, October 22, 1967; *Newsweek*, "Uniting the Underground," November 13, 1967, 26.

19. See *New York Times*, "Leftist and War Foes Set Up Center in Capital," February 16, 1968; John H. Rarick, "Cong Headquarters in Washington," *Congressional Record* 114 (February 26, 1968): E 1156.

20. Mungo, *Famous Long Ago*, 38.

21. Bloom made this point himself after LNS was denounced in the House of Representatives. "The only thing which bothers me is the very unkind notion that we will be mouthpieces for the Viet Cong rather than for ourselves," he told a friend. See Marshall Bloom to "Dan," n.d., MBP, Box 8, Folder 23.

22. Mungo interview.

23. Harvey Wasserman, interview by author, May 24, 2005.

24. Wasserman, "Joys of Liberation News Service," 56.

25. Raymond Mungo, "Dear Friends," Liberation News Service packet 21, December 19, 1967.

26. Wasserman, "Joys of Liberation News Service," 53.

27. Harvey Wasserman, "Rusk Faces the Fulbright Committee," Liberation News Service packet 53, March 13, 1968. The same passage was also quoted in *Time*, "All the News That's Fit to Protest," March 22, 1968, 67.

28. Mungo, *Famous Long Ago*, 42, 41.

29. Mungo interview.

30. Wasserman, "Joys of Liberation News Service," 53–54.

31. Wasserman interview.

32. John Diamante to Marshall Bloom, November 23, 1967, MBP, Box 8, Folder 23. In reply, Bloom indicated that "momentum [was] picking up" in LNS. He was pleased with Allen Young's defection from the *Washington Post*, and he said that a trio of movement heavies—Jeremy Brecher, Arthur Waskow, and Todd Gitlin—had all pledged periodic contributions to the news service. Bloom also humorously added that since the new office occupied only a single floor, there wouldn't be anymore "flying," although he said he could not apologize "for not having with me at all times my phone directory." See Marshall Bloom to John Diamante, n.d., MBP, Box 8, Folder 23.

33. Ryan was arrested along with six other women in March 1965, for sitting in at the White House to demand federal intervention in the civil rights crisis in Selma, Alabama.

While incarcerated at Washington, DC's, Women's House of Detention, Ryan alleged that she had been severely beaten by guards, denied medical treatment, and kept in solitary confinement. See Margie Stamberg, "Sheila Ryan Beaten by Prison Guard," *Washington Free Press*, November 23, 1967, 4; Sheila Ryan, "Sheila's Statement," *Washington Free Press*, November 23, 1967, 4, 8.

34. Sheila Ryan, interview by author, July 21, 2003.

35. See Mungo, *Famous Long Ago*, 101–4; "LNS editors BUSTED again," Liberation News Service packet 65, April 10, 1968, 30.

36. Allen Young interview.

37. Thorne Dreyer and Victoria Smith, "The Movement and the New Media," Liberation News Service packet 144, March 1, 1969, 19.

38. Ray Mungo to John Wilcock, April 10, 1968, JWP.

39. George Cavalletto, interview by author, July 28, 2003.

40. Mungo interview.

41. Cavalletto interview.

42. Allen Young to Marshall Bloom, n.d., MBP, Box 8, Folder 37.

43. Wasserman, "Joys of Liberation News Service," 55. Steve Diamond similarly claimed that "several cadres of political leftists" in LNS had launched a "stealth campaign to take over the news service." See Steve Diamond, "Magical Mystery Tour: A Sixties Memoir for Twenty-somethings of Today," unpublished manuscript in author's possession.

44. Cavalletto interview.

45. Thorne Dreyer et al., "Dear Friends," LNS-NY packet 100, August 19, 1968, 2.

46. Ryan interview.

47. Mungo, *Famous Long Ago*, 154.

48. Marshall Bloom to Raymond Mungo, n.d., MBP, Box 8, Folder 23.

49. Mungo interview.

50. Mungo, *Famous Long Ago*, 155. These labels are used frequently in Mungo's memoir. Although he meant them to be taken humorously, the New York group (plus Young) understandably did not like being called "Vulgar Marxists," especially given Mungo's self-serving decision to call the Washington crowd (plus Diamond) the "Virtuous Caucus." In writing this chapter, I initially tried to avoid using these tendentious labels, before finally concluding that this was all but impossible. Technically, it would be inaccurate to say the schism was between the "New York group" and the "Washington group," because the alliances weren't strictly geographical; nor would it be fair to speak of the "Bloom faction" versus the "Young, Cavalletto, and Ryan" faction, since there were others in each group who played decisive roles, and besides, no one in the New York group wanted to elevate any of their number to leadership status. Finally, regardless of whether or not these terms are appropriate, we're stuck with them. In my research for this chapter, I interviewed nine former LNS members, and every one of them used, or made reference to, the terms "Virtuous Caucus" and the "Vulgar Marxists." Accordingly, I've accepted the labels as well, but only for the sake of simplicity. I don't mean to endorse the loaded connotations that Mungo intended, and occasionally I'll refer simply to "the Caucus" and "the Marxists," without the modifying adjectives.

51. Mungo, *Famous Long Ago*, 154–55.

52. Wasserman, "Joys of Liberation News Service," 55. Support for Mungo and Wasserman's characterization of the conflict came in the form of a letter that LNS received from editors of the highly regarded San Francisco *Express-Times*, in which they registered their disappointment over the deteriorating quality of recent mailings. Whereas the West Coast paper had once been pleased with the "hard political news and engaging panoramas" that originally filled LNS news packets, they sensed that around the time that LNS moved to New York, it started distributing "ponderous political prose decorated with marginal cultural blurbs." "It seems to us," they said, "that at least some of you are assuming that serious stuff has to appear gray and doctrinaire in order to be 'correct.'" Quoted in "Newspapers as Cattle Feed," LNS-Mass packet 100, August 16, 1968, 5.

53. Although the New York faction admitted that a couple of LNSers had managed to insert "simplistic" and rhetoric-heavy stories into the mailings, they implied that these dispatches weren't representative of the group's ideology or intentions. If the quality of recent mailings had suffered, they said, that was only because both LNS factions had been forced to expend so much energy trying to resolve their dispute. See Dreyer et al., "Dear Friends," 4.

54. Dreyer interview.

55. Ryan interview.

56. Cavalletto interview.

57. Young interview.

58. Ryan interview.

59. Mungo, *Famous Long Ago*, 156. By my estimation, the Vulgar Marxists had roughly thirteen members, the Virtuous Caucus about five. It is impossible to be more precise about this because each group challenged the legitimacy of those in the other camp. For instance, the Virtuous Caucus claimed that the Vulgar Marxist faction was packed with neophytes, whereas the Vulgar Marxists pointed out that Mungo would soon be leaving LNS, Wasserman had only worked in the national office for five weeks, and others in their camp only worked part-time. Also, Young objects to Mungo's characterization of the Virtuous Caucus as a Washington-based group, since he feels that by mid-1968, LNS had very few holdovers from Washington, DC. Besides, in addition to Diamond, at least one other New Yorker sided with Bloom—a woman named Hattie Hyman.

60. Allen Young to George Cavalletto, July 14, 1968, MBP, Box 8, Folder 23.

61. Also during this period, an anarchist street-fighting gang, Up Against the Wall, Motherfucker, prowled the Lower East Side, peddling cryptic poetry and angry agitprop, while the city's tactical police force rehearsed maneuvers designed to put down insurrectionists, and the FBI stepped up its campaign to infiltrate and destroy the New Left. According to sociologist David Cunningham, the Columbia uprising "provided the impetus for the establishment of COINTELPRO-New Left on May 9, 1968. . . . The stated purpose of the program . . . was to 'expose, disrupt and otherwise neutralize the activities of [the New Left] and persons connected with it." Some suspect that by this point, the FBI may have already had informants working in LNS. "By 1968," Angus McKenzie alleges, "the FBI had assigned three informants to penetrate the news service, while nine other informants regularly reported on it from the outside. . . . The FBI also attempted to discredit and break up the news service through various counterintelligence activities." See Cunningham, *There's Something Happening Here*, 50; Angus

MacKenzie, "Sabotaging the Dissident Press," in Rips, *Campaign against the Under-ground Press*, 160.

62. Mungo, *Famous Long Ago*, 156.

63. Wasserman, "Joys of Liberation News Service," 56.

64. Dreyer et al., "Dear Friends," 4.

65. Diamond, "Magical Mystery Tour."

66. Mungo, *Famous Long Ago*, 188.

67. Gitlin, *The Sixties*, 186.

68. Although some had suggested that LNS had much to gain by forging an institutional connection with SDS, Mungo writes that they ended up heeding the counsel of maverick journalist Izzy Stone, "who told us to make the news service 'independent' of SDS and everybody else if we didn't want to end up the mouthpiece of an established political group." Mungo says that neither he nor Bloom were ever members of SDS, but in 1968 some in LNS claimed that Bloom belonged to the organization, and in his unfinished memoir, Bloom mentions having friendly relations with many of SDS's national officers. See Mungo, *Famous Long Ago*, 31; Dreyer et al., "Dear Friends," 3; Bloom, "NEWS SERVICE IS DEAD," MBP, Box 8, Folder 46.

69. Mungo to "Dear Friends," Liberation News Service packet 21, December 19, 1967, *Underground Newspaper Microfilm Collection*, Reel 3, No. 10.

70. LNS to "Dear Friends," November 27, 1967, MBP, Box 10, Folder 17.

71. Andrew Nagorski, "Former *Student* Chairman Bloom Heads Underground News Service," *Amherst Student*, April 8, 1968, n.p.

72. Kornbluth, *Notes from the New Underground*, 94–95.

73. *Dialogue*, "From the Editor," May 1967, 2.

74. *Granpa*, November 17, 1967, n.p., SDS Records, Reel 24, Series 3, No. 49.

75. Peter Shapiro, interview by Ron Grele, April 11, 1984, Columbia, 23.

76. Quoted in Robert Cohen, "Underground Connections," fragment, *Connections* Records (1967–68), Box 1.

77. Mungo, *Famous Long Ago*, 38. Bill Blum, who wrote for the *Washington Free Press* in this period, shared Mungo's opinion.

> Our planning meetings [at the paper] had not included discussions of anything so banal as journalistic style or standards, but people's leanings in this direction soon became clear enough when there appeared on the office blackboard the dictum: "Grammer is bourgeois." It was meant in only minor part as a joke. It turned out I was the only one who was truly concerned about the quality of the writing and who seriously and consistently edited the articles, almost all of which needed industrial-strength polishing.

Blum added that although the paper improved with time, "it never quite lost the appearance that it had been laid out on drugs, probably for the obvious reason." See Blum, *West-Bloc Dissident*, 66, 70.

78. Mungo interview. Gary Valenza, who worked briefly at Bloomington, Indiana's *Spectator*, told a nearly identical story. He recalled laborious "Sunday night meetings that "were a paean to the SDS 'participatory democracy' concept, in which anybody— whether or not they had ever contributed to the paper—could attend. . . . There were certainly tacit networks and leadership cadres within this communal mélange, but clearly everyone's input was welcome." Gary Valenza, e-mail to author, June 3, 2003.

79. Eugene Guerrero, interview by Ron Grele, November 10, 1984, Columbia, 85.

80. Mungo, *Famous Long Ago*, 154.

81. Wasserman, "Joys of Liberation News Service," 56.

82. Paul Millman, interview by author, March 20, 2005.

83. Ryan interview.

84. This caused troubles for both of them. As mentioned in chapter 2, Kunkin fell out of favor with many Los Angeles activists after he seemed to be making a handsome profit off the *Freep*. He was also criticized for instituting stricter workplace rules and installing a time clock. In 1967, one irate staffer, John Bryan, left the *Freep* to start a rival paper (*Open City*) after Kunkin refused to print a photograph of a disfigured napalm victim (apparently for fear of offending advertisers). And in 1969 a whole group of staffers left *en masse* to start yet another rival paper, the very short-lived *Tuesday's Child*. (See Learner, *Paper Revolutionaries*, 56–58). In Berkeley, Scherr encountered even more strenuous opposition when someone calculated that the paper was generating considerable revenue while the staff was paid a pittance, and none of the paper's profits were being turned over to the Movement. In June 1969, the *Barb*'s staff revolted, printing a paper called *Barb on Strike*, in which someone editorialized, "It is sheer hypocrisy for the *Barb* to mouth the words of revolution while lining Max's pockets with the people's cash. We [feel] that *Barb* profits should go for bail funds, legal-defense funds, [and] medical clinics." Eventually, Scherr sold the paper, only to buy it back a little while later. But because of all this controversy it quickly fell out of favor in the Bay Area. Many of his former employees, however, helped to launch a new, harshly militant paper, the *Berkeley Tribe*, in which editors were elected and everyone received the same pay of $30 each week. See Learner, *Paper Revolutionaries*, 58–59; Peck, *Uncovering the Sixties*, 159.

85. Millman interview. Other Movement collectives with close links to the underground press, such as New York's Motherfuckers and the San Francisco–based Diggers, presented themselves as radically decentralized, but internally, charismatic leaders exerted a notable influence. In Up Against the Wall, Motherfucker, Ben Morea played a key role; in the Diggers, Emmett Grogan was a ringleader.

86. Ben-Horin, "Journalism as a Way of Life," 242.

87. Steve Halliwell to Jay M. Ressler, August 4, 1967, SDS Records, Reel 19, Series 3, No. 1.

88. Henry W. Haslach, "Thoughts on Leadership," *New Left Notes*, June 16, 1967, 4.

89. Michael Grossman, "SDS Calls for Nationwide Student Strike," *Washington Free Press*, July 21, 1967, 5.

90. Flacks, "Making History vs. Making Life," 143. Flacks also engaged in some of this informal policing himself. In 1965, he wrote a letter expressing his frustration that "polarization" in SDS had recently "occurred around the figures of Steve Max and Tom Hayden" (both of the Port Huron generation.) "These guys should be reminded that they at least implicitly promised to withdraw from top staff or leadership in the organization in an effort to encourage the development of a new generation of leaders. I think . . . everyone would find things a lot happier if they stepped away a little." For his part, Hayden regretted that SDS cultivated "a resentment of anyone with significant authority and a dire fear of formalizing it, even if that authority was based on achievement or could be useful in communicating through the media." See Hayden, *Reunion*, 45.

91. Dreyer et al., "Dear Friends," 2, 4. This is not to suggest, though, that Vulgar Marxists craved control of LNS in order to turn it into an SDS mouthpiece, as the Virtuous Caucus contended. Besides, this would have been difficult to do. By 1968 SDS had perhaps 100,000 official members, spread across nearly four hundred chapters, who embraced a broad spectrum of left-wing views.

92. "Dear Friends," LNS-Mass packet 100, August 16, 1968, 7-C.

93. Mungo interview.

94. Diamond, *What the Trees Said*, 48.

95. See Timothy Miller, *60s Communes*."

96. [Marshall Bloom], "ON MOVING THE MAIN LNS OFFICE TO A COUNTRY FARM," MBP, Box 8, Folder 26.

97. "Dear Friends," LNS-Mass packet 100, August 16, 1968, 6.

98. Bloom, "ON MOVING THE MAIN LNS OFFICE."

99. Minutes of LNS board of directors meeting, August 10, 1968, MBP, Box 8, Folder 36.

100. Mungo, *Famous Long Ago*, 163–66.

101. Some 15 million viewers in England saw *Magical Mystery Tour* when the BBC broadcast it on Boxing Day (December 26) of 1967. After it got almost universally negative reviews, however, NBC canceled a million-dollar deal to broadcast the film in the United States.

102. Diamond, "Magical Mystery Tour."

103. David Bodie, "Magical Mystery," *East Village Other*, August 30, 1968, n.p.

104. Wasserman interview.

105. Mungo, *Famous Long Ago*, 171.

106. Mungo interview.

107. Mungo, *Famous Long Ago*, 166; Mungo interview.

108. Dreyer et al., "Dear Friends," August 19, 1968, 4.

109. As they indignantly put it, "it seemed quite clear to us that the Movement could not be adequately served by Marshall's news service, established in defiance of democratic procedures within a movement group, printing on presses stolen from movement staff, financed by money taken from a movement group through subterfuge—and based, in isolation, on Marshall Bloom's $25,000 farm." See Dreyer et al., "Dear Friends," August 19, 1968, 1. See also Steve Lerner, "The Liberation of Liberation News Service," *Village Voice*, August 22, 1968, 37–38.

110. Dreyer interview.

111. Cavalletto interview.

112. Ryan interview.

113. Mungo, *Famous Long Ago*, 175–76.

114. This was generally the case, anyway. Dan McCauslin, a spokesman for LNS-NY, was quoted by a *New York Times* reporter as having said that "no one had been beaten or held captive" at the farm. This was far from the truth, and McCauslin later complained that he'd been misquoted; he meant to say that no "brutality" took place. Either way, no one disputes that LNS-NY held the rival LNSers hostage at Bloom's farm for about six hours. See John Leo, "Liberation News Service Rocked by Strife," *New York Times*, August 15, 1968, 34.

115. Dreyer et al., "Dear Friends," 1.

116. Mungo, *Famous Long Ago*, 178.

117. Dreyer et al., "Dear Friends," 1. During the siege, some in LNS-NY apparently tried to restrain Hamilton, and later he was purged from LNS. Around this time, a rumor circulated that Hamilton might have been an agent provocateur.

118. Ryan interview.

119. Millman interview.

120. Mungo, *Famous Long Ago*, 178.

121. Dreyer et al., "Dear Friends," 1. In Diamond's unpublished, essay-length memoir dealing with the LNS feud, he glosses over the issue, though he advises readers to consult Mungo's *Famous Long Ago* "for the complete story and all the gory details." In all likelihood, though, Diamond genuinely believed himself to be in danger. According to Cavalletto, Diamond only revealed the existence of the check when he "thought something was happening" to Bloom. See Diamond, "Magical Mystery Tour," n.p; Cavalletto interview.

122. Mungo, *Famous Long Ago*, 180.

123. Dreyer et al., "Dear Friends," 1.

124. "Dear Friends," LNS-Mass packet 100, August 16, 1968, 7A–B.

125. Cavalletto interview.

126. John Leo, "Liberation News Service to go on in Rift," *New York Times*, August 16, 1968, 30.

127. Lerner, "Liberation of Liberation," 38.

128. Mungo, *Famous Long Ago*, 166.

129. Those charged with kidnapping were Daniel McCauslin, George Cavalletto, Peter Cawley, Tom Hamilton, Dino Pabon, Norman Jenks, Thorne Dreyer, Charles Pasternak, Sheila Ryan, Miriam Bosker, Vicki Smith, Sally LaSalle, and Connie Lenham. According to Mungo, it was necessary to file the charges in order to reclaim the $6,000 that had been turned over to LNS-NY.

130. Bodie, "Magical Mystery," n.p.

131. "The Case of the 2 News Services," *New Left Notes*, September 9, 1968, 8. A handwritten copy of this article, also unsigned, survives in the SDS Records, Box 35, WSHS.

132. Dreyer and Smith, "Movement and the New Media," 20.

133. Peck, *Uncovering the Sixties*, 128.

134. Marshall Bloom to "Abbey," n.d., MBP, Box 2, Folder 18.

135. Tad Tekla to "LNS in Montague," September 30, 1968, MBP, Box 8, Folder 25.

136. Margaret Heggen to "LNS in Exile," n.d., MBP, Box 8, Folder 25.

137. Peter Werbe to Marshall Bloom, August 21, 1968, MBP, Box 8, Folder 29.

138. Marc Sommer to Marshall Bloom, September 6, 1968, MBP, Box 8, Folder 29.

139. "Groovy Marc" to LNS-Mass, n.d., MBP, Box 8, Folder 25.

140. Bob Overy to Marshall Bloom, August 20, 1968, MBP, Box 8, Folder 20.

141. Michael von Haag to Marshall Bloom, August 20, 1968, MBP, Box 8, Folder 29. Although the author added the caveat "I am not specifically referring to anyone," one senses that he meant just the opposite. Balanced against all of this, there are only two short notes in the Marshall Bloom papers that are entirely favorable to LNS-Mass. See Christine M. Dwyer to Marshall Bloom, August 29, 1968, MBP, Box 8, Folder 25; Kitty Rhodemyre to LNS-Mass, August 28, 1968, MBP, Box 8, Folder 25.

142. "Brothers and Sister," LNS-NY packet 107, September 27, 1968, A.

143. Nat Hentoff, "Lifeline for the Underground," *MORE: A Journalism Review*, October 1972, 5.

144. See Mungo, *Famous Long Ago*, 187–88.

145. Wasserman interview.

146. Diamond, *What the Trees Said*, 47.

147. Diamond, "Magical Mystery Tour."

148. Marshall Bloom to Abbey, n.d., MBP, Box 2, Folder 18.

149. Bloom said that both were "wonderful people," and he seemed baffled and hurt by this "quarantine" of his personality. "I could have understood if they greeted me with 'Motherfucker, motherfucker . . . ' But not speaking[?]" See Bloom, "LIBERATION NEWS SERVICE IS DEAD," 7.

150. Marshall Bloom to Ray Mungo, n.d., ca. late August 1968, MBP, Box 8, Folder 29. In one article, Bloom was described as a "spoiled brat" who stole LNS's funds simply so he could buy his own farm and become a "News-Service tycoon." See Brian Kelly, "LNS Heist Nets $12,000," *Boston Free Press*, n.d., 9th ed., 16.

151. FBI memo, October 21, 1968, PRA Library. The agent who distributed the missive was instructed to "take all necessary steps to insure that the Bureau is not identified as the source of this letter."

152. FBI, ". . . . . And Who Got the Cookie Jar?" PRA Library; reprinted in Wachsberger, *Voices from the Underground*, 61.

153. Wasserman, "Joys of Liberation News Service," 58.

154. Marshall Bloom to Abe Peck, n.d., MBP, Box 8, Folder 29.

155. Marshall Bloom to Doug, n.d., MBP, Box 2, Folder 18.

156. Marshall Bloom to Ray Mungo, n.d., MBP, Box 2, Folder 16.

157. Young, "Marshall Bloom: Gay Brother," 59–60.

158. In late 1967, Bloom's mother wrote, "It is with a heavy and broken heart that I'm writing to you, but I feel I must, somehow, someway, get thru to you. . . . With your great qualities—leadership, brains, education—how can you do this to yourself? You have changed so much, Marshall." "Mom" to Marshall Bloom, September 20, 1967, MBP, Box 2, Folder 16. Bloom's letters in reply were sometimes plaintive and conciliatory, and sometimes intolerant and angry. Once he wrote, "You must understand . . . that the world is changing. That the young of America, who have grown up in affluence, as I have, are no longer interested very much in making money or starting businesses. Of course many are. But when I say young I mean that those of my age, many of the most talented and most energetic, are excited and stimulated by other kinds of challenges, by their efforts to make the world better. . . . We must learn to respect differences." Marshall Bloom to "family," n.d., MBP, Box 8, Folder 23. Another time, though, Bloom sent a blistering seven-page letter to his father, railing against his support for the Vietnam War and concluding: "To have one's own family on the side of ignorance and bestiality is more than I can bear." Marshall Bloom to "Dad," n.d., MBP, Box 2, Folder 17.

159. Marshall Bloom to "Mom and Dad," October 21, 1969, MBP, Box 2, Folder 19.

160. Marshall Bloom, "Last Will and Testament," November 1, 1969, MBP, Box 1, Folder 6.

161. Jack Newfield, review of *Famous Long Ago: My Life and Hard Times with Liberation News Service*, by Raymond Mungo, *New York Times*, June 28, 1970.

162. Young interview; Katya Taylor, "Katya/Nina's Reminiscences of Liberation News Service," unpublished manuscript in author's possession.

163. "What is Liberation News Service?" n.d., MBP, Box 8, Folder 44.

164. Peck, *Uncovering the Sixties*, 54; Felton, *Mindfuckers*, 178–83. Incidentally, the Virtuous Caucus also was not the only underground media group to engage in polarizing high jinks. The following month, in New York City, about twenty hippies stormed into the live broadcast of WDNT's *Newsfront* program, which was supposed to feature a discussion of the underground media, and hijacked the show for about fifteen minutes, lashing out at the aboveground media and childishly saying "fuck" into the microphones. Seven of the intruders were arrested. See *Newsweek*, "Notes from Underground," July 1968, 76.

165. See note 84.

166. In January 1970, an all-woman group at the *Rat*, led by Jane Alpert, won the right to produce a special "Women's Issue" of the newspaper. Published the following month (with assistance from some LNS women), its centerpiece was Robin Morgan's classic feminist tract, "Goodbye to All That." "*Rat* must be taken over permanently by women—or *Rat* must be destroyed," Morgan argued. The venomous article denounced the entire "male Left" and especially raised hackles among the *Rat*'s male staffers, who began pasting up an issue that was to make light of the feminists. When the women discovered what was in the works, they became enraged and seized control of the entire paper. For a time, the Women's Rat Editorial Collective allowed some men to remain on the staff, but eventually all the men were asked to leave. According to Alpert, before the takeover, the *Rat* was set to expire; "In women's hands, it stuck out another two years, undergoing three more takeovers by splinter groups before it ceased publication forever." See Peck, *Uncovering the Sixties*, 212–15; Robin Morgan, "Goodbye to All That," *Rat*, February 6–23, 1970, 7; *Rat*, "Rat Busted," February 24–March 9, 1970, 2; Alpert, *Growing Up Underground*, 244.

167. John Burks, "The Underground Press: A Special Report," *Rolling Stone*, October 4, 1969, 19.

168. Dreyer and Smith, "Movement and the New Media," 25–26.

Chapter 7

1. Calvin Trillin, "Alternatives," *New Yorker*, April 10, 1978, 118.

2. See Daniel Ben-Horin, "Journalism as a Way of Life," *Nation*, February 19, 1973, 239. The National Association of Newsweeklies became the National Association of Alternative Newsweeklies in 1979, and then in May 1982 it became the Association of Alternative Newsweeklies.

3. James Jacobs, interview by Bret Eynon, October 24, 1984 and July 3, 1985, Columbia, 40.

4. Kornbluth, *Notes from the New Underground*, 6–7.

5. "An Article About Ourselves," *Old Mole*, n.d., ca. late 1970, reprinted in Leamer, *Paper Revolutionaries*, 123.

6. See Newton H. Fulbright, "Underground Press Strives to Fuse Sex with Politics," *Editor & Publisher*, December 27, 1969, 34.

7. Quoted in Goldberg, *Bumping into Geniuses*, 38.

8. After the conference, an LNS member composed a blistering diatribe against the grotesque sexism that she said was omnipresent there. As for the "love-in," she reports that when a few women put their hands over the cameras to disrupt the filming of other

people having intercourse, some of the men cried "censorship," at which point the women threatened to seize their equipment and throw it in the lake. See Nina Sabaroff, "Notes from the First Gathering: An Alternate Media Message," Liberation News Service packet 272, July 15, 1970.

9. Parker Donham, "Media Freaks Act Out Battles of the Radicals," *Boston Globe*, June 18, 1970; Also see Alfred G. Aronowitz, "Vermont Vibrations," *New York Post*, June 19, 1970.

10. Goddard College Business Office to Jerry Witherspoon, June 29, 1970, in author's possession.

11. "Press for Youths Seeks New Image," *New York Times*, June 11, 1973. See also David E. Shipler, "'Underground' Press Coverage Shifts From Rock, Sex, and Drugs to Politics," *New York Times*, March 7, 1973.

12. Trillin, "Alternatives," 119.

13. Forcade was running the Alternative Press Syndicate, which evolved out of UPS. By the time of the Seattle conferences, he'd also written a very good, overlooked book about hippie capitalism, fended off charges that he intended to disrupt the 1972 Republican National Convention, opened a bookstore in Soho, and financed a documentary about the Sex Pistols' 1978 American tour called *D.O.A.* See Forcade, *Caravan of Love and Money*; John Holmstrom, "The Ultimate Hippie: The Life and High Times of Thomas King Forcade," *High Times*, October 1989, 35–44, 77.

14. Trillin, "Alternatives," 120.

15. Gabrielle Schang, interview with author, August 21, 2008. About eight months before he died, Forcade revealed himself to be recklessly in love Gabrielle Schang, who was in a nearby room when he shot himself. "Being without you I feel incomplete, empty, sick, paralyzed," he wrote. "I was thinking about kidnapping you. I am dead serious. I'm a desperate man. I think I am right for you and I love you and I think you love me and it is ridiculous to be apart. I want you, I need you. . . . Please say yes." Tom Forcade to Gabrielle Schang, March 11, 1977, in author's possession.

16. Ed Dwyer, as quoted in Holmstrom, "Ultimate Hippie," 77.

17. The *Texas Observer*, established in 1954, is a member of the Association of Alternative Newsweeklies, but if it were to reapply today, it might not gain admission. As a biweekly, stapled newsletter, published by a nonprofit, with a paid circulation and no listings or ads, it's rather different from other member papers.

18. Quoted in McAuliffe, *Great American Newspaper*, 235.

19. The *Real Paper* was the collectively owned stepchild of a thwarted union drive at its previous incarnation, the *Boston Phoenix*. A good account of its origins, and of the ways that its decentralized working environments caused familiar tensions, can be found in Solman and Friedman, *Life and Death*, 184–205.

20. *Time*, "Press: Notes from the Underground," April 23, 1979, 49–50.

21. Richard Karpel, "Dart to Matt Welch and *CJR*," Association of Alternative Newsweeklies Web site, http://aan.org/alternative/Aan/ViewArticle?oid=129696.

22. See Armstrong, *Trumpet to Arms*, 201–5. See also Brugmann and Sletteland, *Ultimate Highrise*.

23. Alisa Solomon, "Our Hearts Were Young and Gay," *Village Voice*, November 1, 2005, 52.

24. See Conroy, *Unspeakable Acts*.

25. Symington was convicted of bank fraud in 1997, but the conviction was overturned in 1999. On Arpaio, see Clint Bolick, "Mission Unaccomplished: The Misplaced

Priorities of Maricopa County Sheriff's Office," Goldwater Institute Policy Report 229, December 2, 2008.

26. Kristen Lombardi, "Cardinal Sin," *Boston Phoenix*, March 23, 2001; Carl M. Cannon, "The Priest Scandal," *American Journalism Review*, May 2002, 18–25.

27. That state's flagship paper, the *Oregonian*, not only failed to break the story, but also botched its subsequent coverage when it characterized Goldschmidt's repeated statutory rape of a young teenager as an "affair," and expressed sympathy for the former governor. "Even [after the revelations]," the *Oregonian* editorialized, "it is painful to watch him leave." See Jill Rosen, "The Story Behind the Story," *American Journalism Review*, August/September 2004, 44–53.

28. Clif Garboden, letter to author, August 10, 2009.

29. David Carr, interview by author, August 2, 2009.

30. See Weingarten, *Gang That Wouldn't Write Straight*.

31. Stewart McBride, "Underground Papers Come Up on Top," *Christian Science Monitor*, May 22, 1980.

32. Robert A. Roth, interviewed by Jerry Nemanic, April 29, 1985 on WBEZ. Transcript in author's possession.

33. Robert A. Roth, interviewed by Jerry Nemanic, 4–29–85 on WBEZ-FM. Transcript in author's possession. Linda Evans and Joan Collins both starred in the ABC primetime soap opera *Dynasty*.

34. Carr interview.

35. Quoted in Sharon Bass, "Media Stars Remember Their Early Days," on the Association of Alternative Newsweeklies Web site, http://posting.altweeklies.com/aan/media-stars-remember-their-early-days/Article?oid=115918.

36. The *Voice*, though, remained a paid-circulation publication until 1996.

37. Jim Larkin, interview by author, July 28, 2009.

38. Albert Scardino, "Alternative Weeklies on the Rise," *New York Times*, May 29, 1989; Thomas Winship, "The New Curmudgeon," *Editor and Publisher*, July 6, 1991, 18. In 2009, the AAN had 131 member papers.

39. Evan Smith, "The Alternative Press Grows Up," *Mediaweek*, June 21, 1991, 19–21. Creative Loafing filed for bankruptcy in September 2008.

40. See "Press for Youths Seeks New Image," *New York Times*, June 11, 1973; Nathan Cobb, "The Alternative Press Goes Straight," *Boston Globe Sunday Magazine*, June 9, 1974, 6–14; Dan Wakefield, "Up From Underground," *New York Times Sunday Magazine*, February 15, 1976, 4; "Berkeley Newspaper Gaining Respectability and Readers," *New York Times*, February 11, 1979; Stewart McBride, "Underground Papers Come Up on Top," *Christian Science Monitor*, May 22, 1980; Jonathan Friendly, "Transition in 'Alternative' Press Focus of Meeting," *New York Times*, June 17, 1984; Christopher Swan, "Is Success Spoiling the Alternative Press?" *Christian Science Monitor*, July 30, 1987; Jonathan Friendly, "Transition in 'Alternative' Press Focus of Meeting," *New York Times*, June 17, 1984; Albert Scardino, "Alternative Weeklies on the Rise," *New York Times*, May 29, 1989; Kathy Hogan Trocheck, "Alternative Weeklies Are Gaining Respect—and Readers," *St. Petersburg Times*, September 3, 1989; Evan Smith, "The Alternative Press Grows Up," *Mediaweek*, June 21, 1991, 19–21; Ed Avis, "Established Alternatives," *Quill*, January 1, 1995. It's worth pointing out that the trope still has not died completely; in 2008, the Quill published Ed

Avis, "Alternative Newsweeklies: Growing Up," *Quill*, January/February 2008, 16–22.

41. Richard Leiby, "What Alternative? The Avant Press's Conventional Convention," *Washington Post*, July 16, 1994.

42. As quoted in Solman and Friedman, *Life and Death*, 201; the ad appeared after the *Real Paper*'s collective ownership fell apart, and its investors came to include David Rockefeller and future Republican governor of Massachusetts Bill Weld.

43. Kim Campbell, "Free and Quirky," *Christian Science Monitor*, September 7, 2000. In 2000, about 10 percent of alt-weekly revenues came from national ad buys. Tobacco companies especially began using the alternative press as a means for reaching a younger demographic. See Sandra Yin, "The Weekly Reader," *American Demographics*, May 2002, 27; Sepe and Glantz, "Bar and Club Tobacco Promotions."

44. Tim Redmond, "Losing a 'Voice,'" *San Francisco Bay Guardian*, October 26–November 1, 2005, 4; See also Mick Farren, "Alternative to What, Motherfucker?" *Los Angeles City Beat*, October 6, 2005. Brugmann's lawsuit alleged that two New Times papers, the *SF Weekly* and *East Bay Express*, were selling ads below cost in an illegal attempt to put the *San Francisco Bay Guardian* out of business. In March 2008, a jury ruled in favor of Brugmann and ordered *SF Weekly* to pay the *San Francisco Bay Guardian* $15.6 million.

45. Matt Welch, "Blogworld and its Gravity," *Columbia Journalism Review*, September/October, 2003, 21.

46. Russ Smith, e-mail to author, August 12, 2009.

47. Jack Shafer, interview with author, August 3, 2009.

48. Carr interview.

49. Shafer interview.

50. See Stephanie Clifford, "Village Voice Lays Off Nat Hentoff and Two Others," *New York Times*, December 30, 2008.

51. Larkin interview.

Afterword

1. John Holmstrom, interview by author, July 1, 2008.

2. David M. Gross, "Zine Dreams," *New York Times Sunday Magazine*, September 17, 1995, 72.

3. In the 1980s and early 1990s, the zine *Factsheet Five* was an important clearinghouse for information on other personal magazines; today, *Factsheet Five* is published on the Web. See Friedman, *Factsheet Five Zine Reader*.

4. Duncombe, *Notes from Underground*, 14.

5. Rob Chalfen, interview with author, August 11, 2009. See also Pagan Kennedy, "Zines Run Amok!" *Village Voice Literary Supplement*, November 1988, 38; Sally Cragin, "Verbal Agreement: The Small Press Alliance Finds Strength in Numbers," *Boston Phoenix*, June 26, 1987, 6, 13.

6. Duncombe, *Notes from Underground*, 195–96.

7. Matt Welch, "Blogworld and its Gravity," *Columbia Journalism Review*, September/October, 2003, 22.

8. As one journalist has explained, although some conflate the "netroots" with "liberal blogs," technically speaking, the netroots are only a subset of left-wing bloggers that

"are directly involved in political activism, often urging their readers to volunteer for, or donate money to, Democratic candidates." But netroots activists and liberal bloggers are definitely part of the same movement. See Jonathan Chait, "The Left's New Machine," *New Republic*, May 7, 2007, 20.

9. See Armstrong and Moulitsas Zúniga, *Crashing the Gate*; Rich, *Greatest Story Ever Sold*; Greenwald, *Tragic Legacy*.

10. See Trippi, *Revolution Will Not Be Televised*.

11. Careless comments by candidates, which in a previous era would have gone unnoticed, were picked up by bloggers and turned into big news. In March 2007, when innocent Iraqis were being blown up almost daily, Arizona senator John McCain claimed on a right-wing radio show that there were "neighborhoods in Baghdad where you and I could walk . . . today." When a left-wing listener posted the audio from the show online, the remark was broadcast globally (and roundly critiqued). Thirteen months later, a *Huffington Post* blogger recorded Obama telling a roomful of supporters that it's "not surprising" that some economically disenfranchised citizens "get bitter" and "cling to guns or religion or antipathy to people who aren't like them." Coming on the eve of a crucial primary, the remarks threatened his candidacy. See Boehlert, *Bloggers on the Bus*, 201–3, 168–171.

12. Chait, "Left's New Machine," 20.

13. "The State of the News Media," Pew Project for Excellence in Journalism, *The State of the News Media 2009*, http://www.stateofthemedia.org/2009/index.htm.

14. Abbie Hoffman, "An Advertisement for Revolution," interview with Thomas Forcade, *Free Ranger Intertribal News Service*, March 16, 1970, 1.

15. As an organ of the Committee for Nonviolent Action, *WIN* was an unusual type of underground paper, but the difficulties it experienced were common in the New Left press.

16. Gwen Reyes to Julie Weiner, February 24, 1967, *Connections* Records (1967–68), WSHS, Box 1.

17. Kornbluth, "No Fire Exit," 94–95.

Bibliography

Manuscripts and Documents Collections

Allen Young Papers (1962–94). Wisconsin State Historical Society, Madison, Wisconsin.

Alternative Press Collection. Political Research Associates (PRA) Library and Archive, Somerville, Massachusetts.

Columbia. See Student Movements of the Sixties.

Connections Records (1967–68) [WSHS]. Wisconsin State Historical Society, Madison, Wisconsin.

Contemporary History Project (The New Left in Ann Arbor). Bentley Historical Library, University of Michigan, Ann Arbor, Michigan.

John Wilcock Papers (1967–71) [JWP]. Rare Book and Manuscripts Library, Columbia University, New York City.

Marshal Bloom Papers [MBP]. Amherst College Archives and Special Collections, Amherst College.

PEN American Center Archives [PEN Center]. Rare Books and Special Collections Library, Firestone Library, Princeton University, Princeton, New Jersey.

Peter Stafford Papers (1960–71) [PSP]. Rare Book and Manuscripts Library, Columbia University, New York City.

Students for a Democratic Society Records (1960–69). Microfilm. Tamiment Library, New York University, New York City.

Students for a Democratic Society Records (1960–69). Wisconsin State Historical Society, Madison, Wisconsin.

Student Movements of the Sixties [Columbia]. Oral History Research Office, Butler Library, Columbia University, New York City.

Student Protest Files (1965–71). MSU Archives and Historical Collections, Conrad Hall, Michigan State University, East Lansing, Michigan.

Underground Newspaper Collection (1963–73). Microfilm. Lamont Library, Harvard University, Cambridge, Massachusetts.

WSHS. See *Connections* Records.

Interviews Conducted by Author

Berlet, Chip, March 21, 2005, Somerville, Massachusetts
Carr, David, August 2, 2009, telephone
Cavalletto, George, July 28, 2003, New York City
Chalfen, Rob, August 11, 2009, Cambridge, Massachusetts
DeMaio, Don, June 5, 2009, telephone
Dreyer, Thorne, April 23, 2005, telephone
Embree, Alice, April 1, 2005, telephone
Garvy, Helen, May 14, 2004, telephone
Hackett, Margaret, February 4, 2005, East Lansing, Michigan
Hayden, Tom, November 13, 2003, Cambridge, Massachusetts
Holmstrom, John, July 1, 2008, New York City
Jolles, Char, March 16, 2005, telephone
Kramer, Mark, October 20, 2003, Cambridge, Massachusetts
McKelvey, Don, May 17, 2004, Cambridge, Massachusetts
Millman, Paul, March 20, 2005, telephone
Morea, Ben, July 21, 2004, New York City
Mungo, Raymond, March 25, 2005, telephone
Patterson, Phyllis, September 7, 2004, telephone
Peel, David, July 2, 2008, New York City
Price, Mike, February 4, 2005, East Lansing, Michigan
Ryan, Sheila, July 28, 2003, New York City
Schang, Gabrielle, August 21, 2008, New York City
Sinclair, Leni, January 13, 2009, telephone
Tate, Larry, March 4, 2005, telephone
Taylor, Katya (Nina Sabaroff), April 5, 2005
Wasserman, Harvey, May 24, 2005, telephone
Weberman, A. J., June 28, 2008, New York City
Weiner, Rex, February 10, 2009, telephone
Wenner, Jann, June 25, 2009, telephone
Young, Allen, March 11, 2005, telephone

Personal Correspondence

Denson, Ed, to author, August 28, 2003
Diamond, Steve, to author, June 12, 2005
Flacks, Richard, to author, September 4, 2004
Ford, Richard, to author, January 23, 2005
Hirsh, Gary, to author, July 13, 2003
Leitch, Donovan, to author, January 28, 2003, and July 7, 2003
McDonald, Joe, to author, July 20, 2003
Pardun, Robert, to author, February 17, 2004
Sanders, Ed, to author, August 23, 2003
Smith, Russ, e-mail to author, August 12, 2009
Schoenfeld, Eugene, to author, July 22, 2003

Valenza, Gary, e-mail to author, June 3, 2003
Wilkerson, Cathy, to author, February 16, 2004

Major Works, Published and Unpublished

Abbott, Steve. "Karl and Groucho's Marxist Dance: The *Columbus* (Ohio) *Free Press* and its Predecessors in the Columbus Underground." In Wachsberger, *Voices from the Underground*, 332–33.

Abrams, Nathan. "From Madness to Dysentery: *Mad*'s Other New York Intellectuals." *Journal of American Studies* 37 (2003): 435–51.

Adams, Walter. *The Test*. New York: Macmillan, 1971.

Ages, Naomi. "Gather No Moss: *Rolling Stone*'s Counter-Journalism." Honors thesis, Harvard University, 2005.

Alpert, Jane. *Growing Up Underground*. New York: Morrow, 1981.

Anderson, Terry H. *The Movement and the Sixties*. New York: Oxford University Press, 1996.

Anson, Robert Sam. *Gone Crazy and Back Again: The Rise and Fall of the Rolling Stone Generation*. Garden City, NY: Doubleday, 1981.

Armstrong, David. *A Trumpet to Arms: Alternative Media in America*. Los Angeles: Tarcher, 1981.

Armstrong, Jerome, and Marcos Moulitsas Zúniga, *Crashing the Gate: Netroots, Grassroots, and the Rise of People-Powered Politics*. White River Junction, VT: Chelsea Green, 2006.

Atkin, David J. "From the Counterculture to Over-the-Counter Culture: An Analysis of *Rolling Stone*'s Coverage of the New Left in the United States from 1967–1975." In *Studies in Newspaper and Periodical History: 1995 Annual*, edited by Michael Harris and Tom O'Malley, 189–98. Westport, CT: Greenwood, 1997.

Avorn, Jerry L. *Up Against the Ivy Wall: A History of the Columbia Crisis*. New York: Atheneum, 1969.

Bailey, Beth. *Sex in the Heartland*. Cambridge, MA: Harvard University Press, 1999.

Banes, Sally, *Greenwich Village 1963: Avant-Garde Performance and the Effervescent Body*. Durham, NC: Duke University Press, 1993.

Berlet, Chip. "Sex, Drugs, Rock & Roll, Revolution, and Readership." In Wachsberger, *Voices from the Underground*, 66–67.

Berman, Paul. *A Tale of Two Utopias: The Political Journey of the Generation of 1968*. New York: Norton, 1996.

Bizot, Jean-François. *Free Press; Underground & Alternative Publications, 1965–1975*. Foreword by Barry Miles. New York: Universe, 2006.

Bloom, Alexander, and Wini Breines. *"Takin' It to the Streets": A Sixties Reader*. 2nd ed. New York: Oxford University Press, 2003.

Blum, William. *West-Bloc Dissident: A Cold War Memoir*. New York: Soft Skull, 2002.

Boehlert, Eric. *Bloggers on the Bus: How the Internet Changed Politics and the Press in 2008*. New York: Free Press, 2009.

Boskin, Joseph. *Rebellious Laughter: People's Humor in American Culture*. Syracuse, NY: Syracuse University Press, 1997.

Bourdon, David. *Warhol*. New York: Abrams, 1989.

Braunstein, Peter. "Historicizing the American Counterculture of the 1960s and 1970s." In Braunstein and Doyle, *Imagine Nation*, 5–14.

Braunstein, Peter, and Michael William Doyle, eds. *Imagine Nation: The American Counterculture of the 1960s and '70s.* New York: Routledge, 2002.

Breines, Wini. *Community and Organization in the New Left, 1962–1968: The Great Refusal.* New York: Praeger, 1982.

———. "Whose New Left?" *Journal of American History* 75, no. 2 (1988): 528–45.

———. *Young, White, and Miserable: Growing up Female in the Fifties.* Boston: Beacon, 1992.

Brick, Howard. *Age of Contradiction: American Thought and Culture in the 1960s.* New York: Twayne, 1998.

Brody, Leslie Denise. "The Red Suitcase: Hippies, Pinkos and Vagabonds." PhD diss., University of Connecticut, 1998.

Bromell, Nick. *Tomorrow Never Knows: Rock and Psychedelics in the 1960s.* Chicago: University of Chicago Press, 2000.

Bruce, Lenny. *How to Talk Dirty and Influence People: An Autobiography.* Chicago: Playboy, 1965.

Brugmann, Bruce, and Gregor Sletteland, eds. *The Ultimate Highrise: San Francisco's Mad Rush to the Sky.* San Francisco: San Francisco Bay Guardian, 1971.

Buhle, Paul, "The Eclipse of the New Left: Some Notes." *Radical America* 6 (July-August 1972): 1–9.

———, ed. *History and the New Left: Madison, Wisconsin, 1950–1970.* Philadelphia: Temple University Press, 1990.

Calvert, Gregory Nevala. *Democracy from the Heart: Spiritual Values, Decentralism, and Democratic Idealism in the Movement of the 1960s.* Eugene, OR: Communitas, 1991.

Carson, Clayborne. *In Struggle: SNCC and the Black Awakening of the 1960s.* Cambridge, MA: Harvard University Press, 1981.

Carson, Clayborne, David J. Garrow, Gerald Gill, Vincent Harding, and Darlene Clark Hine, eds. *The Eyes on the Prize Civil Rights Reader: Documents, Speeches, and Firsthand Accounts from the Black Freedom Struggle, 1954–1990.* New York: Penguin, 1991.

Caute, David. *Sixty-Eight: The Year of the Barricades.* London: Paladin Books, 1988.

Christgau, Robert. *Any Old Way You Choose It: Rock and Other Pop Music, 1967–1973.* Baltimore: Penguin Books, 1973.

Churchill, Ward, and Jim Vander Wall. *The COINTELPRO Papers: Documents from the FBI's Secret Wars against Domestic Dissent.* Boston: South End, 1990.

Clay, Steven, and Rodney Phillips. *A Secret Location on the Lower East Side: Adventures in Writing, 1960–1980; A Sourcebook of Information.* New York: Granary Books, 1998.

Clinton, James W., ed. *The Loyal Opposition: Americans in North Vietnam, 1965–1972.* Niwot: University Press of Colorado.

Cohen, Mitchell, and Dennis Hale, eds. *The New Student Left: An Anthology.* Boston: Beacon, 1966.

Cohen, Robert, and Reginald E. Zelnik, eds. *The Free Speech Movement: Reflections on Berkeley in the 1960s.* Berkeley: University of California Press, 2002.

Conroy, John. *Unspeakable Acts, Ordinary People: The Dynamics of Torture.* Berkeley: University of California Press, 2001.

Cortright, David. *Soldiers in Revolt: GI Resistance during the Vietnam War.* Chicago: Haymarket Books, 2005.

[Cox, Archibald]. *Crisis at Columbia: Report of the Fact-Finding Commission Appointed to Investigate the Disturbances at Columbia University in April and May, 1968.* New York: Vintage, 1968.

Crowley, Walt. *Rites of Passage: A Memoir of the Sixties in Seattle*. Seattle: University of
Washington Press, 1995.

Cunningham, David. *There's Something Happening Here: The New Left, the Klan, and FBI
Counterintelligence*. Berkeley: University of California Press, 2004.

Davidson, Carl. "The New Radicals and the Multiversity." In *The New Left: A Documentary
History*, edited by Massimo Teodori. Indianapolis, IN: Bobbs-Merrill, 1969.

Davidson, Sara. *Loose Change: Three Women of the Sixties*. Garden City, NY: Doubleday, 1977.

Dellinger, David. *From Yale to Jail: The Life Story of a Moral Dissenter*. New York: Pantheon,
1993.

DeRogatis, Jim. *Kaleidoscope Eyes: Psychedelic Rock from the 1960s to the 1990s*. London: Fourth
Estate, 1996.

Diamond, Stephen. *What the Trees Said: Life on a New Age Farm*. New York: Dell, 1971.

Dickstein, Morris. *Gates of Eden: American Culture in the Sixties*. New York: Basic Books,
1977.

―――. *Leopards in the Temple: The Transformation of American Fiction, 1945–1970*.
Cambridge, MA: Harvard University Press, 2002.

Downie, Leonard Jr. *The New Muckrakers*. Washington, DC: New Republic Book Co.,
1976.

Draper, Robert. *Rolling Stone Magazine: The Uncensored History*. New York: Doubleday,
1990.

Duncombe, Stephen, ed. *Cultural Resistance Reader*. London: Verso, 2002.

―――. *Notes from Underground: Zines and the Politics of Alternative Culture*. New York: Verso,
1997.

Echols, Alice. *Daring to Be Bad: Radical Feminism in America, 1967–1975*. Minneapolis:
University of Minnesota Press, 1989.

―――. *Scars of Sweet Paradise: The Life and Times of Janis Joplin*. New York: Metropolitan
Books, 1999.

―――. *Shaky Ground: The '60s and its Aftershocks*. New York: Columbia University Press,
2002.

―――. "We Gotta Get Out of This Place: Notes Toward a Remapping of the Sixties."
Socialist Review 22, no. 2 (1992): 9–33.

Elbow, Peter. *Writing With Power: Techniques for Mastering the Writing Process*. New York:
Oxford University Press, 1981.

Evans, Sara. *Personal Politics: The Roots of Women's Liberation in the Civil Rights Movement and
the New Left*. New York: Vintage Books, 1980. First published 1979 by Knopf.

Farber, David. *Age of Great Dreams: America in the 1960s*. New York: Hill & Wang, 1994.

―――. *Chicago '68*. Chicago: University of Chicago Press, 1988.

―――, ed. *The Sixties: From Memory to History*. Chapel Hill: University of North Carolina
Press, 1994.

Feigelson, Naomi. *The Underground Revolution: Hippies, Yippies, and Others*. New York: Funk &
Wagnalls, 1970.

Felton, David, Robin Green, and David Dalton. *Mindfuckers: A Sourcebook on the Rise of Acid
Fascism in America, Including Material on Charles Manson, Mel Lyman, Victor Baranco, and
Their Followers*. San Francisco: Straight Arrow Books, 1972.

Ferber, Michael, and Staughton Lynd. *The Resistance*. Boston: Beacon, 1971.

Fero, Kelly. *The Zani Murders*. Austin: Texas Monthly, 1990.

Flacks, Richard. *Making History: The American Left and the American Mind*. New York: Columbia University Press, 1998.

———. "Making History vs. Making Life: Dilemmas of an American Left." In *Toward a History of the New Left: Essays from Within the Movement*, edited by R. David Myers, 125–52. Brooklyn: Carlson, 1989.

———. *Youth and Social Change*. Chicago: Markham, 1971.

Foley, Michael S. *Confronting the War Machine: Draft Resistance during the Vietnam War*. Chapel Hill: University of North Carolina Press, 2003.

Forcade, Thomas King. *Caravan of Love and Money: Being a Highly Unauthorized Chronicle of the Filming of Medicine Ball Caravan*. New York: New American Library, 1972.

Frank, Thomas. *The Conquest of Cool: Business Culture, Counterculture, and the Rise of Hip Consumerism*. Chicago: University of Chicago Press, 1997.

Frankfort, Ellen. *The Voice: Life at the Village Voice*. New York: William Morrow, 1976.

Fraser, Ronald, Luisa Passerini, Daniel Bertaux, Bret Eynon, and Ron Grele, eds. *1968: A Student Generation in Revolt*. New York: Pantheon, 1988.

Friedman, R. Seth. *The Factsheet Five Zine Reader: The Best Writing from the Underground World of Zines*. New York: Three Rivers, 1997.

Frost, Jennifer. *An Interracial Movement of the Poor: Community Organizing and the New Left in the 1960s*. New York: New York University Press, 2001.

Georgakas, Dan, and Marvin Surkin. *Detroit, I Do Mind Dying: A Study in Urban Revolution*. New York: St. Martin's, 1975.

Gitlin, Todd. *The Sixties: Years of Hope, Days of Rage*. New York: Bantam Books, 1987.

———. *The Whole World Is Watching: Mass Media in the Making and Unmaking of the New Left*. Berkeley: University of California Press, 1980.

Glessing, Robert J. *The Underground Press in America*. Bloomington: Indiana University Press, 1970.

Goldberg, Danny. *Bumping into Geniuses: My Life Inside the Rock and Roll Business*. New York: Gotham Books, 2008.

Goldman, Albert. "Living and Dying the Great Adventure." In *High Times Greatest Hits*, 4ff. New York: St. Martin's, 1994.

Goodman, Paul. *Growing Up Absurd: Problems of Youth in the Organized System*. New York: Random House, 1960.

Goodwyn, Lawrence. *The Populist Moment: A Short History of the Agrarian Revolt in America*. New York: Oxford University Press, 1978.

Gosse, Van. "A Movement of Movements: The Definition and Periodization of the New Left." In *A Companion to Post-1945 America*, edited by Jean-Christophe Agnew and Roy Rosenzweig, 277–302. Malden, MA: Blackwell: 2002.

———. *Rethinking the New Left: An Interpretative History*. New York: Palgrave Macmillan, 2005.

Gottlieb, Annie. *Do You Believe in Magic? The Second Coming of the Sixties Generation*. New York: Times Books, 1987.

Graham, John, ed. *"Yours for the Revolution": The Appeal to Reason, 1895–1922*. Lincoln: University of Nebraska Press, 1990.

Greenwald, Glenn. *A Tragic Legacy: How a Good Vs. Evil Mentality Destroyed the Bush Presidency*. New York: Crown, 2007.

Gruen, John. *The New Bohemia: The Combine Generation*. New York: Shorecrest, 1966.

Hagle, Timothy M. "But Do They Have to See It to Know It? The Supreme Court's Obscenity and Pornography Decisions." *Western Political Quarterly* 44 (1991): 1039–55.

Haines, Harry W. "The G.I. Resistance: Military Underground during the Vietnam War." In Wachsberger, *Voices from the Underground*, 190–97.

———. "Soldiers against the War in Vietnam: The Story of *Aboveground*." In Wachsberger, *Voices from the Underground*, 181–98.

Hale, Jeff A. "The White Panthers' 'Total Assault on the Culture.'" In Braunstein and Doyle, *Imagine Nation*, 125–56.

Hannah, John A. *A Memoir*. East Lasing: Michigan State University Press, 1980.

Hayden, Casey, and Mary King. "Sex and Caste: A Kind of Memo." In Bloom and Breines, *Takin' It to the Streets*, 40–43.

Hayden, Tom. "Radical Nomad: Essays on C. Wright Mills and His Time." Master's thesis, University of Michigan, 1964.

———. *Reunion: A Memoir*. New York: Random House, 1988.

———. *Trial*. New York: Holt, Rinehart and Winston, 1970.

Hazlett, John Downton. *My Generation: Collective Autobiography and Identity Politics*. Madison: University of Wisconsin Press, 1998.

Heineman, Kenneth J. *Campus Wars: The Peace Movement at American State Universities in the Vietnam Era*. New York: New York University Press, 1993.

Hodgson, Godfrey. *America in Our Time*. Garden City, NY: Doubleday, 1976.

Hoffman, Abbie. *The Best of Abbie Hoffman*. New York: Four Walls, Eight Windows, 1989.

Hogan, Wesley C. "'Radical Manners': The Student Nonviolent Coordinating Committee and the New Left in the 1960s." PhD diss., Duke University, 2000.

Hunt, Andrew E. *The Turning: A History of Vietnam Veterans Against the War*. New York: New York University Press, 1999.

———. "'When Did the Sixties Happen?' Searching for New Directions." *Journal of Social History* 33 (1999): 147–61.

Isserman, Maurice. *If I Had a Hammer: The Death of the Old Left and the Birth of the New Left*. New York: Basic Books, 1987.

———. "The Not-So-Dark and Bloody Ground: New Works on the 1960s." *American Historical Review* 94, no. 4 (1988): 990–1010.

Isserman, Maurice, and Michael Kazin. *America Divided: The Civil War of the 1960s*. New York: Oxford University Press, 2000.

Jacobs, Paul, and Saul Landau. *The New Radicals: A Report with Documents*. New York: Vintage, 1966.

Jacoby, Russell. *The Last Intellectuals: American Culture in the Age of Academe*. New York: Basic Books, 1987.

Janes, Daryl, ed. *No Apologies: Texas Radicals Celebrate the '60s*. Austin, TX: Eakin, 1992.

Jenkins, Virginia Scott. *Bananas: An American History*. Washington, DC: Smithsonian Institution Press, 2000.

Johnson, Michael L., *The New Journalism: The Underground Press, the Artists of Nonfiction, and the Changes in the Established Media*. Lawrence: University Press of Kansas, 1971.

Johnson, Paul B., David O. Sears, and John B. McConahay. "Black Invisibility, the Press, and the Los Angeles Riot." *American Journal of Sociology* 76, no. 4 (1971): 698–721.

Jones, Glenn W. "Gentle Thursday: Revolutionary Pastoralism in Austin, Texas, 1966–1969." Master's thesis, University of Texas at Austin, 1988.

Kahn, Roger. *The Battle for Morningside Heights: Why Students Rebel*. New York: Morrow, 1970.

Kindman, Michael. "My Odyssey through the Underground Press." In Wachsberger, *Voices from the Underground*, 369–478.

Klatch, Rebecca E. *A Generation Divided: The New Left, the New Right, and the 1960s*. Berkeley: University of California Press, 1999.

Kopkind, Andrew. *The Thirty Years' Wars: Dispatches and Diversions of a Radical Journalist, 1965–1994*. London: Verso, 1995.

Kornbluth, Jesse, ed. *Notes from the New Underground: An Anthology*. New York: Viking, 1968.

———. "This Place of Entertainment Has No Fire Exit: The Underground Press and How it Went." *Antioch Review* 39 (1969): 91–99.

Krassner, Paul, ed. *Best of the Realist*. Philadelphia: Running Press, 1984.

———. *Confessions of a Raving, Unconfined Nut: Misadventures in the Counter-culture*. New York: Simon & Schuster, 1993.

———, ed. *Magic Mushrooms and Other Highs: From Toad Slime to Ecstasy*. Berkeley, CA: Ten Speed, 2004.

Land, Jeff. *Active Radio: Pacifica's Brash Experiment*. Minneapolis: University of Minnesota Press, 1999.

Langer, Elinor. "Notes for Next Time: A Memoir of the 1960s." In *Toward a History of the New Left: Essays from Within the Movement*, edited by R. David Myers, 63–123. Brooklyn: Carlson, 1989.

Leamer, Laurence. *The Paper Revolutionaries: The Rise of the Underground Press*. New York: Simon & Schuster, 1972.

Lemisch, Jesse. "2.5 Cheers for Bridging the Gap between Activism and the Academy; or, Stay and Fight." In *Taking Back the Academy! History of Activism, History as Activism*, edited by Jim Downs and Jennifer Manion, 187–208. New York: Routledge, 2004.

Lieberman, Robbie. *Prairie Power: Voices of the 1960s Midwestern Student Protest*. Columbia: University of Missouri Press, 2004.

Lipton, Lawrence. *The Holy Barbarians*. New York: Messner, 1959.

Long, Howard Rusk, ed. *Main Street Militants: An Anthology from "Grassroots Editor."* Carbondale: Southern Illinois University Press, 1977.

Long, Priscilla, ed. *The New Left: A Collection of Essays*. Boston: Sargent, 1969.

Love, Robert, ed. *The Best of Rolling Stone: 25 Years of Journalism on the Edge*. New York: Doubleday, 1993.

Lovell, Bonnie Alice. "Stoney Burns and Dallas *Notes*: Covering the Dallas Counterculture, 1967–1970." Master's thesis, University of North Texas, 1999.

Lowen, Rebecca S., *Creating the Cold War University: The Transformation of Stanford*. Berkeley: University of California Press, 1997.

Mailer, Norman. *Advertisements for Myself*. Cambridge, MA: Harvard University Press, 1992. First published 1959 by Putnam.

———. *Armies of the Night: History as a Novel, the Novel as History*. New York: New American Library, 1968.

Mankoff, Milton, and Richard Flacks. "The Changing Social Base of the American Student Movement." *Annals of the American Academy of Political Science* 395 (May 1971): 54–67.

Manso, Peter. *Mailer: His Life and Times*. New York: Simon & Schuster, 1985.

Marcuse, Herbert. *An Essay on Liberation*. Boston: Beacon, 1969.

Mattson, Kevin. *Intellectuals in Action: The Origins of the New Left and Radical Liberalism, 1945–1970*. University Park: Pennsylvania State University Press, 2002.

May, Kirse Granat. *Golden State, Golden Youth: The California Image in Popular Culture, 1955–1966*. Chapel Hill: University of North Carolina Press, 2002.

Maynard, John Arthur. *Venice West: The Beat Generation in Southern California*. New Brunswick, NJ: Rutgers University Press, 1991.

McAdam, Doug. *Freedom Summer*. New York: Oxford University Press, 1988.

McAuliffe, Kevin Michael. *The Great American Newspaper: The Rise and Fall of the Village Voice*. New York: Scribner, 1978.

McBride, David. "Death City Radicals: The Counterculture in Los Angeles." In *The New Left Revisited*, edited by John McMillian and Paul Buhle, 110–36. Philadelphia: Temple University Press, 2003.

———. "On the Fault Lines of Mass Culture and Counterculture: A Social History of the Hippie Counterculture in 1960s Los Angeles." PhD diss., University of California at Los Angeles, 1998.

McCarthy, Timothy Patrick, and John McMillian, eds. *The Radical Reader: A Documentary History of the American Radical Tradition*. New York: New Press, 2003.

McMillian, John. "Electrical Bananas: An Epistemological Inquiry into the Great Banana Hoax of 1967." *Believer* 25 (May-June 2005): 18–26.

———. "Locating the New Left." Review of *Rethinking the New Left: An Interpretive History*, by Van Gosse. *Reviews in American History* 34, no. 4 (2006): 551–56.

———. "Love Letters to the Future: REP, *Radical America*, and New Left History." *Radical History Review* 77 (2000): 20–59.

———. "'There's Something Happening Here': The Sexual Revolution in Lawrence, Kansas." Review of *Sex in the Heartland*, by Beth Bailey. *American Quarterly* 53 (2001): 349–57.

McMillian, John, and Paul Buhle, eds. *The New Left Revisited*. Philadelphia: Temple University Press, 2003.

McNeill, Don. *Moving Through Here*. New York: Knopf, 1970.

Michel, Gregg L. *Struggle for a Better South: The Southern Student Organizing Committee, 1964–1969*. New York: Palgrave Macmillan, 2004.

Miller, James. *"Democracy is in the streets": From Port Huron to the Siege of Chicago*. New York: Simon & Schuster, 1987.

———. *Flowers in the Dustbin: The Rise of Rock and Roll, 1947–1977*. New York: Simon & Schuster, 1999.

Miller, Timothy. *The 60s Communes: Hippies and Beyond*. Syracuse, NY: Syracuse University Press, 1999.

Mills, C. Wright. *The Power Elite*. New York: Oxford University Press, 1956.

———. *The Sociological Imagination*. New York: Oxford University Press, 1959.

———. *White Collar: The American Middle Classes*. New York: Oxford University Press, 1951.

Mills, Nicolaus, ed. *The New Journalism: A Historical Anthology*. New York: McGraw-Hill, 1974.

Monhollon, Rusty L. *This is America? The Sixties in Lawrence, Kansas*. New York: Palgrave Macmillan, 2002.

Morgan, Robin, "Goodbye to All That." In *The Sixties Papers: Documents of a Rebellious Decade*, edited by Judith Clavir Albert and Stuart Edward Albert, 509–16. New York: Praeger, 1984.

Morgan, Edward P. *The 60s Experience: Hard Lessons about Modern America*. Philadelphia: Temple University Press, 1991.

Morris, Willie. *North Toward Home*. Boston: Houghton Mifflin, 1967.

Mungo, Raymond. *Beyond the Revolution: My Life and Times since "Famous Long Ago."* Chicago: Contemporary Books, 1990.

———. *Famous Long Ago: My Life and Hard Times with Liberation News Service*. Boston: Beacon, 1970.

Navasky, Victor S. *A Matter of Opinion*. New York: Farrar, Straus & Giroux, 2005.

Newfield, Jack. *A Prophetic Minority*. New York: New American Library, 1966.

———. *Somebody's Gotta Tell It: The Upbeat Memoir of a Working-Class Journalist*. New York: St. Martin's, 2002.

O'Brien, Geoffrey. *Dream Time*. London: Secker & Warburg, 1988.

Oglesby, Carl, ed. *The New Left Reader*. New York: Grove, 1969.

Olan, Susan T. "The Rag: A Study in Underground Journalism." Master's thesis, University of Texas at Austin, 1981.

Orwell, George, and Reginald Reynolds, eds. *British Pamphleteers*. Vol. 1, *From the Sixteenth Century to the French Revolution*. London: Wingate, 1948.

Ostertag, Bob. *People's Movements, People's Press: The Journalism of Social Justice Movements*. Boston: Beacon, 2006.

Palattella, John. "When Poetry Was the Rage." Review of *All Poets Welcome: The Lower East Side Poetry Scene in the 1960s*, by Daniel Kane, and *Digressions on Some Poems by Frank O'Hara: A Memoir*, by Joe LeSeur. *Nation*, June 16, 2003, 35.

Pardun, Robert. *Prairie Radical: A Journey Through the Sixties*. Los Gatos, CA: Shire, 2001.

Pauls, Naomi, and Charles Campbell, eds. *The Georgia Straight: What the Hell Happened?* Vancouver: Vancouver Free Press, 1997.

Peck, Abe. "From Underground to Alternative." *Media Studies Journal* 3 (1998): 156–62.

———. *Uncovering the Sixties: The Life and Times of the Underground Press*. New York: Pantheon Books, 1985.

Pelz, William A. "The Decline and Fall of the Underground Press, 1969–1974." *Indian Journal of American Studies* 10, no. 2 (1980): 58–66.

Perlstein, Rick. "Who Owns the Sixties? The Opening of a Scholarly Generation Gap." *Lingua Franca* 6, no. 4 (1996): 30–37.

Perry, Charles. *The Haight-Ashbury: A History*. New York: Random House, 1984.

Pifer, Matthew T., "Dissent: Detroit and the Underground Press, 1965–69." PhD diss., University of Oklahoma, 2001.

Pilcher, Tim. *Erotic Comics: A Graphic History from Tijuana Bibles to Underground Comix*. New York: Abrams, 2008.

Polletta, Francesca. *Freedom Is an Endless Meeting: Democracy in American Social Movements*. Chicago: University of Chicago Press, 2002.

Raskin, Jonah. *Out of the Whale: Growing Up in the American Left; An Autobiography*. New York: Links, 1974.

Rich, Frank. *The Greatest Story Ever Sold: The Decline and Fall of Truth from 9/11 to Katrina*. New York: Penguin, 2006.

Richards, David. *Once Upon a Time in Texas: A Liberal in the Lone Star State.* Austin: University of Texas Press, 2002.

Rips, Geoffrey. *The Campaign against the Underground Press.* San Francisco: City Lights Books, 1981.

———. "The Campaign against the Underground Press." In Rips, *The Campaign Against the Underground Press,* 37–40.

———. "Dissident Voices." In Rips, *The Campaign Against the Underground Press.*

Rolfe, Lionel. *Literary L.A.* Rev. ed. Los Angeles: California Classic Books, 2002.

Romm, Ethel. *The Open Conspiracy: What America's Angry Generation is Saying.* Harrisburg, PA: Stackpole Books, 1970.

Rosenkranz, Patrick. *Rebel Visions: The Underground Comix Revolution, 1963–1975.* Seattle: Fantagraphics Books, 2002.

Rossinow, Doug. "The New Left in the Counterculture: Hypotheses and Evidence." *Radical History Review* 67 (1997): 79–120.

———. *The Politics of Authenticity: Liberalism, Christianity, and the New Left in America.* New York: Columbia University Press, 1998.

———. "The Revolution Is About Our Lives: The New Left's Counterculture." In Braunstein and Doyle, *Imagine Nation,* 99–124.

Rubin, Jerry. *Do It! Scenarios of the Revolution.* New York: Simon & Schuster, 1970.

Rudd, Mark. "Columbia: Notes on the Spring Rebellion." In Oglesby, *New Left Reader,* 290–312.

Ruvinsky, Maxine. "The Underground Press of the Sixties." PhD diss., McGill University, 1995.

Ryan, Mary P. *Civic Wars: Democracy and Public Life in the American City during the Nineteenth Century.* Berkeley: University of California Press, 1997.

Sale, Kirkpatrick. *SDS.* New York: Random House, 1973.

Sayres, Sohnya, Frederic Jameson, Stanley Aronowitz, and Anders Stephanson, eds. *The Sixties Without Apology.* Minneapolis: University of Minnesota Press: 1984.

Schechter, Danny. *News Dissector: Passions, Pieces, and Polemics, 1960–2000.* New York: Akashic Books, 2001.

Schoenfeld, Eugene. *Dear Doctor Hip Pocrates: Advice Your Family Doctor Never Gave You.* New York: Grove, 1968.

Schulman, Bruce J. "Out of the Streets and Into the Classroom? The New Left and the Counterculture in United States History Textbooks." *Journal of American History* 85 (1999): 1527–34.

Sepe, Edward, and Stanton A. Glantz. "Bar and Club Tobacco Promotions in the Alternative Press: Targeting Young Adults." *American Journal of Public Health* 92 (2002): 75–78.

Shank, Barry. *Dissonant Identities: The Rock 'n' roll Scene in Austin, Texas.* Hanover, NH: University Press of New England, 1994.

Small, Melvin. *Covering Dissent: The Media and the Anti–Vietnam War Movement.* New Brunswick, NJ: Rutgers University Press, 1994.

Smith, Allen. "Present at the Creation . . . and Other Myths: The Port Huron Statement and the Origins of the New Left," *Peace and Change* 25 (2000): 339–62.

Smith, Victoria. "*Space City!* From Opposition to Organizational Collapse." In Wachsberger, *Voices from the Underground,* 165–80.

Solman, Paul, and Thomas Friedman. *Life and Death on the Corporate Battlefield: How Companies Win, Lose, Survive.* New York: Simon & Schuster, 1982.

Stansell, Christine. *American Moderns: Bohemian New York and the Creation of a New Century.* New York: Metropolitan Books, 2000.

Stevens, Jay. *Storming Heaven: LSD and the American Dream.* New York: Harper & Row, 1987.

Stokes, Geoffrey, ed. *The Village Voice Anthology (1956–1980): Twenty-five Years of Writing from the Village Voice.* New York: William Morrow, 1982.

Streitmatter, Rodger. *Voices of Revolution: The Dissident Press in America.* New York: Columbia University Press, 2001.

Taylor, Derek. *It Was Twenty Years Ago Today.* New York: Simon & Schuster, 1987.

Teodori, Massimo, ed. *The New Left: A Documentary History.* London: Cape, 1970.

Tifft, Susan E., and Alex S. Jones. *The Trust: The Private and Powerful Family behind the New York Times.* Boston: Little, Brown, 1999.

Tischler, Barbara L., ed. *Sights on the Sixties.* New Brunswick, NJ: Rutgers University Press, 1992.

Tocqueville, Alexis de. *Democracy in America.* New York: HarperCollins, 2000.

Trippi, Joe. *The Revolution Will Not Be Televised: Democracy, the Internet, and the Overthrow of Everything.* New York: ReganBooks, 2004.

Varon, Jeremy. *Bringing the War Home: The Weather Underground, the Red Army Faction, and the Revolutionary Violence in the Sixties and Seventies.* Berkeley: University of California Press, 2004.

Wachsberger, Ken. A Tradition Continues: East Lansing's Underground Press, 1965-Present." In Wachsberger, *Voices from the Underground,* 233–58.

———, ed. *Voices from the Underground.* Vol. 1, *Insider Histories of the Vietnam Era Underground Press.* Foreword by Abe Peck. Tempe, AZ: Mica, 1993.

Wasserman, Harvey, "The Joys of Liberation News Service." In Wachsberger, *Voices from the Underground,* 00–00.

Weingarten, Marc. *The Gang That Wouldn't Write Straight: Wolfe, Thompson, Didion, and the New Journalism Revolution.* New York: Crown, 2006.

White, Hayden. *Tropics of Discourse: Essays in Cultural Criticism.* Baltimore: Johns Hopkins University Press, 1985.

Wiener, Jon. "The New Left as History." *Radical History Review* 42 (1988): 173–87.

Wolf, Daniel, and Edwin Fancher, eds. *The Village Voice Reader: A Mixed Bag from the Greenwich Village Newspaper.* Garden City, NY: Doubleday, 1962.

Wolfe, Tom, and E. W. Johnson, eds. *The New Journalism.* New York: Harper & Row, 1973.

Wynkoop, Mary Ann. *Dissent in the Heartland: The Sixties at Indiana University.* Bloomington: Indiana University Press, 2002.

Yanker, Gary. *Prop Art: Over 1000 Contemporary Political Posters.* New York: Darien House, 1972.

Young, Allen. "Marshall Bloom: Gay Brother." In Wachsberger, *Voices from the Underground,* 59–60.

———. "Red Diaper Baby: From a Jewish Chicken Farm in the Catskills, to the Cane Fields of Cuba, to the First Gay Protests in New York City." *Vietnam Generation* 7 (1994): 25–33.

Index

Aboveground (Fort Carson, CO), 134

Abrahams, Mike, 127

activism, 4, 9, 10, 15, 19, 37, 45, 53–54, 79, 122, 144

  campus-based, 31, 42, 51, 62, 72, 85, 86, 88 (*see also* individual schools)

  Internet, 187–88

  grassroots, xiv, 5–6, 24, 71, 187

  labor, 22, 32, 54, 143, 174, 196n22

  See also under press

Adams, Walter (of London School of Economics), 86

Adams, Walter (of MSU), 46–47

Adelstein, David, 86–87

advertising, 138

  classifieds, 125, 130, 181, 184

  personal, 63, 175, 178

  See also under press

African Americans, 12, 40

  arts movement among, 194n45

  Black Power Movement, 7, 43, 103, 105

  civil rights of, 5, 14–15, 16, 41–43, 52, 56, 57, 60, 79, 84, 86, 143, 144, 147–48, 158

  discrimination against, 2, 35, 55, 104, 143, 178, 201n22, 206n121 (*see also* racism)

  in Columbia rebellion, 105–13

  segregation of, 25, 56, 58, 86, 187, 210n189

  slavery of, 201n6

  See also Black Panther Party

Agent Orange, 220–21n78

AIDS, 64, 178

Air Force One, 202n31

Albatross, 21

Albert, Stew, 123

Allen, Russ, 207n137

Ally (Berkeley, CA), 134

Alpert, Jane, 135, 243n166

alt-weeklies. *See* press: alternative

Altamont, 1–3, *photo gallery 7*

Alternative Media Project, 175, *photo gallery 10*

Alternative Newsweeklies, Association of (AAN), 178, 181, 182, 183, 244n17

American Civil Liberties Union (ACLU), 131, 133, 207n137

Amherst College, 85–86, 140, 160

Amherst Student, 86, *photo gallery 4*

amnesty, 106, 107–8

anarchism, 25, 50, 52, 57, 60, 64, 84, 115

Anger, Kenneth, 40, 92

Ann Arbor (MI), 20, 37, 120–21

Ann Arbor Sun, photo gallery 4

Annenberg, Walter, 8

Anthony, Susan B., 201n6

Antonioni, Michelangelo, 41

Appeal to Reason (Kansas), 32–33

Armies of the Night, 93

Armstrong, David, 7, 178

Arnold, Martin, 111

Arpaio, Joe, 179

arts, 3, 6, 7, 10, 41, 44, 48, 49, 50, 79, 173,
    181, 185
  reviews in, 34, 60, 62, 72, 73, 74, 76, 119,
    155, 168, 181

assassinations, 148, 174

Associated Press (AP), 83, 102, 103, 158

Asterick (Omaha, NE), 126

authenticity, 11, 16, 55–56, 60, 71, 125, 179

avant-garde, 4, 30, 32, 37, 41, 68, 79–80, 92
  in newspapers, 72, 125, 201n19

Avatar (Boston, MA), xiii, 92, 99, 156, 170,
    189, *photo gallery 3*

Baba Ram Dass, 175

baby boomers, 5, 15, 43, 88

Baez, Joan, 40

Bailey, Beth, 125–26

Baldwin, James, 33

Balin, Marty, 192n9

banana hoax, 66–72, 74–81, 128

Banana Labeling Act of 1967, 67

bananadine powder, 67, 80

Bangs, Lester, 9

Bank of America, 138

Baraka, Amiri, 33

Barnes & Noble, 186

Barron, Fred, 173

Batista, Fulgencio, 107

Beach Boys, 43, 69

beat generation, 33, 38, 201n22

Beatlemania, 2

Beatles, 2, 53, 60, 66, 69, 81, 92, 159, 189,
    194n37

Beckman, Bill, 126

Bell, Arthur, 178

Bell & Howell Company, xiii, 117

Ben Franks, 44

Bergman, Lowell, 8, 132

Bergmann, Frithjof, 18

Berkeley (CA), 55, 75, 103, 122

Berkeley Barb, xiv, 6, 7, 70–73, 75, 76, 122,
    13, 156, 178, 191–92n6, 235n18,
    239n84, *photo gallery 7*

Berkeley free speech movement, 25, 42, 48

Berkeley Tribe, 1, 2–3, 4, 130, 135, 239n84

Berkeley, University of California at, 76

Berlet, Chip, 9, 128, 135

Berman, Louis, 207n137

Bernstein, Carl, 144

Big Brother and the Holding Company, *photo
    gallery 4*

Black Panther Party, 139, 146, 151, 194–
    95n45

blogosphere, 187–88, 190

Bloom, Marshall, 84–87, 89–91, 93, 99,
    102–3, 109, 113, 140–42, 144,
    145–68, 169, 170, 171, 193–94n36,
    photo gallery 4

Bluestone, Barry, 19

Blum, Bill, 238n77

Blum, Shelly, 22

bombings, 2, 120, 121, 124, 131, 132, 135,
    136

Booth, Paul, 27

Bosker, Miriam, 241n129

Boston American Record, 88

Boston Army Base, 89, 134

Boston Globe, 179

Boston Phoenix, 173, 179, 180, 182, 244n17,
    photo gallery 10

Boston University (BU) (Boston, MA), 85,
    87–89, 141, *photo gallery 1, 3*
  See also *BU News*

Boudin, Leonard, 133

Boulding, Elise, 18

Boulding, Kenneth, 18

Bowart, Walter, 73, 92, 118, 215n71, *photo
    gallery 2*

Bradlee, Benjamin, 144

Brecher, Jeremy, 18, 19, 26, 235n32

Brennan, Justice William, 127

Brezsny, Rob, 183

Bright, Susie, 9

Bromell, Nick, 69

Brugmann, Bruce, 183

Bruno's Bohemia, 201n19

Bryan, John, 92, 127, 239n84

BU News, 85, 87–89, 134, 141, 147, 179,
    photo gallery 1, 3

Buckley, William F., 199n70

Buffalo Chip (Omaha, NE), 131

Buffalo Springfield, 43, 45

Buhle, Paul, 9, 37

Bukowski, Charles, 9

Burge, John, 178

Burlage, Dorothy, 17, 210n186

Burlage, Robb, 210n186

Burns, Stoney (aka Brent Stein), 127, 129, 132, 133

Bush administration, 187

Business Week magazine, 214n34

the Byrds, 43

Cage, John, 41

Calvert, Greg, 26, 96, 222n102

Calypso Joe (aka Gen. Hershey Bar), *photo gallery 5*

Cambridge (MA), 55, *photo gallery 3*

Campaign Against the Underground Press, 125

Cannabis Cup, 35

Canter's Restaurant, 44

Capital Records, 130

capitalism, 2, 6, 84, 171, 174, 244n13

Caricature, 201n19

Carmichael, Stokely, 85

Carr, David, 179–80, 184

Carson, Clayborne, 9

cartoons, 184, 213n16
    comics, 51, 74, 230n56
    comix, 9, 126
    political, 3, 13, 35, 80, 83, 126, 183

Case, Harold C., 88

Cavalletto, George, 103, 119, 149–52, 159, 161–62, 164–65

Cawley, Peter, 241n129

center, ideology of, 84, 136, 151, 193n33

Central Intelligence Agency (CIA), 51, 89, 224n130, 227n2

Central Park (New York, NY), 66–67, 77

centralism, democratic, 17, 151, 196n22

Chalfen, Rob, 187

Champaign-Urbana, University of Illinois in, 200n88

Cheetah, 192n12

Chicago (IL), 13, 73, 103, 129, 174, 180

Chicago Reader (Chicago, IL), 173, 178, 179–81

Chicago Seed (Chicago, IL), 73, 76, 122, 127, 131, 168, *photo gallery 4*

Children of God, 162, 163

Chiquita, 215–16n78, 217n101

Chomsky, Noam, 100–101, 188

Christian Faith-and-Life Community, 55

Christian Science Monitor, 144

Chubby Checker, 55

Church, Frank, 229n52

civil disobedience, 96

Civic Wars, xiv

Clark, Kenneth, 227n176

the Clash, 178

Cleveland (OH), 81, 103, 129

Clinton, Bill, 183

clubs, youth, 43, 45, 62

Cobb, Ron, 126

Cold War, 4, 5, 9, 15, 34, 35, 47

Coleman, Henry S., 105

collectives, 14, 165, 186–87, 239n85

College Journalist magazine, 85

College Press Service, 128

colleges and universities, 11, 46, 47–49, 50, 79, 205n111
    authority in 51, 77, 104–13, 130
    censorship in, 10, 51, 76–77, 86–87, 105–7, 122, 207n137
    dropouts, 27, 62, 98, 121
    free, 52, 82–83
    involvement in war, 51, 104–5
    student power, 60, 64
    See also individual schools; press: underground; Students for a Democratic Society

Collins, Stephen, 172

Columbia Daily Spectator, 107, 112, 144

Columbia Records, 122, 130

Columbia University, 83, 103–13, 120, 143, 144

columnists, 3, 8, 34–35, 41, 44, 60, 70, 128, 175, 183, 185

columns, 34–35, 44, 60, 70, 72, 78, 128, 130, 175, 183

comics. *See* cartoons

Commission on Obscenity and Pornography, 136, 139, *photo gallery 9*

Committee for Student Rights (CSR), 46, 48, 50, 52

communal culture, 2, 10, 56–57, 141–42, 151, 155, 166, 170

communes, 120, 121, 141, 147, 149, 158, 165, 167

Communism, 25, 34, 50, 88, 133, 143
  at UT, 54, 58, 59, 199n76

community-building, 4, 6, 16, 23, 37, 52–55, 59–63, 71–73, 82, 92–93, 170, 176, 190

community newssheets, 4, 32, 34, 37, 38, 39–41, 45, 80, 83

Conason, Joe, 8

conformism, 33, 50, 94, 201n22

Congress, U.S. 21, 88–89, 117, 136, 235n21

Congress of Racial Equality (CORE), 38, 43

Congressional Record, 145

Connecticut, University of (Greater Hartford Campus), 127

Connections (Madison, WI), 72, 129, 155

Connery, Colin, 149

Conqueroo, 62

consensus building, 16, 53

conservatism, 54, 55–56, 58, 144

conservatives, 5, 35, 130

Constitution, U.S., 64, 127, 131, 133–38

copyrights, 22, 119, 124

Correspondence, 38

Coser, Lewis, 33

counterculture, 11, 33, 37, 44, 61, 73, 77, 79, 80, 174
  beatnik, 48, 49, 54–55, 62, 78, 172, 201n22, 206n123
  bohemian, 10, 36–37, 39, 41, 43–44, 46, 55, 57–58, 60–62, 73, 80, 123, 177
  commoditization of, 122
  gay, 64
  hip/ hip zones, 4, 7, 35–38, 43–44, 55, 63, 66, 69, 71, 72, 80, 85, 122, 147, 152, 170
  hippie, 1, 3, 10, 11, 12, 33, 38, 41, 44–45, 54, 58, 61–62, 66–67, 71, 72, 75–76, 78, 79–80, 92, 96, 116, 121, 125, 126, 142, 144, 146, 158, 175, 177, 229n33

language of, 4, 8, 122, 125–27, 130, 137–38, 178, 243n164

longhairs, 44, 45, 55, 66, 84, 102

nonconformists, 12, 15, 37, 45, 54, 87, 206n123

oppositional significance of, 212n10

politico, 3, 4, 11, 12, 36, 54, 58, 61–62, 84, 105, 151, 158, 167

subversive power of, 71

youth, 3, 4–7, 9, 11, 32, 44, 52 71, 80–81, 102, 122, 147, 167, 188–89, 190

See also Left: New; newspapers: underground

Counterculture Hall of Fame, 35

counterinstitutions, 4–5, 82–83, 85, 112, 170, 189

counter-revolutionaries, 155

Country Joe and the Fish, 69–70, 189

Cox, Archibald, 107

Cox Commission, 107, 110

Craigslist, 184

Creative Loafing Inc., 181

Crowe, Cameron, 9

Crowley, Walt, 31

Crumb, Robert, 9, 126

Csicsery, George Paul, 2

Cuba, 88, 103, 132, 143, 151
  Missile Crisis, 20, 21, 35

cult, Lyman Family, 64, 156

culture, establishment, 5, 8, 31, 39, 71, 76, 79, 83–84, 106, 212n10, 230n55

Cunningham, David, 237n61

curfew regulations, 44–45, 47, 50, 148

Cutler, Sam, 191n1 (Intro)

Daily Planet (Miami, FL), 128

Daily Texan (Austin, TX), 58–60

Daley, Richard, 129, 230n63

Dallas Notes (TX), 75, 127, 128, 132, 133

Davidson, Carl, 105

Davidson, Sara, 66

Dean, Howard, 188

Debs, Eugene, 13

Dellinger, David, 51, 95, 100–101

DeMaio, Don, 121, 135

democracy, 4, 12, 15–17, 28, 36, 40–41, 48, 142, 170, 188

in Civil Rights movement, 16, 147–48

in institutions, 4

in LNS, 91, 142–43, 146, 148, 151, 153–54, 155, 169

in New Left, 4, 9, 12, 15, 30, 32, 79, 108, 142, 156–57, 170, 190

participatory, 14, 16–17, 21, 54, 142, 146, 151, 153, 157, 170

in SDS, 14, 16, 17, 21, 57, 153, 156–57, 170

in underground press, 14, 40, 54, 59, 63, 80, 93, 155–56, 170–71, 189–90

Democratic National Convention, 2, 152, 230n63, *photo gallery 4*

Democratic Party, 15, 19, 39, 187–88

Denson, Ed (aka "Banana Ed"), 70

Department of Defense, U.S., 96

DeRogatis, Jim, 68

Detroit Free Press, 121

Devine, Dorothy, 93

Diamante, John, 147

Diamond, Steve, 106–9, 114, 150, 152, 158–65, 167, 237n59, 263n43

Didion, Joan, 8, 179

Dickson, Jim, 45

Dickstein, Morris, xiv

Disney, Walt, 69, 142

Dissent, 33, 217n3

Distant Drummer (Philadelphia, PA), 121, 135

DiPrima, Diane, 9

Dixiecrats, 16

Donovan, 66, 68, 71, 81

Doors, 43

Dos Passos, John, 54

Dow Chemical Company, 220n78, 224n130

draft. *See under* Vietnam

Dreyer, Thorne, 9, 53, 58–59, 62, 72–73, 91, 97–99, 129, 151, 162, 164, 171, 210n186, 222n105, 241n129, *photo gallery 9*

"dropping out," 144, 165–66, 176

drugs

advocacy of, 70, 128, 130, 176, 189–90

criminalization of, 46, 58, 77–78, 116, 120, 122, 123, 212n10, 231n90

culture of, 9, 64, 84, 90, 92, 95

ineffective, 69, 213n24 (*see also* banana hoax)

politically motivated persecution for, 120, 122–24, 128, 136

psychedelic, 53, 62, 64–65, 69, 70, 76, 89, 194n37, 211n204, 215n71

trafficking of, 75, 116, 123–24, 176–77

in underground press, 7

use of, 34, 85, 88, 90, 98, 123, 128, 144, 146–47, 151, 170, 175, 176, 238n77

as a topic, 11, 54, 59, 72, 119, 126, 127, 128, 186

violence associated with, 1–3, 64, 121, 174

in youth movement, 3, 62, 124

Duncombe, Stephen, 186–87

Dunne, John Gregory, 8

Dunphy, Tom (aka "Gen. Waste More Land"), *photo gallery 5*

Dylan, Bob, 13, 50, 68, 69, 139, 142, 174

East Bay Express, 246n44

East L.A. Almanac, 38

East Lansing (MI), 31, 46–53

See also *Paper*

East Village (NY), 36, 66, 73, 160

East Village Other (EVO), xiv, 6, 11, 71–75, 80, 91, 92–93, 118, 119, 125, 126, 128, 165, 175, 201n3, 228n13, *photo gallery 1, 2*

Eastern Bloc, 56

Eastman, Max, 32

Echols, Alice, 54

Economidy, John, 58, 60

Editor & Publisher magazine, 106

editorial policies

of *BU News*, 88

of *Chicago Reader*, 179–80

of *Kaleidoscope*, 130, 131

of LNS, 142–43, 146, 154–55, 170

of *Los Angeles Free Press*, 40–41, 74

of *New York Times*, 110–12

of the *Paper*, 50

of the *Rag*, 59

of SDS newsletters, 23–25, 28–29, 142–43, 155

of underground newspapers, 7, 10, 32, 74, 155, 170, 180, 189

editorial policies (*continued*)
  of *Village Voice*, 34
  at *Washington Free Press*, 78, 238n77
  in *WIN* magazine, 189
editorials in mainstream media, 3, 4, 9–10,
    43, 87, 88, 110–12, 181, 225n158,
    245n27
egalitarianism, 21, 29, 142–43, 153, 155,
    156, 171, 177
Epstein, Beryl, *photo gallery* 7
Epstein, Howie, *photo gallery* 7
Eisenhower, David, 85
Eisenhower era, 33
elections, federal, 187, 188, 252
Electric Kool-Aid Acid Test, The, 81
Esquire magazine, 38
Evans, Sara, 197n38
existentialism, 4, 14–15, 55–56, 201n22

Fabrikant, Joel, 175
Face the Nation, 225n158
Factsheet Five, 246n3
Faire Free Press, 39–40
Famous Long Ago, 89, 94, 148, 150, 159, 167,
    169, 234n6, 241n121
Fancher, Ed, 33–34
Farber, Jerry, 44
fascism, 57, 163, 201n22
Fass, Bob, 123
Federal Bureau of Investigation (FBI), 10,
    22, 51, 116, 124, 129–30, 140, 168,
    195n8, 227n2, 237n61
  COINTELPRO, 115–16, 129, 237n61
Feiffer, Jules, 13
Feinstein, Barbara, *photo gallery* 7
Feinstein, Mark, *photo gallery* 7
feminism, 12, 64, 95, 132, 167, 175, 176,
    186, 187, 202n31, 243n166
Ferber, Michael, 222n102
festivals, 1–4, 35, 39, 62, 67, 80, 152
Fields, W. C., 10
Fifth Estate (Detroit, MI), 72, 75, 77, 103,
    128, 166, 201n3
Fifth Estate Coffee House, 41, 44, 45
film, 41, 44, 71
  Almost Famous, 9
  The Battle of Algiers, 145
  Between the Lines, 172–73
  Blow Job, 60
  Blue Fascism, 41
  Camp, 60
  European, 41
  Gimme Shelter, 1–2
  The Insider, 132
  Magical Mystery Tour, 159, 160
  Scorpio Rising, 40
First Amendment, 35, 136, 229–30n52,
    230n61
Flacks, Richard, 18, 19, 37, 157
Fleet Street (London, UK), 118
Fleming, Thomas, 9
Flying Burrito Brothers, 1
Flynt, Larry, 63, 211n201
Foehr, Steve, 176
Foley, Michael S., 134
Foner, Eric, 144, 145
Food and Drug Administration (FDA),
    67, 78
Forbes magazine, 181
Forcade, Thomas King, 7, 116–20, 122,
    123–25, 128, 136–39, 176–77, 186,
    photo gallery 9
Ford, Richard, 208n149
foreign policy, U.S., 10, 21, 25, 51, 146
Franklin, Benjamin, 232n97
Freedland, Nat, 67
freedom
  academic, 86
  of assembly, 229–30n52
  personal, 37
  of press, 129, 131, 137–39, 180
  of speech, 9, 40, 45, 46, 50, 52–53, 60,
    127, 134, 135–37, 139, 229–30n52
Freedom of Information Act, 125
Freeman, Bob, 43
freewriting, 198n65
Freudiger, Larry, 60
Friedman, Thomas, 182
Frontline, 8, 132
Fuck Communism, 35, 208–9n153
Fuck You: A Magazine of the Arts, 68–69, 147,
    193n20

fundraising, 20, 149, 155–56, 159–60
Funkadelic, 178
Fuzak, John, 207n137

Gabriner, Robert, 155
Garboden, Clif, 179
Garson, Marvin, 75, 78, 123
Garvy, Helen, 23–24, 26
gay rights, 11, 54, 145, 178
    Gay Liberation Movement, 168, 178
gender, 5, 12, 19
General Electric, 213n16
Gentle Thursday, 60–62, 76, 80
Georgia State University, 24
Georgia Straight (Canada), 6, 128
Gerth, Jeff, 8
Getz, Michael, 203n62
Ginsberg, Allen, 9–10, 125, 127
Gitlin, Todd, 5, 9, 10, 196n13, 22, 26, 57, 79,
    196n13, 217n101, 217n3, 221n79,
    235n32
Goddard College (Plainfield, VT), *photo gallery 10*
Goldschmidt, Neil, 179
Goldstein, Richard, 121, 178
Goldwater, Barry, 85, 86, 130
Good Times (San Francisco, CA), 123, 133
Goodbye to All That, 132
"Goodbye to All That," 243n166
Goodman, Paul, 33
Goodwin, Richard, 88
Gordon, Ann, 9, 129
Gould, Jay, 147
Grafton, Marvin, 175
Graham, Bill, 118, 159
graphics, 7, 24, 74, 130, 151, 170
    Dadaist, 119–20
    psychedelic, 3, 60, 112, 120, 155, 201n3
Great Speckled Bird (Atlanta, GA), xiii, 127,
    130, 132, 155, 232n96, *photo gallery 8*
Greenspan, Ralph, *photo gallery 7*
Greenwich Village (New York, NY), 32–33,
    36, 48, 55, 77
Grizzard, Vernon, 22
Grob, Benjamin, 130–31
Gruenberg, Alan Howard, *photo gallery 7*
Guerrero, Eugene, 127, 130, 155

Guevara, Che, 107
Guilt without Sex, 35
Gurley, James, *photo gallery 4*

Haag, Michael von, 241n141
Haber, Al, 17, 18, 19, 20, 24, 195n9, 199n70
Haight-Ashbury, 67, 75, 81, 144
Haines, Lionel, 130
Halliwell, Steve, 157
Hamilton, Tom, 108–9, 162, 163, 241n129
Hannah, John A., 50–51
Hansberry, Lorraine, 33
Hansen, Wayne, 92
"happenings," 43, 44, 52, 62, 66, 71–72
harassment of newspapers, 6, 117–18, 121,
    124, 125, 129, 133, 134, 139,
    210–11n200, *photo gallery 9*
    and affiliates, 63, 124, 129–32, 136
    by campus officials, 10, 49, 59–60, 64,
        76–77
    by federal authorities, 10, 14, 115–16, 124,
        125, 129, 132, 140, 145
    by local authorities, 10, 115–16, 120, 125,
        132, 136, 142, 145
    by politicians, 125, 129, 130, 135
    by vigilantes, 10, 125, 130, 131–32
Hari-Krishna, 93
Harlem, 104–5, 108
Harper's magazine, 55
Harris, John, 41
Harrison, George, 159
Harvard University (MA), 67, 89, 107, 182
Hayden, Casey, 19, 20, 210n186
Hayden, Tom, 15–21, 25, 29, 55, 108,
    197n51, 200n88, 239n90
Hazlett, John Downton, 196n10
Heard, John, 172
Hearst Newspapers, 4, 8
Heller, Joseph, 33
Hell's Angels, 1–3, 174
Hendrix, Jimi, 81
Hentoff, Nat, 88, 167, 184
Herschler, Dale, 127
Hershey, Lewis B., 214n41
High Times magazine, 176
Hinckle, Warren, 51, 109

Hirsh, Gary "Chicken," 69–70
HIV, 64
Hoffman, Abbott (Abbie), 75, 78, 99, 123, 189
Holley, Alexander Lyman, 77
Hollywood, 204n88
Holmstrom, John, 186
Holy Barbarians, the, 38
homoeroticism, 40
homophobia, 11, 86, 90, 150–51, 168–69, 175
hootenannies, 41, 55
Hoover, J. Edgar, 115
Hopkins, John, 74
House Armed Services Committee, 134
House Un-American Activities Committee
    (HUAC), 21, 139
housing code reforms, 42, 178
Howe, Irving, 33, 217n3
Huffington Post, 247n11
humor (in the press), 34, 35–36, 40, 50, 54,
    60, 125, 146
Humphrey, Hubert, 62
Hunter, Meredith, 2, 191n6, *photo gallery* 7
Hustler magazine, 63
Hutchinson, Cathy, 161–63
Hyman, Hattie, 237n59

I. F. Stone's Weekly, 33
idealism, 2, 12, 17, 20, 172, 187
imperialism, 12, 134, 174
in loco parentis, 46, 48, 50
In These Times magazine, 184
Indiana, University of, 227–28n3
Indianapolis Free Press (IN), 131
Industrial Workers of the World, 13
Institute for Defense Analyses (IDA), 104–5, 106
Institute of Policy Studies, 220n63
Inter-American Press Association, 144
Intercollegiate Socialist Society, 195n9
Internal Revenue Service (IRS), 40
International Banana Club Museum, 215n75
International Times (IT or *it*), 10, 74
Internet, 178, 184, 187–88, 190
Ireland, Doug, 22
Irons, Greg, 3
Isserman, Maurice, 9
It Ain't Me Babe, 194n45

J. Geils Band, 175
Jacksonian Era, 201n6
Jacobs, Barbara (now Barbara Haber), 17,
    18, 20
Jacobs, Jim, 174
Jacobs, John, 107–8
Jacoby, Russell, 36
Jagger, Mick, 1–2
Jan and Dean, 43
Jaquiss, Nigel, 179
Jefferson Airplane, 1, 3
Jenks, Norman, 241n129
Jezer, Marty, 148
Johnson, Lyndon B., 57, 88, 95–96, 98, 146,
    151, 202n31
Jolles, Char, 52, 53
Jones, Glen W., 61
Jones, Leroi, 3
Joplin, Janis, 209n169
journalism
    investigative, 8, 39, 130, 184, 185
    New Left, 50, 56 (*see also* press:
        underground)
    "professional," 8, 9, 74, 179–80, 182,
        187
    professionalism in, 25, 34, 176
Justice Department, U.S., 182

Kaleidoscope (Milwaukee, WI), 127, 130
Kaleidoscope (Madison, WI), 130
Kalish, Nancy, 126
Karpel, Richard, 178
Katzman, Allan, xiv, 73, 215n71, *photo
    gallery* 2
Katzman, Don, *photo gallery* 2
Kaufman, Arnold, 16
Kazin, Michael, 9
Keast, William, 122
Kempton, Murray, 226n168
Kennedy, John F., 2, 88, 202n31
Keppler, Ernest C., 129
Kerouac, Jack, 87
Kesey, Ken, 35
Kewpeeites, 51–52
Kifner, John, 112
Kindman, Michael, 47–53, 58, 64, 72–73, 74

King, Martin Luther, Jr., 48, 148, 224n130

Kirk, Grayson, 107, 109, 110–11, 224n137, 225n158, n160

Kissinger, Clark, 21

Knickerbocker Hospital, 109

Knobler, Pete, *photo gallery* 7

Knops, Marc, 130

Kois, John, 127–28

Kopkind, Andrew, 84, 216n88

Kornbluth, Jesse, 189

Krassner, Paul, 14, 33–36, 52, 123, 175, 213n24

Kudzu (Jackson, MS), 127, 133

Kunkin, Art, 37–46, 58, 63, 71, 72, 129, 156

Labor Age, 195n9

Lacey, Mike, 183

Laidler, Harry, 195n9

LaMann, Amber, *photo gallery* 1

Landau, Jon, 9

Larkin, Jim, 181

Larsen, Otto N., 139, *photo gallery* 9

LaSalle, Sally, 241n129

layout, 7, 59, 82, 112, 119, 171, 173, 229n35, 238n77

lawsuits, 3, 63, 64, 132, 178, 183

League for Industrial Democracy, 195n9

Leamer, Laurence, 192n12, 194n40, 234n6

Leary, Howard R., 109

Leary, Timothy, 194n37

Left, 43, 56, 79, 82, 185, 187–88, 190

liberal, 14, 34–35, 62 (*see also* newspapers: alternative)

liberals, 5, 11, 15, 39–40, 49, 83, 96, 104, 131, 177

movements

back-to-the-land, 158, 169

Civil Rights (*see under* African Americans)

deaths during, 2, 3, 87, 174

democracy in (*see* democracy)

feminist-punk, 187

peace, 25, 57, 96

youth (*see* Left: New)

Old, 22, 39, 198n59

Left, New, 5–6, 11–12, 31, 51, 53, 64, 79, 174, 189–90

activism of (*see* activism)

anti-elitism of, 19, 22, 74, 142, 154, 174

decline of, 2, 14, 170–71, 173–74, 177, 188

development of, 4–12, 30, 46, 52, 82–83, 113, 143, 189

fragmentation in, 64, 73, 105–13, 142, 161–66, 170–71, 173, 175–76, 234n6

ideological diversity in, 154, 162, 167, 235n18

intellectuals/intellectualism in, 4, 5–7, 14, 15, 24, 26, 33, 36, 37, 40, 69, 82, 188

literature of, xiii–xiv, 9–10, 21–22, 29–30, 31–32 (*see also* newspapers: underground)

militancy in, 32, 95–96, 122–23

politics of, 19, 24, 49, 60, 79, 81, 151

race relations in, 12, 42–43, 105–8, 143–44, 158, 175–76

schools of, 42, 52

sexism in (*see* sexism)

southern, 27, 53–54, 57, 58, 86, 147 (see also *Rag*)

synthesis of politics and culture in, 11–12, 36, 54, 56, 58, 60, 61, 73, 79–81, 106–7, 144, 151, 188–89

white, 11–12, 84, 97, 106, 158, 243n166 (*see also* White Panther Party)

See also counterculture

Leggieri, Peter, 118

Leiby, Richard, 181–82

Lenham, Connie, 241n129

Leninism, 151, 174, 196n22

Lennon, John, 81, 127, 194n37

Lens, Sidney, 22

levy, d. a., 9

Lewis, Bill, 163

libel insurance, 184

liberated zones, 36, 145–46, 155, *photo gallery 3*

Liberation News Service (LNS), xiii, 6, 53, 79, 82, 83, 88, 90–95, 97–104, 106, 108–10, 112–14, 119, 120, 123, 127, 135, 140–71, 184, 210n186, *photo gallery 1, 3, 4, 6, 7*

liberation, personal, 54, 84, 151, 167, 188–89

Liberator (Boston, MA), 32

Liebling, A. J., 114

Life magazine, 44, 111–12

Lipscomb, Mance, 209n174

Lipton, Lawrence, 38

Lombardi, Kristin, 179

London, Jack, 195n9

London American, 87

London School of Economics, 86–87

London Times, 87

Look magazine, 44, 111–12, 227n174

Lorton Prison, 97

Los Angeles (CA), 7, 10, 38–41, 43, 62, 120

Los Angeles Free Press, 6, 31, 37–46, 50, 52, 54,
    58, 63, 67, 71–72, 74, 75, 78, 119,
    126, 129, 132, 156, 194n37

Los Angeles Herald-Examiner, 42

Los Angeles magazine, 204n91

Los Angeles Times, 42–43, 44–45, 136,
    205n108

Los Angeles Underground, 45–46, 205n108

Lott, Trent, 187–88

Love (music group), 43

Lowe, Mike, 132

Lowell, Robert, 100

Lyman, Mel, 64, 156, 170

Lynd, Staughton, 200n102, 222n102

"Lysergic A-Go-Go," 204n93

Macdonald, Dwight, 100–101

MacKenzie, Angus, 130

Mad magazine, 14, 33, 35

Magidoff, Dickie, 22–23

Mahler, David, 59

Mailer, Norman, 33–35, 39, 93, 95, 97, 100,
    101, 216n83

Maine Times, 173, 177

Malone, Bill, 209n170

Manson, Charles, 2, 174

maquis, 73

Marcuse, Herbert, 151, 188, 230n55

Marsden, Steve, 163–64

Marxism, 38, 41, 46, 174, 196n22
    See also Vulgar Marxists

Massa, Robert, 178

Masses (New York, NY), 32

Matthews, Joe, 56

Maui Sun, 177

Max, Steve, 19, 20, 21, 28, 239n90

Maysles, Albert and David, 1–2

MC-5, 121, *photo gallery 5*

McAuliffe, Kevin, 34

McBride, David, 41–42

McCain, John, 247n11

McCarren Internal Security Act, 25

McCarthy, Joseph, 35, 130, 137, 139

McCartney, Paul, 68

McCauslin, Dan, 240n114, 240n129

McDonald, "Country" Joe, 69–71, 81

McKelvey, Don, 23–26

McKenzie, Angus, 237n61

McLuhan, Marshall, 53

McNamara, Robert, 86

Mechanic's Free Press (Philadelphia, PA), 32

Mediaweek magazine, 181

medical clinics, free, 83

Meisner, Lis, 168

"Mellow Yellow," 66, 67, 68, 71, 75–77, 79–80

Melnicoff, Rozzie, *photo gallery 6*

Menand, Louis, 4

Mendocino Grapevine (CA), 64, 178

Michelet, Jules, 98

Michigan, University of (Ann Arbor, MI), 18,
    20, 26, 37, 121, 195n9

Michigan Daily (MSU), 72, 88, 206n129, 207n137

Michigan State University (East Lansing, MI)
    (MSU), 46–53, 64

middle class, 5, 18, 27, 55

Mifflin Street (Ann Arbor, MI), 37

Miles, Barry, 10, 74

militancy, 10
    in New Left, 96–98, 121, 122, 127–74, 177
    in press, 11, 32, 135, 151, 239n84
    in youth movement, 64, 96–98, 105–14,
        121, 122, 158, 177 (*see also* protests:
        violent)

militant groups, 12, 35, 97, 132, 158,
    224–25n143, 229n37
    See also Weather Underground

military, U.S., 40, 64, 92–102, 174, 210n188,
    224n130

Miller, James, 5, 16

Miller, Marvin, 63

Millman, Paul, 156, 163

Mills, C. Wright, 15, 16, 27, 33, 143

Milwaukee Journal (WI), 131

Mindich, Stephen M., *photo gallery 10*

Mitchell, Al, 41, 45

Moby Grape, 76

Monsonis, Jim, 195n9

Montague, MA, 83, 158, 161, 162, 165, 167–68

Moore, Michael, 183

Morgan, Robin, 202n31, 243n166

Morning of the Magicians, 215n71

Morrill Act (of 1862), 205n111

Morris, Willie, 56–57

MoveOn.org, 188

Mother Jones magazine, 184

motorcyclists, 1–4, 40, 60, 62–63, 121, 205n57, 210n183

Ms. Magazine, 194n45

Muhammad Speaks, 194n45

Mulvihill, Kathy, *photo gallery 8*

Mungo, Raymond, 84–85, 87–95, 99–100, 102–3, 113–14, 134–35, 141, 143, 145–70, 179, *photo gallery 1, 3*

music, 1, 31, 38, 41, 43–44, 48, 52, 54–55, 61–62, 69, 78, 84, 121, 124, 151, 159, 186, 214n36

Naked and the Dead, 34

napalm, 220–21n78, 239n84

narratives,

    historical, 5, 98

    in journalism, 179–180

Nation magazine, 184

Nation of Islam, 194n45

National Association of Newsweeklies, 173, 175, 176

National Guardian, 28

National Mobilization Committee to End the War in Vietnam (MOBE), 95, *photo gallery 6*

National Newspaper Association, 131

National Review, 199n70

National Student Association, 89

Navasky, Victor, 193n33

Neiman, Carol, 58–59

netroots, 187–88

New Journalists, 8, 179

New Left Notes, 22, 23, 29, 76, 144, 157, 165, 167, 174, 197n52, 216n97

New Masses, 201n19

New Media Project, 90, 151

New School (New York, NY), 155

New Times (Phoenix, AZ), 178–79, 181

New Times Media, Inc., 181, 182–84

NY Daily News, 9

New York Free Press, 175

New York Observer, 8

New York Post, 111

New York Press, 183

New York Times, xiv, 8, 10, 19, 76, 86, 98, 102, 109–14, 133, 134, 144, 159, 164, 169, 224–25n143, n148, 235n18, 240n114

New Yorker, 38, 173, 180

Newfield, Jack, 79, 84, 93, 110, 111–12, 169

News and Letters, 38

Newsreel collective, 120, 162

Newsweek magazine, 44, 67, 68, 75, 79, 173, 235n18

Newton, Huey, 188

nihilism, 35, 115

Nixon, Richard, 2, 115, 127, 136, 138, 232n90, *photo gallery 9*

No More Fun and Games, 194–95n45

NOLA Express (New Orleans, LA), 133, 230n61

Nolan, Dick, 3

North Beach (CA), 36

Obama, Barack, 188

O'Brien, Jim, 37

obscenity, 10, 40, 54, 124, 127, 128, 136–38

off our backs, 194n45

Olan, Susan, 61

Old Mole (Boston, MA), 174

Ono, Yoko, 127

Open City (Los Angeles, CA), 10, 92, 127, 239n84

Open Process (San Francisco, CA), 155

Oregonian, 245n27

Orlean, Susan, 180
O'Rourke, P. J., 8
Orpheus, 117, 119–20
Orwell, George, 32
Osawatomie, 193n20
Other Scenes, 230n53
Ovshinsky, Harvey, 201n3
Owens, Tary, 62
Ozaukee Press, 131

Pabon, Dino, 241n129
Pacifica Foundation, 38
Paine, Thomas, 117
Palattella, John, 68
Paley, William, 225n158
pamphlets, 14, 32, 105, 117, 134, 155, 186
Paper (East Lansing, MI), 31, 37, 46–47,
     49–53, 54, 58, 63–64, 211n220
Pardun, Robert, 28, 54, 59, 210n186
participant observers, 2, 4, 8, 62–63, 76, 86,
     94, 104
     See also subjectivity
Pasternak, Charles, 241n129
Patterson, Phyllis, 39
Peace Corps, 21
Peck, Abe, 54, 74, 92, 106, 127, 168, 192n12,
     224n137, 234n6
PEN American Center, 9, 125
Pennsylvania State University, 127
Pentagon, 79, 134
     Battle of, 92–102, 113, 120, 146
People magazine, 36
Phoenix (AZ), 7, 117, 118, 119, 120, 123, 178
Pilati, Joe, *photo gallery 3*
Playboy magazine, 60, 215n78
PM, 201n19
poetry, 3, 7, 9, 39, 40, 48, 49, 50, 52, 55, 61,
     68, 72, 92–93, 127, 151, 182, 186,
     194–95n45
police, 3, 25, 41, 44, 51, 70–71, 96, 144–45
     abuse of authority, 77, 110, 124, 125, 128,
          129, 130, 132, 133, 137, *photo gallery
          5 (see also* harassment)
     arrests by, 76, 86, 95, 104, 105, 110–11,
          120, 123, 127–29, 133, 148, 178–79,
          224n134, *photo gallery 5*

narcotics agents, 38, 63, 76, 120
     provocation of, 62–63, 78, 79, 80, 120,
          135, 220–21n78
     violence of, 18, 42–45, 96–102, 106–13,
          120–21, 122–23, 174, 178, 179,
          235–36n33
Polletta, Francesca, 28
Pontecorvo, Gillo, 145
Pool, Joe, 129, 139
Porche, Verandah, 149, 150, 160, 162
pornography, 63, 68, 116, 127–28, 136–37,
     175
pornzines, 175
Port Huron Statement, 12, 15–17, 20, 21, 23,
     24, 29, 32, 37, 40
Port Publications (WI), 130
Postal Service, U.S., 120, 158, 161, 198n55
Potter, Paul, 18
poverty, 6, 42–43, 52, 56, 78, 86, 90, 104,
     141
Powers, Jerry, 128
press
     abolitionist, 201n6
     alternative, 172–3, 175–85, 244n13
          advertising in, 180–81, 246n43
          free circulation of, 178, 180–81
          homogeneity in, 174, 183–84
     anti-Nazi, 6
     consolidation and monopoly of, 8, 182–83
     decline of print media, 187–88
     early American, 32
     graphics in (*see* graphics)
     labor-movement, 201n6
     mainstream, 4, 8, 9, 63, 66–67, 76, 83–84,
          94, 103, 121, 182, 187
          advertising in, 138
          editorials in (*see* editorials)
          failure of, 7, 40, 42–43, 84–85, 104,
               135, 139, 187–88, 245n27
          misrepresentations in, 3, 32, 83–84, 90,
               93–95, 98, 100–102, 109–15, 137,
               145, 171
     underground
          advertising in, 7, 74, 91, 115, 117, 119,
               122, 124, 125, 129, 130, 131, 132,
               138, 175, 239n84

black radical, 194n45

calendars in, 7, 40, 44, 60

circulation of, 4, 6–7, 73, 192n12

death of, 10, 11, 32, 125, 130–32, 136, 170–75, 188–89

embezzlement in, 91, 92, 164, 165, 228n13

in Europe, 10, 74

fake, 116

GI (military), 134, 193n20

harassment of (*see* harassment)

informants in, 38, 63, 77, 115–16, 120, 123, 129–30, 134, 160, 169, 177, 227–28n3, 237n61, 241n117, *photo gallery 5*

internal conflict in, 11, 122, 140–71, 229n37

language of (*see* counterculture: language of)

management structures in

    hierarchical, 84, 93, 149, 155–57, 177, 181, 239n90

    decentralized, 10, 11, 16, 17, 27–28, 54, 59, 63–64, 142–43, 147, 149–50, 170–71, 174, 189, 239n85 (*see also under* democracy)

misrepresentations in, 36, 99–100, 106–10

networks of, 53, 67–68, 73, 80, 92 (*see also* Liberation News Service; Underground Press Syndicate)

obscenity in, 10, 125, 127, 128–31, 230n55

sexism in (*see* sexism)

spread of, 4, 31, 37, 52, 71–73, 80–83, 91, 106, 138–39, 192n12

suppression of, 9, 59–60, 64, 116–18, 124, 136, 220n70 (*see also* harassment)

vending of, 7, 10, 33, 39, 46, 59–60, 82, 124, 128, 132, 133

Priest, Roger, 134

print culture, 30, 142, 176, 188

in SDS, 15, 17, 21, 23, 29–30

printing, 4–7

    desktop publishing, 186–87

    mimeograph, 13–14, 20, 24, 30, 103, 118, 124, 192n12, 193n22

photo-offset, 6–7, 24, 59, 63, 150, 160, 163, 164, 167, 186–87, 193n3, *photo gallery 8*

prisoners, political, 14, 64, 101

Progressive magazine, 184

Project for Excellence in American Journalism, 188

protest, 25, 44–45, 48–49, 57, 71, 86, 94, 144, *photo gallery 5*

    culture of, 4

    peaceful, 1, 2, 21, 26, 42, 45, 48, 52, 62, 66, 77, 87, 105–6, 121, 147, 175, 189, 198n59, 211n204

    violent, 1–4, 42–43, 83, 86–87, 92–102, 104–13, 120, 146, 148, 174, 182, 220–21n78, 235n18, 237n62

the Provos, 60

Pulitzer Prize, 93, 179

Punk magazine (New York, NY), 186

Quan, Lazarus, 159

Quill's Weekly, 201n19

racism, 4, 11, 12, 40, 42, 55–56, 78, 86, 104–5, 127, 129, 143

    See also under African Americans

Rader, Gary, 100

Radical America, 37

radio, 3, 8, 38–39, 41–42, 66, 71, 123, 178, 179, 243n164

Rag (Austin, TX), xiii, 31, 37, 53–54, 58–65, 72–73, 75–77, 97, 126, 129, 133, 232n96, *photo gallery 2*

Rall, Ted, 183

Ramparts magazine, 51, 109, 129

rape, 175, 245n27

Rarick, John R., 145

Rat (New York, NY), 24, 72, 103, 119, 129, 156, 162, 171, 174, 175, 194n45, 210n186, 224n137

Rathskeller (University of Wisconsin), 202n40

Rattiner, Dan, *photo gallery 2*

Reader's Digest, 9, 138

Reagan, Ronald, 9, 69

Real Paper (Boston, MA), 173, 177, 182

Realist, 14, 33–36, 175

Reed, Ishmael, 9

religion, 40, 44, 55, 56, 84, 86, 87, 88, 95, 103–4, 108, 109, 186, 247n11

Republican Party, 92, 187, 244n13

Reston, James, 98

Retherford, James, 119–20, 133

Reuters, 103

Revolution, 201n6

Revolution, French, 98

revolutionaries, 64, 79, 83, 158, 161, 165, 166, 174, 175

  third-world, 32, 84, 132, 174

revolutionary wall painting (RWP), 195n4

Reyes, Gwen, 189

Rhodesia, University College of, 86

Ribicoff, Abraham, 230n63

Richards, David, 64

Riot Grrrl, 187

riots. *See* protests: violent

Rivers, L. Mendel, 134

Rizzo, Frank, 135

Robbins, Tom, 9

Roberts, Cokie, 182

Robinson, Betty Garman, 197n51

Roche, John, 88

Rock and Roll Hall of Fame, 81

Rockefeller, David, 246n42

Rodgers, Jimmie, 55

Rodriguez, Spain, 213n16

Rolfe, Lionel, 39

Rolling Stone magazine, 83, 120, 121, 122, 130, 171, 194n1

Rolling Stones, 1–3, 142

Romm, Ethel, 74, 106, 192n12

Rosenbaum, Ron, 117

Rosenberg, Fred, 45

Rosenthal, Abe, 225n157, 226n164

Ross, Robert, 22–23

Rossinow, Doug, 54–56

Rostow, Walt, 88

Roth, Bob, 179–80

Roth v. the United States, 127

Rubin, Jerry, 77, 123, 175

Rudd, Mark, 105–7, 224n130

Rudnick, Bob, 118

Rusk, Dean, 146

Rutgers University, 24

Ryan, George, 178

Ryan, Mary, xiv

Ryan, Sheila, 119, 122, 147–48, 150–52, 156, 161, 162, 164, 241n129, *photo gallery 6*

Sainte-Marie, Buffy, 48

Sale, Kirkpatrick, 29, 177, 195n3, 200n89

Salon magazine, 8

San Diego Door (CA), 127, 233n110

San Diego Periodicals, 129

San Diego *Street Journal* (CA), 132, 133

San Francisco (CA), 1, 3, 36, 38, 53, 62, 69–70, 155

San Francisco Bay Guardian (CA), 93, 173, 174, 177, 178, 183

San Francisco Chronicle (CA), 71, 192n7

San Francisco Examiner (CA), 3–4

San Francisco *Express-Times* (CA), 237n52

San Francisco *Oracle* (CA), 7, 11, 75, 93, 201n3

Sanders, Ed, 68–69, 193n20

Santana, Carlos, 1

Savage, Dan, 183

Schanen, William, 130–31

Schang, Gabrielle, 244n13

Scherr, Max, 73, 76, 122, 156, *photo gallery 7*

Schiff, Paul, 50

Schoenberg, Arnold, 41

Schoenfeld, Eugene, 72, 175, 213n24

Schweers, Danny, 64

the Seeds, 43

Selective Service, U.S., 214n41

Selma (AL), 86, 235–36n33

Senate Select Committee on Intelligence, 229–30n52

sex, 35, 60, 95, 125–26, 154, 172, 175, 178, 183, 185, 186, 189, 234n6

Sex Pistols, 244n13

sexism, 11, 15, 19–20, 23, 36, 59, 60, 121–22, 125, 126–27, 129, 166, 174–76, 194n45, 243n166

SF Weekly (CA), 181, 184, 246n44

Shafer, Jack, 184

Shahn, Ben, 13

Shakedown (Fort Dix, NJ), 134

Shank, Barry, 55, 62

Shapiro, Peter, 155

Shelton, Gilbert, 126, 175

Shenton, James, 108

Shero, Jeff, 23–26, 28, 30, 32, 56, 60, 72, 103, 119, 129, 156, 198n53, 210n186

Shuster, Mike, 8

Silver, Joan Micklin, 172

Sinclair, John, 121, 123, 128, 229n33, *photo gallery 5*

the Sixties, xiii, 2, 6, 12, 38, 173, 187–88

Slate magazine, 184

Slotin, Moe, *photo gallery 8*

Small, Melvin, 94

Small Press Alliance (SPA), 186–87

Smith, Charlie, 210n183, 210n186

Smith, David, 199n76

Smith, Jack, *photo gallery 3*

Smith, Lane, 172

Smith, Russ, 183

Smith, Victoria, 9, 62, 131, 241n129, *photo gallery 9*

Snyder, Gary, 9

socialism, 32–33, 38, 88, 195n9

Solman, Paul, 182

Sommer, Marc, 146, 166

the South, 50, 53, 58, 86, 197n51

South America, 79, 143

South End, 229n37

Southern Courier, 86, 147

Soviet Union, 35, 54, 56, 151

Space City! (Houston, TX), 131–32, 133, 210n186 *photo gallery 9*

Spectator (Bloomington, IN), 119, 133, 232n96, 238n78

Specter, Arlen, 135

Spiegel, Mike, 167–68

Spiegelman, Art, 9

Spiro's, 49, 52

Spock, Benjamin, 100

Spokane Natural (WA), 75, 133

Spratt, Craig, 159

Springsteen, Bruce, 9

St. Luke's Hospital, 109

St. Mark's Place, 37

standpoint epistemology, 95, 113

Stanley, Owsley, 7

Stanton, Elizabeth Cady, 201n6

Starin, Larry, 75

State News (MSU), 46–49, 52, 207n137

Steinem, Gloria, 194n45

Stockman, David, 9

Stone, I. F. (Izzy), 33, 238n68

Straight Creek Journal (Denver, CO), 128, 176, 177

Streitmatter, Roger, 32

Student Communication Network (SCN), 103–4, 149

Student Nonviolent Coordinating Committee, 16, 197n51, 247n15

Student Peace Union, 23

Student Press Association, U.S. (USSPA), 87, 89–91, 103, 141

Students for a Democratic Society (SDS), 5–6, 13–30, 42, 48, 50, 54, 57, 76, 95, 96, 103–13, 146, 151, 153, 167–68, 173–74, 188, *photo gallery 2*

 chapters of, 20–21, 26, 52, 53, 57–61, 76–77, 104–13, 155, 162, 210n184, 211n220, 240n91

 meetings of, 14–15, 18, 21, 28, 57, 121, 174, 200n88, 210n186, 211n220

 National Council of, 18, 22, 23, 28, 57, 210n186

 publications of, 25, 53, 57, 197–98n52

  Discussion Bulletin (DB), 23–30, 197–98n52

  New Left Notes (see *New Left Notes*)

 Weatherman faction (*see* Weather Underground)

subjectivity

 alternative, 68

 in reporting, 2–3, 4, 8, 47, 50, 62–63, 76, 84, 94–95, 98–99, 101–2, 109–10, 135, 173, 175, 180, 183

 as truth, 8, 94–95, 102, 113

Sulzberger, Arthur "Punch," 109–12

"Summer of Love," 38, 66–68, 144

Sunset Strip, 38, 41, 43–45, 63, 205n104

Supreme Court, California, 203n62, 204n79

Supreme Court, Michigan, 129, *photo gallery 5*

Supreme Court, U.S., 64, 127–28

Sûreté, 51

Swinton, Pat, 135

Symington, Fife, 178–79

Talese, Gay, 179

Tarrantino, Quentin, 183

Tate, Larry, 49, 51, 53, 207n134

taxes, 40, 63

tear gas, 96, 100, 220–21n78

television, 8, 45, 71, 84, 129, 132, 178, 182, 187, 225n158, 232n90, 240n101

teletype machines, 74, 103, 146, 158

Texas, University of (at Austin) (UT), 25, 54–60, 64, 75–77, 133, *photo gallery 2*

Texas Observer, 244n17

theater
    street, 44, 120, *photo gallery 5*
    X-rated, 63

13th Floor Elevators, 62

Thomas, Norman, 195n9

Thompson, Frank, 67, 76

Thompson, Hunter S., 8

Threadgill, Kenneth, 55

Threadgill's Bar (Austin, TX), 55

Thurmond, Strom, 187

Time Magazine, 31, 44, 53, 67, 71, 84, 88, 102, 119, 129, 173, 177

Tocqueville, Alexis de, 9, 98

Tomassi, Carter, *photo gallery 8*

Tomorrow, Tom, 183

Tower Records, 186

Trans-Love Energies Unlimited, 120–21

Trillin, Calvin, 173, 176

Trotskyites, 38

Truman, David, 110, 178

A Trumpet to Arms: Alternative Media in America, 178

Tuesday's Child (Los Angeles, CA), 239n84

Twin Cities Reader (Minneapolis-St. Paul, MN), 179

Underground Newspaper Collection, 221n95

Underground Press Syndicate (UPS), 6, 46, 58, 73–74, 81, 83, 91–92, 112, 116–21, 120–24, 126–29, 135–39, 192n12, 235n18, *photo gallery 1, 9*

Uniform Code of Military Justice, 134

United Auto Workers, 15

United Fruit Company, 75, 78, 79

United Press International (UPI), 102, 103, 158

U.S. Agency for International Development, 47

universities. *See* colleges

University Christian Movement, 103

Up Against the Wall, Motherfucker, 161, 217n61

urban crisis, 5, 36, 43, 85, 90, 104, 158

Valenza, Gary, 238n78

values
    alternative, 80, 83, 113, 187
    American, 5, 37, 56, 78, 112
    humanist, 27
    mainstream, 84, 126

Velvet Underground, 214n36

Venice (CA), 36, 38

Vietcong, 145–46

Vietnam. *See under* war

Village Voice, 13, 14, 33–35, 36, 39, 75, 78, 84, 88, 93, 110, 118, 121, 164, 177, 178, 181–85, 216n76, *photo gallery 1*

Village Voice Media, 181, 182–84

Villager, 201n19

violence, state, 84, 93–94, 97

Virtuous Caucus, 150–53, 157–62, 168

Vizard, George, 59–60, *photo gallery 2*

Vonnegut, Kurt Jr., 33

voter registration, 57

Vulcan Gas Co. (Austin, TX), 62

Vulgar Marxists, 150–53, 156, 159, 160–63, 165, 168, 169, 234n6

Wall Street Journal, 216n88

Walrus (Champaign, IL), 103

Walrus, John, *photo gallery 4*

war, 10, 20, 54, 56, 105, 126, 138, 198n59, 201n22
    Civil, 201n6
    conscientious objector, 169
    Franco-Algerian, 145, 151

Iraq, 247n11

Vietnam, 4, 5, 6, 11, 41, 42, 51, 65, 88, 97, 99, 101, 151, 174, 207n137, *photo gallery 6*

    coverage of, 7, 57, 79, 85, 86, 90

    draft, 5, 7, 72, 86, 88–89, 92, 97, 100, 103, 133, 134, 169, 211n220, 217n10

    opposition to, 13, 26, 42, 50, 51, 52, 57, 61, 64, 83, 88–89, 92–103, 121, 126, 130, 134, 144, 145, 242n158

Warhol, Andy, 60, 214n36

Washington City Paper (DC), 184

Washington Free Press (DC), 72, 76, 77–78, 133, 145, 147, 155, 221n95, 223n114, 232n96

Washington Post (DC), 84, 98, 100, 135, 143, 144–45, 148, 181, 235n32

Waskow, Arthur, 21, 235n32

Wasserman, Harvey, 88, 146, 147, 149, 151, 152, 156, 158–60, 167–68

Water Tunnel (Penn State), 127

Watergate, 107, 136, 144

Way of the Magus, 211n219

Wayne State University, 122

Weather Underground, 2, 135, 173–74, 193n20, 195n4, 196n22, 225n149

Weiner, Rex, 116, 124, 128

Weinstein, Sol, 215n78

Weiss, Nat, 159

Welch, Matt, 187

Weld, Bill, 246n42

Wenner, Jann, 121, 229n35, 232n92

Werbe, Peter, 103, 166

Western Union, 103

White, Hayden, 98

White House, 84, 117, 146, 147

White Panther Party, 121, 122, *photo gallery 5*

Whitman, Walt, 49

Wiener, Jon, 9

Wilcock, John, 73–74, 118–19, 121, 124, 148, 230n53, *photo gallery 1*

Wilkerson, Cathy, 19–20, 167–68, 196n13

Willamette Bridge (Portland, OR), 133

Willamette Week (Portland, OR), 179, 180

Williams, Robert, 126

Wilson, Cicero, 106

Wilson, S. Clay, 126

WIN magazine, 93, 189

Wisconsin, University of, 37, 129, 131

Wittman, Julie, 132

Wizard, Mariann (formerly Mariann Vizard), 59, *photo gallery 2*

Wolf, Dan, 33–34

Wolf, Peter, 175

Wolfe, Tom, 81, 179

Women's House of Detention, 235–36n33

women's rights, 11, 121–22, 201n6

    See also feminism

Wood, Grant, 75

Woodstock, 7, 138, 188

Woodstock West, 1

Woodward, Bob, 135–36, 144

Worcester Punch, 75

working class, 55, 122, 143, 161, 186, 201n6, 229n37

Working Man's Advocate (New York, NY), 32

World War II, 6, 195n9

Xanadu coffeehouse, 39

Yasgur, Max, 1

YMCA-YWCA, 56, 61

Young, Allen, 79, 143–45, 148–53, 158, 165, 168, 222n105, 223n127, 235n32, *photo gallery 6*

Young Socialist Club, 48, 207n137

Youngbloods, 68

Youth International Party (Yippies), 123, 175

youth rebellion. *See* Left: New

Yurdin, Larry, *photo gallery 10*

Zeitgeist, 49, 52

zines, 186–87

Zodiac Mindwarp, 213n16